Champagne Sparkle

Champagne Sparkle

Maggie Mitchell, the First Musical Comedy Star of the American Stage

Thomas A. Bogar

ROWMAN & LITTLEFIELD
Lanham • Boulder • New York • London

Published by Rowman & Littlefield
An imprint of The Rowman & Littlefield Publishing Group, Inc.
4501 Forbes Boulevard, Suite 200, Lanham, Maryland 20706
www.rowman.com

6 Tinworth Street, London SE11 5AL, United Kingdom

Copyright © 2020 by The Rowman & Littlefield Publishing Group, Inc.

All rights reserved. No part of this book may be reproduced in any form or by any electronic or mechanical means, including information storage and retrieval systems, without written permission from the publisher, except by a reviewer who may quote passages in a review.

British Library Cataloguing in Publication Information Available

Library of Congress Cataloging-in-Publication Data Is Available

ISBN 978-1-5381-8355-7 (paperback)
ISBN 978-1-5381-4349-0 (electronic)

Contents

Introduction	1
1 "a wild, restless, spritely little thing"	9
2 "emphatically the People's Pet"	27
3 "quivering masculine hearts"	45
4 Fanchon	59
5 "talked about as much as the war"	77
6 "she will never be more idolized than she was by the soldiers"	95
7 "everything has been deranged"	111
8 "Maggie Mitchell stands unrivaled"	129
9 California and "Cricket Lodge"	149
10 "she does not counterfeit it, but feels it"	167
11 "everything she attempts is Fanchon"	183
12 "bathed in the fountain of perennial youth"	201
13 "she can't quit the stage"	221
14 "completely under his influence"	239

15 "dissipated and untrue"	255
16 "it is the music of the heart"	273
Acknowledgments	285
Index	287

Introduction

On February 17, 1869, the disinterred body of John Wilkes Booth was being prepared for reburial in Baltimore's Green Mount Cemetery. Among the close friends and family surrounding the body in the coroner's workroom were his quietly sobbing mother, Mary Ann, theater owner John T. Ford, and his brother Harry. John's daughter, Annie, began snipping locks of hair from Booth's head, which lay detached from the body. Handing the first lock to Mary Ann, Annie saved another to fulfill the request of actress Maggie Mitchell. Maggie had dearly loved her "John Booth" (as friends knew him) since their early days together in Montgomery, Alabama, on the eve of the War Between the States. He was never far from her thoughts as she toured; in fact, he had appeared to her vividly in a dream in St. Louis on the night of April 14, 1865—the night he murdered President Abraham Lincoln at Ford's Theatre in Washington.

And yet, strangely, Maggie was also a favorite of the late president, who had enjoyed her folksy humor and invited her to tea at the White House. He never knew, or chose to ignore, her sympathy for the secessionist cause. By war's end, she had put those feelings behind her, professing devotion to the Union until her death six decades later.

Her name kept surfacing as I worked on *American Presidents Attend the Theatre* and *Backstage at the Lincoln Assassination*. How did this fiery little actress—whose first entrance in her most famous role entailed clambering through an open window in pursuit of a live chicken—earn the adulation of poets, statesmen, and journalists, adored by millions of fans across the country? How did an unrepentant secessionist at the outbreak of the Civil War become by war's end universally beloved in the North? What made this effervescent actress so appealing, surmounting every challenge, every competitor, remaining triumphant on the American stage in childlike roles for forty years?

Trying to capture her appeal, reviewers exhausted their store of adjectives and metaphors, among them "petite," "vivacious," "hoydenish," "sprightly," "piquant," "elfin," "impish," "mischievous," "winsome," "beautiful," "animated," "electric," "versatile," "chaste," "a darling," "a fascinating little witch," "a materialized sunbeam," "touched by the moon," and "a champagne sparkle."[1]

As a result of her 4'5" stature, most of her roles were a variation of "Little This" or "Little That." But that tiny frame packed a mighty punch. "She isn't as large as fifty ladies we would name," wrote one reviewer, "but then it would puzzle any fifty ladies in our city to equal her in graces of person as well as of mind. Nature . . . gave Maggie perfect symmetry, flexibility and adaptability. She made her a perfect little gem of grace and sprightliness."[2]

A long, graceful waist in a well-developed figure complemented Maggie's dainty (size 1) feet and well-turned ankles. Her cascade of curly, reddish-blonde hair, sparkling gray, almond-shaped eyes—slightly crossed—and enigmatic smile of white, even teeth, just flirtatious enough to pique interest, became her trademarks for generations.

Her costumes, too, were eye-catching—bright colors, scooped necklines, tight breeches, and short skirts (with pantaloons)—but offstage she dressed stylishly and demurely. Eschewing corsets and heavy clothing, she preferred divided skirts, brocaded jackets, "poke bonnets," even an occasional white lace veil. Her skirts were trimmed with lace or embroidery, because, she explained, "in getting in or out of a carriage or a street car it is the underside of the edging that shows, and only that."[3]

She guarded her health and ate well, but fine dining was not to her taste. Few people knew, recalled an actor who toured with her, "with what scientific accuracy and knowledge of anatomy Maggie Mitchell can carve a Thanksgiving turkey, or with what unfailing tenacity of purpose she can, to use a Bowery phrase, 'get outside' of a porterhouse steak." She exercised regularly, swimming, walking, and (her favorite) horseback riding. Although she made every effort to avoid drafty theaters, and her maid wrapped her snugly each time she exited the stage for the walk back to her hotel, she was plagued with recurrent colds, coughs, and sore throats that hindered her performances.[4]

Her temperament remained remarkably placid, humble, and upbeat, as she rose from obscurity to stardom. "She is always the same sunny-tempered, kindly lady," said her maid, who saw her through countless vicissitudes of travel and backstage conditions. Unfailingly generous to stagehands and eleemosynary causes, she performed in countless benefits for indigent or ailing actors and their families, while supporting her own sizable family from an early age. Demands on her time minimized her availability to reporters, but when her schedule permitted, they inevitably found her candid, patient, and personable. She remained "as entertaining in her private life as when on the stage. She touches lightly in private conversation upon the leading topics of the day, and skips from one subject to another with an alacrity that shows she is a great reader." Visitors found her "a most charming hostess," "a good-humored, kind, generous woman."[5]

Backstage was another story. Despite her size, Maggie was a commanding presence: "I was startled when that little elf came on the stage and began to give directions with a vim and exactness that made the old-timers ask themselves what had happened," recalled fellow actor John Barron. "We were all ears and eyes." "A martinet regarding stage discipline," she demanded high standards, recalled another. Everything had to "be done in as artistic a manner as if it were *Macbeth*. . . . Everything must be exactly correct. . . . She knows what she wants and will have it." Yet another thought her "very strict, . . . a perfect disciplinarian. . . . She is very exact, wants everything as she desires, and is consequently sometimes a little unpleasant to people behind the curtains from this fact."[6]

Barron defended that occasional unpleasantness: "If she lost her temper sometimes, it was because someone was positively stupid, or too nervous to get things right." This "involved an enormous amount of labor, especially at rehearsals; but that meant perfect performances, and before rehearsals were dismissed, she was sure that every member of the cast was letter perfect." But she could also be nurturing. "She always has a kindly word for beginners in her profession, and has helped many of them along to success."[7]

And she drove herself equally mercilessly, never stopping from a 10:00 a.m. rehearsal through 11:00 p.m. or later after the last detail was arranged for the next day. "She never required more of the ladies and gentlemen of the company than she herself was willing to do. She never left a rehearsal to anyone; she was the inspiration that affected the entire company."[8]

The remarkable thing about Maggie was not that she gained immediate popularity almost everywhere she played, or that she maintained a lucrative acting career for over four decades—many actors have lasted longer—but that she did so playing child roles until she retired. Justly celebrated for her indelible portrayals of *Fanchon*, *Little Barefoot*, *The Pearl of Savoy*, and *Lorle*, she was arguably the first musical comedy star of the American stage, the template for Lotta Crabtree, Maude Adams, Mary Pickford, and Shirley Temple. No comedienne of the nineteenth century was more famous or maintained a larger, more loyal popular following. Yet she also stretched herself in such serious roles as *Jane Eyre*. For all of this, no nineteenth-century actress better deserves to have her story told than Maggie Mitchell.

Of her 175 roles, *Fanchon* stood alone. "Maggie Mitchell's Fanchon, the Cricket, was for years and years a household word in America. The public loved her and it; one never tired of the wild, loving character or of the exquisite performance of it," recorded theater historian George C. D. Odell. "I still recognize its elemental charm, its magnetic genius; the shadow dance, with its absurd song, and the scene of the beguiling of Father Barbeaud were among the most captivating things ever presented in the theatre. Tiny as she was, this lovely actress could possess the biggest stage with consummate ease."[9]

Her lifetime spanned twenty-two American presidencies. Born in Jacksonian America, she began her career amid the sectional hostility of the antebellum era, maintained it profitably through the Civil War, two major financial waves of panic and the vast expansion of the American West, and died with World War I underway. Wherever she went, despite bad weather, the war, and desperate financial conditions, she usually played to sold-out houses.

An inherent optimism and spunk radiated from her, endearing her to theatergoers, who left feeling confident that they, too, could overcome petty conniving and hatred, transformed like her characters into finer, nobler figures in the end. Warm smiles, spontaneous laughter, waves of applause, and, often, costly gifts flowed to her at every venue, from the largest and most cosmopolitan city to the tiniest, most remote frontier hamlet. No longer dependent on the river travel of her predecessors, she took advantage of the nation's burgeoning rail system to visit 298 different cities and towns during her career.

As her fame grew, she brushed off imitators and competitors with aplomb. Only a handful of other actresses maintained a comparable, but ultimately transitory, following. Some drew crowds in New York but not in the Midwest or West, some in the South but not in New England. Maggie, though, noted reviewers, "seems to please everybody, and at a second appearance anywhere always attracts a larger audience than on a first visit." "None of the 'tragedy queens' attract night after night as do the lighter personations of this vivacious and charming actress." From curtain-up to the last of many encores, there was "no yawning in the audience when Maggie is upon the stage, and no desire to have the curtain fall. And after it has fallen and the audience carry away the memory of a pleasant evening, they are glad of an early opportunity to greet the actress again."[10]

From her first forays into the world of starring tours, Maggie staked out a territory of her own. Capitalizing on her petite build, she embraced the world of charismatic soubrettes rather than face the demands of melodrama and classical tragedy. Although she yielded up the latter a bit begrudgingly, it provided a layer of pathos to her comedy.

Unlike the fans of tragedians Edwin Forrest and Edwin Booth, or of comedians John E. Owens and Joseph Jefferson III, Maggie's adherents from the start came to see *her* as much as her eccentric characters. For the most part, these were the same, leading critics sometimes to ridicule their sameness, only to find themselves bypassed or ignored. Observed the *Brooklyn Eagle*,

"Her audiences abandon all attempts at criticism and accept her as a piquant, delightfully saucy, ever-welcome little being whose peculiar voice and manner bring tears of laughter into their eyes, and whose bright, youthful-looking face and girlish figure furnish their minds with such a pretty picture as time can never destroy."[11]

Anomalous in that era, women flocked to her performances as well as men. "There is probably no greater influence in the success of a play than the favor of women," noted one admirer, for "they delight in the portrayal of love, joy, grief or sorrow." And when it came to an interest in her shows, "where the women go, the men will follow." One young swain remembered many years later that "whenever Maggie Mitchell came around here the boys had to 'loosen up [their funds],' for the girls all wanted to go and see her in the romantic scenes."[12]

Remarkably, at a time when actresses were morally suspect for their bohemian existence, she remained above suspicion. From the start of her career at fifteen, dancing between the acts for the notoriously lecherous Tom Hamblin at his tawdry Bowery Theatre, she managed to avoid the disreputable fate of so many of her peers, becoming "one of the few actresses who have kept out of the tide of filth that has been sloshing over onto the stage." Theatergoers could trust in "the absolute surety that upon the stage where she is can always be found the purity of the home atmosphere and the charming spectacle of a lady whose life both in public and in private is an honor to her sex and to the profession she represents." When Maggie came to town, even "the pious elders and deacons relax a little and drop in for an evening to gaze at the most winsome little woman on the American stage, whose class of plays the most rigid purist could find nothing to object to." She was "a missionary [who] leaves a pure feeling behind her, and makes impressions for good where many a set lesson or elaborated sermon fails."[13]

Her pastoral scripts were "as chaste as a clear mountain stream." They "arouse no base passions, but appeal to the higher and better feelings of human nature." Their themes evoked a "vivid portrayal of childhood's sorrows and joys, of its bitter trials and noble triumphs." They "may not be marvels of literary conception or construction, but the joys and sorrows she portrays are those of good and true women." Her characters melded "the innocent angel" with "the brilliant prodigy as well as the naughty, rebellious child," as any successful nineteenth-century actress of youthful roles had to do.[14]

Most importantly, Maggie remained above suspicion off the stage as well, "an honor to the profession. . . . At no time has the breath of scandal ever sullied the pages of her life." She believed that "an actress must have, or must acquire, the manners of a lady before she can satisfactorily enact one." The "utterance of noble sentiments and the portrayal of scenes in which vice is always punished and virtue triumphant cannot fail to be elevating and refining." Even conservative Midwestern interviewers believed that "perhaps more than any other American woman [she has] purified the atmosphere of the stage, and drawn the better elements of society. . . . Few women have brought to the stage more that is true, good, pure and ennobling than Maggie Mitchell."[15]

A childhood of poverty drove Maggie to succeed. By dint of her energy, focus, and talent, one reporter summarized, "everything she touched turned to gold." That early poverty imbued in her a lifelong shrewdness about investing the hundreds of thousands of dollars she earned, a habit instilled in her early on by her protective mother. Most of it went into judiciously chosen real estate in Manhattan and in Long Branch, New Jersey, which upon her death left her children and husband well provided for. Yet nothing about her childhood could have predicted the remarkable wealth and fame she would acquire.[16]

NOTES

1. *New York Clipper*, Oct. 8, 1859; "Theatric Reminiscences" by "John Carboy" [John A. Harrington], *New York Sunday Dispatch*, n.d. (mid-1880s), clipping, Harvard Theatre Collection (henceforth HTC); American Council of Learned Societies, *Dictionary of American Biography*, New York: Scribner, 1946-58. VII:56.

2. *St. Joseph (MO) Commercial* quoted in *Rock Island (IL) Argus*, Apr. 28, 1876.

3. *Louisville Courier-Journal*, Oct. 19, 1895.

4. Carboy.

5. *Cleveland Plain Dealer*, Mar. 2, 1878; *Cincinnati Star*, Sept. 30, 1879; *Wilmington (DE) News Journal*, Nov. 19, 1886. One old stage doorman recalled in 1907, "There ain't many generous ones left like Maggie Mitchell." *Harper's Weekly*, vol. 51 (1907), 1874.

6. John M. Barron, "Actors of Days Gone By," *Baltimore Sun*, Nov. 11, 1906; *Kansas City Times*, Aug. 10, 1886.

7. Barron.

8. *Ibid.*

9. George C. D. Odell, *Annals of the New York Stage*, vol. VII. New York: Columbia University Press, 1931, 388.

10. *Hartford Courant* quoted in *Lockport (NY) Daily Journal*, May 27, 1876, and *Rock Island (IL) Argus*, Apr. 29, 1876.

11. *Brooklyn Eagle*, Nov. 8, 1885.

12. "Dramatic News," *Minneapolis Star Tribune*, Nov. 1, 1885; *Washington (DC) Evening Star*, June 19, 1921.

13. *Rochester (NY) Democrat and Chronicle*, Jan. 22, 1881; *Philadelphia Times* quoted in *Kansas City Star*, Jan. 10, 1887; *Rockford (IL) Register*, Nov. 18, 1881;

Unidentified clipping, Crawford Collection, Series IV, Box 338, Yale University Library.

14. Barron; *Pittsburgh Gazette*, Mar. 11, 1875; *Washington Sunday Herald*, Nov. 28, 1886; Nan Mullenneaux, *Staging Family*, Lincoln: University of Nebraska Press, 2018, 121.

15. *Brooklyn Magazine*, Apr. 1885 (II:1) 8; *Turf, Field and Farm* quoted in *Cleveland Plain Dealer*, Nov. 6, 1882; *St. Louis Post-Dispatch*, Feb. 2, 1890.

16. *New York American*, Mar. 23, 1918.

Chapter 1

"a wild, restless, spritely little thing"

Maggie Mitchell inauspiciously entered the world on June 2, 1836, in a cramped rented room above a shop on Fulton Street in Manhattan. The year before, her mother, Hannah (called Anna) Dodson Lomax Mitchell, 35, had married Charles S. Mitchell, 30, after the 1832 death from cholera of her husband, Joseph Lomax, soon after they had immigrated from England. Charles had been a small-time actor in his native Dundee, Scotland, but now eked out a living as a bookbinder on Franklin Street. The business had been Lomax's, and Charles had been his manager, but upon Lomax's death, Charles assumed control.[1]

Maggie's "poor but respectable" family "just managed to keep soul and body together." At the time of her birth, it consisted of Anna's four children by Lomax: daughters Sophia, 9, Mary, 4, and sons Joseph, Jr., 7, and John, 3 (born after Lomax's death). Soon after Maggie, three others followed: Charles, Jr., in 1840, Emma in 1841, and Sarah Constance in 1845. (At least one other child died in infancy and another, Emily, in childhood.) Charles would struggle to support his wife and eight children. Maggie as a child knew the keen edge of deprivation.[2]

An Episcopal faith sustained them. Maggie was christened on October 2, 1836, by Rev. William Berrian at St. Paul's Chapel. She spent many a childhood Sunday in its damp basement, looking out onto its graveyard, the girls opposite the boys, for Sunday school. When older, she joined her parents upstairs on St. Paul's hard, high-backed pews for Sunday services, her mother's stern looks quieting her fidgeting. "She was always a wild, restless, spritely little thing," a friend recalled. "Her own childish dreams mingled with the bashful coyness of girlhood. Her very artlessness was artful." Her schooling was minimal and intermittent.[3]

Anna was a strong-willed, protective woman who continued to wear black well after Maggie's birth. There was no time in her life for frivolity. Early in 1848, she did take time to revisit her childhood home in Knaresborough, Yorkshire, parceling out the care of her children to friends. Maggie was placed in a nearby boardinghouse. In the room next door, fortuitously for millions of theatergoers to come, lived actress Mary Provost, who had just debuted at age thirteen at the Chatham Theatre. Hearing Mary rehearsing her lines for an upcoming tragic role, Maggie became fascinated with the process and emulated her by memorizing every piece of dialogue she overheard in the house. Maggie craved knowledge about the world of the stage, so Mary and/or the family with whom Maggie was staying (accounts vary) took her to the Chatham to see Augustus Addams' *Richard III*. Enthralled, she determined to pursue a career in the theater.[4]

In another fortunate happenstance, while returning from England in late summer 1848 Anna struck up a shipboard acquaintance with an engaging thirty-four-year-old British actor named John Moore. When Anna reassembled her brood at 139 Chrystie Street, she met with young Maggie's determination to begin training for the stage. Holding a low opinion of its environment, Anna refused. For months the rebellious child persisted, until Anna finally relented, turning to Moore, now employed at the Park Theatre, for advice and assistance.

First, he advised, Maggie should join an amateur dramatic company, with several nearby. The closest, named for actor James E. Murdoch, rehearsed and performed in a garret on Crosby Street. Maggie was welcomed into the company, most of them older than her. Among them were future stars Frank F. Mackay, William J. Florence, William Goodall, and two she would come to know quite well, James W. Collier and John W. Albaugh. The roles she played there are unknown but would have included a mix of farces, comedies, tragedies, and melodramas.

Moore continued to offer advice and sporadic training. At the end of May 1851, he launched the trajectory of Maggie's career. Through connections at William E. Burton's Chambers Street Theatre, he learned that a diminutive actress was needed there for a minor role in the final performance of the season, a benefit for Emma (Mrs. George) Skerrett on Monday, June 2, coincidentally Maggie's fifteenth birthday. The play was *The Soldier's Daughter*, a new five-act comedy by Andrew Cherry. Moore secured for Maggie the role of Julia, a child. She spent Saturday learning her lines, and Moore coached her throughout the day on Sunday.

On Monday night, from her first entrance, running on in the third scene in a white frock, clutching a doll as she uttered her debut line—"Mamma! Here's a gentleman who says he wants to speak to you"—she knew her course. Burton prophetically proclaimed her "a clever girl, with vital bounce enough to keep her going for the next fifty years." Unfortunately, nearly all critical and audience attention in the city that week was focused on Jenny Lind's concerts at Castle Garden, and no one paid much attention to little Maggie. That would assuredly change.⁵

That summer Moore was hired as actor-prompter at Thomas Hamblin's Bowery Theatre. Close to the end of his life and often ill, Hamblin hired Maggie on Moore's recommendation at $4 per week to play small roles and dance between acts. She would only have to walk two blocks from her itinerant family's latest home at 90 Bayard Street.

Hamblin and the Bowery were notorious for immoral behavior, and actors seldom stayed there long. At a low point financially, facing massively popular attractions at competing venues, Hamblin that fall resorted to staging canine and equestrian melodramas featuring mediocre tragedian Edwin Eddy. The stock company was young and inexperienced but generously provided Maggie with encouragement and advice on stage technique. It was, she remembered years later, "a good school," and she was eager to learn.⁶

Among the most helpful was a twenty-three-year-old comedian named Samuel W. Glenn, who recycled one role, an obtuse "Dutchman" (German caricature) through a variety of farces. His career would intersect with hers over the next two years, and they became good friends. In 1853 Glenn even named his new baby "Maggie Mitchell Glenn." Unsurprisingly, that child too became an actress.

Driven by the need to succeed and the desire to help her family out of poverty, Maggie had virtually no time to herself. "In those days," remembered John Barron, "it was study! study! study! rehearse! rehearse! rehearse! act! act! act! Almost every night I would leave the theatre after playing two parts and not knowing a line of the two long parts for the next night, and so on through a 40-weeks' season." But Maggie was not deterred.⁷

Anna constructed her costumes—an expense each actor was expected to bear—and accompanied her to performances, a "guardian spirit behind the wings—a dear good old lady . . . wearing a dark widow's dress, a plaid shawl, and with a pleasant face, [whose] tender care was around and about Maggie, an aureole of protection."⁸

On Thursday night, September 18, Maggie performed her first two roles for Hamblin, both in dramas and understandably small: Marot, a laborer in Joseph S. Jones' *Carpenter of Rouen*; and Marco in N. N. Belden Clarke's *The Pirate of the Isles*. Both were breeches roles, a common practice of the day whereby women played young men, the better to exhibit their legs in tight pants. Marco provided Maggie with ample opportunities to bound about the stage, sword in hand, itching to assail a host of exotic foes.⁹

A few nights later she reappeared as a princess, Amelia, in the melodramatic *Sixteen String Jack; or, Rann, the Reiver*. These and other insignificant roles in Bowery melodramas were too small to elicit critical notice, but Hamblin felt confident enough in her ability to bill "Miss Mitchell" among the few names in notices for shows.[10]

After a few nights in late February 1852 playing young Prince Edward to Eddy's Richard III, she attained, and brilliantly mastered, her first title role. It was Oliver Twist, with visiting star Fanny Wallack, 29, as Nancy Sykes and hulking company member Bill Goodall, 20, a Murdoch Associate, as Bill Sykes. Hamblin was so impressed by Maggie's performance that he raised her salary to $6 a week. It was doubtful, recalled editor Luther Holden, later a close friend, that Maggie ever "experienced a tithe of the satisfaction and happiness this first modest increase of salary afforded." Hamblin reportedly "took a fancy to the bright little girl and wanted to adopt her" (a sentiment the watchful Anna doubtless scorned).[11]

It was likely Hamblin who arranged for Maggie's sitting for her first formal photograph by an unknown studio. In the best of the lot, she gazes boldly at the camera, shoulders bared below copious dark ringlets. Her adult, feminine gown belies the hoydenish and breeches roles she was performing and conveys a subtle sexuality beyond her years. Countless such sittings would follow over the next four decades as her image appeared on *cartes de visite*, cabinet cards, and a variety of commercial products.

Hamblin began to award her featured roles. On March 19 she stepped for the first time into the breeches of Harry Halcyon, the intrepid hero of William Bayle Bernard's farcical *Middy Ashore*, a role she would keep in her repertoire for years. Monkey Squalls in *Fiends in Human Form* she only played a few nights. In breeches she also played Albert, the earnest young son of Eddy's titular *William Tell*. As Rosa, the plantation owner's daughter in the pro-slavery melodrama *Karfa*, she may have acquired her first understanding of the South, where she would soon become a favorite. Although she continued to dance between acts, Hamblin in April began alternating her with the "physically rich" Gertrude Dawes, whose "dark eyes of witchery" captivated young men's hearts, an effect not lost on Maggie.[12]

But sometime that month Maggie fell from Hamblin's favor and he relegated her to smaller roles with only a handful of lines. He was known to have a "horror of little women," but she may have rejected his unwanted advances. At the end of May, the ever-vigilant Anna pulled her daughter from the Bowery Company due to an unspecified "slight on the part of the management." Maggie then disappears from the historical record until early 1853.[13]

At that time, John Moore again came to her aid. Perhaps sparked by her reception as Oliver Twist, she yearned to act serious drama, and Moore complied, installing her for a week as the opening star in a small theater in Newark, New Jersey. She played Pauline in Edward Bulwer-Lytton's *The Lady of Lyons*, Lady Anne in Shakespeare's *Richard III*, and Young Norval in John Home's *Douglas*. As improbable as these may seem, a tremendously popular fad in the mid-1850s was the performance of tragedies by child actors, notably the traveling Marsh Troupe of child actors. But the Newark theater was poorly equipped, with rowdy, unappreciative audiences and an inexperienced supporting company (whom Maggie, still only sixteen, felt bold enough to advise about wardrobe).

By February, Anna and Moore secured a place for Maggie with another New York theater. A. H. Purdy's National had as little cachet as the Bowery, its bills consisting primarily of farces, songs, dances, and novelty acts. In farces there, some involving songs and dances, Maggie exercised her endearingly bright eyes and smiles and applied her unquenchable sprightliness. In breeches roles, her petite yet well-developed figure gained her a loyal male following. To Harry Halcyon, she added the mischievous Joseph in Edward Stirling's *The Young Scamp* and the eponymous highwayman in J. B. Buckstone's *Jack Sheppard*. She played flirtation with equal skill, like Mary in Buckstone's *The Rough Diamond* and Gertrude in J. R. Planché's *Loan of a Lover*. Her following grew quickly and she filled houses nightly.

Suddenly—with an eye for the main chance—Anna moved Maggie over to the New St. Charles Theatre, Bowery, near Chatham Square, slightly more reputable but still catering to a working-class crowd. Its young manager-playwright, James Pilgrim, would supply Maggie with Irish-tinged scripts for nearly a decade. He offered her better roles (but still required her to dance between acts), more frequent billing, and a salary of $35 a week—the equivalent of a stock leading lady but not a star.

As "Margaret Mitchell," she undertook first the role of Sal Forest, the secondary love interest in Samuel Woodworth's pastoral comedy *The Forest Rose*, opposite the Jonathan Plowboy of veteran comedian James Hall Robinson, 41. It was an instant hit, boosted by Sal and Jonathan's flirtatious repartee, squabbling, and predictable reconciliation. By now, Maggie could more than carry her own in comedy and took on as many roles as Pilgrim would provide.[14]

Primarily, he showcased her in melodrama and farce, usually opposite Robinson, and she shone, especially as the titular Colin in *The Youth Who Never Saw a Woman*. Pilgrim also tried her in serious dramas such as *The Stranger*, *The Willow Copse* (as Rose Fielding, a wild, debauched young woman who drives her father mad), *Don Cesar de Bazan* (as a gypsy), and *Ugolino* (as the lead's love interest), but they seemed a poor fit.

Coincidentally, Maggie's half-sister Mary, now 21, was beginning a career as a tragedienne at Barnum's Museum, nearby. Maggie continued to pine for recognition as a tragic actress, essaying such roles as Juliet, but her perky nature precluded success, and managers dissuaded her from it. One young actor, enamored of Maggie, enthused, "What a Romeo and Juliet we'd be!"

only to receive the retort of an older, wiser actor: "Yes, you as Juliet, of course."[15]

Pilgrim, who specialized in creating colorful Irish characters, crafted a plum role just for Maggie: the heroine of his newest melodrama, *Eveleen Wilson* (and for himself, the ludicrously drunken Irishman Barney O'Slashem). The beautiful, innocent Eveleen must fight off her seducer cousin, escaping his clutches (with Barney's help) to wed her hero. *Eveleen* ran intermittently for several weeks, including Maggie's first New York benefit night, April 20, on which she also performed Young Norval. Her name was sufficient to guarantee successful benefits—usually on a Friday night—for thirty years until she discontinued the practice.[16]

Through the end of that season, she enacted virtuous maidens in a string of forgettable melodramas but found her calling in comedy (notably as Susan in *The Lottery Ticket* and Lize in *A Glance at New York*). Summer brought scattered engagements, including a night at the Albany Museum as Young Norval, and benefits for Moore (who must have been proud of his little discovery) and the orchestra leader of the St. Charles, followed by a stint back in Newark in breeches and farces.

Then, in fall 1853, her long career of touring began. Robinson was organizing his tour, to begin with four weeks in Boston starting August 9, and invited Maggie to join, accompanied, of course, by Anna. Boston, competing with New York as a discerning theater center, was in 1853 still subject to Puritan suspicion of the morality of the stage. One jeremiad proclaimed that any young man who attended the theater "becomes dissipated, spends his time, loses his credit, squanders his property, and at last sinks into an early grave."[17]

Robinson had booked the cavernous Eagle Theatre, previously a home for circuses and far from prestigious. There, "Margaret Mitchell" reprised Jack Sheppard, Young Norval, Lize, The Young Scamp, and Eveleen Wilson, and took on new leads in *Beauty and the Beast*; a dramatic adaptation of Susanna Rowson's Revolutionary War–era romantic novel, *Charlotte Temple*; and a Buckstone farce, *Nan, the Good for Nothing*.

This last role, which Maggie would keep in her repertoire for decades, was typical of the hoydens which suited her so well: a disheveled, untutored, undisciplined, willful wild child orphan prone to pranks, whom no one knows what to do with. Repeatedly told she is "good for nothing," she chances one day to save a drowning child, proving that she is "good for something." In Boston, having "gained many admirers by her graceful and spirited delineations," she received her first glowing notices. Her friendliness and propriety were deemed as valuable as her evident talent.[18]

But again, Anna saw a quicker route to star billing for Maggie. Rather than allowing her to move on with Robinson, Anna took her to Baltimore, where

George Joseph Arnold, a New York actor in tragedy and melodrama, who had been in Hamblin's Bowery Company with Maggie, was trying his hand at management. His new Arnold's Olympic on Baltimore Street was to be a house of light comedy and farce, despite his background. Already hired were Sam Glenn (also from the Bowery, a comfortable presence), John A. and Effie (Euphemia) Ellsler, and Charles Burke (brother of comedian Joseph Jefferson III). Arnold, though, had doubts about Maggie: "There isn't enough of her to last," he complained. "She's too little. She'll make one of your fussy women who'll prance about the stage till she catches the man she wants; then no more stage, only marriage, babies, and the rest of it." But he took a chance on her and was proven wrong.[19]

On September 17, 1853, at seventeen she received her first billing as a star. Furthermore, she would no longer have to dance between acts. She worked diligently, cultivating with Arnold's encouragement a wider repertoire of breeches and soubrette roles opposite Burke or the Ellslers. But the venture was failing and Arnold lacked the funds to keep it going. After the November 7 performance, he fled the city ahead of his creditors. At the actors' urging, the thirty-one-year-old Ellsler, who would later become a nationally respected manager, took over and for two weeks attempted to make it pay.

But nothing worked, and on November 26 Ellsler shut down the operation, grousing that Baltimore was never "a paying theatrical town." Unwilling to put these earnest, desperate actors out of work, Ellsler decided to undertake a small-scale tour. Burke bailed out, but the others stayed and a few new actors signed on, including Tom Owens, brother of comedian John E. Owens, and William Goodall (another Bowery veteran) who had been playing leads at the Baltimore Museum. Goodall and Effie Ellsler would play leads, and Maggie—still chaperoned by Anna—would carry comedies and farces with Owens. Ellsler would later claim that it was he who "discovered" Maggie Mitchell and made her a star.[20]

The troupe headed by train to a three-night engagement in remote Cumberland, Maryland, which sported just one small theater. Ellsler decided to open with *The Stranger*, with Effie and Goodall as the leads, with Maggie ("with a song") as the maid to Effie's Mrs. Haller. Quipped Goodall, "I wish I *was* a Stranger to this place." Cumberland, he griped, was a "God-Forsaken land" of inexpressible boredom. Just before the second night's *Lady of Lyons*, nine members of the troupe, including Maggie, her mother, Effie, and Owens, fell ill with typhoid fever, precluding any performance. Maggie, resilient as ever, recovered soonest and nursed her mother, but some of the group remained laid up in Cumberland for two months.[21]

Ellsler took the healthy ones, including Maggie (sans Anna) and Goodall, on to Martinsburg, Virginia, where the only venue was the train depot's dining room, which could hold three hundred people. The intrepid actors moved tables together to form a stage and set up scenery and footlights. Maggie, never one to shy from a challenge, took on the leading roles that had been Effie's, beginning with Pauline in *Lady of Lyons*. The 6:30 p.m performance was suddenly interrupted by the arrival of a train, which disgorged passengers demanding dinner. The actors hastily jumped down and disassembled their stage, resuming only after the seated passengers had departed. For the rest of the week, they began their performances earlier.

After bumping in wagons over the mountains in the snow to Hagerstown, Maryland, they found a hall appropriate for a few performances, and then returned to Cumberland for two weeks, concluding with a benefit for Goodall as Hamlet. This doubtless required considerable doubling of roles, Maggie's remaining unknown—most likely First Gravedigger and Osric, although Ophelia would not have been out of the question given Effie's continuing illness.

Ellsler then received an offer to manage a theater in Utica, New York, to which he took the healthy members of his company (but still paid everyone). They would then tour other towns in upstate New York, including Troy, Rochester, and Syracuse. But, except for a memorable Topsy (in blackface) in the newly ubiquitous *Uncle Tom's Cabin*, Maggie chafed under Ellsler's casting. In early 1854 she refused to play an assigned role and Ellsler fired her in Troy.

But fortune always seemed to smile on Maggie. Around the same time, a Troy theater manager named John G. Cartlitch was forming a stock company for a theater in Cleveland under E. T. Nichols (a cousin of P. T. Barnum, who sent his entire company from New York to help). Cartlitch intended to satisfy Cleveland's "*moral* and *religious* community" by eschewing anything "of an improper or immoral tendency." Maggie seemed a perfect fit, and he offered her a star spot.[22]

But she declined, returning to Manhattan to care for Anna, still quite weak. That spring Maggie only played occasional benefits, including one on March 20 in Philadelphia—her debut there—for Chestnut Street Theatre manager James Quinlan, as Constance in *Love Chase*. (She never played the role again, many years later admitting that "there was too much elegant naughtiness" in the role for her and "too little of hoydenish nature.")[23]

By April, Cartlitch was still seeking stars, especially soubrettes. His first choice was young Agnes Robertson, who had recently immigrated from Scotland and debuted to acclaim in New York. Unable to secure her, he sought the best alternative and contacted Anna, who agreed that it was time for Maggie to tour as a star in her own right. She accepted Cartlitch's offer for Maggie to play three weeks in Cleveland beginning June 12. As a later reviewer expressed it, "In years and stature a child, but with talent and courage, not to say audacity, enough for a giant, she soon dragged her mother off upon a starring tour."[24]

A solo starring tour was a daunting undertaking, but Maggie faced it squarely. Together, mother and daughter organized its route and selected roles best suited to Maggie's personality and performance style. A few were in breeches: Halcyon, Young Scamp, Sheppard, Albert, and the wandering minstrel, Carlo, in Thomas Archer's *Asmodeus; or, the Little Devil's Share*. In some, she switched sexes in the course of the script, like Fanny, who disguises herself as her Cousin Tom, who "pretends" to be Fanny, in Edward Morton's *The Eton Boy*; and cheeky milliner Charlotte Clapier, who disguises herself in military dress, in Stirling's *Captain Charlotte*, which became one of Maggie's favorite roles.

She loved playing impish soubrettes like *Nan*, Milly in Buckstone's *The Maid with the Milking Pail*, Fanny in J. H. Siddons' *An Object of Interest*, and Catharine in Buckstone's *A Husband at Sight*. Most of these were British, adapted from French farces, unprotected by any international copyright law. No Americans were yet churning them out quite as profusely as Stirling and Buckstone.[25]

The soubrette she played most often until dropping it in the 1870s was the titular *Katty O'Sheal* in Pilgrim's two-act farce of palace romantic intrigue. The "madcap" Katty is the maid and confidential go-between of Florence O'Connor and her secret husband, Captain O'Lynn. Irish to the core— "Faith, . . . don't ye be spoilin' your blushes wid the blarney"—she banters with upper-class courtiers, delivers wry asides on their foolishness, and meddles in their affairs. Whenever the outcome of her meddling is in doubt, she sings "Trust to Luck," which quickly became a popular melody. (Her Irish jig drew equal favor.) By play's end, Katty helps set all matters aright, notably the happily revealed marriage of Florence and O'Lynn.[26]

The Maid with the Milking Pail she played consistently for over a decade. Derided as "the most inaccessible, thickheaded little monster," Milly only appears unrefined. With blatant foreshadowing, she resembles the beautiful lost love of an aristocrat. An artist asks her to pose for a portrait and hands her a newspaper to read to complete the picture and steady her nerves, despite her professed illiteracy. Suddenly, Milly drops the newspaper and reveals that she has been dissembling all along: she is a well-educated, highborn lady who has been in hiding from an abusive husband, whose death she has just learned of in the newspaper. She is indeed the lost love of the aristocrat, with whom at play's end she is rapturously united. As Maggie played her, Milly was "rustic but not vulgar, natural yet refined." "She retains enough of the court lady to make the milkmaid doubly charming."[27]

Such soubrettes often speak with a discordant provincial accent, Katty being a prime example. They laugh easily, shun praise or compliments, although deserving of both, and can sing beautifully and dance with abandon. While innocently engaged in working-class pursuits, they meddle in the romantic entanglements of others, fend off the overtures of lecherous older men—Milly repels the advances of Lord Philander—and pine for a cultured man above their station. At the penultimate moment, a twist of fate reveals their true, refined identity or grants them a belated inheritance, raising them to his level, and they blissfully wed. The soubrette shares her intrigues with the audience in frequent asides and in a concluding speech cements their affection.

"With her tricks, her winks, her songs, her shock of flaxen hair, and her baby voice," the soubrette was "a bit of a fraud," observed playwright Charles Dazey, who created several for Maggie:

> She appeals to you one moment by her weakness, yet [can] wrestle with the bold, bad man of the play and come off victorious. . . . She affects a tone infantile in the extreme, yet she has an understanding of worldly affairs—especially of legal matters. . . . With unerring accuracy she detects the true hero and attaches herself to his fortunes. She guesses by intuition the contents and hiding place of the missing will, and you feel certain that before such superhuman prowess villainy is helpless. . . . She is densely ignorant until the last act, when, after a series of most surprising achievements, mental and physical, she is transformed in a breath from the rough, uncultured hoyden into a refined and elegant young lady.[28]

Maggie's breeches characters conducted themselves much like these soubrettes, similarly meddling in the romantic complications of others while improving their stations in life, often gaining, in the end, the hand of a highborn lady.

In early June, Maggie, just eighteen, embarked with Anna and fourteen-year-old Charles, Jr. on her first starring tour aboard the nearly new railroad line to Cleveland. That city of over 25,000 had entertained itinerant acting troupes for thirty years but had only seen its first permanent theaters in 1848. Its dramatic critics espoused high standards. "The day has passed," asserted one, when theatergoers would tolerate actors who "rant in the worst style of the worst actors of the Bowery or to grin at the footlights and repeat the latest cant of the barrooms."[29]

Cartlitch's Atheneum, built to accommodate Jenny Lind's tour in 1851, seated 1,500. But when Maggie arrived, she found British comedienne Julia Bennett (later Barrow) receiving top billing. "Margaret Mitchell from the New York theatres" would perform only in farces, beginning with *Middy Ashore*. She would exist in the limbo of "stock star," worthy of featured billing but not well-enough known to carry a production alone. Either Cartlitch had overpromised or he and Anna had miscommunicated.

Nevertheless, Maggie accepted the circumstances as an opportunity to observe and learn. One night, for instance, Bennett performed a "protean" (multiple-character) role, The Mysterious Stranger in Charles Selby's *Satan in Paris*, who alternates identities and sexes by scene (a tuxedoed Satan, a beautiful Polish princess, an apprentice thief, a dashing military officer, and an angelic young woman). Observing its success, Maggie added the role to her repertoire and began looking for similar "protean" roles. Versatility would become another arrow in her quiver.

She was an instant hit. A "Maggie Mitchell craze" erupted, with "Maggie Mitchell" hats, scarves and other apparel seen everywhere on the streets. Young men swooned. Among them, from her first night on, was a haberdasher two months older than Maggie who fell immediately and (for now) hopelessly in love with her. Henry T. (Hank) Paddock would spend the next fourteen years pining for her, but later dismiss her in these early years as "hardly anything more than a stock star, . . . a little girl in short dresses."[30]

Clevelanders would claim for decades that it was they who first discovered Maggie Mitchell. Critics there were certainly smitten: she was "an immense favorite. . . . If Miss Robertson comes here, she must look to her laurels." Possessing "more dramatic talent than anyone we have ever seen," Maggie was "destined to take a prominent and honorable position amongst the rising actors of America." "There is a naiveté, a freshness in her delineations that is most charming, and an audience never wearies with her presence." Her benefit drew a shower of bouquets and an overflowing box office.[31]

Her popularity unquestioned, Cartlitch engaged her for another three weeks of farces, now with top billing. She began to give interviews, fudging her age as fourteen in one and sixteen in another (initiating a lifetime of public speculation about that topic), downplaying her training under Hamblin and Ellsler and stressing her dependent family. Interviewers pronounced her an enchanting, natural prodigy, with

> . . . a fine form, and an eye and a head indicating a superior mind and a high order of intellect. Her voice is clear, strong, and sweet, filling with ease the largest halls with its musical inflections. Her style of acting is entirely natural and original. . . . Never having been practiced upon the stage and trained in stock companies to imitate stars, she plays from her own impulses and conceptions, never mistaking her characters, being taught by nature and not by the stage manager. . . . That she is bound soon to [rank with] stars of the American stage there can be no doubt.[32]

Buoyed by her success as Norval and Jack, Maggie continued to entertain thoughts of playing tragedy. She undertook more serious roles, including Madeline in Donizetti's *Daughter of the Regiment* and the title role in *Thérèse*. The former, for her second Cleveland benefit, was a resounding success, bringing her another shower of bouquets and two beribboned white turtle doves tossed from an upper box amid clamorous applause.

A rival Cleveland manager, Joseph C. Foster, also managed a theater in Pittsburgh and knew a good thing when he saw it. He already had a dancer-soubrette, the beautiful Sallie St. Clair, but he promptly booked Maggie for a week in Pittsburgh. A week after closing in Cleveland, she opened for Foster—sharing billing with St. Clair—on August 1 in *Middy Ashore* and *Eton Boy*, followed by her customary singing and dancing and chipper soubrettes. Pittsburgh reviewers lauded her as enthusiastically as those in Cleveland had. Her benefit drew a full house.

Anna now began purchasing local newspapers and clipping rave reviews to use as advance publicity for Maggie's upcoming performances, and booked the next in Detroit, at MacFarland's Metropolitan Theatre. To her growing repertoire, Maggie added Paul in Buckstone's three-act comedy (with frequent songs), *The Pet of the Petticoats*, another breeches role which Laura Keene had recently made famous in New York. It became a mainstay for years, especially for benefits. Paul, the sheltered nephew of an abbess, is innocence incarnate, the "pet" of the convent's young inhabitants, two of whom are married and held against their wishes. Outside the convent, bewildered by worldly life, Paul encounters their husbands, two randy military officers. He foils their plan to seduce a visiting actress and through a clever ruse reunites them with their wives. Detroit critics, too, showered praise on Maggie.

She won as many hearts in Detroit as she had in Cleveland, collecting love letters from smitten admirers for months. One, which she kept all her life, reported that since she left, life had been dull. He wished that her copious talents would continue to receive "that true reward they so justly merit." In a P.S. he hoped she would count his many inkblots as kisses.[33]

Whereas experienced stars took restorative summer vacations, Maggie's family's financial straits led her—apparently without Anna's demanding it—to work through these early summers. She moved on to Buffalo for a week in September, then back to Cleveland, where Cartlitch had hyped this "Pet of the Public," as the opening star for his fall season, opposite the familiar William Goodall. Every night for a week full houses greeted her with enthusiastic applause, and reviewers were kind.

Foster by now was impressed enough with Maggie to bill her as the opening star on October 11 of his fall season in Pittsburgh. After two weeks of farces, still yearning to perform serious drama, she played Nancy in *Oliver Twist* for her benefit night but paired it with *Pet*. There, and for two more weeks in Detroit with MacFarland, she drew full houses, the walls of which "nightly reverberate with the applause of the enraptured audience," and enthusiastic reviews.[34]

Foster recommended Maggie to his former partner James Quinlan, now manager of the aging Chestnut Street Theatre in Philadelphia. Billed as "the great original American Fairy Star," she opened there on December 4 in *Pet* and *Object of Interest* but for the first time faced significant competition. Robertson and her playwright-actor husband Dion Boucicault were holding forth at the prestigious Walnut Street Theatre. Descriptions of Robertson were remarkably similar to those of Maggie: "a delightful little creature with a perfect figure, a beautiful face and a voice full of rippling music," whose versatility was "artistic in the extreme." Young men fell over themselves to declare their adoration. Still, Maggie drew equally good houses and praise for her "graceful ease and vivacity." But after her second night, Quinlan, who had been struggling for five seasons, abruptly closed the theater, discouraged by the deterioration of the neighborhood. Maggie and Anna retreated to Manhattan for the holidays.[35]

For 1855 Anna mapped out an aggressive tour, beginning with two weeks at the Albany Museum, on its last legs under managers Henry Meech and Charles T. Smith. Paired with farces, Maggie took on more dramatic roles: Juliet, Norval, Rose Fielding, Jack Sheppard, the bold Olympia Cigniani in J. S. Coyne's *Queen of the Abruzzi*, and the willful Christine [sic] of Sweden in Charles Shannon's *The Youthful Queen*. These were young, intrepid, high-spirited characters appropriate to Maggie's demeanor and personality. But it was becoming evident that she was unsuited for such roles. She was eventually "dissuaded"—it is unclear by whom, but likely by Anna and by the tepid audience and critical response—from continuing in this vein. For another decade, though, she couldn't resist an occasional Juliet, and at times even Romeo.[36]

In Albany, a visiting manager from Troy stopped by to evaluate Maggie but balked upon seeing her diminutive form: "W-h-a-t! That there Miss Mitchell! . . . That snip of a girl is the actress? . . . I don't want her. . . . I thought she was a woman!" It would be another year, under new management, before Maggie played Troy, but it became important to her personally.[37]

The next test of her embryonic fame was Chicago, which had enjoyed professional theater for less than two decades. Manager John B. Rice, of the highly successful Chicago Theatre on Dearborn Street, contracted with Anna for Maggie to perform there for two weeks at $50 a week (over $1,400 today) with two benefits, a reasonable star salary at that time. Despite heavy snowfall, she opened to one of the largest houses of the season on February 19 as *The Mysterious Stranger* and *Milly*, bringing in $267.50 (with tickets averaging about thirty-five cents). In her first week, Rice took in nearly $1,500; receipts on the night of her benefit were $347 (over $10,000 today). Her second week was almost as profitable: $1,323, with that week's benefit bringing in $414. That second benefit was a tour de force of nine roles in four scripts. In addition to The Young Scamp and Milly, she played Marie (later published as Josephine) in Buckstone's *Child of the Regiment*, with songs. To these, she added another "protean" script which she would play over a hundred times in the next six years.[38]

James Pilgrim had adapted *The Ladies' Stratagem* specifically for Maggie from a 1775 two-act farce by Irish playwright Robert Hitchcock. In it, she enacted five roles: Maggie Wilton; Moll Tozer, with an Irish jig; Alexis, a Greek Boy, with the song "Why Don't the Men Propose?" and a Greek Dance; Capt. Eugene Charlemagne, a French officer; and Gizelle, "the Night Dancer," who sang "Banks of the Blue Mozelle" (later supplanted by "Love's Parting" and then "The Red Petticoat"—Maggie was flexible). It was an evening of astounding versatility for an eighteen-year-old actress. After her final curtain, several prominent men of Chicago, including Senator Stephan A. Douglas, presented her with a gold watch which she treasured for life.[39]

One night in Chicago she barely escaped injury from a falling wall of scenery which pitched her across the stage. This luck would continue throughout her career, allowing her to elude several potentially fatal accidents. The city's critics were as eager as those in Cleveland to celebrate what they, too, considered their discovery, praising her "expressive face, noble forehead and beautiful eyes," "genial sunny face and clearly cut profile." She exhibited "undoubted genius" and "a high degree of spirit" that carried "glorious promise."[40]

After returning to Detroit, she expanded her territory to St. Louis, opening there on April 9 at the People's Theatre, focusing on protean characters. While lauded for her moral character—as she would be throughout her career—she drew criticism for overuse of certain gestures, particularly an abrupt "singular throw of the arm and hand with a crack or catch of the fingers." Since this complaint did not recur, she learned from her mistakes.[41]

Back in Pittsburgh, she picked up another serious role: the titular lead in Thomas Talfourd's verse drama *Ion*, a foundling and potential assassin who kills himself to end the plague of Argos. But she would soon drop it from her repertoire in favor of lighthearted fare. That spring, she also jettisoned the name "Margaret," to be henceforth billed as "Maggie Mitchell," more conducive to her sprightly persona.

In May she played two weeks at the Albany Theatre on Green Street (the Museum having gone under), again for Smith. In his company was Emma Skerrett, for whose benefit she had debuted four years before, doubtless surprised to see her newfound stardom. In her usual farces played to full houses, Maggie garnered more plaudits and jewelry, including a pair of diamond earrings from Smith's hopelessly enamored partner, David M. Barnes. (He even took out ads in New York newspapers posing as her manager, to no avail. Anna still tenaciously filled that role, consulting with veteran New York agent Charles Henry Wilson.)

Following two weeks at William Fleming's National Theatre in Boston—a step up from Robinson's Eagle—including a benefit for Skerrett, whose husband had just died, Maggie returned to Green Street in Albany. There she tried out another new lead breeches role: Irish schoolboy Bob Nettles in *To Parents and Guardians*, Boucicault's alteration of a Tom Taylor play. The character perpetrates a run of practical jokes—the audience always in on them—on a hapless schoolmaster. Emulating Robertson, who had played Bob to sold-out houses in New York in 1853, Maggie kept Bob in her repertoire for fifteen years.

She was supported on her June 22 benefit night by two of her sisters: Mary, 23, coming off a successful run as Topsy in a touring production of *Uncle Tom's Cabin*, and Emma, 14, who had debuted as a dancer in New York two years before. To Maggie's Rosalind in *As You Like It*, Mary enacted Celia and Emma danced the Highland Fling between acts. The next night, Maggie and Mary teamed as Catharine and Augusta, respectively, in *Husband at Sight*. Both of Maggie's siblings, opined the *Albany Argus*, "share the remarkable beauty of their sister, and the former is a most pleasing actress, while the latter is a charming little dancer." Their "triple beauty excited no little admiration and enthusiasm." Mary would prove so attractive to Albanians that she would remain in that stock company and later marry its manager. A minority opinion, the *Argus* thought Maggie's future lay in the "higher walks of the drama" like *As You Like It*.[42]

Regardless of her choice of material, her future held nationwide stardom.

NOTES

1. Many variations of Maggie's birthdate exist and there is no birthdate on her gravestone. The most commonly repeated erroneous date is 1832, but Anna and Charles did not marry until three years after that, after Lomax's death. The most accurate, specific date is that of her christening on the roster at St. Paul's, which I have used. Anna provided an incorrect birthdate of 1805 for herself in U.S. census records, perhaps to appear the same age as Charles, who may not have known her true age.

2. *Cleveland Plain Dealer*, July 7, 1854; *Cincinnati Daily Gazette*, Feb. 22, 1878.

3. *St. Joseph (MO) Commercial* quoted in *Rock Island (IL) Argus*, Apr. 28, 1876.

4. Other accounts have the first theatrical performance she witnessed being one by comedian Barney Williams, who did perform in New York at the National Theatre in August 1850. There are also mentions of her acting child roles (which she did all her life) and being briefly employed as a child sweeping out Barnum's Museum, but none of these can be verified.

5. Andrew Cherry, *The Soldier's Daughter* in *The English and American Stage*, London: The Dramatic Repository, Shakespeare-Gallery, 1807, III:12; Carboy.

6. *Rochester (NY) Democrat and Chronicle*, Dec. 25, 1881.

7. John Barron, "The Stage Before the War," *Baltimore Sun*, Nov. 4, 1906 and Jan. 20, 1907.

8. *NYH* Aug. 18, 1850; *Rochester* [NY] *Democrat and Chronicle*, Dec. 25, 1881; Carboy. Maggie was not a "ballet girl," as some accounts state, since Hamblin that fall could not afford a *corps*. She later remembered her first salary as being $4.50 a week.

9. For a thorough review of the practice of breeches roles, see Elizabeth Reitz Mullenix, *Wearing the Breeches: Gender on the Antebellum Stage*, New York: St. Martin's Press, 2000.

10. On November 7, 1851, future Broadway director-choreographer Julian Bugher Mitchell was born, and controversy endures as to whether he was Maggie's son or nephew. In later legal documents he lists his parents as Sophia Mitchell (Maggie's half-sister, then 24) and her husband Alfred Mitchell, 33 (Maggie's father's younger brother). Lacking DNA proof, it is impossible to tell whether Maggie gave birth during this interval and gave the baby to Sophia and Alfred to raise, or Sophia herself gave birth to Julian. He was raised as Sophia and Alfred's child, and the preponderance of contemporary references to him are as Maggie's nephew. He was not invited to either of Maggie's weddings, nor mentioned in her will. Furthermore, it is difficult to believe that with Maggie's petite frame, playing breeches roles, her pregnancy would not have been evident in late September 1851. The possibility cannot be discounted however, given Hamblin's notoriety for seducing teenaged actresses, that he may have impregnated Maggie, that being the unrecorded offense "on the part of management" which led Anna to remove her daughter from the Bowery company as soon as her contract expired in spring 1852.

11. Luther Holden, "Maggie Mitchell," *Famous American Actors of To-day*, eds. Frederic Edward McKay and Charles E. L. Wingate, New York: T. Y. Crowell, 1896, 313; MM interview in *Rochester* [NY] *Democrat and Chronicle*, Dec. 25, 1881.

12. *New York Times*, Oct. 2, 1887.

13. Actor George Joseph Arnold in Carboy; Holden 313. It is possible that Maggie's disappearance from May 1852 until the following winter was a confinement of pregnancy with Julian and his birthdate was fudged backward by a year for his entire life. Again, it is only possible at this remove to conjecture.

14. Woodworth's characters were appropriated from Royall Tyler's 1787 *The Contrast*.

15. Carboy.

16. On a benefit night, an actress claimed all box office proceeds, minus incidental expenses of the management.

17. *New England Farmer* (Boston), Sept. 10, 1853.

18. Boston correspondent for *Spirit of the Times*, Sept. 17, 1853.

19. Carboy.

20. John A. Ellsler, *The Stage Memories of John A. Ellsler*, ed. Effie Ellsler Weston, Cleveland: The Rowfant Club, 1950, 91.

21. Goodall to "Dear John" [possibly Ellsler], Jan. 2, 1853, HTC.

22. *Forest City (OH) Democrat*, Feb. 27, 1854.

23. *New York Sun*, Mar. 3, 1889.

24. *Spirit of the Times*, June 28, 1862. Carlitch, 61, had been a renowned equestrian actor in England, notably the original Mazeppa.

25. *Katty O'Sheal* was billed under a wide variety of spellings over the years.

26. James Pilgrim, *Katty O'Sheal*, New York: Samuel French Inc's Standard Drama CCXCV, 1870.

27. John Buckstone Baldwin, *The Maid with the Milking Pail*, London: T. H. Lacy, 1853; *Spirit of the Times*, June 28, 1862.

28. *New York Times*, Sept. 17, 1893.

29. John Vacha, *Showtime in Cleveland*, Kent, OH: Kent State University Press, 2001, 19.

30. *Syracuse Standard*, Dec. 27, 1881.

31. *Cleveland Plain Dealer*, June 13, 19, 29 and 30, 1854.

32. *Cleveland Plain Dealer*, July 7, 1854.

33. Thomas C. McNabb to MM, Mar. 12, 1855, MM Papers, MS Collection 4552, New York Public Library (henceforth NYPL).

34. *Detroit Free Press*, Oct. 31, 1854.

35. John M. Barron in *Baltimore Sun*, Nov. 25, 1906; *United States Gazette and North American*, Dec. 4–5, 1854; Weldon B. Durham, ed. *American Theatre Companies, 1749–1887*, New York: Greenwood Press, 1986, 200.

36. New York Correspondent for *Wheeling Register*, Oct. 9, 1886.

37. Carboy.

38. James Napier Wilt, "The History of the Two Rice Theaters in Chicago from 1847 to 1857" (PhD diss., University of Chicago, 1923), 317–22. Buckstone's play is not to be confused with *Daughter of the Regiment*.

39. Pilgrim's play is not to be confused with Hannah Cowley's *The Belle's Stratagem*.

40. *Chicago Tribune*, Feb. 20. 1855; *Chicago Sunday Times*, May 10, 1876.

41. *St. Louis Democrat*, Apr. 6, 1855.

42. *Boston Post*, June 7, 1855; *Albany Argus*, June 22–23, 1855.

Chapter 2

"emphatically the People's Pet"

Overnight stardom was one thing. But how to sustain it? It would take fortitude, just the right repertoire, and expanding her following. For three years Maggie would tackle all three. With the guidance of Anna and perceptive managers, Maggie had chosen roles fit for her natural spunky energy that allowed her with a wink to charm audiences. She displayed not just an innate, versatile talent, but a youthful freshness combined with a preternatural maturity, a free-spirited effervescence (and *lack* of formal stage training), unquestioned physical beauty, and the obvious goodness of a pure heart.

Fame could be ephemeral. To sustain it would require constant effort and refining her repertoire, always pursuing the perfect star vehicle. Driven by the twin needs of her career and her family's financial stability, she again plunged through the summer with no break, spending July and August 1855 in Chicago, St. Louis, and Cleveland performing farces. In St. Louis she discovered a protean "operetta" (with songs) by Bernard in which she portrayed all of the titular *Four Sisters*: the sensible Caroline Merton; Diana, a jockey "fond of whipping and spurring"; romantic Eugenia, "fond of moonlight and melody"; and domestic Ellen, "fond of comfort and chattering." She would charm audiences with this quartet for over a decade.[1]

Refining her "line" of characters that summer, she added those in droll burlettas. Her sense of impish fun, enhanced by frequent glances out to the audience, left them feeling that they were in on the joke. Her Polly Ann in O. E. Durivage's *Lady of the Lions* spoofed Pauline (and indirectly her aspirations in tragedy) in *Lady of Lyons*; her *In-Go-Ma*, by A. R. Smith of St. Louis, satirized the turgid *Ingomar the Barbarian*; and her Jenny Leatherlungs poked fun at Lind's widespread fame. She would also try, but quickly discard, roles in full-length plays which failed to suit her, including Lady Gay

Spanker in Boucicault's *London Assurance* and Martha Gibbs in Thomas and John Maddison Morton's *All That Glitters Is Not Gold*.

During the 1855–56 season, with Maggie's name a selling point, managers promoted her starring engagements well ahead of her appearances. But travel was tough. When she returned to the road in September she faced the usual grueling inconveniences—what theater historian Thomas Postlewait has delineated as "a series of train stops, delays, breakdowns, missed connections, boarding houses, cheap hotels, filthy rooms, poor restaurants, inadequately equipped theaters, incompetent musicians, bad weather, poor management, drunken companions, exhaustion, illness, social prejudice, and uncertain pay."[2]

Nevertheless, she launched herself into Syracuse, Detroit, St. Louis, Chicago, Cleveland, and Pittsburgh, performing *Maid with the Milking Pail, Satan in Paris, Captain Charlotte, Lady of the Lions, Eton Boy, Middy Ashore, Ladies' Stratagem, Husband at Sight, Nan, Four Sisters, Young Scamp*, and others of their ilk, "causing more side-ache than can be cured in a month." "Emphatically the People's Pet," she continued to accrue valuable tokens of that affection. On her last night in St. Louis, she garnered "a beautiful set of sable furs, the cost of which was $300, and also a handsome set of jewelry." The correspondent for the *New York Herald* summarized her appeal: "the legs, it would seem, rather beat the head."[3]

As remarkable as Maggie's rise had been, during the same two years her chief competitor, Agnes Robertson, had attained stardom in large Eastern cities, playing the same soubrette and breeches roles, many created (or adapted) by her husband. She had debuted in one of his protean pieces, *The Young Actress*, in five different roles: "Maria, the Manager's Daughter" images herself as first Effie Heatherblossom, a singing Scottish lass; then Cheshire vocalist Sally Bacon (later mutated into two different opera stars); Paul, a French minstrel boy (later becoming Hans, a German minstrel); and Corney, a singing Irish bogtrotter. Not to be eclipsed, Maggie appropriated this protean role, debuting it in Cleveland on December 6.

More to her liking was *The French Spy; or, The Siege of Constantina*, by John Thomas Haines, which had brought exceptional fame to Céline Céleste, whose versatility and sinuous, unrestrained physicality provided Maggie with a stylistic model. Its protean lead role consisted of three vividly different characters: Omar, a Wild Arab boy (who performs a deranged, mystic dance); Henri St. Alme, a lancer in the French Army (who despite Maggie's tiny frame required her to fight a battle wielding a broadsword); and Mathilde de Marie, a desirable French lady attired in a gauzy white harem outfit. About this time, she (or Anna) began to promote this ability to play a variety of roles in one night. Her limit was ten, generally reserved for benefits.

Realizing the opportunities that *French Spy* afforded to showcase her acting, mime, song, dance, and shapely figure, Maggie played it for the first time before a full house on December 14 for her benefit in Pittsburgh. Drawing enthusiastic critical response, she played it regularly for a decade. A week later she took on the soubrette role of Gertrude, a precocious child, in Augustus Harris' two-act comedy, *The Little Treasure*, which she kept in her repertoire for fifteen years.

During Christmas Week she returned to Baltimore a far bigger star with a broader repertoire than had been the case under Arnold only two years before. The manager of the Charles Street Theatre there was John T. Ford, who would become a dependable supporter and lifelong friend. The following spring he would introduce Maggie to audiences in Washington, D.C., generating admiration from the highest levels of government. Baltimore critics attributed Maggie's appeal to her "exquisite naturalness. There is a wild, airy freedom and vivacity in all she says or does," and an "intuitive undulatory grace in every movement." The "genius" of this "vivacious little creature" lay in her "delightful abandon."[4]

As she had done the previous year, Maggie began 1856 in Albany. Hailed as "the American Fairy Star" and "the Star of the West," she filled two weeks with her exuberant farces. The management also served up a new production of Charles Dickens' *The Cricket on the Hearth*, adapted for the stage by Albert Smith. Maggie played the endearing Dot Peerybingle, who proves loyal to husband and family, keeping an important secret in the process and abetting young love. The titular cricket, a portent for the family's good fortune, presaged Maggie's phenomenal fortune and her most famous role, still five years in her future.

In Albany, she added another new role, which further displayed her versatility: actress Peg Woffington in Charles Reade and Tom Taylor's comedy, *Masks and Faces*. The role was simultaneously a fetching love interest, a cunning schemer who has risen from rough Irish roots to Thespian fame, and a sharp-tongued skewer of critics and two-timing husbands. The play provided a privileged glimpse of life "before and behind the curtain," including a fanciful description of a "green room": "the bower where fairies put off their wings, and goddesses become dowdies—where Lady Macbeth weeps over her lapdog's indigestion and Belvidera [*Venice Preserved*] groans over the amount of her last milliner's bill." A weeklong snowstorm failed to deter attendance or the warmth of Maggie's critical reception.[5]

In January she appeared for the first time in Providence, Rhode Island, at William C. Forbes' theater, attracting immense audiences. Forbes, 48, a Bowery veteran and middling tragedian who had become a successful manager in southern cities, quickly gained Maggie's trust and friendship. She would return regularly to Providence for over thirty years.

It may have been Forbes who steered Maggie to her next new territory. In February she moved into the South, an area of the country that had long been hospitable to performers. Opening in Richmond on the 18th at the Marshall Theatre with *Little Treasure* and *Maid*, followed by *Katty, Middy, Pet, Stratagem, Lions, Young Actress*, and *Charlotte*, she quickly became a favorite. On the eve of the Panic of 1857, Richmond's population of nearly 34,000—many of them new Irish immigrants—thrived in an economy built on cotton, tobacco, the Tredegar Iron Works, and a robust slave trade. Being seen at the theater was *de rigueur* for fashionable citizens, and a frequent attendee was Governor Henry Alexander Wise, an early, fervent secessionist. Maggie would have gleaned in Richmond her first comprehension of the strength of that cause. While not advisable in a staid New York or Boston company, Maggie's willingness in Richmond to throw aside restraint and address the audience directly, improvising as she went, boosted her popularity. Playing leads opposite her was Linington R. "Len" Shewell, 23, on the cusp of a New York and Boston career that would intersect with Maggie's.

Encouragement to perform in Richmond may also have come from Ford, who would soon take over the Marshall's management, and who in early March brought her to his National Theatre in Washington. Despite its status, the nation's capital in 1856 remained a cultural backwater, its citizens far from sophisticated. Maggie's feisty soubrettes, exuding boundless good humor, satisfied their entertainment needs. Her petite figure, expressive features, and graceful movement wowed men and women alike. "The soul of animation," she "seems to impart a portion of her spirit to the whole company. In versatility [protean roles] she has no superior." She was no doubt cheered by favorable comparisons to the "bewitching piquancy of Agnes Robertson—quite as attractive in person as that universal favorite—and with far more physical power."[6]

Then it was back to St. Louis (her third time in a year), where after a two-day travel delay she opened for manager George Wood on March 12 as Katty, Milly, and Nan. Critics praised her "irresistible" "natural genius" and her "sprightly abandon." Her "hearty laugh" helped "dispel the general [financial] gloom."[7]

Next, she debuted in Cincinnati, a town known for its strong religious opposition to the theater (where actors had to travel to their next engagement by steamboat, as its trains did not run on Sundays). Nonetheless, at the People's Theater, managed *in absentia* by Wood, Maggie drew crowded houses and laudatory reviews. Her farces were "admirably adapted to [those] who, fatigued by the business of the day, seek relief in light vivacious entertainment. There is no flagging in her acting, but one continuous round of joyousness."[8]

Crossing the Ohio River, she expanded her territory into Louisville, Kentucky, whose citizens she won over as quickly as those of other cities. Especially popular were her five characters in *Stratagem* and her song, "Trust to Luck," in *Katty*. The former, performed on three nights, began in her hands to morph into a fluid series of vignettes rather than a coherent script, indicating the licenses she was taking with it. Such would be the case for a number of her scripts over the years, beefing up her central role. In doing so she paralleled the amplification of such roles as Lord Dundreary by E. A. Sothern in *Our American Cousin*, Rip Van Winkle by Joseph Jefferson, and Solon Shingle by John E. Owens in *The People's Lawyer*.

Then it was back up the river to Wheeling, Virginia, where she was again an immediate success, "the greatest attraction which has ever visited this city." Her best assets continued to be her youthful energy, her beauty, her amalgam of innocence, flirtatiousness, and wit, and her manifest song-and-dance talent. Here, she tried another new work, also soon abandoned, a three-act ethnic comedy by J. H. Amherst called *Ireland as It Is*, she as Judy O'Trot.[9]

Her fifth appearance at the Pittsburgh Theatre, still under Joseph Foster's management, did nothing to diminish her following. To mollify any inhabitants' moral opposition to theatergoing, the *Pittsburgh Post* touted her "private character of unsuspected purity." Maggie herself reinforced that point, in character, near the conclusion of *Masks and Faces*: "When hereafter... you hear harsh sentence passed on us, whose lot is admiration, but rarely love; triumph but never tranquility—think sometimes of poor Peg Woffington, and say, stage masks may cover honest faces, and hearts beat true beneath a tinseled robe."[10]

Maggie turned twenty near the end of this grueling season, spending June in Troy, Albany, and (for the first time) in Columbus, Ohio. This "most bewitching little creature we have ever seen upon the stage" seemingly inspired the other performers: their "acting seems quite impregnated with the effervescing spirit of the charming Maggie." In Albany rumors circulated that she was soon to marry a young local lawyer, but like countless such rumors for the next decade, it was false. Even Maggie's father had to occasionally deny such gossip.[11]

For three weeks in July, she drew well at Rice's Theatre in Chicago. Prominent among the otherwise unremarkable stock company was a new "first old man," a twenty-four-year-old Bostonian who would perform with Maggie for much of the rest of her career, Robert F. McClannin. Her benefits brought her an average of $240 (over $7,000 today), a fine close to her exhausting second season touring as a star.

Anna and Maggie spent a three-week break in August back in New York, charting out an expanded tour for the 1856–57 season. It would last a full year, comprise twenty-one cities and towns (eight of them new) and cover over 7,300 miles—one of the most extensive tours of Maggie's entire career.

She began on September 3 in Baltimore under the supportive Ford, who had recently taken over the Holliday Street Theatre which he would guide for another twenty-five years, to which he would always welcome Maggie. Although most of her performances were in farces and protean pieces (notably *French Spy*), she dipped a bit back into melodrama. She added a new work, written for her by James Pilgrim, entitled *Our Maggie; or, the Star of the West*. No script of it is extant, and it was never published, but it seems to have been a one-woman show, a sort of Night with Maggie Mitchell. In it, she played five different characters (including a male in blackface) and delivered a variety of songs and dances. One jaunty number, "Maggie By My Side," she sang and danced for two years as an olio act and inserted improbably into several different scripts. But after two seasons, as she refined her repertoire, *Our Maggie* yielded to better vehicles.

For two weeks in Wheeling, she stuck to the same farces, but for a benefit night as Juliet, which was not reviewed. In Columbus in October she dabbled in serious drama, following again in the footsteps of Céleste, playing Marco in Charles Selby's *The Marble Heart*. Marco, a woman of the world, is by turns alluring and scornful, ultimately breaking the heart of a young sculptor, driving him to madness. (The double role also entailed portraying a diaphanously draped "nude" statue.) Maggie performed the role creditably despite an uneven supporting company.

From Columbus, she submitted papers applying for membership in the fairly new (1848) American Dramatic Fund Association, its mission in keeping with her own strong beliefs of the need to aid ailing and destitute fellow actors. Truthfully asserting that she had earned her livelihood as a professional actress for at least three years, she questionably provided a birthdate which appears on no other documents in her life: June 14, 1838. She was accepted and maintained her membership though the group's merger with the Actors' Fund of America in the 1880s. She would never need to draw from its funds, but readily and repeatedly supported its charitable efforts.

November took her back to Wood's People's Theatre in St. Louis in her usual farces, her sister Emma joining her. Her Rosalind in *As You Like It* drew favor, and in *French Spy,* she was deemed a close second to the definitive Céleste. Her acting showed more polish, with "a finishing grace that renders her efforts immeasurably superior to those of any artist in the same class of characters. . . . Her voice is more matured, her physical charms now more fully developed" (contributing, no doubt, to the growth of her devoted male following). "We now see instead of the volatile, crude, but pleasing actress an artiste of exquisite taste and refinement."[12]

On November 5, performing *Satan in Paris*, she ran afoul of Wood's actor-stage manager James McVicker. For two nights McVicker refused her request to lay down a carpet to cover the bare stage floor which dirtied her dresses. Equally strong-willed, they took their case to the audience, which hissed McVicker. When he threatened to close the theater, Maggie simply decamped to the rival St. Louis Theatre, where she was wildly applauded as Juliet opposite a breeches Romeo. Moving on to Chicago, at Rice's Theatre her box office figures topped those of her previous appearance by 26 percent, and her first week's benefit—in *French Spy*, *Stratagem*, and as Nanette in Buckstone's *Mischief Making*—brought her an astounding $578.12 (over $17,000 today).[13]

Expanding her territory further, Maggie and Anna next headed 900 miles south, where she got off on the wrong foot by arriving nearly a week late to Ben DeBar's St. Charles Theatre in New Orleans. Whether this was a scheduling error, miscommunication, or complications of winter travel remains unknown, and DeBar filled in with other actors. Although the rotund, notoriously hard-working DeBar held everyone to high standards, Maggie met them, for this engagement began a twenty-one-year professional and personal relationship that ended only with DeBar's death. She would provide him with 223 performances, more than any other star.

When she tardily opened on Saturday, December 13, she was visibly nervous and encountered indifference and critical skepticism. To gain popular favor, she agreed to perform the following night despite a lifelong aversion to performing on a Sunday. As the week went along, she visibly improved. On her benefit night, she played an exhausting nine characters in three plays and "received cheer after cheer, with the waving of hats and kerchiefs, and all the bouquets that were in the house." She had become "the best and most brilliant star that has shone in our theatrical firmament this season."[14]

The *New Orleans Creole*, though, begged to differ with the "lunacy" of fellow critics who exalted Maggie "to the seventh heaven of luminous stars." They "must carry a huge telescope, for we have not been able to see the luminosity so be lauded." "The truth" was that

> ... the so-called "Fairy Star" was a pleasant little lady, who jigged, sung [sic] and capered herself into the good graces of the peanut-crackers of the pit and very susceptible young gentlemen of the dress circle. She had considerable merit as a vaudeville actress, but never was entitled to be dignified with the name of "star." She is a two-and-sixpence dramatic steamboat running up a small dramatic stream, ... a pretty little goldfish swimming gaily up a brook, of no particular consequence to the angler.... Her natural sprightliness enables her to invest trifles with some interest, [but she requires] study, years and experience ... to make her a shining light.[15]

Whenever such critical carping arose throughout her career, Maggie simply took it in stride, refined her repertoire, strove to improve, and continued her tour, head held high. She began 1857 with two new southern cities: Mobile and Memphis. Well received for two weeks in Mobile, Maggie became a special favorite in Memphis, extending her initial one-week contract at David Ash's Memphis Theatre to an extraordinary five weeks. Part of her draw there was her circumspect decorum. This "estimable lady has passed through that fiery ordeal [a career in the theater] and has come forth unscathed. Her mother, an intelligent and worthy lady, accompanies her" (the tacit implication being that Anna helped keep Maggie "unscathed"). Still, there was some opposition to the "inexcusable" use of "uncalled for and unexpected" profanity in her scripts, including "too much 'damned,' 'damnation,' 'devil,' etc."[16]

Undaunted, she defied naysayers by introducing during this engagement one of her naughtiest roles, another in which Robertson had excelled in New York: Cleopatra in Charles Selby's 1837 burletta of *Antony and Cleopatra* played as a saucy "grisette" (young working-class Frenchwoman) with an exceedingly flirtatious demeanor. Maggie carried it off by striking the ideal blend of sweetness, naiveté, and allure.

Despite weeks of harshly inclement weather, she filled the house every night. There had been some skepticism due to Ash's advance hype, "but we were not prepared for the triumph she has achieved. . . . No actress that has appeared at the Memphis Theatre within several years has so won upon audiences as this lady has." Her engagement was the most successful of the season, "a perfect triumph from beginning to end." Her farewell benefit was "literally jammed, [with] a larger number of ladies than usually attend, while the remaining seats, and every place where a person could stand, were occupied by gentlemen." Ash "hit the taste of the Memphis public exactly in securing an engagement with Miss Mitchell, and she will always be a favorite here." So, the South had embraced Maggie as warmly as the North had.[17]

Returning 800 miles upriver to Chicago, Maggie opened on February 23 at Perry Marshall's Chicago Theatre, Rice having retired. From the start, she began "crazing the heads of the young gentleman . . . by her charms of person and graceful coquetry of winning smiles, pretty hair, sparkling eyes, &c., which are such formidable weapons when a lady who knows how to use them holds them." As some reviewers acknowledged, "Miss Mitchell is by no means much of an actress, and probably don't profess to be, but she is nevertheless popular, and a very pretty little "titbit" of a woman, with a something of the sylph in her airy movements, and of the nightingale in her voice." She added a sixth character to *Our Maggie* while still enacting the five in *Stratagem* and *French Spy*, the four in *Four Sisters*, and an occasional serious drama, including *Marble Heart*.[18]

Another new script, Thomas de Walden's *Margot the Poultry Dealer*, provided her with yet another sassy-yet-sensible, rustic soubrette who outsmarts the machinations of a titled man to lure her into dishonor. Never published, it proved so popular that Maggie played it hundreds of times for fifteen years.[19]

April took her back to Richmond and Baltimore, billed as "Our Maggie." Whether she chose this appellation either from her protean revue or from the massive press coverage two years earlier of the abduction in New York of a twelve-year-old girl termed "Our Maggie" (and found alive in Chicago in 1856, her captor arrested) is unknown. In both cities, full houses applauded her versatility and vivacity. For her Baltimore benefit, she played ten different characters with four dances and three songs. Her dramatic skills (and fetching figure) were evidenced by three nights—including a benefit—of *Marble Heart*.

The supporting stock company at Ford's Holliday Street Theatre was exceptionally strong. "First Walking Gentleman" Harry Langdon would perform opposite Maggie for several years and come to know her, her sister Mary, and both of Mary's husbands well. The troupe generated two of the biggest comedic stars of the American stage in the second half of the century: Joseph Jefferson III and Stuart Robson. The extent of Maggie's popularity there can be measured by the gift she received from grateful Baltimoreans upon her departure: "a magnificent diamond finger-ring, a large cluster of diamonds encircling a costly opal stone."[20]

From Baltimore, she returned to Forbes' in Providence, hailed there as a "beautiful child of genius." After a quick week each in New Bedford, Massachusetts (a new venue) and Boston, supported by Forbes' stock company, she returned to Wheeling. Four of the next five towns were new, beginning with Lexington, Kentucky, where she opened June 8 at Hough's Varieties to effusive reviews and large, fashionable houses that increased each night, showering her with bouquets. On June 19, while enacting Peg Woffington for her benefit, she suffered another potentially lethal accident. A stagehand's pistol exploded in the wings a few feet from her, scorching her face and neck, ending that night's performance as well as her engagement in Lexington.[21]

She recovered sufficiently by June 22 to open for DeBar in St. Louis in *Stratagem* and *Pet*. With the support of his competent company, she tried another serious role, Narramattah in William Bayle Bernard's adaptation of James Fenimore Cooper's *The Wept of Wish-Ton-Wish* (a fictional frontier settlement in Connecticut). It, too, had brought acclaim to Céleste, and now stretched Maggie's skills. The anguished Narramattah is torn between the white family from whom she was abducted by Narragansetts and their chief, Conanchet, to whom she is wed and to whom she has borne a child. When Conanchet is taken prisoner and condemned to die, "Maggie Mitchell does not rant it or tear it, or imitate the doing of it." Instead, "you see and know and feel the very moment when her heart strings break." Returned to her Caucasian family, she fails to recognize her father and sister until the latter croons a poignant melody from their infancy. "At the sounds, and touched by the magic spell of association, memory awakens with a cry, that thrills to the heart. She throws herself upon the breast of the anxious man, calls him by the endearing name of the father, while she reaches one embracing arm toward the sister whom she simultaneously recognizes." It provided a striking contrast to her farces: "In Narramattah she makes your heart bleed—in Katty O'Shiel [sic] she makes your side ache. Dear, charming, enchanting Maggie Mitchell!"[22]

Joining her in St. Louis was her old comrade Sam Glenn, with his "Dutch" characters. For unknown reasons, possibly among them the nomadic nature of Maggie's itinerary that season, he took over from Anna the scheduling of their 1857–58 tour. Anna, though, would still travel with her.

Again with no summer break, Maggie headed in July into more new territory: Peoria, Decatur, and Bloomington, Illinois, drawing crowded houses in all three towns. Among the stock company of the Gaiety Theatre in Bloomington was her fellow youthful amateur, James W. Collier, who in 1853 had married Maggie's half-sister Mary. Audiences liked his pleasant, florid face, with its blue eyes, brown hair, high forehead, and bristle mustache, and his warm voice. For his July 30 benefit as Marquis Beauseant in *Lady of Lyons* (the drama, not the farcical *Lady of the Lions*), he asked Maggie to perform in breeches as Claude Melnotte. Unwilling to drop her serious aspirations, she agreed, and the reception was so positive that she remained in Bloomington a few extra days.

Her dilatory departure from Bloomington and an unplanned stop in Cleveland (perhaps to see Paddock?) prevented her timely arrival in New York, where Glenn had arranged for her first appearance there as a star, at Burton's New Theatre. Considerably larger and further uptown than Burton's Chambers Street Theatre where he had first encountered little Maggie, it was a managerial risk that would soon fail in the Panic of 1857. Glenn's explanation for her delay was "unforeseen circumstances," later amended to "sickness" and then "illness of a sister." Her failure to appear as advertised on August 3 led Burton to replace her with young, beautiful, talented Susan Denin, who proved more than satisfactory to his audiences.[23]

Arriving on August 6, she hit the ground running with three consecutive nights of *French Spy* and *Katty*, eliciting favorable comparisons to Céleste. New Yorkers recalled the Maggie of four years ago as merely a "clever and promising presenter of eccentric female roles" who "did not make any very extraordinary sensation." But in the intervening years, her performances had improved considerably. Denin was forgotten as Maggie, called out for repeated ovations, "made a decided hit," establishing herself in "the very first rank" of American soubrettes.[24]

Throughout August and September, supplemented by Glenn's "Dutch" humor, Maggie filled houses in Manhattan, Albany and Rochester, earning an "enviable reputation as a superior versatile actress." Her greatest assets were her "lovely, light and graceful figure," which she applied with "the greatest *abandon*," and "the surprising rapidity, grace, ease and expressiveness of her posturing. Every turn of the body, inclination of the head, and gesture, however minute, is full of meaning, and she produced the most striking effects."[25]

In Chicago in October at North's nearly new National Theatre, to her well-received Narramattah and her established repertoire, she added for her benefit another serious drama: *The Young Prince*. Adapted from the French by Charles Gayler and retitled *The Love of a Prince*, Laura Keene had performed its lead role, Prince Charles Frederick, in New York in May. Maggie had Pilgrim cut its three acts to two, playing it successfully until 1863 when she was stayed by Gayler's court injunction, copyright occasionally being enforced.[26]

Glenn had arranged for a supporting company from St. Louis to meet them in their next town—another new one—Dubuque, Iowa. There, Maggie's performances yielded her a gift of jewelry worth over $100. She and Glenn then returned east, to Richmond's Marshall Theatre, whose young but talented stock company included three men she would come to know well: the handsome John W. Albaugh, 20, another adolescent amateur ally who would become family; John M. Barron, 22, who would later tour with her and serve as her advance manager; and Edwin Adams, 23, who would become a close friend and a comedy star in his own right. In *Wept* and other, lighter pieces (notably *Katty*), she provided Richmonders "unalloyed satisfaction.... Miss Mitchell has improved (if such a thing were possible) since her last visit." Her performances "would anywhere be considered creditable to a much older and more experienced artist."[27]

She introduced on November 16 another role in which Céleste had found fame, and which she had seen Fanny Wallack perform back in her Bowery days. In Buckstone's melodramatic *Green Bushes*, another dual role showcasing her diversity, she transformed wild frontier native Miami into the refined yet miserable Madame St. Aubert. Success with it in Richmond led Maggie to perform it for another three years. She risked going a little too far for her Richmond audience by adding a suggestive dance to her burlesque Cleopatra. On nights it was announced, ladies stayed away, and she was urged to withdraw it. But she knew what she was doing, for this "production which requires but little modesty . . . drew the masculine portion of playgoers like a mustard plaster."[28]

Maggie and Glenn then opened more new territory by hopping a steamboat to Norfolk, Virginia (its railroad line still under construction). Her alluring charms remained on ample display: "We would caution our susceptible young men beforehand to be on their guard against her witchiness," warned the *Norfolk Day Book*. Shrewdly, she included *Antony and Cleopatra* on the bill for two of her six nights there, drawing tremendous (male) applause.[29]

By fall 1857 the ravages of the financial panic were everywhere in evidence. The *New York Clipper* estimated that it would be difficult to find two theaters in the United States able to meet expenses. Yet, astoundingly, Maggie continued to fill houses. When she played Baltimore in December the Holliday Street Theatre "was literally packed, from parquette to dome, from the footlights to the street, with a mass of people greater than we have ever seen within its walls." Hundreds of disappointed ticket-seekers were turned away.[30]

Later that month she and Glenn added two more new towns: Savannah and Augusta, Georgia, where she proved hugely popular with audiences and critics alike. Her Narramattah and her Arab Boy in *French Spy* were especially praiseworthy. "Beautiful beyond description, with a figure fit for a Venus, her lithe form seems . . . the very impersonation of lively reality." Opposite Glenn in *Katty*, she was "glee, made a living thing."[31]

That winter an increasing number of laudatory odes, songs, and dances, including "The Maggie Mitchell Polka," began appearing, especially in the South. Proclaimed one admirer of "sweet Maggie":

> Oh! How my heart went pitty-pat/ When first her sweet voice I heard;
> Just like a man entranced, I sat/ But could not speak a word. . . .
> She wins all hearts where'er she goes/ And does so without trying;
> She won my own and well she knows/ For herself it is, I'm dying.

Another wished,

> Oh! Maggie, may you ever/ Remain as bright and fair,
> And may that young heart never/ Be dimmed to dark despair.[32]

Maggie came to regard the South as a warmly hospitable second home. Northern correspondent George Alfred Townsend "never wondered why many actors were strongly predisposed toward the South. There, their social status is nine times as big as with us." Northerners tended to socially ostracize actors, he said, while "the South took them into affable fellowship."[33]

That maxim held during Maggie's return to Ash's Memphis Theatre at the start of 1858. For three weeks she and Glenn, supported by an unusually capable stock company, filled houses that included a healthy share of ladies. She had "no equal in her line," and even "the severest critic cannot find room for censure." Countering those who might object to her roles' flirtatiousness, one paper reminded patrons that "all her pieces have a moral tendency—to hold up truth and virtue—and this alone ought to recommend her to the patronage of her sex and an enlightened community."[34]

With the Mississippi River breaking up in an early thaw, Maggie and Glenn followed its tortuous course up to Louisville on the steamboat *Memphis*, opening at Mozart Hall on February 1. But the rigors of incessant travel and a week of winter weather took their toll on Maggie. She fell seriously ill, unable to perform, leading manager Benjamin J. Duffield to substitute other productions, then close the Mozart for two days. Fortunately, Maggie was comforted in her illness by her half-sister Mary Collier, who played soubrettes opposite her husband in Duffield's company. When Maggie did resume acting, she found Louisville audiences disappointing.

Her next engagement, in Lexington, generated an embarrassing situation. In the habit of receiving courtly gentlemen in her hotel suite (where was Anna?), she one evening received there an elderly unmarried judge, but after a short while abandoned him, ducking into another room to entertain "a young gentleman." The disconcerted judge graciously withdrew, and Maggie did not emerge until the following morning, accompanied by the young man. Their excuse was that they had not heard the hotel porter locking them in, as "both being interested in their lively chat, neither had heard the turning of the key." The judge took the incident in good humor, but Maggie needed to be more circumspect.[35]

She found a familiar face managing in Cincinnati, her next stop. George Wood now catered to Cincinnati's working-class audiences, who embraced Maggie's March 1 opening with enthusiasm. Hers was the most successful engagement of Wood's season, and his business markedly fell off when she and Glenn moved on to Columbus. There, she was proclaimed "a nonpareil." "It is no wonder that the people rush to see her." "If Miss Mitchell continues playing [Milly] in this captivating sort of manner, . . . it is not safe for a great many of the nice young men who go to the theatre every night."[36]

Returning to Ford's Holliday Street Theatre in Baltimore, Maggie and Glenn both tried out new roles. He moved from "Dutch" sketches to full-length comedies, and she took on a new farce, a new Irish drama, and a heroic melodrama. The first of these, *My Son Diana*, by Augustus Harris, was poorly received and she never played it again. The second, *The Wild Irish Girl*, Pilgrim had loosely adapted specifically for Maggie from—to the point of being a burletta of—an 1806 romantic novel of the same name by Lady Morgan (Sydney Owenson). In it, Maggie played the intriguing Countess Zytomir.

The melodrama, *Jessie Brown*, ostensibly written for Maggie by Pilgrim, closely echoed—and was pirated from—the identically titled work by Dion Boucicault which was enjoying a long run on Broadway with Robertson in the title role. Depicting the brutal events of the Sepoy rebellion in India the previous year, *Jessie Brown* required the intrepid Maggie, amid omnipresent bagpipes and assorted spectacle, to defy the wrath of the evil Nena Sahib, scale his palace walls, share her final morsel of food with a starving child while deliriously envisioning her mother's grave, and single-handedly inspire a regiment not to surrender. Ultimately, the attack of the Sepoys is "gallantly repulsed" with "terrible slaughter of the rebels by a bombshell thrown from the wall by Jessie," and all ends well. Maggie played *Jessie* in various cities until its topicality wore thin.[37]

That spring, in newspapers across the country, rumors appeared of her impending engagement to "a young Clevelander" (likely Paddock, and plausibly started by him). This, of course, would be terrible news to the "troops of infatuated young men who have so persistently chased the sparkling little comedienne through the country." Glenn, as Maggie's manager, did his best to quash the rumors, but they cropped up from time to time until eventually proven true.[38]

When Maggie and Glenn traveled north to Providence, they found a theater in dire financial straits. William C. Forbes had had to periodically close his theater due to the aftereffects of the Financial Panic. On some nights his box office yielded less than $20 against expenses of nearly $150. Although Maggie did comparatively well, drawing the largest houses of the season, with nearly as many fashionably dressed ladies as men, Forbes closed the theater for good after she left. Her benefit on April 23 was boosted by the reappearance on the stage of her sister Emma, now 16, who paired with Maggie—both in breeches—in Mordecai Noah's *The Wandering Boys*.

In May, good houses and favorable notices greeted Maggie at North's National Theatre in Chicago and Foster's New National Theatre in Pittsburgh. The latter venue was suffering the same financial difficulties as Forbes, but Foster provided Maggie with ample production resources and she reversed its fortunes for a time. Even those with meager resources managed to scrape together the cost of admission when Maggie came to town.[39]

June took her back to Columbus for her erstwhile manager, John Ellsler. Maggie had no way of knowing that nineteen-year-old Lizzie Maddern, who teamed with her there for *Wandering Boys*, would in a few years give birth to a future star, Minnie Maddern Fiske. Two of Lizzie's sisters, Emma and Mary, would perform in the original cast of Maggie's famous *Fanchon*, and Lizzie and Emma would emerge as Maggie Mitchell imitators. In Columbus Maggie earned some of the most effusive reviews of her early career from the smitten critic of the *Daily Ohio Statesman*: "The beauty, piquancy, vivacity, and versatility of this great favorite of the public are unsurpassed on the American, or any other, stage. Her faultless charms, in which the diamond lens would not have revealed the slightest imperfection, are extraordinary." She radiated "a concentrated essence of wit, beauty, and accomplishments, regulated by a cultivated taste. . . . When lighted up by the sparkling animation [of her acting], the expression of her face is vivid and brilliant to an extraordinary degree." He wished in vain that Maggie might appear in Shakespearean comedies, possibly *As You Like It* or *Twelfth Night*.[40]

Ellsler also managed now in Cleveland, Maggie and Glenn's next destination. For the past two years Ellsler had found initial success there, patronized by the city's fashionable elite, but now he, too, was foundering. He had taken the theater over from Foster, who had failed when he over-optimistically modified the house to accommodate 2,000 people, unreasonable for a city whose population hovered around 30,000. The prosperity Maggie had brought to Providence and Pittsburgh failed to save Ellsler, either. For a week in mid-June she and Glenn struggled to attract crowds, but "theatricals are at very low ebb in Cleveland," lamented the *Plain Dealer*. Despite appealing to "chivalry" on Maggie's behalf, "no attraction seems to draw."[41]

Her childhood poverty always in the back of her mind, Maggie managed to escape the fortunes of these managers. Several newspapers in 1858 assessed the personal wealth of prominent actors, and Maggie at only age twenty-two was reportedly worth about $7,000 ($197,000 today). By comparison, Edwin Booth, three years her senior, was then worth about $5,000. Her comfortable status can be discerned from purchases made during her touring; in Baltimore, she had bought $186.87 ($5,500 today) worth of cloth, ribbon, paper, shawls, robe, gloves, capes, and handkerchiefs.[42]

Finally, now that Glenn was arranging Maggie's schedule, she took the summer off to rest at home in New York, performing only two benefits for other actors. For the first, at Holliday Street in Baltimore on July 3 honoring Glenn, she performed *A Husband at Sight* with Mary in her Baltimore debut. A week later, back at the Bowery Theatre, she teamed up with Mary's husband, James Collier, in *Antony and Cleopatra* on behalf of actor T. W. Newton. For the next four seasons, Collier would tour steadily with Maggie, and through him, she would meet and grow close to his friend John Wilkes Booth.

NOTES

1. Nov. 24, 1834 playbill in *The Era Almanack*, 1872.

2. Thomas Postlewait, "The Hieroglyphic Stage," *The Cambridge History of American Theatre, vol. II 1870–1945*, eds. Don B. Wilmeth and Christopher Bigsby, New York: Cambridge University Press, 1999, 150.

3. *Cleveland Herald*, Oct. 27, 1855; *St. Louis Democrat*, Oct. 30, 1855; *Detroit Free Press*, Dec. 6, 1855; *New York Herald*, Nov. 19, 1855.

4. *Baltimore Patriot and Commercial Gazette*, Dec. 24, 1855; *Baltimore American and Commercial Advertiser*, Dec. 25, 1855; *Spirit of the Times*, Jan. 5, 1856.

5. Tom Taylor and Charles Reade, *Masks and Faces*, New York: Samuel French, 1854, 32.

6. *Washington Daily Union*, Mar. 5, 1856; *Washington Evening Star*, Mar. 7, 1856; *Daily American Organ (Washington DC)*, Mar. 8, 1856.

7. *Missouri Democrat*, Mar. 13, 15 and 21, 1856.

8. *Spirit of the Times*, Apr. 12, 1856.

9. *Wheeling Daily Intelligencer*, May 9, 1856.

10. *Pittsburgh Morning Post*, May 30, 1856; Taylor, 57.

11. *(Columbus) Ohio Statesman*, June 24 and 25, 1856.

12. *Missouri Democrat*, Oct. 28 and 31, 1856.

13. Wilt 389–90.

14. *New Orleans Daily Crescent*, Dec. 22, 1856.

15. *New Orleans Daily Creole*, Dec. 17, 1856.

16. *Memphis Daily Appeal*, Jan. 23, 1857; *Memphis Public Ledger*, Mar. 27, 1875.

17. *Memphis Daily Appeal*, Feb. 1 and 17, 1857; *Memphis Eagle and Enquirer*, Jan. 25 and 31 and Feb. 7 and 18, 1857.

18. *Western Railroad Gazette (Chicago)*, Feb. 28, 1857.

19. *Margot* was originally adapted by de Walden for Lola Montez from J. R. Planché's *The Pride of the Market*, in turn adapted in 1846 from a French comedy.

20. *Miner's Journal (Pottsville, PA)*, May 9, 1857.

21. *Providence Daily Post*, May 5, 1857.

22. Durham 248; *Louisville Courier*, Sept. 25, 1860; *Rochester (NY) Union and Advertiser*, Sept. 8, 1857.

23. *New York Daily Tribune*, Aug. 4, 1857; *Spirit of the Times*, Aug. 8, 1857; Odell, VI:529.

24. *New York Herald*, Aug. 7, 1857.

25. *New York Herald*, Aug. 7 and 12, 1857; New York correspondent for *New Orleans Sunday Delta*, Aug. 16, 1857.

26. The 1856 act of Congress granting American playwrights rights of public performance of their plays was largely unenforced, but efforts such as Gayler's were sometimes successful. Pilgrim, like other playwrights, freely adapted the material of other authors and then claimed ownership.

27. *Richmond Dispatch*, Nov. 5 and 6, 1857.

28. Richmond correspondent in *Boston Saturday Evening Gazette*, Dec. 5, 1857.

29. *Norfolk Day Book*, Nov. 17, 1857.

30. *Baltimore Patriot* quoted in *Savannah Morning News*, Dec. 1, 1857.

31. *Savannah Morning News*, Dec. 12, 1857; *Augusta Constitutionalist*, Dec. 22, 1857.

32. *Savannah Morning News*, Apr. 27 and June 10, 1858; Louisville correspondent quoted in *New York Clipper*, Nov. 10, 1860.

33. George Alfred Townsend, *The Life, Crime and Capture of John Wilkes Booth*, New York: Dick and Fitzgerald, 1865, 22.

34. *Memphis Daily Eagle and Enquirer*, Jan. 14, 1858.

35. *Spirit of the Times*, May 8, 1858.

36. *(Columbus) Ohio Statesman*, Mar. 16, 1858; *New York Clipper*, Mar. 27, 1858.

37. *Baltimore Sun*, Apr. 6, 1858.

38. *Cleveland Plain Dealer*, Mar. 23, 1858.

39. A rival Chicago manager, David Hanchett, for whom Maggie had performed in Wheeling, unsuccessfully sued her for breach of contract, alleging she had agreed to perform for him instead of North.

40. Anonymous critic of the (Columbus) *Ohio Statesman*, June 5–8, 1858.

41. *Cleveland Plain Dealer*, June 18, 1858.

42. Bill from Baltimore dry goods dealer Robert W. Dryden, NYPL MS Collection 4552.

Chapter 3

"quivering masculine hearts"

For 1858–59 Maggie would perform thirty-five different scripts but narrow them down to ten standards, playing each dozen of times: *Katty, French Spy, Young Prince, Margot, Milly, Ladies' Stratagem, Wept, Four Sisters, Pet,* and *Satan in Paris*. Except for the tragic *Wept*, these displayed her as saucy, sprightly and intrepid, showcasing her physical charms and protean versatility.

All of twenty-two, she opened her fifth season as a star on August 23 in Boston, still under Glenn and accompanied by Anna, at James Pilgrim's newly redecorated, 2,500-seat National Theatre. Despite that city's fallout from the Panic of 1857, for two weeks she drew immense audiences. Her "bewitching vivacity" filled its 76'-wide stage in a repertoire understandably favoring Pilgrim's plays, and most nights he joined her onstage. The costumes and pageantry of his lavish staging of *Young Prince* would have bankrupted many a smaller theater.[1]

By September 13 Maggie was back in Richmond at the newly renovated Marshall Theatre, where comanagers George Kunkel and Thomas Moxley had assembled a strong stock company. One handsome new utility player would become a special friend: twenty-year-old John Wilkes Booth. Among other roles, he enacted Uncas, the heartless Mohican chief in *Wept* who executes Narramattah's husband, Conanchet. His electrifying performances, even in small roles, promised greater fame. "When he walked the stage," said John Ellsler, "sparks of genius flashed" from his "large, dark and expressive" eyes and animated features. "Upon his shoulders, nature had placed as handsome and intellectual a head as ever crowned her handiwork." Actress Clara Morris adored "the ivory pallor of his skin, the inky blackness of his densely thick hair, [and] the heavy lids of his glowing eyes [that] gave a touch of mystery to his face.... As the sunflowers turn upon their stalks to follow the beloved sun, so old or young, our faces smiling, turned to him."[2]

Booth gained immediate popularity in Richmond, associating with "all the best men and many of the finest women," recalled fellow actor Edward Alfriend. "With men, John Wilkes was most dignified in manner, bearing himself with insouciant care and grace, and was a brilliant talker. With women, he was a man of irresistible fascination because of his superbly handsome face, conversational brilliancy, and a peculiar halo of romance with which he invested himself and which the ardent imagination of women amplified." It is no wonder that Maggie's charisma and Booth's magnetism bonded instantly. They went riding together and corresponded freely. It took no time for rumors to fly.[3]

How close did they become? Despite contemporary rumors and modern speculation, absent any extant record of the degree of their emotional and sexual involvement, it is impossible to say exactly what transpired between Maggie and Booth. But it is clear that they grew quite close, a fondness she treasured for the rest of her life.

Returning to the nation's capital, Maggie opened on October 4 at Kunkel and Moxley's new Washington Theatre on Pennsylvania Avenue at 11th Street. Night after night she surpassed expectations and the lingering aura of Céleste's recent engagement. Critics adored this "beautiful and sparkling young comedienne, whose witchery and joyous abandon" were enhanced by "a vivacity, archness, and abandon of style, wholly irresistible."[4]

On the way to St. Louis, she and Glenn ran into transportation issues again, arriving late at Wood's Theatre, embarrassing manager George Wood. Before her delayed arrival on Tuesday, October 19, he had arranged for bills to be posted around the city that morning proclaiming her "enthusiastic reception" the *previous* night. But as the *Missouri Republican* observed after Maggie's week of crowded houses, those bills "would not have been very far wrong if published another morning later." Maggie was happy to find among Wood's company the dependable Robert F. McClannin, who supported her in thirteen different productions, including *French Spy* and *Katty*. At her closing benefit, citizens presented her with $150 and a silver service, which she proudly sent on to New York.[5]

Following two weeks in Cincinnati, Glenn had scheduled them to arrive in Memphis on November 22. But to save a few dollars, instead of an overland train they unwisely took a steamboat, which for three days ran into one difficulty after another. In Memphis, manager William Crisp was forced to refund ticket money to openly disgruntled patrons. Newspapers deemed Maggie's delay "unpardonable."[6]

Yet after she sent word on the 25th guaranteeing she would appear that night, a large, fashionable audience gathered at Crisp's Gaiety Theatre for *French Spy* and *Four Sisters*. The slapdash rehearsal which preceded them yielded a poor performance by the stock players and the orchestra. But by the end of the night, all was forgiven. Maggie had again triumphed, even though one critic pronounced *French Spy* "destitute of interesting plot or literary merit." This "inexplicable dumb show" required "no other gift than that of a well-proportioned person." Maggie, exactly that, "held her appreciative auditors in rapt attention." As her two weeks in Memphis went along, Crisp warmed to her, as did Treasurer Matthew W. Canning (a close friend of Booth), on whom Maggie would later rely as a manager in the South. Stage manager John Cartlitch, who had helped start her career in Cleveland, worked to improve the level of her support. But audiences diminished day by day due to heavy rains and the Gaiety's chilly interior.[7]

An all-day and all-night Sunday rail journey took her next to Nashville, arriving barely in time to conduct Monday's rehearsal. But Crisp also owned that city's Gaiety Theatre, and for two weeks he provided no better level of support than he had in Memphis. The actors required constant, audible prompting and mugged excessively to get cheap laughs. One play dragged on because of slow changes of amateurishly painted backdrops (scenes from one side bleeding through to the other, showing a different location). A faulty stove in the orchestra pit, to compensate for the unusually cold, rainy weather, belched smoke onto the stage and into the audience. Surprisingly, due to Maggie's name, crowded houses attended. Remarkably, "several churchgoers are known to have slipped in and taken back seats, and seemed to enjoy the fun as well as the rest."[8]

Critics in these southern towns were not rubes. Memphis and Nashville had seen visiting professional actors since the early years of the century. Granted, early attempts to form resident stock companies had produced mixed results, but standards and competency were rising, only to be crushed by the Civil War and Reconstruction. Some managers, like Crisp, had organized "circuits" for their stars. George F. Marchant operated a four-city "southern circuit," which Maggie began during the Christmas holiday in Charleston, her first time there. She opened with *Mysterious Stranger* (her new title for *Satan in Paris*, probably changed to appease religious scruples), followed by several nights of farces and serious roles: *Masks and Faces*, *Wept*, and *Douglas*. Surprisingly large houses attended despite bad weather and competition from a nearby opera company.

Maggie and Glenn parted ways in January 1859, he going north to Baltimore to arrange the rest of her tour, and she to Marchant's Concert Hall in Augusta, Georgia. There, she kept her sometimes-rowdy audiences—likely reminding her of the Bowery—"entranced and spellbound." Her Milly, pronounced as improved from her previous visit, was "the very embodiment of Irish piquancy and sprightliness." But as one discerning critic observed, "Miss Mitchell cannot divest herself of her own identity. . . . She always wears the air and face of 'charming Maggie.'"[9]

In Savannah, Maggie played "Marchant's Varieties," in reality St. Andrew's Hall, a large brick building with a stage thrown up at one end. But Marchant's stock company provided excellent support. Competing with the hugely popular Marsh Troupe of child actors at the nearby Athenaeum, she drew crowded houses for a week, sticking with lighter fare. Her "genuine, rich, unctuous Irish brogue [was] the best we have ever heard." She drew praise for her beauty, voice, versatility and "artlessness—her entire truthfulness to nature—her complete identification of herself with the part, . . . which makes one forget that she is acting at all." Heavy rain on her benefit night did little to deter attendance, and she closed her engagement the next night by singing "Maggie By My Side" (becoming her signature song) to the largest house of the season. At the curtain, Savannahians presented her with a hefty sum of cash.[10]

She was not as wildly hailed at her next stop, two weeks at Marchant's Thalian Hall in Wilmington, North Carolina, her first time there. She drew modest houses, heavy rains keeping patrons away, yet she played with her usual verve, and audiences slowly improved.

February brought her back to Richmond for a week at the Marshall, where she reconnected with Booth, his Uncas again terrifying her Narramattah. In other, lighter roles, she filled the house, employing "the merry twinkling of those cunning eyes." "It seems that the people will go to see Maggie, when they wouldn't go to see anybody or anything else."[11]

Kunkel and Moxley sent along most of their Richmond Company to support Maggie at their Phoenix Hall in Petersburg, Virginia, another meager venue. Its stock of scenery was sufficient, but its stage and house were dimly lit and its seating—with no class divisions—consisted of hard-backed chairs. The Richmond actors were unimpressed, regarding Petersburg as "a God Forsaken Town" whose residents did nothing but drink whiskey and sell slaves. "To act and give an effective performance [in Phoenix Hall] required dramatic talent of superlative talent." Nevertheless, Maggie soldiered on, attracting sizable audiences.[12]

She provided Petersburg theatergoers with a bold surprise on her last night, February 24. In addition to performing the protean *Four Sisters*, she played Romeo to the Juliet of Mrs. I. B. Phillips (Booth played Paris), earning Maggie afterward an $85 diamond ring. When she volunteered to repeat the role back in Richmond, the *Richmond Dispatch* spoke for many: "That piquant little imposter, Maggie Mitchell, who has been making everybody believe she was simply a comedienne and winning over so many hearts in that role, is to appear in tragedy and give the public another proof of her versatility in rendering the character of Romeo—who could have believed it! The romping, Merrie Maggie as Romeo!"[13]

From there it was back to Ford's Holliday Street Theatre in Baltimore in early March. Her return "was hailed with an enthusiasm bordering upon rapture," especially by countless "quivering masculine hearts." Ford provided another strong supporting company, which included Helen Muzzy, who would play important Old Woman roles for Maggie for over a decade in Baltimore and Washington, and as First Walking Gentleman her friend John M. Barron brought up from Richmond. Ford billed Maggie as the "Minne-ha-ha of the Drama," due to her success in *Wept*, and took out massive newspaper ads with "Maggie" spelled out acrostically with words of praise.[14]

For her first benefit, Maggie performed an astounding three full-length plays: *French Spy*, *Four Sisters*, and the title role (in breeches) of Centorino in *The Pirate Prince*, a new melodrama by Pilgrim (being of negligible literary worth and only tolerably received, within two months she dropped it). She also tinkered with the roles and songs in her "protean burletta," Pilgrim's *Ladies' Stratagem*. These became: Margaret Wilton; a Greek Boy who incongruously sang "Why Don't the Men Propose?" and performed a Greek Dance; Moll Tozer, with an Irish Jig; Capt. Charlemagne; and Gizelle, "the Night Dancer," with the song "Love's Parting." She would continue to make such changes for the rest of her career.[15]

Maggie, rejoined by Glenn, opened in Chicago on March 21. The manager there was James H. McVicker, 37, with whom Maggie had had the run-in in St. Louis over the carpet, but who would become a warm, lifelong friend, in whose theaters she would perform regularly for many years. He had opened his eponymous theater two years before, just when the financial panic struck, but had stuck it out and now was able to fill houses with a strong stock company. One of the finest theaters in America, it was immense, seating 2,000 with a stage 80' wide and 60' deep, more than sufficient for McVicker's trademark spectacular melodramas. An ebullient low comedian, he usually took leading roles in farces. Already a beloved fixture in Chicago society, he would over the next four decades become the dean of Chicago theater, notable for his vigorous defense of his art in the face of religious opposition.[16]

After stops in Lexington and Frankfort (a destination she never repeated), Kentucky, Maggie was again late to St. Louis, opening for George Wood on May 3. For two weeks she earned laughter and positive reviews that often focused on her physicality. In *French Spy*, this meant her "reckless abandon" and "well-formed and voluptuous figure, which is exhibited to advantage in the picturesque Arab costume she wears. . . . All were enchanted with the exhibition of a form of indescribable loveliness displayed with tantalizing grace and taste in a costume well adapted to present its most prominent charms to the best advantage." Immense audiences were "in raptures."[17]

Her songs were equally compelling. She kept "Trust to Luck" and her jig in *Katty*, but moved "Why Don't the Men Propose?" again, to another new piece, a J. M. Morton farce called *The Little Savage*. In this, she played Kate Dalrymple, a supposed heiress fought over by two ardent swains, who feigns insanity and rudeness to expose the more mercenary one. Maggie kept it in her repertoire for over two decades.

In Cincinnati, playing leads opposite her at Wood's Theatre were her mentor, John Ellsler, and her brother-in-law, James Collier. She rotated farces to see which ones struck and continued tinkering with her songs, moving "Why Don't the Men Propose?" yet again (its sentiments being universal) to the burlesque *Antony and Cleopatra*. She played to overflowing houses.

On June 6 she opened with part of Kunkel and Moxley's company in Lynchburg, Virginia, (another new town) in Dudley Hall, sticking with pieces the Richmond Company already knew. In *Wept*, Booth again played Uncas. She returned with these actors to Petersburg's Phoenix Hall, repeating her Lynchburg repertoire, and then moved with them to Richmond, closing their season with a benefit for Kunkel on June 26.

By this time, it was widely known that Maggie loved fast horses, a love she would nurture as long as she was able. She likely rode with Booth now, as they later did in other cities. At the close of Kunkel's benefit, the citizens of Richmond presented her with a handsome riding horse, which they preemptively named "Maggie Mitchell." Returning now to New York, she may quietly have sold the horse, as she would have had nowhere to keep it. A different, but identically named racehorse, a bay mare, appeared in racing columns for years, winning a fair share of its races.

Other than volunteering for a July 16 benefit for A. H. "Dolly" Davenport at Niblo's Garden, Maggie enjoyed five weeks of well-deserved rest with her parents on Staten Island. That summer Anna reclaimed control of Maggie's touring when Glenn signed on to act with Ford in Washington. Mother and daughter planned the 1859–60 season, which would feature a wider array of scripts (forty-one in all, with most in breeches or as multiple characters), but maintain nearly the same core repertoire (with *Wandering Boys* and *Husband at Sight* more frequent, and *Wept* and *Pet* less often). By far the most frequent piece was still *Katty*, a consistent crowd-pleaser.

Maggie opened her last antebellum season on August 29 in Baltimore at Ford's Holliday Street Theatre, playing ten characters (with songs and dances) in *Satan in Paris* and *The Four Sisters* with even stronger support than previously. Along with Stuart Robson was James W. Wallack, Jr. on the cusp of major stardom, and Wallack's wife, née Ann Waring, another Hamblin-Bowery alumna. Maggie's half-sister, Mary Collier, joined her in *Wandering Boys* for a benefit night.

Mary, now 27, was encountering moderate success in serious drama, but their sister Emma, 18, was not, sporadically performing small roles and olio acts. Mary traveled with Maggie to her next venue, the Pine Street Theatre in Providence, where Mary would join the stock company. It was poorly located, poorly equipped, and housed a barely respectable stock company (even with Mary). Maggie's engagement did little to help its bottom line, and the entire venture proved so unprofitable that the new managers soon closed.

She did far better in Philadelphia at the end of September. At Mrs. M. Augusta Garrettson's Walnut Street Theatre (Maggie's first time there, a step up from Chestnut Street); she earned full houses and a crowd of new admirers. Reviewers admired her ability to transition on the same night from the grief of Narramattah to the gaiety of Katty, and her impulsive energy: "the blood seems to run like lightning through her veins." But discerning critics also knocked her imperfect Irish jig, uneven accent, and lack of education reflected in incorrectly pronounced words. But on balance "she is young enough to make up for her short-comings (and they are not many)." And regardless of critical carping, sizable audiences cheered and her popularity soared.[18]

Beginning a two-decade trend, that fall her name became a valuable commercial commodity. "Maggie Mitchell" cigars and twists of chewing tobacco went on sale for five and ten cents. She lent her endorsement to (and likely reaped healthy royalties from) such products as a "skin beautifier" called "Jules Jared's L'Email de Paris," which she supposedly used regularly, finding that "it instantly imparts a natural bloom and freshness to the complexion."[19]

On October 10 she opened in Richmond for Kunkel and Moxley, whose stock company still included the charismatic Booth, with whom she grew even closer. She would publicly admit to no more than seeing Booth as "a very handsome and agreeable man," but two such compelling, beautiful young people—he 21 and she 23—were naturally mutually attracted. In Richmond, Maggie added another new role: Beauty in J. R. Planché's "fairy spectacle" *Beauty and the Beast*. This lavish new production provided scenes in the "Bower of Roses," "Garden of Delights," "Magnificent Fountains," and, suggestively, "Beauty's Boudoir," along with an onstage locomotive, "twinkling stars," and several fairy dances and songs—Maggie delivering most. She was "bewitching and fascinating" in this "gorgeous and enchanting spectacle." Among the smitten in the audience was Virginia Governor and future Confederate General Henry Wise, who named his thoroughbred "Maggie" after her.[20]

The last two months of 1859 took Maggie and Anna illogically to Memphis, then Boston, then Cincinnati. At the New Memphis Theatre, manager William C. Thompson provided a far stronger stock company than Crisp had. Maggie easily filled houses. In *Satan in Paris*, "she made that individual so charming that . . . for the first time in our lives, we were half in love with the Evil One." When she ventured out during the day to attend the Memphis races, she was the "cynosure of all neighboring eyes, . . . as charming off the stage as upon it."[21]

In Boston, she played two weeks at the Howard Athenaeum for struggling manager E. L. Davenport, a respected, versatile actor. Her popularity helped him, boosted by her well-attended Thanksgiving Day matinee, but not as much as Davenport might have hoped. She was "sprightly and mirth-provoking," "a champagne sparkle, a sunbeam," and "a fascinating little witch," with enough spirit to "quicken the course of the red current in one's veins" (especially men's), "but possessing scarcely dramatic power enough [to] fill what may be termed a 'star theatre.'"[22]

Back with Ellsler in Cincinnati for two weeks, she earned decent, if not effusive reviews. She was again injured, wounded in the cheek during the feverish fencing scene in *French Spy*, but returned to the stage the next night for the premiere of a three-act adaptation of Emma Southworth's wildly popular, recently serialized gothic romance, *The Hidden Hand*. In it, Maggie played fearless street waif Capitola Black, first disguised as a boy. While the role fit the hoydenish Maggie like a glove, the script itself, possibly by Robert Jones or George L. Aiken (of *Uncle Tom's Cabin* fame), was wretchedly maudlin. Mary joined Maggie there for a few nights before returning to Canning's southern company and dealing with pressing marital woes (within months she would divorce Collier for his adultery with prostitutes).[23]

Maggie began 1860 in Lexington and Louisville, then returned to Ford's Holliday Street Theatre in Baltimore. Ford, one of her biggest supporters, again ran massive promotional ads, and audiences flocked to see her. Still, it chafed her that she had to alternate nights with a French comic opera troupe. Adding to her frustration was being unable to go to Memphis when she received news of the death there of the wife of her half-brother, John H. Lomax, leaving him with two small children. When tragedy again befell him some years later, she would immediately intervene.[24]

She returned on February 7 to the new Washington Theatre, which Ford had taken over from Kunkel and Moxley as part of his search for a permanent presence in the capital. Its stock company was strong, among them Glenn, who also stage-managed. He portrayed himself in the city as being Maggie's manager but did not tour or perform with her for another two years.

Ford's orchestra leader was the talented but self-important William Withers. Late one evening he marched his orchestra over to the National Hotel to serenade Maggie with new pieces dedicated to her and was rewarded with a bouquet tossed from her balcony and a request to compose an overture and some incidental songs for her. These he promised to have by summer, telling her fawningly that he knew "no other person to bestow with satisfaction a compliment so worthy and becoming as yourself," as to be granted a composition by him. Photographer Mathew Brady similarly celebrated her appearance in Washington, bringing down from his New York studio a large watercolor portrait on porcelain of her which he hung in his reception room two blocks from her hotel. For two weeks Washington audiences and critics alike were enthralled. Maggie was "the protean delineator" whose "blue eyes [sic] and pretty flaxen curls have proven an attractive card, and the house is nightly filled by the elite of Washington."[25]

Anna arranged for Maggie next to cover a circuit of southern towns with William Fleming and his "Star Dramatic Company." For their eight-week tour to Savannah, Macon, Columbus, Atlanta, Augusta, Columbia, and Wilmington, they would blend their repertoires. For Maggie, this meant that in addition to her protean farces and comedies she had to dust off her Jack Sheppard, her Marco in *Marble Heart* and her Lady Gay Spanker in *London Assurance*. Relying on Fleming's company was a calculated gamble, but it beat the questionable support to be found in these southern towns. She drew good houses, in Savannah the largest of the season.

In mid-April she and Fleming parted ways, he going north into Virginia and she back to Thompson's New Memphis Theatre, drawing respectable crowds. She closed out the 1859–60 season with a week in Newark, New Jersey; a benefit in Philadelphia for Garrettson; and two weeks in Troy and Buffalo. Increasingly, the same theatergoers returned to see her night after night, "the feast of one evening only sharpening the appetite for the next." For her closing benefit in Troy, she performed *Margot*, *Four Sisters*, and *Wandering Boys* (teaming again with her sister Emma), prompting an astute critical assessment that dashed her hopes of acting serious drama: "In the role of light comedy, Miss Mitchell excels. . . . She will never touch the heart keys with Charlotte Cushman; she will never succeed in being so interestingly melancholy as Julia Dean; nor so tragically wicked as Mrs. [Emma] Waller. Let her and her friends be thankful for her disqualifications in tragedy, so long as she is capital as 'Margot,' 'Caroline Merton,' and 'Paul,' and can sing so exquisitely."[26]

The house Maggie and Anna returned to that summer in Manhattan was a crowded one. Fifteen people resided at 87 Thompson Street in the Eighth Ward (a step up from Maggie's origins on Fulton Street in the Second Ward), her family still dependent on her income. Her uncle (half-sister Sophia's husband) Alfred headed the household, with his bookbinding shop nearby. The only other wage-earners were her brothers Joseph and Charles, now a doctor and clerk, respectively. Maggie's father was unemployed. It may well have been this summer that Maggie first yearned for, and began planning for, a summer home in the country.

By now her name was known to nearly everyone, and newspaper ads for the upcoming season trumpeted not the title of an upcoming script, but the name "Maggie," her surname increasingly superfluous. By fall 1860 everyone from Maine to Florida was choosing sides in the impending sectional conflict, and Maggie too would become embroiled in it, eventually suffering in the North for her justifiably perceived Southern sympathies. She began the 1860–61 season on August 13 safely in the North in the supportive atmosphere of McVicker's Chicago Theatre. He knew of the success in London and New York of Tom Taylor's three-act comedy, *Love's Telegraph*, and foisted its lead role now on Maggie for her opening bill. The lead role, Princess Blanche, who transforms from a convent novice to a shrewd monarch, was a poor fit for Maggie, but she gamely undertook it. The Princess enjoys meddling in palace intrigue, competing with her lady-in-waiting, Alice, a former convent friend, for the hand of her secretary. (He and Alice secretively "telegraph" their feelings for each other via signals with fan and glove.) At play's end, the Princess relinquishes her claim and bestows her love on a neighboring prince, sacrificing personal happiness for the good of her subjects. Despite its lacking songs or dances, Maggie curiously kept it in her repertoire for two years.

She followed it with *French Spy* and another new title role: Maggy McFarland in Charles Selby's 1858 farce, *The Bonnie Fish Wife*. Maggy, an "ugly, red-haired, gawky hoyden," first appears with a basket of fish on her back, spouting a thick Scottish brogue and bewailing her drunken father. This, however, is only a disguise of the refined Lady Thistledown to test the character of handsome young Wildoats Heartycheer, whose father is horrified. As Maggy, she intrigues Wildoats with a song, "Caller Herring," and as Lady Thistledown later enchants him with "The Soft Dew Is Sleeping." Smitten, he proclaims his love, she reveals her true identity to the father's relief, and all dance a Highland Fling. Maggie played it for three more years.[27]

Both of these new roles served her well at her next stop, DeBar's in St. Louis, where she was now famous enough to be his season-opening star attraction. The city, still feeling the effects of the financial panic, nevertheless turned out for her performances, applauding her "high animal spirits, pretty face and figure, and roundly developed limbs." Among DeBar's uncharacteristically mediocre company—its comedian was "a buffoon with very little genuine low comedy talent"—she relied heavily on actor-stage manager Robert McClannin.[28]

Next, for two weeks each at John Bates' National in Cincinnati and John T. Lorton's New Louisville Theatre, she drew full houses despite inclement weather. But she was caught on the horns of a dilemma: as much as she wished to be taken seriously as an actress, the more her provocative side drew male admirers. She worked to submerge her identity into a character, rewarded by reviews that proclaimed, "It was not 'Peg' [Woffington] but it was Maggie" and if Narramattah "is a specimen of Miss Maggie's ability, we unhesitatingly pronounce her an actress of transcendent power." But her wild Arab dance in *French Spy* was becoming wilder, and her gauzy attire was becoming gauzier, "admirably adjusted to the exquisite symmetry of her limbs." She acted these roles "with precious little 'kiverin' [covering] but to the evident satisfaction of all [presumably male] beholders." "Eve wore a fig leaf. Maggie wore scarcely more. . . . Were we a South Sea cannibal we should feel inclined to eat her."[29]

French Spy, perhaps more than any other piece, divided critical and popular opinion. It was "as mongrel a piece of absurdity as was ever conceived or put upon the stage," yet no one could deny that it satisfied the popular taste. Even when "careless in her reading and taking all sorts of liberties with the traditional proprieties of the stage, she wins more than our forgiveness by her saucy originality. . . . We can't help liking in her a style which we should be very likely to consider in anyone else as presumptuous and inartistic." She was "such a cunning little thing that she charms criticism out of its reason by her piquant little impertinences."[30]

In Cincinnati, an amusing incident occurred late one night at her hotel. Running through her lines for the melodramatic *Queen of the Abruzzi* in the corridor outside her room, she at one point loudly commanded her minions to carry out a violent murder. A nervous old farmer in the next room, fearing for his life, drew his trusty horse pistol and rushed out to confront the would-be murderess. The diminutive Maggie laughingly explained, introducing herself and disarming the sheepish octogenarian with a smile and a distinctive Katty O'Sheal curtsy.

As election day approached, secessionist talk and martial preparations proliferated throughout the South, where Maggie headed next. In Louisville, she incorporated into *French Spy* along with her "celebrated military dance" a Grand Parade and Review by the Louisville Zouaves, who serenaded her post-show at her hotel. Similarly, in Memphis, she integrated the "splendid military bearing and faultlessly executed" drills of their Zouaves, thrilling audiences. Her versatility shone as she shifted from her Wild Arab Boy to Mathilde. In *Love's Telegraph*, "Her final rendition of the heart-broken but forgiving lover was made with exquisite grace and telling effect, as was indicated by the storm of applause which greeted her." *Wild Irish Girl* gave "entire and perfect satisfaction."[31]

The courtly South provided Maggie some of her most effusive praise. "A.T.G." of Louisville offered up a gushing ode to her allure, which began: "Oh! Pretty little Maggie/With form in fairy mold,/With cheeks of blooming softness/And hair like crested gold." Then came fulsome stanzas celebrating her eyes, lips, voice, and laughter, concluding with the wish, "Oh, Maggie! May you ever/Remain as bright and fair,/And may that young heart never/Be doomed to dark despair." There would be many such over the coming years.[32]

Her antebellum sweep of the South took her next to Nashville and Mobile, to well-filled houses and critical raves. When she hit New Orleans just after Abraham Lincoln's election as president, she encountered theater managers uncertain what the political climate meant for their continued viability.

On October 29 Southern firebrand William Lowndes Yancey had spoken in the city, which "had a somewhat malign effect upon the theatres." At the St. Charles Theatre, Ben DeBar, who had recently expanded south from St. Louis, debated whether to stick it out, but remained for now. Opening for him on November 12, Maggie was supported by his St. Louis Company, including the capable McClannin and leading man Charles Pope, also to figure prominently in her career. She drew full houses every night, her last one generating $1,250 for DeBar and forcing him to turn away four hundred people.[33]

But New Orleans critics, who prided themselves on their high standards, were not kind. The most caustic was *True Delta* literary/theatrical critic John W. Overall, a man "remarkable for cleverness and malignancy." He considered *Wild Irish Girl* "a poor play, . . . poorly performed." Maggie fell "far below the mark in attempting to represent the [final] princely lady." She "paints her lips so thickly red as to sometimes interfere with her articulation." Her voice was too weak, her Irish brogue was inconsistent, and she danced with uncontrolled abandon. She persisted in a habit "of nearly closing her eyes, of tossing her pretty head from one side to the other and looking at the person addressed precisely as a bird looks with a single eye. There is, too, a sudden and singular twitch of the muscles of the limbs . . . which is not graceful." As a comedienne, "Miss Mitchell cannot come within a thousand rods of Céleste." "Take her all in all, Maggie is not a 'star.'" With impeccably poor timing for Maggie, that week P. T. Barnum phenomenon Tom Thumb chimed in from New York, maligning her as "unfit to hold the position of a ballet girl at a Metropolitan Theatre."[34]

Vicksburg and Mobile in mid-November were equally inhospitable: "Maggie Mitchell has spoiled her theatrical reputation in the South by giving 'farewell benefits' in the middle of the engagement and then taking the people by surprise the next week. Her engagement was thus made in Mobile a miserable failure." Since she had always scheduled her farewell benefits on Fridays it is difficult to understand, if the reports were accurate, why she changed this now, unless she attempted to cut short her obligation due to poor attendance amid secession fever. Audiences were so slim that "drama is in a languishing condition." On some nights fewer than two hundred people attended. It had become "impossible for actors to play with any spirit under such circumstances."[35]

But then, with head held high, Maggie marched on to Montgomery, Alabama, and conquered all.

NOTES

1. *Boston Traveller* [sic], Sept. 6, 1858.
2. Effie Ellsler Weston, ed. *The Stage Memories of John A. Ellsler*, Cleveland: The Rowfant Club, 1950, 123; Clara Morris, *Life on the Stage*, New York: McClure, Phillips and Co., 1901, 97–100.

3. Edward M. Alfriend, "Recollections of John Wilkes Booth," *The Era*, Oct. 1901, 604.

4. *Washington Daily Union*, Oct. 3–7, 1858; *Washington Evening Star*, Oct. 5–6, 1958.

5. (St. Louis) *Missouri Republican*, Oct. 19–25, 1858.

6. *Memphis Appeal*, Nov. 23, 1858; *Memphis Avalanche*, Nov. 24, 1858.

7. *Memphis Appeal*, Nov. 27, 1858. Crisp had driven David Ash out of business in Memphis.

8. Nashville correspondent for *Charleston Mercury*, Jan. 3, 1859.

9. *Augusta (GA) Evening Dispatch*, Jan. 11 and 15, 1859.

10. *Savannah Morning News*, Jan. 19–24, 1859.

11. *Richmond Dispatch*, Feb. 9 and 12, 1859.

12. Edwin Eddy letter to "My Dear Tom," Richmond, Apr. 23, 1858, HTC; John M. Barron, "Acting in the South in the Drama's Palmy Days," *Baltimore Sun*, Dec. 9, 1906.

13. *Richmond Dispatch*, Feb. 25, 1859.

14. *Baltimore Republican*, Mar. 1, 1859; *Baltimore Sun*, Mar. 2, 1859.

15. *The (Cincinnati) Israelite*, May 27, 1859.

16. Jay F. Ludwig, "James H. McVicker and His Theatre," *Quarterly Journal of Speech*, 46 (1960):14–25.

17. *St. Louis Morning Herald*, May 3–12, 1859.

18. *Philadelphia Press*, Oct. 5, 1859.

19. Countless ads in newspapers across the country, for example, *Baltimore Daily Commercial*, Apr. 13, 1866.

20. *St. Paul (MN) Globe*, Oct. 2, 1881; *Richmond Dispatch*, Oct. 15 and 17, 1859.

21. *Memphis Daily Avalanche*, Oct. 27, 1859; Memphis correspondent for *Charleston Mercury*, Nov. 10, 1859.

22. *Boston Post* quoted in *Wheeling (WV) Daily Intelligencer*, Dec. 1, 1859; *Spirit of the Times*, Dec. 17, 1859.

23. There were dozens of dramatizations of this exceptionally poplar novel. Perhaps the best was Tom Taylor's, well after Maggie had ceased to enact Capitola.

24. MM to Job Carpenter (treasurer of Forbes Theatre in Providence), Baltimore, Jan. 30, 1860, author's collection.

25. Withers to MM, Aug. 12, 1860, MS Collection 4552, New York Public Library; Washington correspondent for *New Bern (NC) Daily Progress*, Feb. 17, 1860.

26. *Troy Daily Whig*, June 12 and 22, 1860.

27. Charles Selby, *The Bonnie Fish Wife*, New York: Robert M. De Witt, 1858, 19.

28. *Missouri Democrat*, Aug. 25, 1860.

29. *Cincinnati Press*, Sept. 8, 1860; *Louisville Courier*, Sept. 25, 1860; *Louisville Daily Democrat*, Sept. 29, 1860; *New Orleans True Delta*, Nov. 18, 1860.

30. *Cincinnati Commercial Tribune*, Sept. 6, 8 and 13, 1860.

31. *Louisville Courier*, Sept. 28, 1860; *Memphis Avalanche*, Oct. 13 and 20, 1860.

32. *New York Clipper*, Nov. 10, 1860.

33. *New Orleans Picayune*, Oct. 30, 1860.

34. Emilie M. W. Cowell, *The Cowells in America*, ed. Willson Disher, London, n.p., 1934, 64; *New Orleans Daily Delta*, Nov. 14, 1860; *New Orleans True Delta*, Nov. 18, 1860; *Memphis Avalanche*, Nov. 19, 1860. Overall later shot and killed an actor who attacked him over an especially nasty review.

35. *Chicago Tribune* and other papers, Nov. 28, 1860; *Montgomery (AL) Weekly Advertiser*, Nov. 28, 1860.

Chapter 4

Fanchon

Montgomery on the eve of the Civil War was a city shifting into a higher gear. Its 9,000 residents, over half enslaved, continued their daily routines amid cotton warehouses and palatial homes while secessionist fervor buzzed around them. "Dixie" was heard everywhere, and the Metropolitan Guards drilled on Court Square, ready to protect the city from northern aggression. On November 17, 1860, Alabamians had gathered in the city to elect delegates to a January secession convention.

Ground zero for gatherings and fiery speeches was the new $45,000 Montgomery Theatre at Perry and Monroe Streets where Maggie was to appear on November 29. From its stage that winter would ring cries for secession. Built with slave labor, it had just opened on October 22 to accommodate 1,280 patrons, with acoustics and lighting unparalleled in the South. Manager Mat Canning, whom Maggie already knew, had recruited his company in New York. They had performed for a month in Columbus, Georgia, before opening in Montgomery, and by the time Maggie arrived they were a polished, cohesive group. It would be her only appearance in Montgomery during her career. She did not have a hard act to follow. The previous star, Kate Bateman, had not drawn well, "owing to the election, and the excitement attending it."[1]

Leading lady there was Maggie's half-sister Mary, her eyes already on one of its handsome leading men, John Albaugh. Emma Mitchell played small roles and performed olio songs and dances. Low comedian James Lewis and "heavy" Sam Chester would later support Maggie in her tours. John Wilkes Booth was there too, on the cusp of major stardom but recovering from a firearm accident two weeks before (shot in the leg while tussling with Canning). He and Maggie only had three days together before he departed for the North (ironically under a cloud for uttering Unionist sentiments), but as their friendship deepened over the next five years, they continued their flowery correspondence. Actor James Kelley, who shared a dressing room with Booth, asserted that Booth's magnetism elicited "scented letters from beautiful women.... He often read me excerpts from letters couched in particularly endearing terms, and he always laughingly exclaimed that not one of the writers compared with Miss Mitchell."[2]

The biggest favor Maggie did for Booth in Montgomery was bringing him into her spotlight by contributing her talent to his first benefit night as a star on December 1. She performed *Katty* and he, the title roles of *Rafaelle, the Reprobate* and Act V of *Richard III*. A good-sized crowd attended since "Miss Maggie never fails to fill the house." Called before the curtain afterward, Booth gracefully accepted a gold-headed cane from the citizens of Montgomery. From that night on he no longer hid behind the billing "John Wilkes," having sworn to use his famous surname only when his stardom was assured.[3]

For three more weeks, despite bouts of strong rain, ever-present mud, and an unseasonal ice storm, Maggie rode a wave of rapturous applause, full houses and critical acclaim in a theater kept cozy by Canning's new stoves. She and Canning distributed passes to the local militia, the Montgomery True Blues, soon to be shipped out to besiege Fort Pickens in the Florida panhandle, who attended several nights *en masse* in uniform. The engagement overall was unlike anything Maggie had encountered to date. Every joke "told," every pose and grin and grimace brought down the house, every song and dance necessitated encores. There was no more talk of her needing further training, further experience. She was "no taught puppet, but thoroughly understands what she attempts to portray, and invariably carries the audience with her." Her "impersonation of the deceptive, coquettish, marble-hearted Marco" in *Marble Heart* was "an achievement of which she may well be proud."[4]

The first of only two sour notes came when Maggie indulged her penchant for tragedy and again essayed Romeo. It came across as more ludicrous than tragic, especially when the diminutive star attempted to carry Mary as Juliet. The other was *Hidden Hand*, perceived as anti-southern, its lowbrow content off-putting. Pandering to "citizens who value lofty, patriotic sentiment from the lips of blackguards and brigands . . . speaking a lingo known mainly to house breakers and other nocturnal artists," it presented "a set of white people and negroes who never possibly existed—a mass of the most stupid incongruities that the human mind ever conceived." Its "inartistic," "unnatural" plot was "miserably stupid and only half developed. The whole is a wretched libel on human nature and fit only for . . . Northern literary trash sensation papers."[5]

Canning hyped Maggie's December 14 benefit for days. Two of the most potent symbols of nascent Secessionism were the wearing of a blue cockade and the singing of "The Southern Marseillaise," and that night she embraced them both. The *Montgomery Mail* urged attendance by militia members, assuring them that "Miss Maggie enters into the spirit of the song most fully," providing words to all four verses and chorus should the audience wish to sing along. Canning included all of this in his playbill and requested singers from the Montgomery Saengerbund to join Maggie and the entire company in the song's rousing delivery. Furthering the symbolism of the evening, "a committee of young gentlemen" would present her with a flag, "a deep blue field, with a single star in the centre, and the name 'ALABAMA' blazoned above. We are, thank God, free from the stripes, or likely to be very soon."[6]

That night, between her performance as Dot in *Cricket on the Hearth* and the burletta *Antony and Cleopatra* with Albaugh, she delivered. Fronting a tableau with the singers, she belted out, "To arms! To arms! Ye brave! Th' avenging sword unsheathe! Now, now the abolition storm is rolling, which treacherous states, fanatic raise," and on through all four verses. Presented with the Alabama flag, she assured "the largest and most brilliant and fashionable audience of the season" that the occasion "shall ever be treasured in the happy pearls of memory." In the worst gaffe of her career, she then impulsively "dragged the Stars and Stripes from the right-hand box and trampled it underfoot," eliciting "rapturous applause." Repeating the song on at least one other night in Montgomery, she had by the time of her departure on December 23 "endeared herself to everyone."[7]

She gained countless new admirers, predominantly male. "It was a common delusion of nearly every young gentleman who saw her [that her] vivid glance was directed at him in particular." Reportedly "among her *most* ardent admirers" was Confederate guerilla John Hunt Morgan. Another was Alabama Quartermaster General Reuben Thom, 40, a Montgomery resident and friend of Canning's who would become the first officer appointed to the Confederate Marine Corps and who as a captain commanded marines aboard the ironclad *CSS Virginia* (formerly *USS Merrimack*). For the duration of the war, he wrote Maggie long, tender, melodramatic letters, looking forward to the time he might see her again in Mobile or New Orleans. Each time—even when he admittedly had not written his own family—he asked after Maggie's mother and sisters.[8]

At least for the moment, she stood committed to the Southern cause. How sudden her conversion was, and how firm her conviction, is open to debate. She was surrounded by warm new friends in a company which had resolutely embraced Secessionism, with Albaugh and Chester among its strongest proponents. She may also have been influenced by DeBar, who after quitting the city for St. Louis in summer would be arrested for his widely acknowledged Southern sympathies, a belief said to affect his choice of actors. Maggie was revered nightly by southern audiences cheering her every word and action, leaving her little recourse but to appease them. The circumstances demanded it and she complied.

She would not have been influenced by Booth in their brief time together, as he was at that time still anti-secession. She may have sought to emulate two of her competitors, actresses Caroline Richings and Annie Miller, who had sung "The Southern Marseillaise" from stages in Richmond and Georgia, respectively, with Richings also trampling on an American flag. In any case, Maggie was young, she was impressionable, and she reveled in the moment. But consequences were not long in coming.[9]

By January 1861, as southern states began to secede from the Union, northern newspapers picked up the Maggie/flag story, just as Richings was vehemently denying her singing of the South's adopted anthem. Maggie, bemoaned the *Pittsburgh Post*, "has gone over to the enemy. . . . Alas for Maggie! What must her Republican admirers here in the North think of her now?" In May the *New York Clipper* lamented that "Miss Maggie Mitchell is accused of being astride the Union fence, throwing bon bons and kisses on each side. Oh, Mag!"[10]

Over the next year, as word of the contretemps spread to other northern cities, most editors gave Maggie the benefit of the doubt. The *Buffalo Commercial* defended her loyalty, believing her to have been caught up in the moment back in Montgomery. "Maggie Mitchell Not 'Secesh,'" announced the *Brooklyn Eagle*. Although it printed her denials, that paper averred that "Maggie has unjustly, it is said, lost some of her popularity on account of a rumor that she is a little petticoated rebel." The *Clipper* halfheartedly admitted in April 1862 that Maggie "has pretty well refuted some of the lies told about her, and taken the ground in regard to other charges upon which we have always stood in regard to the matter. . . . We gave Maggie Mitchell the benefit of our columns, because she did contradict what had been urged against her. We may yet hear further upon that subject." Periodically, it would resurface.[11]

For now, billed as the Star of the South and the Pet of the West, she was warmly embraced on January 14 by the people of New Orleans, if not its critics. The city was awash in secession fever, with four states—South Carolina, Mississippi, Florida, and Alabama—already having voted themselves out of the United States. As in Montgomery, "nearly all of the theatrical performers in this city have informally enrolled themselves as a military company in defense of the South," reported the *New Orleans Bee*. At the Varieties Theatre, manager John E. Owens had formed a company, himself as Captain, which would include several of Maggie's future co-stars. DeBar, at whose St. Charles Theatre she performed, joined other managers in capitalizing on the frenzy, very much "alive to the prevailing tastes of our people" by avoiding anything too serious.[12]

Strangely, Maggie began with *Hidden Hand* despite its denunciation in Montgomery, yoking it first to *French Spy*, then *Katty*. But "the attempt was flat and crude," although "considerably relieved by the singing and dancing." In *French Spy*, "a handsomer Arab Boy could hardly be imagined." She was "young, pretty, has a good bust, good arms, and a knee round as a period," and happily for the young bucks of New Orleans she was willing to "strip for it like a young pugilist." Still, "almost any actress with a pretty face, fine physical development, and a fair idea of pantomime expression" could succeed in it. Maggie, though, was still "a long way behind Céleste." The harshest critic was still John Overall: "Aside from the *French Spy* and her little dancing characters, the 'star' shines as feebly as the feeblest light ever seen on the boards."[13]

But, of course, the crowd loved it. In the dramatic denouement of *French Spy*, Maggie's character, Mathilde, is rescued from peril by French troops storming in to save the day. The script then calls for the Barbary (enemy) flag to be hauled down and the French tricolor waved triumphantly. Recklessly reprising her Montgomery bravado, Maggie reportedly substituted the northern Stars and Stripes for the Barbary flag and the Stars and Bars for the French, trampling the former. No contemporary accounts mention this action, but a charge was made secondhand in 1862 by a disgruntled former Union Army veteran that she did. When that accusation arose, Maggie emphatically denied ever trampling on the American flag, in Montgomery, New Orleans, or anywhere else. But then, she also denied ever singing the "Southern Marseillaise," which numerous people heard her do in Montgomery.[14]

Katty pleased the audience but further nettled Overall, who derided her brogue as crude and inconsistent, her voice, whether speaking or singing, too weak for a large theater. "Her enunciation was often indistinct, her elocution poor, her pronunciation very faulty. . . . She depends entirely upon youth, a prepossessing face, and the Terpsichorean bits introduced in almost every piece." She was "as piquant and rollicking as it is possible for female grimace, ogling, ejaculating, capering and wriggling" to be.[15]

On January 21, "the wettest, nastiest, muddiest, and chilliest day" of that winter, Maggie veered back to the serious with *Wept*, but her Narramattah fared no better at Overall's hands. *Stratagem* succeeded only "because, for once, the pretty little player was natural, and left off attitudinizing." (Maggie did momentarily fall out of character, though, and deliberately mugged for cheap laughs, by cracking up when a fiddle in the orchestra struck some squeaky notes during one of her songs.)[16]

Inexplicably, despite Overall's harsh assessments of Maggie's ability, he had been urging her and Anna while they were in New Orleans to take a look at a new work by his good friend, composer-playwright August Waldauer, the thirty-five-year-old German émigré who was DeBar's orchestra conductor.

Waldauer had seen a production in German of Charlotte Birch Pfeiffer's adaptation of George Sand's 1848 pastorale set in Cossé, France, called "La Petite Fadette," which he thought had potential. He had spent the summer of 1860 in St. Louis crafting an English version, which he titled *Fanchon, the Cricket*, submitting it for copyright protection. That fall, at Overall's urging, he had offered it to tragedienne Julia Dean, who rejected it.

Now, Waldauer thought its pixyish lead character was perfect for Maggie. It had few songs or dances, no tableaux, and no emotional "points" to make, so she and Anna were apprehensive. But Maggie determined to channel her nervousness into her character's restiveness. DeBar was so sure *Fanchon* would fail that he paired it for its premiere with *Bonnie Fish Wife*.[17]

On Wednesday evening, January 23, 1861, the fortunate audience to witness for the first time the most enduring role of Maggie's career watched the curtain rise not on her but on Robert McClannin and Jennie Johnson McManus as Father and Mother Barbeaud, comfortable French peasants, the parents of twin brothers. Didier (Alvin Read), something of a scapegrace, has disappeared, worrying them greatly. Landry (Charles Pope), the handsome, favored twin, fears that Didier has run off due to Landry's having spent time lately with the fetching Madelon (Mary Maddern), and has just returned from a fruitless search for him. The only person who might discern the boy's whereabouts is a "horrible old witch" named Fadet (veteran actress Adeline Knight Hind, 47) who hates the Barbeauds for past wrongs.[18]

Fadet treasures her granddaughter, Fanchon, called the Little Cricket, "a poorly clad, wild, shrewd, harum-scarum girl," the role Maggie would inhabit for the next thirty-one years. Landry calls her "as inquisitive as a bird, talkative as a magpie, and ugly and lazy," yet, "like a Cricket, she is merry." She spoke in a "voice not especially sweet or musical," yet her every utterance was "lightning quick, and every movement, gesture, pose electric with energy; her laugh a wild, careless, jubilant child's laugh, resonant, ringing, and perfectly natural."[19]

As the Barbeauds fret, a chicken (guided by unseen wires) flies in their window and alights on the grandfather clock. Right behind it clambers the disheveled Fanchon to exclaim, "Ah, you rascal, I've got you now!" She accuses the Barbeauds' dog of chasing the chicken, the loss of which to her she slyly compares to that "if you were to lose Didier." This of course, gets their attention, but Fanchon only unleashes a litany of her ill treatment by the Barbeauds and others of the village. She runs off, Landry in pursuit.[20]

The second scene reveals Fadet's home. On that premiere night, it was not well rendered. "Not a dash of the brush or a blow of the hammer had been made to get up scenery," Maggie recalled. Fadet enters hunched, her voice "pointed and screechy" as she dispenses herbs and concocts potions. Didier enters, numb from hunger and fatigue. He wants to die over the loss of his brother's company, to which Fanchon snorts, "*poor, stupid boy.* . . . A good beating, that's what you need." Yet she relents, offers him bread, and shows him a hiding place.[21]

As soon as they leave, Landry enters, breathless. Fadet mocks him until Fanchon returns and reminds Landry of their shared childhood and her saving his life when he stumbled into the river returning home late from last year's St. Andoche festival. He had been too proud to thank her, but had offered to grant her any favor. Then, she had demurred; now, she demands a favor to reveal Didier's hiding place. He gives his solemn word to grant her anything she wishes, then using her information, goes to find Didier. Fanchon intends to make him keep his word at this year's festival, taking place the next day, in front of all the village. The night before it, she capers fiendishly in the moonlight, laughing and rejoicing, "I've got you after all, handsome Landry!" For this premiere, she merely sang a gloating ditty, but would in the coming weeks amplify this moment into her famous Shadow Dance.[22]

Act II opens in a large hall in the village inn. Joyous young folk gather for the festival, teasing one another. When Landry appears with Didier, Madelon grabs him to dance, stopping short when they see Fanchon approach wearing ridiculously outré garb—her version of finery—which the villagers mock. To them, she appears "half-witch, half-crazed," someone to shun. It is her eighteenth birthday. She reminds Landry of his promise and demands that he dance seven dances with her. He honors his pledge for the first one, with Fanchon light on her feet, as Madelon and the others jeer. Surely, they sneer, she has bewitched him with a medallion locket she wears around her neck. Landry is repelled by Madelon's conduct.[23]

When the villagers surround Fanchon, viciously taunting her, demanding the locket, she turns in terror to Landry for protection. He withdraws from it a piece of paper and reads the "mother's prayer" written there, then steps between Fanchon and the villagers. "Hold! Let no one raise his hand against her," he warns. "She is here under my protection!" With Didier at his side, he chastises their scurrilous behavior. "Gratified beyond measure," Fanchon releases Landry from the rest of his promise, and everyone disperses.[24]

Act III opens back at Fadet's as Fanchon confronts her over her stigmatized upbringing: "I don't want to be a laughingstock any longer. . . . If I had known how I looked, how they hated and despised me, I'd never have disgraced Landry by forcing him to dance with me." Fadet screams, "That poisonous offspring from the twin farm? Are you in love with the fellow?" No, she assures Fadet, and the crone's rage ebbs as the two embrace, weeping. Fanchon in a pique throws her "finery" into the nearby river and dons anew her rags.[25]

She lies there "with her scrawny arm before her red eyes, her tangled hair looking as if the bats had slept there, bewailing in a tear-choked voice that Landry will not love her because she is 'the ugly Fanchon.'" He enters, startled to find her weeping, and asks why. "I cry because heaven has created such a miserable thing as I am," she moans. Surprised at his own feelings, Landry is moved, drawn to her in pity. In a remarkably tender scene they share their innermost thoughts, including Fanchon's grief over losing her mother at age seven, leaving her "a poor, forsaken orphan." Landry comforts her, noticing as if for the first time that "you are not ugly," and have "splendid" eyes. They declare their friendship, embrace and are about to kiss when they hear villagers approaching. "Run, Landry, run," she cries. "You shall kiss Madelon tomorrow, but never poor, unhappy Cricket."[26]

Act IV opens with Landry bewailing Madelon's continued rejection. Suddenly he realizes, "Pshaw, I don't care! It is Cricket that causes my uneasiness.... I could tear myself to pieces for having been so foolish." Didier enters to relate that their father is angry over Landry dallying with Fanchon and has gone to make peace with Madelon's father. Didier relates having passed a clean, well-dressed Fanchon going to make peace with Madelon herself. Landry retorts, "Let her mind her own business, not mine!" and warns Didier, "Keep your distance from Cricket, let me advise you; she is very dangerous!" Didier, puzzled, leaves, and Landry soliloquizes his confusion until surprised by the entrance of Fanchon and Madelon, whereupon he darts behind a pump to listen.[27]

Madelon is quarrelsome; Fanchon responds with quiet reason. Madelon sneers; Fanchon lauds Landry as "a noble boy, of whose love you ought to be proud.... He's not only the handsomest and the richest boy in the whole country, but also the most honorable!" Abashed, Landry emerges and renounces any love for Madelon, who sulkily yields him to Fanchon, warning him to be careful "that your sweetheart doesn't fly on a broomstick through the chimney some fine evening." Landry professes his admiration and love for Fanchon: "You are handsome inside and out. You are also better, more sensible, and braver than all others." From the night of the St. Andoche Festival, "I saw no other girl than you, and see you everywhere, even where you are not." Fanchon, trembling, thinks Landry is joking. He reaches to embrace and reassure her, when Didier, their father, and Madelon's father (T. J. Hind, Adeline's husband) enter.[28]

Father Barbeaud upbraids Landry, who defends his feelings for Fanchon, telling Madelon's father he expressed himself to Fanchon "exactly the same that my father told my mother when he was wooing her." Both fathers are stunned. Fanchon, silent to this point, steps up and speaks her heart. Despite being dressed in rags, "I never asked anybody in my life for a sou, nor have I ever accepted one." By citing her poverty, she is not seeking to win his favor nor "force myself into your family.... I shall never desire a husband whose station in life is above me." Rather than unjustly claim Landry's love, she yields the field and exits, he rushing after her. Both fathers think him bewitched.[29]

In a second scene of the act, Fanchon implores Fadet to allow her to go away to "the city." Fadet agrees, knowing that in her absence Landry will torment his father. Fanchon goes into another room to prepare for her departure. Father Barbeaud enters to clumsily offer Fadet three thousand francs to send Fanchon away. Fadet mocks his pride as matching his avarice, telling him twenty thousand would not be enough, and leaves. Fanchon emerges to tell Barbeaud that she has overheard, and that she is going away: "You've got for nothing what no person in the world could have bought of me!" She asks only that he care lovingly for Landry. As soon as he exits, a distraught Landry rushes on and throws himself at Fanchon's feet. He begs her not to go, but Fanchon thinks him mad to disobey his father's wishes: "Since [smiling painfully] I am a witch, I know of no other expedient than to get out of your sight." She only asks his word that he not attempt to follow her and that he meet her a year hence on that very spot. He promises, and she tearfully offers him her locket, her "holiest gift, . . . the only souvenir I have of my poor mother." In a year she will ask for it back. They pledge their bond as the curtain falls.[30]

The final act takes place a year to the day later, in the Barbeaud home. All four are miserable. Fanchon returned to the village to care for the dying Fadet, but sent no word to Landry and refused to see him when he came to her door, beseeching her. When Fadet died, as Mother Barbeaud relates, "the girl didn't leave her coffin for three days and nights." Didier adds that yesterday, at Fadet's burial, Fanchon appeared subdued, modest, a transformation noted by the entire village. Father Barbeaud is irate that his sons attended the burial, their defense being that it was their Christian duty. Both extol Fanchon's character and new demeanor. Landry asserts that now that he is of age, he can do as he pleases, if Fanchon will have him. But if she will not, he will join the army. Didier adds that if Landry does not marry her, he will. Even Mother Barbeaud avers that both twins have been changed for the better by Fanchon. Their teaming up against Father only angers him more.[31]

At the height of this contention, Fanchon enters in deep mourning. She is completely transformed—the kind of transformation for which Maggie had already demonstrated a skill for conveying and which she would continue to demonstrate for another thirty years. She is now refined, ladylike, her manner composed and her voice simple and sweet. Her business, she says, is with Father Barbeaud, alone, and the others leave. Then transpires a scene which became a metaphor for any young woman's winning over an intractable man. Fanchon acknowledges their past grudges, she flatters him, she references her difficult life after losing her mother, and amid her eloquence he thaws. He stuns her (and the audience) by telling her that he knows "how to restore your good name in the whole country around." He has been dissembling. He had her observed during the past year and is now willing to tell everyone in the village "that your behavior in the city was without reproach," she being "the most industrious, modest, and pious girl" anyone there had known. He believes, now, that all she needs to cement her good reputation is a good husband—and he knows just the one![32]

Conveniently, at that moment Landry bursts in demanding to see Fanchon. With mock gruffness, Father Barbeaud asks what he wants of her. It is to return the locket, which he has worn by his heart every moment, and ask for her hand in marriage. Joyously, verbosely, sentimentally they profess their mutual love to the astonishment of Didier and Mother Barbeaud. Father Barbeaud asks Fanchon's forgiveness for the wrongs he has done her. To seal the bargain, Fanchon reveals that she has inherited from Fadet a life savings of twenty thousand francs, which matters not to Landry: "No king could have made her richer than she already was. . . . Holy be the Cricket, who without money, brings happiness and blessing to our hearth!" They form the requisite final tableau as Father and Mother intone, "it may be so for all time to come."[33]

From that night forward Fanchon was Maggie, and Maggie, Fanchon. It became the most celebrated character she would ever play, in a script hailed as universal, "innocent as childhood, and captivating as the first steps into the enchanted land of romance." It provided Maggie with the ultimate opportunity to showcase her versatility, "including high comedy (as in the last act), low comedy (in the meeting with Didier in the first act), sentimental (the separation of the lovers), and vividly dramatic (the struggle with the rabble at the festival)." And at every turn she matched its demands: "From skipping about the scene laughing spontaneously, she dropped to sudden mysterious melancholy or flashed into elfin rages."[34]

As if the storm of applause which followed *Fanchon*'s debut were not enough, Waldauer, DeBar, Maggie and the entire cast soared on word from the early reviews. All of their pre-show nervousness had been for naught. *Fanchon* was pronounced one of the greatest successes of the American stage, "a success in the fullest sense of the word." It "far exceeded in interest anything of the kind." Maggie "charmingly" and "bravely" triumphed in a challenging character, conveying "the different phases of feeling through which the wild and independent gypsy girl of the country" emerges into "the staid and dignified lady of the city." The rest of the cast drew raves as well, especially Hind's Fadet. Commendably, Fanchon was a moral exemplar "of that class which makes good wives and deserves to be mother of a gentleman's children." *Fanchon*'s pure moral tone "is what we want now, seeing that the stage is so often degraded by vulgar trash." It was "a broom which would sweep the Augean stable clean."[35]

Overall was quick to praise the work of his friend Waldauer and, belatedly, Maggie: she was "the right person in the right place as Fanchon. . . . It could not have been better suited to her in physical conformation, facial expression, and youthful appearance." She had conveyed Fanchon's emotions perfectly, whether they be "rollicking hilarity or momentary depression . . . or love or giving expression to earnest determination or undeniable truth, she seems so naturally alive to the meaning of the author that none but the veriest hypocrite could fail to be pleased." Despite Overall's prior pans, Maggie later credited him as the biggest factor in *Fanchon*'s early success.[36]

In 1861 she could never have guessed the thousands of performances of the wild, winsome character that lay ahead of her, nor the extent to which it would define her career. Still, the event was almost eclipsed by the celebrations in New Orleans of Louisiana's joining the embryonic Confederate States of America—the sixth state to do so—on Saturday, January 26, the night of Maggie's closing benefit. When the news reached the city by telegraph from Baton Rouge at 1:00 that afternoon, cannon salutes, church and fire bells and Louisiana "Pelican" flags filled the air amid unbounded cheering. "Business was to a large extent suspended, and the streets were crowded with people, surging to and fro, exchanging congratulations." That evening, the city erupted in illuminations, its streets jammed with citizens and militia parading for hours.[37]

Inside the St. Charles, Maggie soldiered on with *Fanchon*, closing by thanking the audience for their "kind reception." She hoped to return, she said, reminding them, "when you hear the chirp of a cricket on your peaceful and happy hearth, give one thought to the 'Cricket' who did her best to enliven [her] kind friends. . . . Whatever may take place, you and I at least will never *secede* from each other." Possibly because the smallish audience due to the festivities, Maggie broke her rule against performing on a Sunday to perform *Fanchon* and *Wept* the following night before departing for Montgomery.[38]

The atmosphere she encountered there was even more vibrant than it had been in December. The "Southern Marseillaise" boomed out everywhere, and anyone within earshot sang along. A martial spirit reigned, as a Home Guard of over a hundred citizens supplanted Maggie's adoring Montgomery True Blues, now mired off Pensacola. Strangers flocking into the city could be seen everywhere on the street and in the Exchange Hotel (where Maggie and Anna likely stayed) a block from the theater. Many were journalists from papers South and North, as Montgomery now commanded the interest of the entire nation. Canning and Albaugh provided strong support for Maggie's opening *French Spy* on Friday, February 1, which drew the "largest and most fashionable audience of the season." The following Monday, the Confederate Constitutional Convention came to order in Montgomery. Thirty-six delegates from six states officially anointed the city the provisional capital of the new Confederate States of America.³⁹

Supported again by Mary and Emma, Maggie for a week drew strong attendance and critical reception. The only glitch was the unceasing bawling one night of the infant used onstage in *Wept*, causing a lengthy wait until a substitute could be obtained. But all was forgiven after Maggie apologized to the audience. During her second week attendance dropped off as excitement mounted for the anticipated arrival of Jefferson Davis, elected February 8 to be inaugurated on the 18th as the first president of the Confederacy. Although *Fanchon* on Friday the 15th drew a packed house, Maggie's farewell benefit the following night drew poorly as everyone swarmed to the railroad depot to greet Davis, arriving on the ten o'clock train.⁴⁰

She may have attended Davis' inauguration on Monday the 18th with Canning and Albaugh. The likelihood of her being present for it is reinforced by an account by diarist Mary Chesnut on February 28 of a recent dinner with virile, handsome Alabama Governor Andrew Moore, who had attended the inauguration: "They say the old sinner has made himself ridiculous with that little actress Maggie Mitchell." Furthermore, Maggie uncharacteristically began her next engagement, with DeBar in New Orleans, on a Thursday, February 21, instead of a Monday, despite its proximity. In 1862 the same disgruntled Union Army veteran who complained about Maggie's behavior in December 1860 claimed that she, dressed to represent the state of Louisiana in a pageant of seceded states, stood on the rostrum behind Davis on the day of his inauguration. As with the flag-trampling accusation, she denied doing so, and no contemporary accounts—including many by eyewitnesses—corroborate the charge or even mention such ladies on the rostrum, despite Maggie's being a popular, recognizable star.⁴¹

In New Orleans she predictably opened with *Fanchon*, which was again enthusiastically received, especially by Overall: "There is enough of life-romance, of life-reality, of semi-witchcraft about it to make it popular." Maggie had only "increased in public favor since her admirable [first] delineation." But amid the political climate, attendance ebbed and New Orleans managers began folding their tents. Varieties Theatre manager Owens returned to Baltimore for the duration, forfeiting a previously profitable lease and an expensive inventory of new scenery, costumes, and furnishings. DeBar, telling a friend, "Business here is very bad. Nothing thought of but arguments about Politics &c &c," departed New Orleans for over a decade. Despite the initial expectation that the war would be of short duration, these managers, skilled in foresight, realized that the necessary rail transportation and funding for scenery, costumes, scripts and stars would no longer be available, and that dire straits awaited anyone who stayed.⁴²

Maggie closed her last New Orleans engagement until war's end with a successful benefit, then left with Anna for Mobile, and then Memphis. Her final appearance in the antebellum South began on April 2 back in Montgomery with Canning, Albaugh, her two sisters, and the same capable stock company. At first, everyone in the Confederate capital loved "this gifted and charming little actress, who turns the heads of *all* the young men, and those of about half the *married* ones." But within days Maggie failed to "excite sufficient interest to induce even a moderate attendance" for Margot and Milly and a misguided turn as young Norval in *Douglas*. That night, a small audience "seemed to enjoy the entertainment very little, and the players appeared correspondingly indifferent," so that "everybody and everything looked gloomy." The remedy? *Fanchon*, of course, which Maggie triumphantly supplied on April 5. But Canning, too, threw in the towel and closed the season early with a series of benefits, including one for Emma Mitchell on April 8 with Maggie contributing *A Husband at Sight* and one for himself on April 12—the evening after Confederate guns opened on Fort Sumter in Charleston—with Maggie as Rosalind in *As You Like It*.[43]

Her journey north to Louisville was complicated by heavy rain and war-disrupted rail lines, causing her to arrive a day late for her announced April 15 opening. To her dismay, Louisville was ablaze with dissension over President Lincoln's call for 75,000 ninety-day troops to suppress the rebellion. Governor Beriah Magoffin refused to provide any, and within a week five companies of Louisville volunteers shipped out to fight for the Confederacy. Others went north on their own to enlist. The news that week that Virginia had become the eighth state to secede did nothing to calm matters. No one had time for anything as frivolous as the theater. Despite Maggie's "most successful engagement of the season when here last" and appeals to the chivalrous impulses of "bachelors who [otherwise] have no occasion to secure seats," paltry houses greeted her. In her second week she tried *Fanchon* for four nights, including her farewell benefit, but it fared no better. The nascent war was already impeding her career.[44]

Now, likely influenced by the pragmatic Anna and aware of the exodus from the South of theatrical personnel, Maggie publicly embraced the Union. She must have communicated this to her Confederate admirer, Captain Thom, for he wrote her that month, "You my Dear Miss Maggie will be on the one side and I on the other in this great struggle for liberty, but that will not interfere with our friendship. I shall think of you as often and as kindly as ever." Some Southerners remained unaware of Maggie's newly professed loyalty, however, for as late as that October the *Richmond Enquirer* praised her and Owens for their devotion to the Confederate cause.[45]

As far as can be determined, she never actively contributed to the Union cause, as did numerous others. Waldauer enlisted in the Union Army, earning a Captain's commission organizing army bands for General John C. Frémont. Actor James Murdoch, who lost his son fighting for the North, provided weeks of inspirational campfire readings for Union troops. Another, Lawrence Barrett, served as a captain in a Massachusetts regiment. Charlotte Cushman enacted numerous benefits for the U.S. Sanitary Committee. Many others in the profession followed their examples.

Maggie's next stop, Milwaukee, did force her to take a public stand on the national schism. Two days before her scheduled arrival on April 29, a notice appeared in the *Milwaukee Sentinel*: "It having been currently reported that, during one of your engagements at a Southern theatre, you stamped upon the glorious Stars and Stripes, and raised the Palmetto flag [of South Carolina] in triumph over your head, we, as loyal citizens of the Union, ask you to give us through the press a true version of the affair, before your appearance at the Academy of Music," signed, "The Milwaukee Public."[46]

At the close of her performance on April 30, Maggie came to the edge of the stage to thank the audience and defend herself against these "false reports of the basest kind, . . . a fabrication of the deepest dye, too horrible for me to contemplate. I was born under the stars and stripes and hope always to live under them." She was rapturously applauded. The Academy management took out newspaper ads defending her, earning her gratitude, but also one rebuttal: "The managers are mistaken. Maggie did sing the 'Southern Marseillaise' not very long ago." Hearing of the controversy, Overall of all people leapt to her defense: "'Fanchon' never meddled with politics in any way. This sort of warfare [in Milwaukee] is contemptible."[47]

The first few nights of Maggie's return to St. Louis yielded lackluster houses, even in *Fanchon* with her original Landry, Charles Pope. Then, the reality of war intruded most immediately. On May 10 Union Captain Nathaniel Lyon successfully attacked Fort Jackson outside the city, held by the Missouri militia. When Lyon marched hundreds of prisoners through downtown St. Louis, violence erupted. His regiments, "finding themselves sorely pressed, turned and fired upon their tormentors," resulting in the deaths of seven soldiers and twenty citizens. The fictitious grief of *Fanchon* was supplanted by the real sorrow in those homes. "Life had suddenly become too serious to permit public attention to be devoted to the stage." With martial law imposed, Maggie played to a nearly empty house, and DeBar the next morning closed the theater, ending the season.[48]

In the long run, Maggie and *Fanchon* would become overwhelming favorites in St. Louis. Her *Fanchon* would become DeBar's most-produced play, even more so than *Hamlet*. The play's author and origin appealed strongly to St. Louis' German immigrants, who comprised about a third of the city's population. But for now, the war took center stage.[49]

Maggie retreated to New York, where for four months she lay low except for two weeks for Moses Kimball at his venerable Boston Museum. From June 3 through 15 she held forth in her usual repertoire, along with *Fanchon*—its first time in Boston. In this heart of the Abolitionist movement, she drew a supportive, if not fervent, following, with no mention made of her Southern proclivities. Kimball brought in Maggie's half-sister Mary to play Fadet and did as much as he could to hype *Fanchon*, producing it every night during her second week and adding Wednesday and Saturday matinees, an increasingly popular American tradition.

While not the nationwide rage it became after its New York debut, *Fanchon* proved popular in Boston, and critical response was favorable. Maggie was "without a rival," exhibiting "the higher powers of dramatic genius." She "never fails to delight an audience. There is not just such an actress on the American stage." She left having "made hosts of friends and will henceforth be one of Boston's greatest favorites."[50]

But New York would be the true crucible for *Fanchon*.

NOTES

1. *New York Clipper*, Nov. 24, 1860.

2. *Atlanta Journal*, Jan. 20, 1924. Despite her Scots-English heritage, there is no evidence that Maggie attended the St. Andrews Society dinner on November 30 to which Booth had been invited, nor that he himself attended.

3. *Montgomery Daily Mail*, Dec. 3, 1860. As has been erroneously repeated, Maggie did not "sponsor" Booth's first star benefit; it was initiated by the citizens of Montgomery and she agreed to participate.

4. *Montgomery Weekly Advertiser*, Dec. 19 and 26, 1860.

5. *Montgomery Daily Mail*, Dec. 13, 1860.

6. *Ibid.*, Dec. 12 and 13, 1860. See also *New York Clipper*, Mar. 8, 1862.

7. *Montgomery Daily Mail*, Dec. 14, 15 and 20, 1860; *Montgomery Weekly Advertiser*, Dec. 19, 1860. No contemporary Montgomery newspaper mentions the flag-trampling, but the *Richmond Dispatch* of Dec. 19, 1860 does, and two eyewitnesses, assistant property master Frank O'Brien and Cora Semmes Ives, sister of Confederate Senator Thomas Jenkins Semmes do, in strikingly similar accounts, both, however, at the remove of over forty years (*Montgomery Advertiser*, Nov. 24, 1907; T. S. DeLeon, *Belles, Beaux and Brains of the Sixties*, New York: C. W. Dillingham, 1907, 113).

8. *Spirit of the Times*, June 28, 1862. Thom's letters in MM Papers, MS Collection 4552, NYPL.

9. For a cogent account of Booth's anti-secessionism in fall 1860 see Terry Alford's definitive *Fortune's Fool: The Life of John Wilkes Booth*, New York: Oxford University Press, 2015, 97–98 and Nora Titone's *My Thoughts Be Bloody*, New York: Free Press, 2010, 232–33.

10. *Pittsburgh Post*, Jan. 11, 1861; *New York Clipper*, May 25, 1861.

11. *New York Clipper*, Apr. 19, 1862; *Buffalo Commercial*, Apr. 12, 1862; *Brooklyn Eagle*, Apr. 18, 1862.

12. *New Orleans Bee*, Jan. 21, 1861.

13. *New Orleans Daily Delta*, Jan. 15, 1861; *New Orleans True Delta*, Jan. 17 and 20, 1861.

14. *New York Clipper*, Apr. 5 and 12, 1862. The same accuser claimed that Maggie had two brothers in the Confederate Army, but her one brother and at least one of her two half-brothers could not have been. The first, Charles S. Mitchell, Jr., was practicing bookbinding in New York with their father. Of the other two, Joseph D. Lomax was in medical school in New York from 1860 to 1862, and then appointed to practice at the Marshall Infirmary in Troy, New York. Maggie insisted that the other, John H. Lomax Mitchell of Memphis, was deaf and unqualified for military service. A thorough search of Confederate and Union enlistment records in National Archives revealed nothing for him.

15. *New Orleans True Delta*, Jan. 20, 1861.

16. *New Orleans Crescent*, Jan. 22, 1861; *New Orleans True Delta*, Jan. 22, 1861.

17. Waldauer had seen Pfeiffer's version, *Die Grille* (the Cricket) acted in German. He and/or Overall may also have known of the success of a pantomimic version of *La Petite Fadette* in New York in 1855.

18. August Waldauer, *Fanchon, the Cricket*, New York: Samuel French Inc's *Standard Drama* CCCXXXIV, 1860.

19. *New Orleans Crescent*, Jan. 24, 1861; L. Clarke Davis, "Two Artists of Comedy," *The Galaxy*, vol. 6 (Aug. 1868), 245; Waldauer 5.

20. Waldauer 5–6.

21. *Detroit Free Press*, Mar. 14, 1880; Waldauer 7–9.

22. Waldauer 12. St. Andoche was a Greek priest martyred in A.D. 177. Sand identifies the Feast of St. Andoche, the patron saint of Cossé, as occurring in late September.

23. Davis, *Galaxy* 247.

24. *New Orleans Crescent*, Jan. 24, 1861.

25. Waldauer 19–20.

26. Olive Logan in *Cincinnati Enquirer*, reprinted in *Bellefonte (PA) Centre Democrat*, Dec. 4, 1879; Waldauer 21–23.

27. Waldauer 24–26.

28. Waldauer 27–30.

29. Waldauer 31.

30. Waldauer 32–38.

31. Waldauer 39–41.

32. Waldauer 42–46.

33. Waldauer 47–48.

34. *Colorado Chieftain*, Nov. 22, 1884; *Detroit Free Press*, Mar. 11, 1884; "Mitchell, Margaret Julia," *Dictionary of American Biography*, Dumas Malone, ed., New York: American Council of Learned Societies, 1984, 56.

35. *New Orleans Crescent*, Jan. 24, 1861; *New Orleans Delta*, Jan. 24, 1861.

36. *New Orleans True Delta*, Jan. 27, 1861; *Detroit Free Press*, Mar. 14, 1880.
37. *New Orleans Crescent*, Jan. 28, 1861.
38. *New Orleans Delta*, Jan. 27, 1861.
39. *Montgomery Confederation*, Feb. 3, 1861.
40. *Montgomery Confederation*, Feb. 17, 1861.
41. *New York Clipper*, Apr. 5 and 12, 1862; Mary Chesnut, *The Private Mary Chesnut*, eds. C. Vann Woodward and Elisabeth Muhlenfeld, New York: Oxford University Press, 1984, 16.
42. *New Orleans True Delta*, Feb. 24 and Mar. 1, 1861; DeBar to Sol Smith, Dec. 13, 1860, Sol Smith Collection, Missouri Historical Society.
43. *Montgomery Advertiser*, Mar. 31 and Apr. 6, 1861.
44. *Louisville Courier*, Apr. 17 and 19, 1861.
45. Thom to MM, Apr. 19, 1861; *Richmond Enquirer*, Oct. 9, 1861.
46. *Milwaukee Sentinel*, Apr. 27, 1861.
47. *Milwaukee News*, May 2, 1861; *New York Mercury* reprinted in *Milwaukee Morning Sentinel*, May 16, 1861; *New Orleans True Delta*, May 12, 1861. Previously an ardent Southerner, Overall postwar became a staunch Unionist.
48. Davis, *Galaxy* 246.
49. Grant Herbstruth, "Benedict DeBar and the Grand Opera House in St. Louis, Missouri, from 1855 to 1879" (PhD diss., University of Iowa, 1954), *passim*.
50. *Boston Transcript*, June 5, 7 and 11, 1861.

Chapter 5

"talked about as much as the war"

Maggie, Anna, and Mary returned to a New York agog with patriotic frenzy. American flags and banners promoting the Union cause unfurled from almost every building. Ubiquitous recruiting centers created endless new regiments. New York State eventually provided almost three hundred of them—nearly 17 percent of the total northern war effort. Recruits were camping and drilling on every available plot of land, especially Union Square, the Battery, and City Hall Park.

The city's economy was gearing up as well. Manhattan and Brooklyn industries churned out clothing, foodstuffs and urgently needed materiel, their shipyards working around the clock to get it to anxious quartermasters and foreign markets while building more naval vessels. The city's tempo ratcheted up even higher when news came in of the Union rout at Bull Run on July 21.

Business was not booming that summer of 1861 at New York's theaters. Most had closed for the summer, leaving Maggie few options if she wished to see what the market held. The only house providing full-length productions was Laura Keene's Varieties at 622 Broadway. Known for melodramas and spectacles, its bill had remained unchanged since November, an "operatic, spectacular, diabolical, musical, terpsichorean, farcical burletta" called *The Seven Sisters*. When it finally closed on August 10 it had completed a record-setting 253 performances. Its hodgepodge of song and dance may have appealed to Maggie's sense of the outré.[1]

She and Anna were not yet ready to try *Fanchon* on Broadway. The economic climate was still not amenable, and Maggie remained unsatisfied with the script, parts of which she considered dull. She spent much of the summer making adjustments to it, condensing several tedious speeches by Fadet into shorter, incisive comments which softened the character, and beefing up the role of Father Barbeaud. She embellished certain dramatic moments, such as Fanchon's huddling grief-stricken at the loss of Landry while village girls pass by singing gaily, and added a new Maypole dance and the soon-to-be-famous Shadow Dance.[2]

Fanchon executes it in jubilation after securing Landry's commitment near the close of Act I. She espies her shadow in a secluded dell, then (with the help of a trained "Drummond light" follow-spot operator atop a stepladder) dances with her shadow, "spreading out her ragged skirts and kicking up her frowsy heels in girlish delight." The moment was "unique in its grotesque action, its wild and almost unnatural exuberance of animal life, its mocking laughter, and the little witch's earnest and real companionship with her black familiar." One manager believed Maggie's "Fanchon, dancing in the moonlight with her imaginary partner" was "one of those perfect bits of acting before which even the chronic fault-finder is dumb."[3]

But Maggie needed to earn a living, and the 1861–62 season beckoned. Aware of the evolving military needs and concomitant disruptions of the rail network, she and Anna restricted the upcoming tour to six cities, returning to two—Cincinnati and St. Louis—several times each. She also put out feelers about going with Anna to California which were quickly picked up and spread by reporters. Something about the idea gave her pause, however, and she dropped it.

Again, she consolidated her repertoire. She would be increasingly dependent on *Fanchon*, performing it twice as often as she had the previous season, usually making it the entire bill due to its length and rigorous emotional and physical demands. She dropped several frivolous farces (leaving only half as many as three years ago) and on the road would add four new pieces (none very successful). Besides *Fanchon*, her core scripts remained *Katty, French Spy, Bonnie Fish Wife, Wept, Margot* and *Wild Irish Girl*.

She opened in Buffalo on September 9 at the Metropolitan Theatre, where large audiences applauded her heartily and critics praised her "real and superior dramatic genius." The only script poorly received was *French Spy*: "We had hoped that this absurd production would never be suffered to be presented upon the boards in this city again."[4]

All summer Ben DeBar had planned to reopen his theater in St. Louis, booking such surefire attractions as Maggie, slotted for a mid-September engagement. Military authorities, though, had a different idea, fearing the consequences of any mass gathering should Missouri bushwhackers swoop in looking for revenge for Fort Jackson. Plus, DeBar's reputation was tainted; he even took his name off billings due to his (accurately) perceived southern sympathies. Maggie finally opened for him on September 25 with *Milly* and *Katty*. After an emergency military proclamation closed the theater again the next night, she performed *Wept* on the 27th. DeBar and comedian Stuart

Robson carried a few farces and the latter participated in boxing matches, which the soldiers cheered.

Next up was Detroit, at Agnes Land Perry's 1,200-seat Metropolitan Theatre. Mary Mitchell and John Albaugh had joined Perry's stock company to play leads. After only five nights in Detroit, though, Maggie boomeranged back to St. Louis to help DeBar with a benefit for the survivors and families of fire victims at the Continental Theater (formerly the National) in Philadelphia on September 14; several young dancers had burned to death. She took time for a benefit night for herself as well, performing *Pet*.

In Cincinnati, her southern hijinks caught up with her. "Maggie, like Caroline Richings, had the misfortune to play in the South last winter," reported the *Cincinnati Enquirer*. "Hence, she is made the subject, notwithstanding her sex, of abuse." But the paper reassured theatergoers that Maggie had "doubtless shelved her secession songs and is as ready to chant the 'Star-Spangled Banner' to an American audience as the 'Southern Marseillaise' to a rabid mob of Secessionists." For now, no further ado arose, but that would not be the case for long.[5]

After only four nights in Cincinnati, she dashed back to Detroit for two weeks, the second mainly consisting of *Fanchon*. Attendance was wretched, though, except for a full house on her benefit night, acting *Wept* opposite Albaugh. The engagement averaged only $22.67 a night, with a dress circle and orchestra priced at 50¢.

Fanchon dominated two weeks back at Wood's Theatre in Cincinnati in mid-November, this time to better results, some nights seeing standing-room-only crowds. Maggie seemed "the very Cricket. . . . From beneath the guise of rudeness and ill-nature . . . there shoots forth a spark of the pure, rich fire beneath, which lights a reciprocal flame in the heart of the listener that makes him, like Landry, love her."[6]

Her next engagement was far less pleasant. For a week, Pittsburgh Theatre manager William Henderson (who had been Maggie's Romeo in Albany seven years before) had hyped her upcoming appearance but ran into strong dissent. It was bruited about in the city that Maggie had sung "secession hymns in the South, calling the chivalry to arms." The afternoon of her scheduled opening on November 25, a notoriously rowdy, drunken Union Army captain named Baum shouted out in a saloon near the theater, "She's a rank Secessionist! I saw her pull down the American flag and trample on it in a theatre in New Orleans." There was reportedly "not a man in the place who did not want to shoot, hang, and quarter the actress." Among the calmer patrons was former Montgomery Theatre manager Matt Canning, a friend of both Maggie and John Wilkes Booth. Canning leapt to Maggie's defense and hot words nearly led to blows before others separated the men. Canning rushed off to warn Henderson.[7]

That night, only a few hundred people attended Maggie's opening in *Satan in Paris* and they were a grim lot. She was greeted on her first entrance with an icy silence. As she soldiered on, she could hear hissing. At its end, she received no applause and rushed in tears to her dressing room. Baum and his cronies in the front row of the balcony rose, inciting the crowd to violence. Henderson urged Maggie to return to the stage and explain, but she sat paralyzed with fear. Determined to defend her honor, he strode onto the stage and announced that Maggie had never shown disrespect to the United States flag. What Baum had seen, he said, must have been a scene from *The French Spy* involving a tricolor French flag (which, splitting hairs, it was). Henderson called to the stage two company members who had been performing with Maggie in the South and who now substantiated Henderson's account. Baum, he told the crowd, "was in the same [drunken] condition in New Orleans that he is often in here, and could not tell the red, white and blue of the French standard from the red, white and blue of the Stars and Stripes." The crowd turned, the moment was won, and Maggie was allowed to proceed with her next piece, the *Bonnie Fish Wife*. Baum was ushered out by other officers, who placed him under arrest.[8]

Most newspaper editors, North and South, defended Maggie. The *Cleveland Herald* opined, "May be Miss Maggie has indulged in little disloyal peccadilloes to 'bring down' the Southern houses," but that was no reason for the officer's boorish behavior. To the *Cincinnati Enquirer*'s Scottish editor, Baum was "an ass. Miss Maggie neither belongs to the North or South; she is a Scotch lassie, and we suppose considers herself under an engagement to sing any song to suit the latitude in which she is cast—be it 'Yankee Doodle,' 'God Save the Queen,' or the traitorous 'Marseillaise.'" But the issue was not over for her.[9]

Uncharacteristically, she left Pittsburgh on a Saturday morning, December 7, en route to St. Louis, and stopped over in Cincinnati. That night Booth closed his Cincinnati engagement and left Sunday morning for his next one, in Louisville. The two warm friends could easily have traveled together to Louisville before she moved on to St. Louis, along with the protective Anna.

In St. Louis, Maggie played older pieces, reserving *Fanchon* for benefit nights. Presumably, she shared her adjustments to it with Waldauer, still conducting DeBar's orchestra. Among her ardent admirers in St. Louis was a Missouri State Militia cavalry officer. Col. H. S. McConnell wrote to her on December 27, "A month since [ago], I had no thought but for ambition, and now as I told you this morning (hallowed morning!), the one great object of my life will be to procure your permission to have me devote my existence to a constant effort to render you happy." His letters to her from the front (chasing Confederate guerrillas in Southeastern Missouri) kept up for months and gush with devotion. Watching her prancing on the stage might have filled the heads of lesser men with lascivious thoughts, but McConnell overcame his:

> I know I love your dear self, for though I have seen you at *moments when degrading and unworthy thoughts would be most likely to intrude* [emphasis his], . . . I have never had a wish or an idea concerning you that I could not at any moment have told you. . . . And when I think of you, your goodness, your purity, the blood [illeg.] to my forehead when I reflect upon my presumption in asking you to accept one so wicked as myself. . . . I do promise upon my honor as a gentleman, an honor without a tarnish, that I will do all in my power to render myself worthy of you. . . . God grant I may have your love, Sigh.[10]

As for her reciprocating his affection, he intended to "Trust to Luck." Although he (apparently fruitlessly) sought replies from her and his letters tapered off (he survived the war), Maggie kept them her whole life.

She and Anna headed back to Manhattan for the holidays, and then opened 1862 back at Wood's Theatre in Cincinnati with *Fanchon* on January 6. Adeline Hind, Fadet in the original New Orleans production, had come north and now reclaimed the role with Maggie. Wood was charging lower "war prices" and the result was full houses. Anticipating the many Fanchon imitators who would follow Maggie, the prescient *Commercial Tribune* decreed, "She has so identified herself with it that the success of another actress in the same part would depend very much on a strict adherence to Miss Mitchell's representation." Joining her on stage for her second benefit, in *Wandering Boys*, was her sister Emma, whose career was struggling. Fleeing Montgomery with Mary soon after Maggie, Emma had failed to find work as her sisters had and now, about to turn twenty, depended on Maggie's largesse.[11]

Emma traveled with Maggie and Anna to Baltimore, to the Front Street Theatre of George Kunkel, John Ford's former partner. (Ford was preparing to open his new Athenaeum in Washington, which would star Maggie, while nominally still managing the Holliday Street Theatre, now primarily a venue for tragedy.) Despite slush-filled streets, theatergoers crammed the house nightly for *Fanchon*, *Wept*, and older farces. Her new shadow dance came in for special praise, being alone "compensation enough for the outlay." *Fanchon* was again championed for being "untainted with the vulgarism which predominates in the mass of the modern sensation dramas of the present day."[12]

Maggie had brought Hind with her to Baltimore as Fadet, joining Maggie's old touring partner Sam Glenn as Father Barbeaud. It may have been Glenn, an inveterate promoter, who encouraged Maggie to start billing *Fanchon* implausibly as having been performed "for 200 successive nights . . .

in the Eastern States." This puffery would balloon in the coming decades to an equally impossible 2,000 and then 3,000 times, a figure picked up and repeated erroneously by countless biographers and theater historians. Emma joined Maggie for both of her benefits (in small roles and dancing an Irish jig), the second of which completely sold out.[13]

Closing on February 8, Maggie was to go on to Washington, but Ford was not ready to open, leaving her and Anna stranded in Baltimore for several weeks, during which they may well have walked four blocks over to the Holliday Street Theatre where Booth was performing. On March 3, Maggie reopened at the Front Street and on March 11 she, Booth and Kunkel's Ethiopian Nightingales (blackface minstrels) participated in a special benefit for Kunkel. For her final benefit on March 14 (competing head-to-head with Booth's at the Holliday Street), she enacted another new soubrette, Marie in *The Vivandiere*, a ballad opera by secessionist John Hill Hewitt which included a ballad, "Darkness Is the Lover's Friend."

A harsh assessment of Maggie's acting appeared at the close of this second Baltimore engagement. Frank Queen, the founder, owner, and editor of the *New York Clipper* denounced her as an actress "who imagines that variety constitutes genius. [Her] characters are destitute of that elegance of style, beauty of finish, and skill which denote the well-educated artist. She is bright, pretty, versatile, possesses a beautiful form, dances well and sings agreeably, [but] her manner is too coarse—of that style which is usually found in a Western [unpolished] actress." Anna took action on Maggie's behalf. Returning to New York from Baltimore, she stormed into the *Clipper* offices to upbraid Queen for his harsh words and to refute charges that Maggie was less than an ardent Unionist.[14]

Back in Cincinnati, Maggie opened on April 21 with *Margot* and *Katty*, but for the most part stuck with *Fanchon*, drawing immense audiences. It was "talked about as much as the war and a person who has not seen Maggie Mitchell in *Fanchon* is now considered as much out of fashion as a man in a semi-military stock and swallowtail blue coat with brass buttons."[15]

From there she headed with Anna and Emma back to St. Louis, DeBar and the enjoyable company of Booth, whom she succeeded. During the first week of May, before Booth headed to Boston, they spent considerable time together, including afternoon coffee with Waldauer and his wife. Also present were DeBar's niece (and adopted daughter) Blanche Booth DeBar. Like her uncle, who was repeatedly admonished by the St. Louis Provost Marshal for "pandering to rebel tastes on the stage of his theatre," Blanche was "an unmitigated rebel" who idolized, and wrote poetry to, Confederate officers. Over coffee, Waldauer pressed Booth for his views on the war. Booth asserted his intention as an actor to remain neutral, "but one thing is certain," he swore, "I should never lift a hand *to fight against the old flag* [emphasis Waldauer's]." That week Booth and Maggie went riding with Blanche, who idolized her handsome "Uncle John." This became a regular activity whenever the three could be together. Booth and Maggie exchanged forget-me-nots, and rumors reached the east coast of their engagement, but nothing ever came of it.[16]

Maggie's repertoire in St. Louis was a conflation of the old and the new. To the predictable *Fanchon, Katty, Bonnie Fish Wife*, and *Four Sisters*, she added the role of Marie in what had been Talfourd's *Ion*, now *The Foundling; or, Love and Duty*; and the title role in a "new fairy drama," *The Home Fairy* (adapted from Boucicault's *Dot; or, the Cricket on the Hearth*). These retitled and altered scripts were Maggie's way of evading copyright laws. She and Emma teamed again for *Wandering Boys* for Maggie's May 9 benefit.

In wartime St. Louis Maggie was often surrounded by "many sighing swains, [both] in the profession and out of it." Recalled one, "We followed her around the stage, sent our big bouquets and were just as sick and dreamy over her as young fellows usually are over their first love. The Sunday she left the whole fifty of us went to the Planters' House, stood in a row and bade her good-bye. Then . . . we followed her over the river in the ferryboat and stood on the platform at the station waving her [sic] handkerchief and throwing kisses as the train disappeared in the distance. That sort of thing seemed to do us all good."[17]

Stopping in Cincinnati, Maggie caught a performance of the emotional star Matilda Heron in *Belle of the Season*, in which Heron had sold out the Winter Garden on Broadway for weeks. Heron was being paid an astounding $400 a night ($10,000 today), which may have inspired Maggie to soar to commensurate heights, for immediately upon arriving in New York, Anna arranged for *Fanchon*'s Broadway debut at Keene's Varieties (a seven-block walk from the Mitchell home). Despite the success of *Seven Sisters*, Keene continued to struggle due to the financial panic, problems with her health, and the outbreak of war. Now the pressure was on Maggie to produce a profitable summer season. About to turn twenty-six on June 2 and emerging somewhat from the managerial shadows of Anna, she would for this engagement be her own manager, hire her production staff, and cast *Fanchon* herself.

In Keene, she had a commendable role model, a meticulous, imperious manager who demanded perfection from every performer and every aspect of staging—necessary to compete in a male-dominated world. She no doubt shared with Maggie not only the intricacies and mechanics of the venue but also some of her methods of achieving perfection. Although her genteel comedic acting style was different from Maggie's exuberance, her audiences expected only the finest acting.

With assistance from Keene and two of Maggie's former colleagues, playwright, and acting manager James Pilgrim and stage manager Dolly

Davenport, Maggie assembled a competent cast and began rehearsals. Fadet would again be Hind, whose husband T. J. would play Father Caillard. Father Barbeaud would be James H. Stoddart, 34, a holdover from Keene's company, and the spiteful Madelon would be Stoddart's wife, Matilda, 36, a former Keene actress. Maggie knew the couple from Baltimore in 1859. Mother Barbeaud would be Mrs. H. P. Grattan, 52, with whom Maggie had acted at the Bowery a decade ago. For Landry, Maggie needed someone she knew well and turned again to Mary's former husband, James Collier, now 26. Having grown into a handsome, brawny actor and sometime pugilist in the mold of Edwin Forrest, whom he consciously emulated and with whom he would later tour, Collier had lately been playing "heavies" at Niblo's Garden. Boyish low comedian Davenport, 34, was a perfect fit for Didier.

Among the dancing, singing villagers (utility players) were Stoddart's daughter Adele, fifteen-year-old Kitty Blanchard (later a minor star in her own right), and a "Miss Emma," likely Emma Mitchell, 20 (the type of billing used by actors to obscure nepotistic connections; Booth first acted as "J. B. Wilkes"). The ensemble was versatile enough to carry roles in other plays should *Fanchon* not succeed or audiences demand variety.

Opening night was set for Monday, June 9, 1862, amid considerable competition, some of it seemingly designed to thwart Maggie. Across the street and a block up, the Winter Garden trumpeted a "spectacular, magical burlesque," *The Wizard's Tempest*. A little further up Broadway, Mr. and Mrs. W. J. Florence were performing melodrama at Wallack's. Five blocks west, at Niblo's, Caroline Richings was enacting the kind of roles Maggie specialized in. Less than a mile south lay a triple threat: Barnum's Museum playing domestic comedies, the Old Bowery churning out lurid melodramas, and the New Bowery with the uninhibited Adah Isaacs Menken, whose attire was even skimpier than Maggie's and whose repertoire included *French Spy* and a near-nude *Mazeppa*.

Maggie would have to prove herself to the toughest audiences and the most discerning critics in America, with New York having already lionized other soubrettes, including Robertson and Richings. Plus, Lotta Crabtree, nearly a Maggie clone, was coming up fast on the inside, having established herself securely in the West and would take New York by storm in a few years.

Word of mouth about *Fanchon* generated healthy ticket sales. Maggie had played it enough times to be confident but still felt unusually nervous. Then, from her first entrance chasing her flyaway chicken, she was energized beyond anything she had ever felt:

> Her arms, her legs, her feet, her hands, her head and tongue, are all in motion. . . . The fiery spirit in the tiny form imparts to it an eternal unrest. It is scarcely possible to look at the curiously dressed figure, which seems to be strung upon wires and impelled by electric shocks, as it gives way to laughter

or subsides into tears, whose voice suddenly sinks from the most boisterous mirth into the most profound depths of pathos in a breath, without feeling that the girl's mind has suffered some rude shock. Yet when her clear, strange voice breaks into speech, its music is wedded to words of noble simplicity. When sorrow moves them, they fall upon the ear as softly as rippling water, in slow, measured cadences; but when an ugly wrong has wrought upon her mind, the actress, who is utterly forgotten in the part, flings them out with quick and savage hatred; they rise and swell and fill the air until each hurtling word seems potent as a curse or witch's spell.[18]

As she knew it would be, Maggie's "shadow dance" became that night iconic. For the rest of her career, no moment in any other script she undertook could top it for dramatic effectiveness. Starting it, Fanchon is

full to the brim with a simple, childish joy, which at first finds vantage ground in wild, exuberant laughter and in mad, frolicsome gestures which are interrupted presently by her catching sight of her own weird and fantastic shadow in the moonlight. The rays fall through a break in the trees, forming a sort of fairy circle, into which she steps, and to a blithesome song that bubbles up from her full heart, she begins a strange, fantastic dance, full of artless grace and freedom. Her whole body vibrates, moves to and fro in the measured rhythm of her song. The lithe limbs, the undulating body, the bending head crowned with its wealth of hair, are instinct with happiness, swayed and impelled by the music of her own voice. Directly her shoe falls off, and she stoops to put it on, still singing, but in a softer key, her jubilant song to which still sways her body and bends her head. But as she stoops lower, the tiny, tawdry figure and its shadow meet and start appalled apart, then the sweet song dies on her lips, an awful pain fills up her face, a terror, very pitiful to see in any child, animates her form and, bending still lower till her loose hair touches the little black shadow of herself, she addresses it familiarly, bitterly, as if it had life and were sentient as her own self. All this action lasts scarcely longer than a minute. But in that minute *the shadow has shown her herself*; she has seen in that little moment how her childhood has been abused by circumstance, how tawdry, eccentric and mean is her dress, her fantastic and uncouth appearance, and her lack of all that is debonair and beautiful in childhood, and though the few words with which she addresses it are a child's simple language, they are so full of nature, so burdened with her trouble, loss and pain, so nearly underlying all human sympathy, that no one who looks upon the actress now sees any actress there, but only a little child to succor, to whom he would like to stretch out loving, helpful hands—a little child who has wetted his cheeks with unusual tears.[19]

When the villagers mock Fanchon in Act II,

no [other] actor has thrown into any single situation the nervous force and bewildering concentration of scorn and hatred which the actress hurls upon her tormentors in this scene. Her words seemed to blister and scorch the creatures they fell upon, the tiny gestures were charged with a nameless evil, . . . the little, trembling body was regnant, fiery with a passion that had power to wither or to kill; her very laughter, that had been but a moment before soft and melodious as the music of the dance, was full of stinging, savage bitterness, creating an atmosphere of poisoned malice.[20]

When Fanchon lies weeping by the riverside as night comes on,

She sobs as if her grief had exhausted physical nature and she could weep no more; but she stretches her hands out straight before her with infinite weariness, clasps them about her neck as her head droops to her breast; her eyes are swollen and dry, her dress disordered, and all that is heard is the sound of the painful, tearless sobs; but underneath all this the spectator sees that a child's heart is breaking. She does not speak; her pain and wrong and misery are too deep for words, and they find more suitable expression in a certain nervous caressing of her arms and hands and face which are more pitiful to see than language would be to hear. The tenderness and pathos of the picture are unutterable.[21]

"When Maggie Mitchell walked off the stage of Laura Keene's little theater that beautiful summer's night," declared journalist L. Clarke Davis, "she knew she was famous, and that her fortune was secure." Taking the critics by surprise, she was more than just successful; she was "a triumph" in "a part of rare difficulty and demanding much study and intelligence." She demonstrated "how in the heart of a rough, eccentric and apparently half-witted girl, a flower of pure love springs up, . . . making it beautiful and fragrant forever." Her "matchless impersonation" was "better than many sermons."[22]

Like Robertson, Maggie was "one of those bright little sympathetic actresses that somehow insinuate themselves into the affections of the public before the public has time to make up its mind on the subject of criticism." There was "a charming freshness and originality about her that forestalls without defying criticism, and that makes you feel at once she is not to be carped and caviled at, but to be studied and appreciatively understood." Her Fanchon "put fault-finding out of the question; one can only find for it the heartiest admiration." Significantly, "It would have been a signal failure if any other actress in the country had appeared as the Cricket."[23]

She was "a cunning, wee thing, so handsome and exquisitely formed as to remind one of a fairy," "a beautiful child and still an actress of marvelous power." "There was none of the magpie rote and mechanical action" of other young stars. Here was "a cherub soul, arch, bright, and full of mirth, in girlish and angelic shape, wonderfully lovable. You felt towards her as some mariners to some beautiful bird from the land, which has settled upon their spars when they have been long at sea. You longed to caress her, but withheld your hand for fear she might unfold her wings and fly to the heavens away."[24]

Although Waldauer's script was considered overly didactic, he had eschewed "trick or violence, relying on simple, natural beauty and pathos, to win the audience. The characters are homely, yet how true; the incidents naturally evolved but interesting; the language never stilted, but often touchingly pathetic.... Old men and maidens are alike affected to tears." Still, the dialogue was "rather flat. There is no sparkling repartee, no wit, nor humor, when Fanchon is not upon the stage.... The thin sentimentality of the piece compels her to work her natural pathos very hard in order to produce the effects the author has feebly aimed at."[25]

The entire cast, especially Collier, Davenport, and Adeline Hind came in for praise as well, along with Davenport's stage direction. Nor had Anna's influence gone unnoticed: "Such beauty as [Maggie's], and such homage ... would have intoxicated and been dangerous to many; but strong principles and regard to the precepts of an excellent mother have rendered them harmless to her."[26]

By the end of June, Maggie was elevated to that gold standard of Victorian excellence, "genius." She "undoubtedly possesses genius," having created "a quaint and most difficult character with a power and originality of conception which could only be reached through the possession of genius." Her "delineation of Fanchon is the most unique, quaint, startling, natural and charming piece of acting that we have witnessed for years." This "new child of Genius" exhibited "a *petite femme* very trim, well-proportioned, with a face that can look prettier in repose than many others when excited, ... a figure which can be distorted into a hundred elfish shapes in a moment or sink in repose into the noblest little statue ever seen." She performed with a rare naturalness: "There is a freshness in her gestures, movements, form and voice that excites your attention and then attracts your admiration. Never was an actress less stagy, [as if she] suddenly, when no one was looking, stepped quietly over the odious barrier ... between Nature and the Dramatic Art."[27]

There remained "no little curiosity to witness her conception of some other character." Maggie happily complied, initiating on July 3 two weeks of *Katty, Young Prince, Margot, Four Sisters, Treasure*, and *Pet*. These "fully confirmed the favorable impression produced by her *Fanchon* and proved the versatility and strength of her resources." In these roles, too, she "first surprised her audiences, then made them think, and finally won them over to appreciation of those daring flights of natural emotion which abound in all of her impersonations." How, asked the *New York Times*, could Maggie "have remained so long contented with the plaudits of provincial crowds"? She would henceforth be always welcomed and embraced in Manhattan.[28]

Despite oppressive heat that was costing other managers dearly, some closing their theaters, Maggie's farewell *Fanchon* benefit on July 18 was sold out, and "by unanimous desire" was repeated the next night to accommodate those turned away. Called before the curtain and showered with bouquets at the close of each act, she concluded the evening with a gracious speech of gratitude to the audience. It felt, she told them, "like having my friends around me for a quiet little chat." She also expressed her debt to the press for *Fanchon*'s success. She admitted the trepidation with which she had undertaken this New York venture and conveyed her relief at how well it had gone. Predictably, a perfect "mania" of playwrights began churning out *Fanchon*-like pieces for "the eccentric genius of Miss Mitchell," nearly all of which fell short of her consideration.[29]

Basking in all of this attention and affirmation, Maggie sometime that month went to Mathew Brady's New York studio to sit for a series of *cartes de visite*, most in poses from *Fanchon*, some with Collier. These became the most widely disseminated images of Maggie for generations.

Her task for 1862–63 was to replicate the New York success of *Fanchon* across the country. For this, she hired respected theatrical agent William F. Brough, 64, as an advance man (the precursor to today's press agent). He would make sure that each theater was ready for her arrival, its stock company prepared to adequately support her, especially in *Fanchon*, and that newspapers ran ample notices of her upcoming appearance.

Fortunately, the stock company for her season-opener on September 3 at Louisa Lane Drew's Arch Street Theatre in Philadelphia was an exceptionally strong one. Mrs. Drew, in her second season of management, was like Keene discerning in her hiring, diligent in her training, and demanding in her rehearsals. She and Maggie collaborated on preparing *Fanchon* and it succeeded wonderfully, Maggie investing her character "with an interest which never flags."[30]

She then traveled south to Washington with Anna, with whom she spent nearly all of her offstage time, to open September 15 at Ford's new Atheneum [sic] on Tenth Street, supported by a strong stock company, formed chiefly for comedy. A lavishly furnished, well-ventilated venue with the latest stage equipment, Ford's seated 2,500.

The wartime capital was a far different place from that of her last visit in early 1860, its population unsettled and wary. Regiments camped and drilled on every available parcel of ground, including that of the U.S. Capitol, with horses and cattle in rude stockades on the grounds of the truncated Washington Monument. News at the end of August of another Union disaster at Bull Run preoccupied government officials at every level. As Robert E. Lee's Confederate army marched into Maryland, President Lincoln, his new commander George B. McClellan, and all Washingtonians braced for invasion.

Nevertheless, for a week Maggie cycled through her pre-*Fanchon* repertoire while Ford, stage manager Humphrey Bland and orchestra conductor William Withers (a recent Union Army veteran) prepared everyone for *Fanchon*, slated for September 22. During Maggie's performance of *Four Sisters* on September 17, news arrived of the pyrrhic Union victory at Antietam Creek, just outside Sharpsburg, Maryland—the bloodiest single day of the war.

Remarkably, the war news did not affect attendance at Ford's. As Lincoln's secretary, John Hay, observed, Washington that fall "is now jollier than ever before. . . . I have seen nowhere since the miserable war began, a people so volatile, so pleasure-loving, so nonchalant, as that which forms the population of Washington." Catering to their whims, Maggie dished up escapist fare. Night after night the house was full, admirers tossed bouquets, and reviewers praised her vivacity, grace, good looks, versatility, and modest offstage demeanor. (Since her New York success, Maggie was downplaying the sauciness of her soubrettes.)[31]

Countless men, many in uniform, flocked to worship her, some serenading her under her hotel balcony. One of their numbers, writing almost twenty years later, remembered well "when Maggie played at Ford's Theatre in 1862 and infatuated aide-de-camps [sic] used to spend all their pay in boxes and bouquets. Maggie could have married any officer in the army she pleased, including the writer, but she didn't." Newspapers reported that she "has turned the heads of half the spoony [sic] shoulder straps in Washington. Nightly the stage is flooded with bouquets, and frequently with more substantial evidences of admiration, until the greenhouses of Washington and the pockets of her admirers are about equally empty."[32]

For years Maggie had been "peculiarly captivating to susceptible young men." Hank Paddock had been smitten in Cleveland, an obsessed Baltimore hotelier had sold his business to follow her, and rumors abounded about a Maggie Mitchell engagement and/or impulsive marriage. The most persistent had it that while playing Richmond in the mid-1850s, Maggie had eloped after a Saturday night performance to marry a "handsome young stranger." Anna, though, had supposedly opposed the union and Maggie never lived with the man, who left the scene while she went back to work on Monday. It was reported over twenty years later that "the people in the theatre in Richmond knew all about it," and a divorce was quietly facilitated "many years afterward" by Chicago Judge Robert Wilson. Unfortunately for anyone seeking corroboration of this, but helpful to rumormongers, the municipal records of Chicago were lost in the Great Fire of 1871.[33]

However, in late September 1862, Maggie did impulsively follow her heart—and this time left a paper trail. It was her habit to go riding early each morning, and in Washington, a handsome male companion sometimes joined her. William Virgil Wallace, 24, a fellow New Yorker, was a musician and minor actor at Ford's. Tall, dark-complected, brown-eyed and brown-haired, he may have reminded her of John Wilkes Booth or had simply caught her fancy, but their rides ventured farther and farther afield from Ford's until, on the morning of Friday, September 26, they drew up to the courthouse in Bladensburg, Maryland, and took out a marriage license. The following morning they were secretly wed.[34]

Returning to her hotel with Wallace, Maggie blithely informed Anna that they were husband and wife. Anna, furious, ordered Wallace out, commanding him never again to see or contact Maggie in any way. He was, she announced, "not exalted enough to win such a wife." Maggie obediently acquiesced. The marriage was never consummated and divorce was quietly arranged in Baltimore. Or so it was later reported—no record of the divorce is extant.[35]

Maggie's engagement at Ford's stretched to a remarkable six weeks, with *Fanchon* its centerpiece, drawing houses so crowded that dozens were turned away every night despite intense competition from nearby theaters. Nothing failed to hit the mark, from *Wept* to *French Spy*, to *Wild Irish Girl*, to *Pet*, to *Milly*, to *Masks and Faces*, to *Satan*, and more—even shopworn pieces like *The Vivandiere* (which she spiced up by inserting, and conducting, a musket drill of sixteen lovely chorines). Crowds flocked to Ford's.

By the end of Maggie's third week, Ford added Saturday *Fanchon* matinees. Significantly, her audiences included many fashionably dressed women who "seem to be in perfect rapture with Miss Mitchell and *Fanchon*." This "has created a perfect furore, a sensation far exceeding that of any other play represented for years." As an added attraction, by mid-October Maggie brought in two of her sisters, with Mary assuming the role of Fadet and Maggie and Emma in *Wandering Boys*. All three performed together in a farce, Richard Ayton's *The Rendezvous*.[36]

"Never was there a success more instant and decided," recorded Hay. "Her wonderful personation of the elfish witch-child of the mountains, with a beautiful nature turned momentarily awry by the world's unkindness, brought by a true love out of the shadows of early neglect and abandonment to the light and beauty of perfect womanhood, touched the hearts and compelled the admiration of all who saw it—The wild and startling grace of the Moonlight Dance with her shadow—the simple pathos and modest dignity of her dialogue with her peasant lover in the gathering twilight . . . were delineated with that exquisite naturalness which we thought had vanished from the American stage." He rejoiced to see in wartime a theater "nightly filled to excess with an intelligent crowd who come to listen to a simple uneventful story of a humble life, as proper as a sermon and as pure as a prayer." He was especially glad to see Maggie "turn from Protean farces to a five-act drama of domestic life, to throw her past behind her, and venture alone upon a higher future."[37]

A surprising number of fans in the capital were clergy, who found it "an attractive moral example, calculated to teach the bright reward of virtue." Indeed, *Fanchon* "may be witnessed by the most puritanical without any fear of being allured from their devotions." It evoked "all the noble passions of the soul, . . . causing all to fall in love with virtue." Maggie thus "has won for herself an unsullied name and set an example that will keep many of her profession from falling victims to the temptations that surround them."[38]

Her benefits brought in wildly enthusiastic audiences and more flowers than she could hold, including a basket of them (enclosing jewelry), lowered from a private box on tricolored ribbons. When another actor stepped up to cut these loose for Maggie, she drew "thunders of applause" when she proclaimed, "No, do not sever the red, white and blue." Also bestowed on her were such lavish gifts as a solid-gold cricket brooch, which she promised to wear as an emblem of her refinement in the final scene of *Fanchon*.[39]

But the highlight of her Washington visit was an invitation to tea with the Lincolns in the Executive Mansion. Even though the president had not yet seen Maggie perform, he had likely heard Hay's raves, and sent over a carriage for her and Brough. Lincoln greeted her most kindly: "He shook my hand and looked me steadily for a minute, and then he said, 'I hearn [sic] of you so much, young woman, that I wanted to meet you.'" For Maggie, it was "the greatest day of my life."[40]

1862 had been a magical year, but new challenges awaited.

NOTES

1. Odell VII:311.

2. Waldauer and Overall insisted that these elements existed in the original *Fanchon*, but Maggie repeatedly insisted they were her inventions. Reviews from 1860–61 productions do not mention them. The earliest extant script of *Fanchon* is that of 1862, published by Samuel French in New York, which includes all of these embellishments.

3. *The Michigan Argonaut*, VI (1887–88), 81, reprinted from *Louisville Courier-Journal*; *Chicago Tribune*, Nov. 5, 1893; Augustus Pitou, *Masters of the Show*, New York: Neale Publishing Co., 1914, 104 and 402.

4. *Buffalo Commercial*, Sept. 13 and 21, 1861.

5. *Cincinnati Enquirer*, Oct. 13, 1861.

6. *Cincinnati Tribune*, Nov. 20–21, 1861.

7. *New York Evening Post*, Nov. 30, 1861; *New York Times*, May 16, 1886. Canning may have been traveling with Maggie and helping Anna arrange her tour, a possibility reinforced by his managing Booth's tour, which somewhat paralleled hers.

8. *Pittsburgh Chronicle*, Nov. 30, 1861. It was apparently a former army comrade of Baum's who wrote the *Clipper* describing Maggie's supposed flag substitution and trampling. See *New York Clipper*, Apr. 5, 1862.

9. *Cleveland Herald*, Dec. 2, 1861; *Cincinnati Enquirer*, Dec. 1, 1861.

10. McConnell to MM, Dec. 27, 1861, MM Papers, MS Collection 4552, NYPL. McConnell is not to be confused with Captain (later Major) Hall S. McConnell of the Confederate infantry.

11. *Cincinnati Commercial Tribune*, Jan. 6, 1862.

12. *The South* (Baltimore), Jan. 30, 1862.

13. *The South* (Baltimore), Jan. 28, 1862.

14. *New York Clipper*, Mar. 15 and Apr. 12, 1862. It is unclear whether Maggie returned to New York with Anna; there is no record of her performing there or elsewhere from mid-March to mid-April. It is unknown whether she spent any unaccompanied time with Booth.

15. *Cincinnati Commercial Tribune*, Apr. 28, 1862.

16. William C. Edwards and Edward Steers, Jr., *The Lincoln Assassination: The Evidence*, Urbana: University of Illinois Press, 2009, 99–100; Waldauer letter to Alfred Becks, July 17, 1895, Harvard Theatre Collection; Blanche DeBar letter to Leslie Traylor, Minneapolis, MN, May 12[?], 1925, in E. H. Swaim Papers, Georgetown University Library; *St. Louis Republic*, July 25, 1897; Alford 146 and fn. 14, 380. Waldauer concluded from this discussion and from time spent with Booth in New York during the summer of 1864 that Booth remained loyal to the Union. Waldauer was subsequently shocked when Booth announced his intention to cease acting and even more so when he learned of his assassination of the president. Blanche's mother, DeBar's sister Clementine, had been abandoned by Booth's brother, Junius Brutus Booth, Jr.

17. "Theatric Reminiscences" (Carboy); *St. Louis Post-Dispatch*, Jan. 31, 1883.

18. Davis, *Galaxy* 248.

19. *Ibid*.

20. Davis, *Galaxy* 249.

21. *Ibid*.

22. Davis, *Galaxy* 250–51; *New York Herald*, June 10, 1862.

23. *New York Times*, June 10 and 17, 1862; *Spirit of the Times*, June 28, 1862.

24. *Ibid*.

25. *Ibid*.

26. *Ibid*.

27. *New York Times*, July 14, 1862; *New York Saturday Courier* quoted in *New Orleans Times-Picayune*, July 13, 1862; *Frank Leslie's Illustrated Newspaper*, June 28 and July 5, 1862.

28. *Frank Leslie's Illustrated Newspaper*, July 5 and 19, 1862; *New York Times*, July 14, 1862.

29. *New York Tribune*, July 19, 1862; *Frank Leslie's Illustrated Newspaper*, July 26, 1862; *New York Herald*, July 21, 1862. The *Richmond Dispatch*, perhaps disillusioned with the formerly pro-secessionist Maggie, wrote on September 25 that her New York engagement was "a financial failure."

30. *Philadelphia Inquirer*, Sept. 3, 1862.

31. Michael Burlingame, ed. *Lincoln's Journalist: John Hay's Anonymous Writings for the Press, 1860–1864*, Carbondale: Southern Illinois University Press, 1998, 320.

32. (Washington) *National Republican*, May 26, 1881; Washington correspondent Oct. 23, 1862, for *Indiana State Sentinel*, Nov. 3, 1862.

33. *Spirit of the Times*, Mar. 15, 1856. The chief sources for the elopement story were the *New York Times*, Mar. 5, 1889, and the *New York Herald*, Mar. 7, 1889, at the time of Maggie's divorce from Paddock, both citing an anonymous Chicago source. The Baltimore hotelier was a Billy Wilkeson. See also *Louisville Democrat*, May 28, 1863, and *New York Clipper*, May 31, 1863.

34. Wallace was born July 23, 1838, in Litchfield, CT. Passport Application No. 16080, Nov. 11, 1864, National Archives and Records Administration, https://www.fold3.com/image/60537409; marriage license recorded Sept. 26, 1862, "Margaret Julia of New York" to "William Virgil Wallace of New York," Record of Marriages, Upper Marlboro, Prince Georges County, Maryland, 1777 to 1886, Part 04, File I-M.

35. *Nashville Tennessean*, Apr. 9, 1889; Washington correspondent to *Cincinnati Enquirer*, reprinted in *St. Paul Globe*, Apr. 21, 1889, who narrates a thorough, yet ultimately unsuccessful, search for records of the Baltimore divorce.

36. *National Intelligencer*, Sept. 26, 1862.

37. Burlingame 321–22.

38. *National Intelligencer*, Sept. 24, 1862; (Washington) *National Republican*, Sept. 30, Oct. 8 and 13, 1862.

39. *Cincinnati Commercial*, Oct. 29, 1862.

40. *Pittsburgh Post*, Nov. 1, 1862 and Mar. 26, 1918. Several of Maggie's obituaries erroneously date this event as Spring 1865, when she was touring in the Midwest, by which time Lincoln had already met her and seen her perform at Ford's.

Chapter 6

"she will never be more idolized than she was by the soldiers"

Word of *Fanchon*'s success in New York and Washington spread quickly and imitators began to crop up thanks to stolen copies of Maggie's promptbooks. The first and most persistent of these was Charlotte Thompson, who would plague Maggie for twenty years, beginning with a *Fanchon* in Philadelphia as soon as Maggie had left there. Maggie and Waldauer threatened lawsuits against managers who violated copyright protection, to no avail.

Some comparisons were unfavorable. Thompson was touring widely in the Midwest—Maggie's stomping ground—with an unauthorized *Fanchon*, and Ettie Henderson, the wife of Pittsburgh manager William Henderson, had been doing so in London. The *Cincinnati Enquirer* asserted, "Only in the first act can Maggie approximate to Miss Thompson. In the others, she is comparatively nothing. Miss Mitchell's great attraction is wit, sprightliness, and vivacity. Miss Thompson possesses these requisites, combined with a force and pathos that render her irresistible. [Thompson's] face is the most expressive we have ever seen, her gestures are graceful, and her eyes fairly talk."[1]

Still, as a few discerning critics observed, "Maggie has no cause to 'fear a rival near the throne.' . . . Stars of a minor stamp have most unscrupulously appropriated this piece, although the copyright is the sole property (by purchase) of Miss Mitchell, [who need] be under no fear of rivalry, as her genius is the true copyright." "Several really talented *comediennes*" trotted out their *Fanchons* over the years, noted her friend Luther Holden, but "none ever made an impression on the public which in the slightest degree tended to dim the lustre of the American original."[2]

Southern papers clamored for Maggie's return, but the Confederacy was anathema to her now. Urged to perform in Virginia and Georgia, she demurred, saying she was unable to "on account of the numerous trunks of wardrobe which she endeavored to bring with her." In rebuttal, the *Augusta*

Constitutionalist jibed, "Maggie certainly wears less clothes than any actress the editor has ever seen on stage."³

Instead, she headed west with Anna, spending November in Cincinnati at Wood's Theatre, in Chicago at McVicker's, and in Louisville at the Louisville Theatre. At each, *Fanchon* comprised at least half of her performances and met with universal acclaim. Her Didier in Chicago was McVicker himself, now in his forties and rather heavy.

She continued to look for new scripts that might bring success commensurate with *Fanchon*'s. For her farewell benefit in Louisville on December 5, she tried the title role of *Hermance, the Child of Fortune*, a five-act pastoral comedy in the mold of *Fanchon* translated from the German by J. G. Methua and J. R. Fisk. Boarding school girl Hermance protects the honor of a classmate and is expelled for refusing to share her secret and is thus disowned by her duchess grandmother. Seeking refuge in a rustic cottage with her old peasant nurse, she predictably finds true love with the handsome Anatole. The script was wholly formulaic: "Nobody in the piece has to do anything but come on and talk and exit." Still, Maggie had paid Laura Keene $1,000 for the rights to *Hermance*, so she played it intermittently for three more seasons.⁴

Leaving Louisville for St. Louis, she experienced a fright when changing trains outside Seymour, Indiana. Realizing she had forgotten her purse as she disembarked, she stepped back aboard just as the train started up again, throwing her to the ground. Fortunately, her injury was not serious enough to prevent her arrival in St. Louis on time to perform for DeBar on December 8. There she drew packed, fashionable houses that included many ladies. She tried *Hermance* for two nights, including her farewell benefit, with better results this time. Succeeded by Booth, she either remained in St. Louis for the holidays—which, given the DeBar's previous hospitality and Booth's proximity, was quite possible—or returned to New York, for her next appearance was not until January 5, 1863, in Boston.

In that city virtually untouched by the Civil War she performed for Wyzeman Marshall at the Howard Athenaeum, drawing well with just *Fanchon*. Backed by a good stock company and "exceedingly beautiful and picturesque" scenery, *Fanchon* was an "unqualified success." It was reviewed by a delighted nineteen-year-old Bostonian named Henry James, his first published work. Over forty years later he reminisced about "Maggie Mitchell, over whom I went fantastically mad, though she was undoubtedly a barbarian and would nowadays be taken for such." But that first night, he gushed with typical Jamesian verbosity, that

> [s]he makes the heart and body labor in concordant action. She does not express throbbings and tremors of emotion by the recognized rules of declamatory

eloquence, but by the guiding impulses of the heart. She leaps upon the stage like the child of nature skipping over the green fields of waning spring, and her face looks flushed with the health of fresh breezes. . . . Her whole acting emanates from impulse. . . . The wild and reckless scenes of childhood she delivers with the most delicious vivacity and effect, while the tenderest chords of pathos are exhibited in that untutored sorrow which we might anticipate in a roving child. . . . The exquisite abandon which she throws into every scene . . . is among the most characteristic and entertaining features of her acting.[5]

In late January she alternated *Fanchon* with older pieces and the persistent *Hermance* in Providence at J. C. Myers' Academy, selling out nightly with hundreds turned away. Her "artless manners and rustic abandon" drew critical acclaim. "Her childish glee and sorrow were so truthfully rendered as to move the most stoical." Her benefit drew "the largest audience ever assembled at the Academy."[6]

Brough publicized her next performance, at the Brooklyn Academy of Music, but its manager had contracted with another performer, leaving Maggie up in the air. This and a similar scheduling error in March could account for Maggie's not renewing her association with Brough after this season. She opened instead on February 2 back in Washington, which giddily celebrated her return. If anything, it was more successful than her previous engagement. At the close of her benefit, her love of riding widely known, she was presented with "a splendid horse, with elegant trappings to match, a superb Spanish saddle, the bits of solid silver." She was forced, however, to perform at the smaller, rundown Washington Theatre, as Ford's had burned down on December 30. Maggie's vastly improved financial status since her New York triumph with *Fanchon* allowed her to purchase several $500 shares in Ford's rebuilding effort. She would become a welcome star upon its completion until its ill-fated closure on April 15, 1865.[7]

In Washington, *Fanchon* predominated, and audiences and reviewers alike marveled at Maggie's transformation from "an untaught, neglected, lonely child in search of her stray pet chicken" into "a delicate, lovely, truthful woman." She was irresistible, "one of those witches who rob men of their senses every day with their beautiful eyes and winsome ways." Best of all, "those who know her say that she is good, and pure, and true as Fanchon herself." Two nights of *Hermance*, though, met with failure. "A composition of school-girl nonsense, without interest," it was deemed unfit for production, with Maggie struggling "to make something out of nothing."[8]

Presumably leaving her new horse to be stabled in Washington, she left the city immediately after her Saturday, February 21 performance, heading with Anna by train to her next engagement in Boston. Her sudden departure may have been due to the receipt of the news of the death that morning in Boston of Mary Devlin Booth, the young wife of Edwin Booth, who was performing in New York. Edwin made it to Mary's deathbed too late, and his brother John, performing in Philadelphia, rushed to Boston out of fear of Edwin's committing suicide in his grief. For four days in Boston, John was a frequent visitor to Maggie's dressing room at the Howard Athenaeum. There is no evidence, however, that Maggie, who opened Monday to an overflowing house with *Fanchon*, attended Mary's funeral the next day. On Wednesday a massive snowstorm, with ice and hail, hit New England. Marshall kept the Howard open, though, and Maggie soldiered on through a week of *Fanchon*. Then she again tried *Hermance* but withdrew it after two performances.

With her next two experiments with new scripts, both during this engagement, she was far more successful. She knew that anything she tried would be measured against the yardstick of *Fanchon*. It had to contain an endearing, dynamic central character, compelling minor characters, a dose of humor, some entertaining songs and dances, and a strong moral message. Fortunately for Maggie and hundreds of thousands of her future fans, both new works would more than fill the bill.

The first was Charles Zachary Barnett's adaptation of Gaetano Donizetti's 1842 opera *Linda di Chamounix* called *The Pearl of Savoy; or, a Mother's Prayer*. Sometime during the winter of 1863, Maggie discovered it, realized its potential, and began rehearsing it with Marshall's company in Boston. On Monday, March 9, she performed it for the first of over five hundred times.

She played its lead, Marie Lonstalot, an Alpine shepherdess forced to leave her village to escape the lust of The Commander, who is in league with a cruel landlord threatening to evict her impoverished family. Fleeing to Paris, she earns her keep as a street singer, dubbed the Pearl of Savoy. Joining her there are two friends from her village, the rustic Pierrot and the ambitious Chouchon, whose songs and dances with Marie provide delightful diversions. Both in her village and now in Paris, Marie is counseled and tutored by the handsome yet secretive Andre, who professes his love for her. He is, in reality, a marquis named Arthur whose mother demands his marriage to a noble mademoiselle. His uncle is the lecherous Commander, who follows Marie to Paris and renews his attempts to seduce her, but Pierrot and Chouchon aid her in escaping his clutches. Arthur's mother threatens Marie's arrest on trumped-up charges unless he marries within his class, and he relents, first lavishing costly gifts on Marie. When her destitute father shows up and sees her newly acquired wealth, he disowns her for supposedly dishonoring the family. This, coupled with Arthur's impending marriage drives her into madness. Pierrot and Chouchon lead her back to their village, where her mother's plaintive song brings her out of her madness just in time for the arrival of Arthur, who has jilted his highborn lady. Best of all, he is now their landlord and guarantees Marie's family an untroubled life in their humble Alpine home.

On its opening night, *Pearl* was well received, with Maggie repeatedly called before the curtain to copious applause. Reviewers, too, were supportive. She brought "a tear to every eye." Her "pathos is the pathos of nature."[9]

A week later she played another new work for the first time which would predominate along with *Fanchon* and *Pearl* for the rest of her career. It was Waldauer's *Little Barefoot*, a five-act domestic drama in which Maggie played relentlessly good-hearted, devout Amry Grievenot. She and her half-witted brother Jemmy (William Scallan), whom she dutifully protects, are orphans in yet another peasant village. Initially going about unshod, she toils as a maid to the Hempfarmers, who provide her with shoes and a nice dress for the village festival, where she is bowled over by the handsome William Peace (James Duff). He finds her charming and dances with her to everyone's dismay. He owns a sizable farm and is looking for a proper wife. The local matchmaker pairs him with Rose (Kate Newton), haughty sister of Amry's employer, but William has his own "wife mirror"—a series of tests for a future spouse. When he visits the Hempfarmer home, Amry hides her face and her feelings for Rose's sake. But when William returns unnoticed and witnesses Rose's mistreatment of Amry and other failures of his tests, he speaks his heart and proposes to Amry. She passes every test with ease. When William's stern father angrily withholds his consent, Amry wins him over (just as Fanchon won over Father Barbeaud), having saved his life years ago. All embrace just as a traveling troupe of musicians arrives to play the songs Amry and William danced to at the festival.[10]

Maggie got to deliver some touching songs, including "Fly Away, Sweet Bird" which encouraged the flight of a pet pigeon upward to heaven, where Amry's deceased parents appear in a scrim opening in a stage flat. That song was quickly published, as was "Little Barefoot" that the villagers sang about Amry. Both sold well. The initial critical response was lukewarm, and for now, Maggie did not repeat it. It was considered good, with some intriguing situations and clever dialogue, but *Barefoot* was not equal to *Fanchon* and Amry was not Fanchon.[11]

Verse tributes to Maggie began appearing, the first allegedly by Ralph Waldo Emerson, entitled "The Shadow Dance" and (after her departure) "Maggie's Gone." Emerson, however, denied their authorship and believed them to be the work of essayist Edwin Percy Whipple. The first lauds the "lovely reveler in the moon" and asks, "Is that your shade, fair dancer, or are you both but dreams?" The other laments that "only one can restore the grace and beauty that lately illuminated the place" now that "Maggie's gone."[12]

Through the efforts of Brough and/or Anna, quotes from laudatory Boston reviews appeared almost immediately in Baltimore papers, where Maggie opened on March 23 at Ford's Holliday Street Theatre. Full houses cheered her and, and critics outdid themselves with praise, going so far as to ask,

"Do we Americans estimate properly the debt of gratitude we owe Miss Mitchell?" "It is impossible," avowed the *Baltimore Sun*, "to conceive a more touchingly simple or chastely attractive play" than *Fanchon*, to imagine anything "more wholesome and entertaining." "We cannot fancy a soul so lost or so dead to the beautiful appeals of virtue as to be insensible to the sympathetic effect of this play [or] without being conscious of some elevation of Christian sentiment."[13]

That theme of redemption was echoed in a letter Maggie received during her next engagement, back at Wood's Theatre in Cincinnati. A Union Army officer stationed across the river at Fort Mitchell attended two nights in a row. On the second night,

> A merchant from eastern KY, a noble, pure minded, honorable man, but not a habitual theatregoer, accompanied me to Wood's. At the period in the play where you first begin to realize that your wardrobe is too scantily supplied, and that you do not dress as other girls, my friend with breathless interest remarked, "Capt., *if I can only see her come out with a better dress on than any of those fools, I will go home satisfied* [emphasis his], and delighted!" [I myself] am better for having heard you. None but a pure heart can claim the impulses that enable you to hold so fully up to nature the impersonation of the Noble Cricket. . . . Should you ever marry, may you find your Landry and be immeasurably blessed in his profession [sic], as in all things you deserve.[14]

"Winning all hearts by its sweet sympathy and naivete," *Barefoot*, too, drew praise. "No one can sit through *Little Barefoot* and fail to see the sparkle which shines through it." Maggie's acting had noticeably improved as well, especially compared to that of the ineluctable Robertson: "She has lost all trace of mannerism, and her acting is now fresh, sweet and unaffected."[15]

Among the nightly crowded houses were many soldiers, as was the case in Indianapolis at Metropolitan Hall and in Chicago at McVicker's, who knew his audience: *Barefoot* featured "farmers' daughters [wearing] dresses that only reach to their knees" and "flesh-colored tights." However, one Chicago critic thought *Barefoot*'s first act one of "unparalleled dullness," during which he acknowledges taking "a few brief naps when Maggie was off[stage]." He also disliked the slapdash manner in which Amry's deceased parents appeared "though a ragged hole in a rainbow-colored stone wall."[16]

Maggie closed out her 1862–63 season with Louisville, St. Louis, and Pittsburgh, where all appeared to be forgiven. *Fanchon*, *Barefoot*, and *Margot* dominated her repertoire as lesser farces dropped away. Again, her unaffected persona and the moral purity of her characters drew commendation. "Not a particle of rant, that common and odious crime of players, can be detected. . . . Her face at times is luminous, and those almond-shaped eyes beam either with love, scorn, pity, fear and reverence. . . . The young and pure can profitably witness [her performances] to embibe [sic] moral and religious impressions whilst enjoying dramatic amusement of the most innocent description."[17]

Aside from the trinkets she picked up from admirers—including a gold watch in St. Louis—Maggie was steadily accruing wealth. According to the *New York Times*, from her nine months of touring just completed, she cleared $9,000 [$181,000 today]. For the first time, *Fanchon* had comprised well over half of her performances. She now touted—likely at Brough's hands—*Fanchon* as having been played over three hundred times (over a hundred more than actuality), with *Pearl* and *Barefoot* increasing in frequency.[18]

According to John Ellsler, it was Anna who first managed Maggie's money and insisted on its investment in real estate, but Maggie proved an astute student. They returned to New York on June 27 to a far nicer home, acquired with funds from touring. It was a new brownstone rowhouse at 26 W. 54th Street, a thinly settled middle-class block between Fifth and Sixth Avenues. Despite some shantytowns and dumps on still-undeveloped lots, this represented an investment in the future of Manhattan. Central Park construction was well underway five blocks to the north. Maggie's father was there, too, once again employed as a bookbinder. In addition to providing for her family—an overriding commitment—home represented to Maggie a haven and stability in an otherwise itinerant life.[19]

For two weeks the Mitchells enjoyed a tranquil existence, receiving the good news on July 4 of the Union prevailing at Gettysburg and the simultaneous surrender of Vicksburg. However, on July 13 the city was rocked by horrific rioting in lower Manhattan in response to new draft laws (Booth was also in the city that week, staying with his still-grieving brother, Edwin, but there is no evidence that he met with Maggie, nor even that he wandered far from the Booth residence on Seventeenth Street, amid the worst rioting).

For the 1863–64 season, her third during wartime, Maggie culled her repertoire further, down to twenty roles, with a core of five: Fanchon, Barefoot, Pearl, Margot, and Katty. She began performing only one main piece each night, keeping it on the boards for a week at a time. This was easier not only on her but for the company of each theater she visited.

An increasing concern for her was the extent to which she still had to depend on those local stock companies for capable Landrys, Arthurs and William Peaces. For her first engagement, a remarkable six weeks at John Ford's rebuilt theater in Washington beginning on September 21, Ford fortunately provided a strong company, pulled from among the more than one hundred men and women that he rotated among his four theaters. Among his leading men were future stars John T. Raymond and James A. Herne and standout actress Helen Muzzy, who would play Fadet.

Ford's Theatre, in which Maggie had invested, had just reopened following the fire of last winter. Seating 1,640, its elegant interior, decorated in white and gold, attracted the elite of the city, including a goodly portion of military and political figures. Its stage equipment and dressing rooms were of the latest design, and its ventilation was excellent, based on consultations with the Smithsonian Institution. Skilled scenic artist Charles Getz created vast, gorgeous backdrops, and conductor William Withers led an able orchestra. Ford faced competition from two venues operated by his arch-rival, Leonard Grover, who featured top-tier stars at his eponymous theater and less-savory attractions at Canterbury Hall.

Maggie countered these with *Barefoot* and *Fanchon*. From her first night, over 2,000 patrons jammed into Ford's nightly, with hundreds turned away and reviewers again ecstatic. Her "lovely emotional picture of the gladsome, pure-hearted little Cricket is one of the most delightful marvels of the modern stage." More than ten thousand Washingtonians bought her *cartes de visite*, on sale between acts. Across the city, "professors of dancing are all busy forming steps for shadow dances" and musicians were occupied "in composing Cricket Polkas or Fanchon Overtures."[20]

A few reviewers did object to the emotional pandering of works like *Fanchon*. Chief among them was the discerning yet acerbic American critic for *Albion*, William Winter, who deplored the "vast amount of trash [which is] thrust upon the public, who must swallow it whether or no [sic], thus encouraging ... theatrical quacks to continue their nauseous deeds."[21]

Such opinions mattered not to Maggie, who gained a new fan on October 12 when esteemed tragedienne Charlotte Cushman attended *Fanchon*. Cushman was in the city to enact Lady Macbeth at a benefit at Grover's for the U.S. Sanitary Commission (Maggie may have contributed a similar effort for wounded soldiers at Campbell Hospital, as she received onstage one night an 18″-diameter bouquet from its patients). Backstage afterward, Cushman told her, "You have three fortunes in hand [with *Fanchon*]—one in America, the second in France and the third in Germany." Only the first of these would come to fruition, as Maggie steadfastly spurned entreaties to perform in Europe. She realized that the rustic Cricket would not translate to European tastes.[22]

By October 7 she began introducing other works but soon was back to *Barefoot* and *Fanchon*. Nothing slowed the Maggie juggernaut, including an injury incurred while riding early on October 15. Thrown from her horse and stunned, she nevertheless attended rehearsal later that morning at Ford's for the upcoming *Pearl*. It opened on October 19 to acclaim, further prompting church leaders to relax their opposition to the theater. Its high moral tone earned the "admiration of all who have ever felt the tender endearments of a virtuous home or learned the accents of religious prayer at that most hallowed of earthly altars—a Mother's Knee." Among those moved to tears upon witnessing Maggie's Marie regaining her senses at the knee of her dying mother was Washington socialite Kate Chase, escorted to Ford's by John Hay. Like Marie, Chase knew well the sting of a father's disapproval, hers being Lincoln's self-righteous Secretary of the Treasury.[23]

The ultimate approval in the capital came on October 30 when the president, again perhaps encouraged by Hay, attended Maggie's benefit of *Fanchon* with his wife and several cabinet secretaries. Fortunately, he was seated in a reserved box, as the aisles that night were jammed with chairs, campstools, and standees.[24]

Herne and Raymond migrated with Maggie on November 2 to Ford's Holliday Street Theatre in Baltimore, where leading lady Alice Gray took over Muzzy's role of Fadet. For four weeks, opposite Herne's Landry, William, and Arthur, Maggie played *Fanchon*, *Pearl*, and *Barefoot* to huge crowds. For her first benefit, hundreds were turned away. Her Thanksgiving Day matinee of *Barefoot* drew an especially large house.

From there Maggie moved north, opening November 30 at Marshall's thoroughly renovated Boston Theatre, her first time in that venue. Its conductor was as talented as Withers: George F. Suck, a violinist and later professor of music at Boston University. He scored and published "Maggie Mitchell's Songs and Dances," including "Little Barefoot Waltz," "Savoyard Song," and "Fanchon Polka," which she immediately incorporated into her performances. (Withers had written but not published a "Cricket Polka" for her.) Boston artist T. R. Burnham began producing Maggie Mitchell miniatures, which sold briskly.

Maggie had to scamper to cover the Boston's 48' wide, raked stage, and despite its seating 3,140, she played to full houses, including many fashionably dressed ladies, with many patrons standing, through two weeks of *Fanchon*. Each time she tried a few nights *Barefoot* or *Pearl*, she quickly returned to *Fanchon*, even adding Saturday matinees of it to accommodate families with children. "A greater popular success was never witnessed in Boston," crowed reviewers, despite Maggie's following Edwin Booth. "Those who imagined 'little Maggie' would be lost in so large a theatre were sadly at fault, for not only did her voice fill the spacious edifice, but her acting, abounding as it does in delicate points, was full as effective." She was pronounced as powerful as Booth, Forrest, or Cushman.[25]

Either in the mood to try something new during this engagement or yielding to the influence of a prominent Bostonian, Maggie tried at the close of the year a new play entitled *La Petite Marie* by earnest young lawyer John D. Long. Billed as filled with "coquetry, jealousy, 'gilded misery,' retribution and restoration," it awkwardly reflected Long's Harvard erudition. Its scholarly verbiage and 4½-hour running time left her and the audience exhausted and the critics calling it "a damned poor play," a "theatrical abortion" with an inconsistent plot, and "outrageously unnatural." Trimming it by an hour availed little and Maggie dropped it. It was *Fanchon* that filled Maggie's and Marshall's purses. Various contemporary estimates placed their proceeds from her five-week engagement at between $6,000 and $8,000 for each of them.[26]

Maggie required a full week—likely including a stop in Manhattan—of circuitous rail travel to get her next to Nashville, her first return to the South in three years. There, she faced a native population chafing under Union occupation, in place since February 1862. Many residents had lost sons and husbands in the Confederate cause. It was "a city over which the shadow of gloom hung darkly," bemoaned one. "It is literally the City of Woe." The occupying soldiers, however, sought diversion. Seeking to curry favor with Union generals—among them Ulysses S. Grant and William T. Sherman, both of whom enjoyed theatre and attended at least once in Nashville—managers kept their theaters open, "more from political motives than from any prospect of pecuniary profit." Only Nashville, Richmond, and New Orleans—the last of these Union-occupied almost as long as Nashville—had maintained any continuity of theatrical activity in the South since the war began.[27]

At J. R. Allen and William Simon's New Theatre, Maggie opened on January 11 with *Margot* and *Four Sisters*, followed by similar tried-and-true pieces. By order of the Provost Marshal, each of her performances opened with patriotic airs. She required an entire week with the cobbled-together stock company to generate a viable *Fanchon* since by 1864 few men of fighting age remained to perform. For a week, she played it to overflowing, cheering houses, composed almost entirely of uniformed men, with a smattering of officers' wives. Native Nashvillians hoarded their meager resources and dreaded citations for violating curfew, not to mention fear for their safety from drunken soldiers. The *Nashville Gazette* spoke for many when it decried the presence in theaters of "a nomadic class among us, whose patronage served to drag down the stage to the level of a brothel."[28]

But, oh, the young soldiers who swooned over Maggie! Remembered one over a decade later,

> When the army was massed around Nashville, Maggie Mitchell was cheered to the echo night after night, and at the fall of the curtain each boy in blue confessed himself dead in love with her. On the lonely picket walk, or stretched at full length under the swaying canvas, he dreamed of the bright eyes of the Cricket, and thought that his sum of happiness would be complete if he could only take her in his arms and call her wife. Ah! Those were grand triumphs for Maggie Mitchell. Should she live a thousand years, and bloom afresh each June with the roses, she will never be more idolized than she was by the soldiers, who

left not even standing room in the theatre. At the front, where cannon frowned and bayonets glistened in the morning sun, the simple rustle of a woman's dress was enough to set the heart in a flutter. When Fanchon appeared upon the scene, with her winning ways, she carried everything before her. She made an impression upon the heart which will not fade until the heart ceases to beat.[29]

Retreating into Union territory, Maggie opened in Cincinnati on January 25, at Pike's Opera House. (By 1864, the term "opera house" was coming into vogue as a glorified way of rebranding theaters as cultural development pushed further into the frontier. Most became gathering places for civic affairs, with the elevated, nearly ubiquitous name being a way of avoiding the stigma of things theatrical. Their construction and their offerings remained as humble as their surroundings, and almost none staged legitimate opera.) Despite its substantially larger capacity than her previous venues in Cincinnati, Maggie had no trouble filling houses for the first week. After that, business dropped off. As she ran through *Fanchon*, *Pearl*, *Barefoot* and a handful of other pieces, she faced competition at nearby Wood's Theatre from her half-sister, Mary, in melodramas.

Supporting Maggie at Pike's was a capable stock company, which included a petite "walking lady" named Alice Kingsbury, 24. Within months of observing the original during this engagement, Kingsbury began touring *Fanchon* in the West. Dubbed the "Elfin Star," she became for a decade one of the most dogged imitators of Maggie, drawing the most favorable comparisons, with some reviewers claiming she surpassed Maggie. And Kingsbury was not alone. Short, roundish twenty-six-year-old Kate Denin and twenty-nine-year-old Cecile Rush were touring smaller towns with *Fanchon*, and more copycats would appear during the next few seasons. Most quickly relinquished the role, though, and only a handful would approach Maggie's level of popularity.

While playing at McVicker's in Chicago in February, Maggie encountered vestigial rumors of her former southern sympathies. A newspaper article here, an overheard conversation in a hotel lobby there, elicited a full-bore defense of her patriotism by a pseudonymous fan, whose purpose was to "entirely obliterate all such doubts and prejudices." Maggie, he/she argued, wholeheartedly "desires a vigorous prosecution of the war, a speedy and permanent peace," and the according of full honor to "the brave soldier [and] the suffering wounded and dying." This defense was effective, for now, as Maggie filled houses nightly.[30]

She was important enough of a star by this time that managers outside of New York held slots open in their schedules to attract her. In Louisville, George Wood bumped John Wilkes Booth to make room for her the first two weeks of March. There, she confronted competition at the nearby Louisville

Theatre during the same two weeks by Thompson in *Fanchon* and *Barefoot*. Thus, ensued a cat-and-mouse game of competing bills and benefits. In response to copyright threats from Maggie and Waldauer, Thompson refashioned her *Fanchon* into *Little Fadette, the Cricket*, but the plot was essentially the same. For one benefit, Maggie brought in Mary, who had recently performed to acclaim in Louisville, to costar in *Husband at Sight*, *Wandering Boys*, and a joint "Maggie Mitchell Polka." The night after Maggie performed *Pet*, Thompson countered with her own "Pet Polka." The size of their respective audiences and critical reception tilted toward Maggie, but at least one reviewer considered them equals. Maggie would remain on her guard against Thompson.

Complications of train travel delayed her a day getting to St. Louis, where she opened for DeBar on March 22. Most nights she played *Fanchon*, *Barefoot*, and *Pearl* or a few oldies like *Wild Irish Girl*. Another missed train connection caused her to arrive a day late in Columbus for her old friend John Ellsler, now the dominant manager in Ohio. She had intended to open with *Fanchon*, but lacking sufficient rehearsal time, she performed *Margot* and *Katty*. The audience, although disappointed, forgave her and for the rest of the week filled Ellsler's Atheneum [sic], applauding her enthusiastically in *Fanchon*. She already knew and trusted her Landry, J. C. McCollom, from Buffalo, and her Father Barbeaud, Ellsler himself, who even joined Maggie between acts in an Irish jig. She may or not have noticed a teenaged ballet girl playing one of the taunting villagers. It was Clara Morris, who later became a celebrated tragedienne noted for the profound, convincing depth into which she sank portraying her characters.

Much like John Ford, Ellsler circulated parts of his stock company among several theaters. Maggie closed out her Columbus booking—which had purposely coincided with the state legislature's session—and migrated with him and his actors to Cleveland. (The people of Columbus were far from pleased with the company which replaced them, despite its leading lady, Alice Kingsbury, and her *Fanchon* and *Barefoot*.)

From there it was on to Pittsburgh (with still no fallout from her earlier encounter there) and then, in mid-May, to Boston, where she closed out her season with five weeks back at Marshall's immense Boston Theatre. During her engagement, Maggie and Anna settled into their coziest accommodations on the road, Amelia Fisher's renowned Theatrical Boardinghouse at 2 Bulfinch Place, just behind Beacon Hill. Fisher provided a prim, cosseted environment, albeit at a cost considerably above that of a regular hotel, but well worth it. She accommodated actors' hours and paid special attention to protecting the honor of young actresses, having been one herself, and as the sister of actress Clara Fisher Maeder.

Another resident there that month, playing a long engagement at the Boston Museum (the last of his touring career), was John Wilkes Booth. One Sunday evening as Maggie, Anna, and Booth settled in for tea, they were joined by a starstruck clerk from the War Department, Harrison Huguley, who was so taken aback at Booth's intemperate, even treasonous, views on the war that he excused himself, intending to report Booth to Secretary of War Edwin Stanton. Booth felt no compunction about expressing strong pro-Confederate views in front of Maggie.[31]

Virtually every night from her opening on May 16, Maggie drew full houses, again including many fashionable ladies, for *Fanchon*, *Barefoot*, and *Pearl*, supported by Marshall's highly capable company. Despite *Fanchon*'s widespread acceptance by the religious community, Boston's Rev. John Weiss wrote her a new, moralistic, sentimentalized fifth act for it, including Fanchon's visiting Fadet's grave. Maggie gamely tried it but, finding it far too somber, promptly and politely abandoned it.

Her closing benefit on June 10 proved exhausting but rewarding. A visiting delegation of Russians, escorted by the Mayor of Boston and "pretty much the entire population of the city," called her in front of the curtain between every act, clapped and sang along with her songs and dances, and demanded reprises of several. "It was fun for the audience, and Miss Mitchell, who has the soul of a steel spring, didn't mind it." At its close, Marshall presented Maggie with a $150 silver vase inscribed with words expressing his and Bostonians' gratitude. Her audiences had been the largest of the season, partially helped by Marshall's arranging for special trains to ferry theatergoers from outlying towns such as Lowell, thirty miles away.[32]

Characteristically generous, Maggie remained for two nights past her announced closing, performing in benefits for the theater's doorkeepers and ushers and for Marshall. He had every reason to celebrate her engagement, noting that she "carried away hard upon ten thousand dollars [$155,000 today]." By 1864, Maggie was already serving as a benchmark for financial success at the box office, with assessments appearing in papers comparing the earnings of other stars to hers.[33]

Also, she was becoming so identified with Fanchon that critics had begun equating her character with such signature roles as E. A. Sothern's Lord Dundreary, John E. Owens' Solon Shingle, Frank Chanfrau's Mose, and Mrs. D. P. Bowers' Lady Audley. But that identification was a two-edged sword. Opined one Boston critic, "she does herself an injustice and we fear may do herself injury by following too long a single line of characters." Noted another, "She does not seem so much to lose herself in her characters as to show herself through them." But the people thronged to see Maggie herself and not the characters.[34]

And so far, in a country slogging through a horrific war, her career was thriving.

NOTES

1. *Cincinnati Enquirer*, Jan. 15, 1863.
2. *Baltimore Sun*, Oct. 23, 1862; *Missouri Democrat*, Dec. 12, 1862; Holden 316.
3. *Augusta Constitutionalist*, Nov. 25, 1862.
4. *New York World*, Apr. 10, 1866; *Albany Argus*, Apr. 12, 1866.
5. Sheldon M. Novick, "Henry James's First Published Work: 'Miss Maggie Mitchell in *Fanchon the Cricket.*'" *The Henry James Review*, 17:3 (1996), 300–302; Witter Bynner, "A Word or Two with Henry James," *The Critic*, Feb. 1905, 46.
6. *Providence Evening Press*, Jan. 20, 1863; *New York Clipper*, Jan. 31, 1863.
7. Unidentified Boston clipping, Mar. 1, 1863, HTC.
8. Washington correspondent for *Springfield (MA) Republican*, Feb. 21, 1863; *New York Clipper*, Feb. 28, 1863.
9. *Boston Saturday Evening Gazette*, Mar. 14, 1863.
10. Augustus Waldauer, *Little Barefoot*, New York: Samuel French, 1863. Waldauer's version relied heavily on the German story *Barfüssle* by Moritz Reichenbach, after Berthold Auerbach.
11. "Fly Away Sweet Bird," words by Thomas B. Long and music by J. C. Meininger; "Little Barefoot," words and music by Frank Howard.
12. "Our Maggie: The Shadow Dance, by R. W. Emerson," Bill for Ford's Theatre, HTC; Ralph L. Rusk, ed. *The Letters of Ralph Waldo Emerson*, New York: Columbia University Press, 1939, V:321; Jackson, TN, *Whig and Tribune*, Apr. 12, 1873; *Louisville Democrat*, May 17, 1863.
13. *Baltimore Sun*, Mar. 21–27, 1863.
14. MM Papers, MS Collection 4552, NYPL.
15. *Cincinnati Commercial*, Apr. 9 and 16, 1863.
16. Chicago correspondent for *Milwaukee Sentinel*, May 7, 1863.
17. *Louisville Democrat*, May 21, 1863; (St. Louis) *Missouri Democrat*, June 8, 1863.
18. *New York Times*, June 28, 1863.
19. Ellsler, *Stage Memories*, 98.
20. (Washington) *National Intelligencer*, Oct. 5, 1863; (Washington) *National Republican*, Oct. 6, 1863.
21. *Albion*, Oct. 24, 1863.
22. *New York Herald*, July 27, 1879.
23. (Washington) *National Republican*, Oct. 20, 1863.
24. *Ibid.*, Oct. 23, 1863.
25. (Boston) *Saturday Evening Gazette*, Nov. 28, 1863; *Boston Herald*, Dec. 2, 1863; *Providence Press*, Dec. 4, 1863; *Boston Advertiser*, Dec. 1, 1863.
26. Holden 318; "Journal of John D. Long," *Proceedings of the Massachusetts Historical Society*, Third Series, 70: 99–100; "Letter from Boston, Jan. 10, 1864" in

Sacramento Daily Union, Feb. 8, 1864; (Boston) *Saturday Evening Gazette*, Jan. 2, 1864.

27. Letter from John A. Rawlins to unnamed recipient, Jan. 16, 1864, James H. Wilson Papers, Library of Congress; Edward Dicey, *Six Months in the Federal States*, 2 vols., London, n.p., 1863, I:79.

28. *Nashville Gazette* quoted in Oscar G. Brockett, "Theatre in Nashville During the Civil War," *Southern Speech Journal*, 23 (1957):72.

29. *Buffalo Express*, Apr. 5, 1878.

30. *Chicago Tribune*, Mar. 1, 1864.

31. It is unknown whether Huguley reported Booth or not. There is no evidence of any intimacy between Maggie and Booth during their simultaneous stay at Fisher's, and Fisher's character and standards suggest it would not have been permitted.

32. Unidentified clipping, June 11, 1864, HTC; *Boston Advertiser*, June 11, 1864.

33. Marshall letter, undated (but end of 1863–64 season, as he then relinquished management of the Boston Theatre) to J. B. Wright, HTC.

34. Unidentified clipping, June 11, 1864, HTC; *Boston Transcript*, May 16, 1864.

Chapter 7

"everything has been deranged"

Two worries beset Maggie during the summer of 1864. Most urgently, her half-sister Mary lay seriously ill with heart disease in Washington, where she had been performing at Ford's Theatre. It was not until mid-August that she recovered enough to travel with Albaugh to perform in Detroit.

Another concern for Maggie was the increasing number of imitators performing scripts for which she believed she held exclusive rights (with copyright protection only haphazardly enforced). It was fine that Mary had been performing some of Maggie's older pieces, such as *French Spy* and *Satan in Paris*. But now Charlotte Thompson and Alice Kingsbury were seen as equaling if not surpassing Maggie, the former perceived as conveying more tenderness and pathos. In New Orleans—in the very theater where Maggie had originated Fanchon—Kingsbury was performing the role, compared favorably to Maggie. Emma Maddern, a taunting village girl in Maggie's original New Orleans *Fanchon*, had played Fanchon in the same theater for the same manager, Ben DeBar, and was now touring in it, proclaimed by some to be Maggie's equal. Ida Vernon and Ada Webb were doing so as well. That fall, simultaneous with Maggie's *Fanchon* at Niblo's in New York, Mollie Williams would perform it at the New Bowery. And there were others: Mrs. J. W. Lanergan's *Fanchon* was close to Maggie's, and Kate Estelle was performing *Katty*, "as played by Maggie Mitchell."

To fend off this assault, Maggie had to remain wary and proactive, maintaining her existing following while gaining new adherents. She would focus in the 1864–65 season almost exclusively on *Fanchon*, *Barefoot*, and *Pearl*, with *Fanchon* comprising over two-thirds of her performances. She would play significantly fewer cities, for longer engagements.

She began in the city where she had acquired some of her greatest accolades, Washington, at a familiar theater that would tragically close before the end of the season. She opened at Ford's Theatre on September 26 to large, fashionable audiences, with a generous share of Union officers and politicos and their wives. To underscore her patriotism, Maggie teamed with comedian John T. Raymond in a benefit for the Enrolment Fund to Relieve Drafted Men. She also loaned $500 to a young actor who was drafted and unable to pay for a substitute. (Hired as a clerk by the government, he eventually repaid her in full.)

Ford provided the best-supporting company he could muster in wartime, with mixed results. Landry was W. J. Cogswell, a young Buffalo comedian and Union veteran who had been recovering in a Washington hospital. Ironically, Didier was Ned Emerson, a staunch secessionist whose revered older brother had been killed fighting for the Confederacy. At least Fadet, Helen Muzzy, whom Maggie had known for years, was capable and experienced. By and large, the players fell short of the mark, "as much out of place on the stage of a theatre pretending to be first class as a bull in a china shop." Maggie's "admirable" performances "were frequently marred by the obtrusive dullness of the unimpressible [sic] clodhoppers around her."[1]

Her reviews were stellar, though: "Miss Michell has passed that hour of her histrionic reputation when criticism could pronounce severely upon her performances. Satisfying the strictest demands of the harshest critic, ... when this lady essays a character she throws her whole soul into it." Her performance was "so life-like in verisimilitude that it does not seem like acting at all."[2]

In mid-October Maggie reunited with Mary at Wood's Theatre in Louisville, where—her early hopes for a career in tragedy briefly resurgent—she enacted Juliet to Mary's Romeo. Then it was on to New York City for four weeks at William Wheatley's venerable Niblo's Garden in the wake of the "Great American Tragedian," Edwin Forrest. In the more than two years since her triumphant New York debut in *Fanchon*, the hunger for it among the citizenry had only grown.

Some in the supporting company were accomplished actors she knew well, minor stars in their own right. Landry was again James W. Collier. Her Didier, George Becks, would perform with her for more than a decade. Fadet was the estimable Mary Ann Russell (Mrs. George P.) Farren. Madelon was the cherubic Mrs. Emma Skerrett, for whose benefit Maggie had debuted in New York in 1851 (Skerrett, like Maggie, made a career out of playing characters far younger than herself). Some of the minor players, however, resembled "a company of confirmed sticks." It took a few nights for the actors to shake off stylistic detritus from supporting Forrest, such as "sledge-hammer demonstrations with the fist upon the chest being used by one prominent character [likely the muscular Collier, a virtual Forrest clone] as expressive of ... depth of affection."[3]

Maggie, too, came in for critical carping. Prominent among her perceived defects were overacting, "the habit of using the nose as an organ of speech" and the use of "the most vulgar of colloquial style [as if] Fanchon was acquainted with the Bowery." True, "Her lightness of foot and activity of body are wonderful," and "Nothing could be more quaint than her shadow-dance," but other moments resembled "the 'low-like gambols' of Topsy [in *Uncle Tom's Cabin*]." But the audiences that crammed into Niblo's nightly, applauding, cheering, calling her before the curtain between acts, cared not a whit for such assessments.[4]

Maggie also received a congratulatory letter from Charlotte Birch Pfeiffer, the original adapter of *Fanchon*. Less-welcome attention came in a letter from a wealthy retired Manhattan merchant offering to keep her in lavish style. "Witch or no witch, you half bewitched me," he confessed. He "wondered if you were not as pure and good as you seemed to be," and might perhaps "make one of the choicest little companions in the world. . . . I am in need of a darling Pet." Whether she answered or not is unknown, but she kept the letter for the rest of her life.[5]

After closing at Niblo's on November 20, she remained in the city to observe Thanksgiving with her family and perhaps take in the sole performance at the Winter Garden of the only onstage gathering of all three Booth brothers. To raise money for a statue of William Shakespeare in Central Park, their *Julius Caesar* on November 25 starred Edwin as Brutus, John Wilkes as Antony, and Junius, Jr., as Cassius.

Next, Ford had booked her *Fanchon* in Washington beginning December 5, followed by it and *Pearl* at the Holliday Street in Baltimore. She had no other engagements until January 9, 1865, in Cincinnati. Sometime during this winter likely transpired the last moments she would share with John Wilkes Booth. He was in Washington intermittently through much of December, and a teenaged Blanche Chapman—later the wife of manager Harry Clay Ford—reported seeing Maggie wearing onstage a bunch of violets that Booth had bought her as a pledge of his affection.

A snowstorm caused her to arrive in Cincinnati a day late, but as soon as she arrived she had to rush back to New York upon learning of the death there of her uncle, Alfred (Sophia's husband) in a railway accident. Such occurrences were a frightfully frequent event; in 1864, 140 rail accidents cost the lives of 404 people, the most in a decade. Anna's health was declining, too, and Sophia would take on the role of traveling chaperon for Maggie until Maggie's marriage in 1868.[6]

The citizens of Cincinnati were understanding of the delay, and Maggie opened on January 16 at Wood's Theatre with *Fanchon* and *Pearl*. Mary, who had interrupted her touring schedule for Alfred's funeral, teamed with Maggie again in *Romeo and Juliet* for Maggie's farewell benefits. Maggie was deemed at best an average Juliet and Mary unsuited for Romeo. But criticism was again moot: "We can hardly call to mind an actress that from the start has maintained so firm a hold upon the affections of the Cincinnati public." After all, "Maggie's petite figure, as it bounds upon the stage, brings with it a ray of sunshine that is not reflected from the footlights" and managers "know upon which side their bread is buttered."[7]

February 1865 took her South, to Wood's Theatre in Louisville and Duffield and Flynn's "Old" Theatre in Nashville. If anything, the demand for tickets to her shows had increased. Both of Nashville's theaters were jammed despite the troops of Confederate General John Bell Hood dug in south of the city. Quipped one reporter, that "If Hood were to bring up his ragged legions to Nashville tonight, and hurl his shells and cannonballs into the heart of the city, it would not affect diminishing the numbers of the vast throng rushing to see 'the play.'" Part of the demand can be attributed to the city's civilian population explosion over the past three years, from approximately 30,000 to 75,000, some quite unfashionable: "Thieves, gamblers and disreputable of both sexes swarmed in from all over the country."[8]

Maggie's reviews were mixed. "In some of her pieces, there was too much display of mannerism—too much pandering, too much 'clap-trap' foolishness—or, in other words, a disposition to overplay the part." Most offensive was her "habit of playing as it were directly to the audience ... as though it was a direct appeal to the audience for its approbation." But that, of course, was a significant factor in Maggie's continued popularity."[9]

That winter it had been General Sherman whose exploits filled the pages of newspapers north and south. After capturing and burning Atlanta on November 15, he had led his forces on a scorched earth policy southeast to the coast, reaching Savannah by Christmas. Union Adjutant Samuel H. M. Byers, imprisoned in a Confederate camp in Columbia, South Carolina, composed a celebratory song, "When Sherman Marched Down to the Sea," which became an instant sensation in the North. When Maggie appeared back in Louisville in late February, the soldiers in her audiences clamored for the song. Nightly, she obliged, sublimating any vestiges of Southern sympathy. "It was from her lips that we first heard the words," recalled one grateful young man. "Each night she was nearly buried in an avalanche of flowers."[10]

On her way to Chicago in mid-March, Maggie detoured to Cincinnati, where Mary was still performing for Wood. For Mary's benefit night, Maggie volunteered *Fanchon* with Mary as Fadet. Back at McVicker's by the 20th, she performed a wider repertoire: not only *Fanchon*, *Barefoot*, and *Pearl*, but also *Katty*, *Margot*, *Husband at Sight*, and *Pet*. This may have been due to the inability of McVicker's company to fulfill all *Fanchon* roles to her liking. Her Landry, Joseph E. Nagle, 37, was an overweight tragedian, and her

Fadet, Anna Cowell, made that role overly tragic (she had recently played Lady Macbeth).

On April 9, the morning after Maggie closed in Chicago, Confederate General Robert E. Lee surrendered his forces to Union General Ulysses S. Grant, effectively ending the Civil War (exclusive of mopping up in North Carolina and scattered guerrilla attacks). For the rest of her life, Maggie claimed, in an account repeated in numerous papers and some of her obituaries, that she was in Mobile, Alabama, that weekend and gloriously waved the Stars and Stripes. In an 1881 interview, however, she asserted that she was in St. Louis that week, at the Lindell Hotel, presumably performing for DeBar, and that Mary had joined her (after performing in Nashville with Albaugh). But actress Kitty Blanchard (by then) Rankin said in 1908 that Mary was performing with her that week in Louisville. Furthermore, all St. Louis theaters were presenting other attractions the week of April 10. If Maggie was scheduled to perform the following week, her engagement would have been canceled by events.

By her 1881 account, she had a disturbing dream the night of April 14: "I saw John Wilkes Booth leap from the private box of the President at Ford's Theatre to the stage. He was dressed as usual, with inimitable taste and neatness. He wore a short Spanish cloak, lined with crimson satin. As he leaped upon the stage from the box, hurriedly and excitedly, his cloak flew open and disclosed a little white poodle dog under his arm. He ran past me and made his exit by the [upstage right door]." The next morning, she said, she was relaxing with Mary and friends at breakfast and had just shared her dream when "a waiter came up to us with a scared look on his face ... asking if we had heard the news. He then said that President Lincoln had been shot the night before, and in less than ten minutes we were all electrified with the astounding news that the assassin was John Wilkes Booth, about whom we were talking when the head waiter interrupted our chat."[11]

Due to Booth's profession, theaters were disproportionately affected by his rash act. On Easter Sunday, April 16, preachers from coast to coast rained judgment down on anyone and anything connected with his vile occupation. For weeks, few attended any theater, due to "hostility to the stage developed by and since the assassination of the President." Many of Ford's actors, managers, and stagehands were arrested and interrogated. "Everything has been deranged by the atrocious crime," lamented the *New York Clipper*, "engagements broken, time curtailed, entertainments postponed, speculations ruined, hopes deferred, and aspirations nipped in the bud." In mid-May, *Frank Leslie's Illustrated Newspaper* reported that "the theatrical diversions have received such a stunning blow as they never felt before, and at the time we write are hardly on their legs again."[12]

Maggie and Mary retreated to the family home in New York, where theaters remained closed until April 26, the day after Lincoln's funeral procession. Sometime that week, Maggie received notice of Booth's death in a burning tobacco barn in northern Virginia but left no record of her reaction to this news.

Opening on May 1 for five weeks back at Niblo's Garden, Maggie's *Fanchon*, advertised in black-bordered newspaper columns, faced relatively little competition except for comedian John E. Owens at the nearby Broadway Theatre in Solon Shingle, his greatest star vehicle. He and Maggie were simultaneously hitting career strides—and muting their previous southern sympathies—both providing New Yorkers with escapist comedy following the horrific war. Still, Maggie played to full houses. Even a fire in the carpenter's shop on May 21 only cost her a night's performance.

Just below City Hall, P. T. Barnum, the quintessential showman, was running his usual sensations, oddities, and humbuggery at his American Museum. To rattle Maggie, Barnum hired a fourteen-year-old blue-eyed blonde named Emilie Melville who resembled Maggie in face, figure, and voice. (Melville had had ample chance to observe Maggie while engaged as a ballet girl at Ford's Theatre.) Melville opened on May 22—Maggie's missed performance—and demonstrated "numerous personal charms, a pleasing voice, and an unaffected manner." Barnum conjured up a different translation of *Fanchon* (thus evading copyright protection) by Frederick Lubin, and on June 12 put Melville on in its lead. She drew well but, unfortunately for Barnum, did so well she received better offers and took her *Fanchon* on the road for over a year—another headache for Maggie. Within a year she was being proclaimed as good as Maggie, if not superior in some respects.[13]

During that time, still another Maggie clone, young Kitty Blanchard, set forth, earning equally fulsome accolades. Soon novice actress Noemil De Marguerities would play *Fanchon* in Philadelphia, and shortly after that Matilda Stoddart, Maggie's original Broadway Madelon, would launch a tour as Fanchon. So would young Jennie Hight, who had observed Maggie from the ranks of the stock company in Richmond in 1857. In New York, even a minstrel show came up with a Maggie satire, *The Pearls of Savoy in Their Little Barefeet*.

The most compelling threat, however, was petite, impish Lotta Crabtree. Only seventeen—and looking no older than fourteen—Lotta was being touted as the new Maggie Mitchell, who was about to turn thirty. A whirlwind of energy like Maggie, whom she closely resembled in face and figure, Lotta had gotten her start as a child playing banjo in the mining camps around San Francisco, a city Maggie had yet to visit. During the war, Lotta had toured up and down the West Coast, attracting a growing following, largely male (her skimpy skirts and spunky flirtatiousness assisting). "The same elements always appeared in Maggie Mitchell-Lotta characters," observed the *New York World*: "youthful vim, ever-ready bravery, snow-white goodness and bubblesome [sic] impudence—while the plays through which the popular soubrettes romped were ingenuous combinations of farce and melodrama."[14]

Under the guidance of her stage mother, Mary Ann, Lotta came east in June 1864, appearing in smallish New York venues, but failed there and migrated to Chicago, where she won instant acclaim at McVicker's. Now, she had been touring and had staked her claim to protean and breeches roles and gamines as Maggie had. In Buffalo, where Lotta drew jammed houses, the critic for the *Commercial* threw down a gauntlet: "If she should undertake to play Fanchon the Cricket, I would advise Miss Maggie Mitchell to look to her laurels." By 1867 the *New York Herald* would be calling Lotta "a dangerous rival" to Maggie. In the next few seasons, as Lotta did begin to perform *Fanchon*, the two women would sometimes appear at competing theaters in the same city, and their rivalry would intensify. Critics began to speak jointly of the "Maggie Mitchell and Lotta" style, or school, of acting.[15]

But that summer in New York nothing cut into Maggie's audiences. Some of the loudest applause in Niblo's came the night of June 1 when General Sherman attended *Fanchon*. But the cheering and close crowds became so oppressive that Sherman had to sneak out between acts, "his first retreat," jibed the *New York Times*.[16]

Four nights after Sherman's visit, Maggie finally changed the bill to give New Yorkers their first chance to see her as Marie in *Pearl*. Since Collier, who had enacted Landry, had to leave for an engagement in London, Wheatley provided John W. "Handsome Jack" Blaisdell, 25, for the role of Arthur, and Thomas E. Morris, 36, as the lecherous Commander. Otherwise, Mary Ann Farren, who had embodied Fadet, enacted Marie's virtuous Mother Margaret; Emma Skerrett again played for youth as Chouchon; and comedian William Scallan, Maggie's original Pierrot in Boston, resumed that role. Thirty-five-year-old Mary Wells had done so well as Mother Barbeaud and again as Arthur's mother, The Marchioness, that she would carry those roles for Maggie for another fourteen years.

But *Pearl* itself, and Maggie's performance, were flawed. It became evident that despite the versatility she had shown in her "protean" roles, that trait failed her now. "There is a sameness of manner, of speech, and . . . artistic subterfuge that cannot escape notice. Her personality is rarely lost sight of. Miss Maggie appears *in* a part, not as the part." As for the "trifling" script, "We are called upon for our tears before we have even become acquainted with, much less interested in, the story of the characters [and thus] we are pretty sure to become callous to and unsympathetic with [their] misery." The worst part was, the evening was nearly four hours long.[17]

The *New York Times* labeled *Pearl* "rather trite. . . . In all respects it was so strangely wrong and grotesque that we marveled at the patience of an audience that could be thus imposed upon." Exhibiting a "general tendency to hysterics," Maggie was "a silly person who knows nothing of her profession, and who, in fact, is an imposture on it. [She] is no artist, and her success before the public is the accident of a dramatist. . . . Her knowledge of art is so paltry that it is simply disgraceful. . . . A worse performance of a principal part we have never seen." Capping this diatribe, the *Times* resurrected her flag-stomping: "Miss Mitchell's feet are lively. They danced on the American flag when she tore it down with her own hands, they dance with animal vitality on everything else."[18]

This triggered Anna's maternal fury. Her response appeared in the *Times* on June 13. To bring up the flag incident now that the war was over, she asserted, was "coarse, harsh and unjust." Its depiction "is not only wholly at variance with the truth, but it has often been publicly denied and refuted in this city and elsewhere. . . . While I do not question your right as an editor to fairly and even severely criticize Miss Mitchell as an artist, I cannot believe that you will claim the right to publish statements wholly untrue, and calculated to fasten upon her the odium which attaches to conduct alike disloyal and unbecoming to a lady." Maggie filed a libel suit against the *Times*, but no record remains of its disposition or a *Times* retraction or apology.[19]

On June 21 Maggie brought out *Barefoot*. Blaisdell having washed out, she borrowed James Duff, her William Peace in Boston two years ago, from New York's Park Theatre for that role. Scallan played the foolish Jemmy, and Wells the tolerant Mrs. Hempfarmer. The *Times* did not deign to review it, but others considered it "a charming combination of levity and pathos blended with as rapid changes as clouds, sunshine and showers on a summer landscape." Despite Maggie's "exuberant glee" and "naïve simplicity," there were "periods when the young lady's exuberance and volatility are apt to become oppressive, . . . when her simplicity touches upon the dangerous verge of transparent artifice."[20]

With Duff only on loan, she needed a new Landry for her final week of *Fanchon* starting July 3. She took a chance on W. E. Sheridan, 26, a Union Army veteran making his New York debut. The rest, including Scallan as Didier and Farren as Fadet, sufficed. But box office lagged amid scorching heat, with Maggie and Wheatley reportedly losing about $500 a week (although "all our theatres are losing money"), bringing it all to an end. Nevertheless, she had completed a remarkable ten weeks in the toughest theater city in America—four more than in 1862 at Laura Keene's. The *Times*' nastiness aside, she could reflect with satisfaction how far her career had come in fifteen years.[21]

She spent what remained of the summer at home on 54th Street arranging her 1865–66 tour. It would entail fewer roles, with *Fanchon*, *Barefoot*, and *Pearl* comprising over 80 percent. As Keene had done for several years, Maggie now gathered a handful of actors to tour with her to carry major roles. Such a practice, observed historian George Odell, represented "perhaps the entering wedge for the destruction of the stock company." Her first choice was Collier, her original Landry. He would be back from London by fall but under contract to Niblo's. She would borrow him when she could and work on securing him more often.[22]

Waiting for his availability, she opened the season later than usual, on October 9 at the Boston Theatre, where manager Henry C. Jarrett had succeeded Wyzeman Marshall. In addition to Collier, she also borrowed from Niblo's George Becks to play Didier and J. G. Burnett for Father Barbeaud. Boston actress Fanny (Mrs. E. L.) Davenport covered Fadet. A packed house on her opening night generated over $1,800, and full houses continued for four weeks, with Maggie taking away $10,000. (Still, Charlotte Thompson was that fall pulling in nearly $3,000 for twelve performances.) When Collier returned to Niblo's, Maggie switched to *Barefoot* and *Pearl*, replacing him in leads with Frank Mayo, 26, fresh off a huge success in *Streets of New York*. The *Boston Journal* quipped that Maggie geared *Barefoot* and *Pearl* to "tender-hearted play-goers, who value a performance as a harpooner would a whale—by the amount of blubber which it produces."[23]

After a brief run of *Fanchon* in mid-November in Norfolk, Virginia, for her old friend Sam Glenn, Maggie returned to Ford's Holliday Street Theatre in Baltimore. Freed from his post-assassination imprisonment (although never charged), Ford had lost tens of thousands of dollars and been forced to shutter three of his five theaters. Maggie, who had lost her investment in the Washington one, would help him recover. He had lost many of his actors in the interim, but the remainder adequately supported her through three weeks of *Fanchon*, *Barefoot*, and *Pearl*. She drew well despite stiff competition from Owens at the nearby Front Street Theatre.

She began 1866 back in the nation's capital, where Ford's keenest rival, Leonard Grover, was flourishing in his eponymous theater, using actors displaced from Ford's, some of whom—like those in Baltimore—had been in the cast on the fatal night. She again drew houses "full in every part from floor to ceiling, including the aisles and private boxes."[24]

One night, performing *Fanchon*, her quick wit turned what might have been an embarrassing interruption into a minor triumph. In their scene beside the river, Fanchon at first fails to notice Landry slipping his arm around her, then with "a look of shocked modesty" says, "Why Landry Barbeaud, just see where your hand is." Before she got her line out, a rube in the gallery "cried out to one of his chums, 'Say, Jim, he's got her.' Quick as light, Maggie flashed her eyes toward the gallery and in a tone of loving and complete surrender, . . . said, 'Yes, Jim, I guess he has,' and then she nestled a little closer to her lover. The audience recognized the quick wit and exquisite timing of Maggie and greeted her with round after round of applause." Maggie could always improvise and knew instinctively how to win over an audience.[25]

Enlisting some of the actors from Grover's company, she took *Fanchon* and *Pearl* to New England, to Providence, Hartford, and New Haven (Maggie's first appearance in the latter two). "Her figure is *petit* but graceful," observed the *Hartford Courant*, "and her voice is full and rich, and under admirable control. In her power of expression she possesses wonderful genius; swelling with indignation one moment she will electrify an audience, and in the next . . . her pathetic exhibition of voice and gesture will suddenly stifle applause and touch the keenest sensibilities."[26]

Back at Niblo's, with Collier as Landry, Becks as Didier, Farren as Fadet, Burnett as Father Barbeaud, and Maria Maeder (the Farrens' daughter) as Madelon, Maggie drew the usual crowds. Pearl and Barefoot, with the same actors, succeeded as well. She continued her Saturday matinees, a practice she maintained off and on for the rest of her career. In a shot across the bow of actresses like Thompson and Melville, the *New York Evening Post* reminded readers that as Fanchon, "Miss Mitchell has no rival."[27]

She had planned to try out another new role during this engagement. Augustin Daly's melodramatic *Leah the Forsaken* had served as a vehicle for Kate Bateman at Niblo's three years before but had been assailed by critics. Daly had urged Maggie to give it new life, but Wheatley put his foot down. Maggie wrote to Daly that Wheatley had returned the script to her

> in the most indignant manner, calling it Trash—absurd—improbable, and that he would not allow any such piece to be produced at Niblo's Garden. He was exceedingly ungentlemanly during the interview. Speaking in the most uncomplimentary terms of your piece and endeavored [sic] to impress me with a due sense of his *misfortune and of the honor* he conferred by *allowing anyone* [emphasis hers] to play in his theatre. I am really disappointed. . . . I trust you will acquit me of all blame, as I have made every effort for its production."[28]

During this protracted engagement, Maggie stayed with her family on 54th Street, by now "a handsome house of her own, beautifully fitted and furnished. . . . Her drawing rooms are very handsome, containing, among other things, some fine statuary; and she has a large and well-selected library." She also maintained an active social life. Her callers included General George Custer, who one Sunday evening enjoyed "a delightful visit. Her manners are so pleasing, her conversation so refined you would not suppose she had been on the stage." Unfortunately, one evening in late February, while Maggie performed the house was burglarized. She lost many valuable items acquired in her touring. Her resources were sufficient that spring, however, to donate through John Ford's daughter Annie $100 for the Southern Relief Fair.[29]

Initiating a twenty-year professional relationship, Maggie next performed for "Colonel" William E. Sinn at his New Chestnut Street Theatre in Philadelphia, a city in which she had not appeared for nearly four years. Returning to Brooklyn's Academy of Music, she followed the alluring Kate Bateman, 22, coming off a successful round of performances in London. It may have been Bateman who planted the seed for Maggie's renewed consideration of a London tour, or it may have an offer from Dion Boucicault to play at his new theater being built there, or an attempt to counteract the success as Fanchon of British actress Amy Bruce, who was coming to the United States that summer. In any case, rumors circulated that Maggie was preparing "her departure for Europe. She goes to the old world in search of a triumph as great as that which rewarded Miss Bateman, and will doubtless readily obtain it." But no sooner had she announced her intentions than she retracted them, giving the cause as the Austro-Prussian War, although that was far afield from London.[30]

She closed the 1865–66 season back in New England. In Boston at Jarrett's Boston Theatre beginning May 14 she again utilized Mayo, but audiences were underwhelmed. She didn't help herself in her choice of material for her benefits. For one she undertook the part of Parthenia in the turgid *Ingomar the Barbarian* she had satirized nearly a decade ago, with Mayo in the title role. For another, she chose Pauline in Bulwer-Lytton's outdated *Lady of Lyons*, which she had also satirized. Overall, though, she bested Bateman, taking in between $700 and $1,200 a night. On June 2, she took a rare evening off, celebrating her thirtieth birthday, and then finished up in Providence and Springfield, Massachusetts (her first time there, a harbinger of future forays to smaller towns).

In a rare, well-deserved vacation, she relaxed for a few weeks in New Hampshire's White Mountains. As she passed through Connecticut returning home, she learned that Connecticut sculptor Truman H. Bartlett had completed a bust of her, "a splendid portrait, full of character, and with all the peculiar expression of the charming original. The hair is arranged in the Grecian style. The drapery is light, simple and pleasing." According to mutual friends, it was an excellent likeness. That fall it would be exhibited at Tiffany's in New York.[31]

That summer aerialist Harry Leslie, who had famously crossed Niagara Falls on a high wire the summer before, was demonstrating his skills from a hot-air balloon tethered a thousand feet above Central Park. On July 18, an exceptionally hot day, Maggie impulsively decided to ascend with him, accompanied by an unnamed "old lady relative" (possibly Sophia, not yet forty, or Anna, as unlikely as that seems). Soon after they reached their zenith, a massive thunderstorm—later reported to be a small tornado—broke.

Workers hauled in the balloon as fast as possible, in the process knocking down part of the amphitheater surrounding the site. To Maggie's cries of "What shall I do, what shall I do!?" Leslie calmly replied, "Hold me tight." She complied and all was well, but the "venerable lady" took some time to shake off her fright.[32]

On July 29 Maggie attended the New York wedding of her half-sister Mary and John Albaugh. The following summer Mary would give birth to a future actor and manager, unsurprisingly the start of a new generation of theatrical Mitchells and Albaughs. Compared to the rocky marriage Mary had with Collier, for the rest of their time together she was, recorded one who knew them well, "a true helpmate to [Albaugh] in all the relations of life, a good actress, a careful manager, a faithful mother, and a loving wife."[33]

Over the past few seasons, through John Ford, Maggie had come to know Baltimore playwright Clifton W. Tayleure, 35, who would become a friend for life. During stints as an actor, attorney, and journalist in Baltimore and Richmond during the war, he churned out original plays and adaptations from novels. In those cities, his southern-centric version of *Uncle Tom's Cabin* (1853) was highly popular, and in New York, his *East Lynne* (1862) had struck gold. Then he had turned to management, taking over the Brooklyn Academy of Music where Maggie had just performed and planned now to open her 1866–67 season. Like Owens and Ford, Tayleure and Maggie postwar were assiduously casting off any erstwhile pro-South beliefs.

Tayleure that fall began crafting specifically for Maggie an adaptation of Charlotte Brontë's *Jane Eyre* which would serve her well in the coming decade. (Tayleure would also provide Lotta with her first big break in Manhattan.) Until it was completed, 93 percent of Maggie's repertoire would consist of *Fanchon*, *Barefoot*, and *Pearl*, with *Fanchon* comprising nearly half. Only a handful of the old scripts would remain, including an occasional *Margot* or *Little Treasure* on benefit nights. She would again count on Collier, who had signed on with her for the entire season (All hard feelings had dissipated within the family, and Collier, Albaugh, and Mary remained friends).

She opened for Tayleure in Brooklyn on September 4 with *Barefoot*, followed by *Pearl* and *Fanchon*, a pattern she repeated in Cincinnati starting on September 17 at the renovated National Theatre. From there it was back to New York, where a four-week engagement at the massive Broadway Theatre awaited. Seating 4,300, it had recently housed Owens and Mr. and Mrs. Charles Kean and would be the biggest venue Maggie had ever played. Its manager was her friend George Wood, building on the success he had achieved in "the West." She filled the house nearly every night, with standing room only and many turned away, despite intense competition from the massively popular, risqué *The Black Crook* at Niblo's.

New York critics found it "really remarkable how this little creature, without much physical power or any special grace, or a voice either rich or round, produces the effects she does." *Barefoot* was "a sort of second edition of *Fanchon*, and to witness the two plays on successive nights seems like the latter production in ten acts." "Saved from excessive tediousness only by the young actress' natural, fresh and captivating style," *Barefoot* "abounds in cheap dialogue and sentimental platitudes. . . . The heroine so frequently refers to her mother, the angels, Heaven and the All-seeing Father that we are led to conclude she is under the immediate protection and even patronage of the celestial powers." Maggie's "hundred thousand friends of New York are so familiar [with *Fanchon*] that should the Little Cricket be taken 'suddenly indisposed' some evening, a hundred pretty girls in the audience could step forward and play the part for her without missing a word or forgetting a gesture."[34]

That many of those "pretty girls" empathized with Maggie's characters was demonstrated one night during this run in this most sophisticated city: "In the fourth act [of *Barefoot*] where William Peace asked Amry if she would be his wife, some intensely interested young woman—from the country, probably—cried out, 'Say yes! Do take him, Maggie [tellingly, not 'Amry']!' This unexpected speech from the front brought down the house and caused general laughter, in which the young artist herself could not refrain from joining." Maggie was truly, wholeheartedly theirs, and knew it well.[35]

Varying her nucleus of touring companions, she added to Collier that winter two known quantities, George Becks and Adeline Hind, to play comic young leads and old women (e.g., Jemmy and Fadet), and took a chance on Charles Hale, 47, to play old men (e.g., Father Barbeaud and Farmer Peace). On the advice of her new business manager, Brown Atkins, she dipped her toe into management, leasing several theaters in smaller New England towns. Thus, she would cultivate new audiences for *Fanchon*, *Barefoot*, and *Pearl*.

Not yet the grueling, frantic tours she would undertake when her career began to wane, it was nevertheless a challenging schedule. The first town was Springfield, Massachusetts, where her mini-company, supported by stock actors in smaller roles, played two nights in early November, a different show each night. A third night saw them in Hartford and a fourth in Providence. The fifth and sixth took them to Lowell, Massachusetts. In each town, Maggie drew crowded houses, one of the few attractions to do so that season. In Worcester, Massachusetts, despite the legendary nurse Clara Barton lecturing at a nearby venue, Maggie took in "the most money for two nights ever taken by anyone at the Worcester Theatre, except Forrest, and in numbers of audience is ahead of him. Forrest charged $1.50; Maggie, 50 and 75 cents."[36]

In Albany, her first return in nine years and the first time she enacted *Fanchon* there, she and her small company attracted one of the largest, most fashionable audiences to that point. In Syracuse, her first appearance in eleven years, the same held true. As Fanchon, "She charmed from the moment when in rags she bounded upon the stage, until at the last when she stood the self-poised woman with love crowning her life of trial." Anticipating her return, "We cry like little children for more."[37]

In Rochester, religious opposition to the theater was as strong as it had been when Maggie had visited nine years before, but she knew *Fanchon* promulgated Christian morals and appealed to all ages. Touting it as such, she was disappointed: "The majority of the audience was composed of clergymen and their families, and people who seldom or never go to the theater. They sat stone still all through the play" without applauding once. "It was very depressing. At the close of the play, they all sat in their seats until the manager went out and told them the play was over."[38]

Heading for a December 3 opening in St. Louis, where she knew DeBar would provide good support, Maggie let Becks, Hind and Hale go, keeping only Collier. She successfully counteracted Melville's *Fanchon* nearby, as she would do elsewhere against Ada and Emma Webb as Fanchon and Fadet, respectively, and Mr. and Mrs. William Gomersal (she a beautiful young comedienne) as Landry and Fanchon, and a few flash-in-the-pan imitators like M. E. Gordon, Amy Stone and Leona Cavender. Jeannie Gourlay, a Ford's Theatre actress who had seen Maggie perform *Fanchon*, also toured in the role throughout New England for several years. Critical response bordered on ennui: "It is needless to say anything in praise of the performance of *Fanchon* by Maggie Mitchell, for everybody has heard of its excellence." No one "will stop to criticize it, and every night a crowded audience witnesses the play with delight" despite exceptionally cold weather. (The entire 1866–67 winter across the country was one of the most severe of the century, with rail travel severely constrained.)[39]

Maggie and Collier closed out 1866 in Bloomington, Illinois, drawing mediocre houses, and Columbus, Ohio, where audiences were larger. They inaugurated 1867 for John Ford at the leased National Theatre in Washington, D.C., supported by a strong, known stock company. Again, crowded, fashionable houses left hundreds turned away. Nearly a week of tedious, circuitous travel on war-battered rail beds took Maggie and Collier to New Orleans, opening February 4 at the Varieties Theatre which Owens had relinquished at the war's onset. Its manager now was W. R. Floyd, with whom Maggie had acted years ago. Its stock company fell well short of the antebellum standards Owens had set, but Floyd was relying on stars to bring in the crowds.

Maggie complied. She threw in a few nights of *Little Treasure* and *Margot*, but *Fanchon* predominated. Critics shrugged as crowds, hungry for entertainment, flowed in: "We have nothing more to say of Miss Mitchell's *Fanchon* [which] is in full communion with the town, and the town will not stay away." Admittedly, Maggie was "not so youthful-looking" as on her last visit, and Collier "did not strike us as particularly brilliant."[40]

Celebrities always attract rumors and Maggie was no exception. As she headed with Collier to Mobile and war-ravaged Vicksburg, rumors swirled in eastern newspapers—mostly to gin up circulation—that she would soon marry. In some the intended groom was unspecified, in others, he was "a journalist in Boston who has been long devoted to her," who would insist she retire from the stage. Others were certain that she already had a husband, or that Maggie "is reported to be opposed to matrimony," advising "all actresses to remain single." Rumors on a different subject speculated that Maggie and Collier were to perform for an exorbitant amount in London next summer, but these were equally baseless.[41]

Four weeks in April back at the Broadway Theatre in New York, under the new management of Barney Williams and William A. Moore, yielded more crowded-to-overflowing houses, more wild applause, and more critical yawns. The same held true through another four back at the Howard Athenaeum in Boston. Although "hackneyed and worn out," *Fanchon* was "neither better nor worse than she has played it hitherto, and her popularity appears to be undiminished." Occasionally, there came a nugget of praise: "you are surprised into a laugh where you expect to cry, and in the midst of merriment, one sad touch makes you sober again." Collier still supported her ably. Although probably "long ago sick and weary of the platitudes he utters night after night, there is no evidence of it on the stage. He is ever earnest, faithful, conscientious, and full of intelligent *esprit*."[42]

Almost every Saturday, "Maggie Mitchell matinees" drew in families, and tributes of all kinds continued. A New Orleans poet cranked out an ode to "Charming little Maggie Mitchell," asking, "Where do you get all that laugh from, clear as crystal and no giggle?/And those sobs you pop and smother, while your little foot you wriggle?" In Boston, she was serenaded one night by a brass band at her boardinghouse. In Charleston, South Carolina, that spring the yacht "Maggie Mitchell" began winning regattas. Its mention in racing columns, like the racehorse "Maggie Mitchell," was soon a regular occurrence. In 1868 a "Maggie Mitchell" vein of silver out west would prove extremely rich.[43]

And the money kept rolling in. By now, it was said, only Edwin Booth and Maggie could fill the largest theaters. Accounts of her worth varied widely, and she remained secretive, but they ranged from $100,000 to $175,000 (close to $3 million today). She was variously reported as earning between $1,000 and $1,500 per week (between $17,000 and $25,500 today), at a time when the average weekly wage for a working woman in America was about $1.85. Booth, by comparison, was making about $2,000 per week and Lotta about $900. An average stock company leading man could expect about $75 a week. Eschewing an extravagant lifestyle, concerned primarily with her family's comfort and saving for future investments, Maggie maintained control of her funds (as opposed to the silly headed Lotta, whose mother tightly controlled her finances well into Lotta's fifties).

Maggie and Collier closed out their 1866–67 season on June 1 at the Brooklyn Academy of Music. Her last three shows were billed as farewell performances before a European tour, but it would be a well-deserved pleasure tour, not to perform.

NOTES

1. *Washington Chronicle*, Oct. 23, 1864.
2. *Ibid.*; *Washington Evening Star*, Sept. 27, 1864; (Washington) *Constitutional Union*, Oct. 3 and 14, 1864.
3. *New York World*, Oct. 25, 1864; *Frank Leslie's Illustrated Newspaper*, Nov. 19, 1864.
4. *New York Times*, Oct. 27, 1864.
5. Letter to MM from "Hamilton," Nov. 18, 1864, MM Papers, MS Collection 4552, NYPL.
6. *Cincinnati Commercial Tribune*, Jan. 13, 1865; *New York Herald* quoted in *Pittsburgh Gazette*, Jan. 5, 1865.
7. *Cincinnati Commercial Tribune*, Jan. 19 and 28, 1865.
8. *Nashville Union*, Nov. 27, 1864; Walter T. Durham, *Reluctant Partners: Nashville and the Union, 1863–1865*, Knoxville: University of Tennessee Press, 2008, 277.
9. *Nashville Union*, Feb. 15 and 17, 1865.
10. (Washington) *National Tribune*, July 11, 1901.
11. MM interview with Cincinnati correspondent in the context of the nation's mourning the death of President James Garfield on Sept. 19, 1881, in *Louisville Courier-Journal*, Sept. 28, 1881.
12. *Cleveland Leader*, May 2, 1865; *New York Clipper*, Apr. 29, 1865; *Frank Leslie's Illustrated Newspaper*, May 13, 1865.
13. *New York World*, May 23, 1865.
14. *New York World*, Feb. 13, 1912.
15. *Buffalo Commercial*, July 22, 1865; *New York Herald*, June 11, 1867.
16. *New York Times*, June 2, 1865.
17. *New York World*, June 6, 1865; *New York Evening Express*, June 6, 1865.
18. *New York Times*, June 7, 1865.
19. *New York Times*, June 13, 1865.
20. *New York Herald*, June 22, 1865; *New York Tribune*, June 22, 1865.
21. New York correspondent for *Sacramento Union*, Aug. 21, 1865.
22. Odell VIII:145.
23. *Boston Journal*, Jan. 18, 1866.

24. *Washington National Intelligencer*, Jan. 9, 1866.
25. *Washington Evening Star*, June 24, 1923.
26. *Hartford Courant*, Feb. 8, 1866.
27. *New York Evening Post*, Feb. 20, 1866.
28. MM to Daly, Mar. 21, 1866, Daly Papers, Folger Shakespeare Library.
29. *Cincinnati Gazette*, Feb. 16, 1866; *Washington Evening Star*, Aug. 30, 1867; Custer to wife Elizabeth, Apr. 1, 1866, in Marguerite Merington, ed., *The Custer Story: The Life and Intimate Letters of General George A. Custer*, Lincoln: University of Nebraska Press, 1987, 180.
30. *Buffalo Commercial*, May 7, 1866.
31. *Boston Advertiser*, May 28, 1866.
32. *New York Times*, July 19, 1866.
33. Henry P. Phelps, *Players of a Century*, Albany, NY: J. McDonough, 1880, 10.
34. *New York Herald*, Oct. 23 and 30, 1866; *New York Sun*, Oct. 9, 1866.
35. *New York Herald*, Oct. 30, 1866.
36. (Worcester) *Massachusetts Spy*, Nov. 16, 1866.
37. *Syracuse Standard*, Nov. 22, 1866.
38. MM interview, *Boston Weekly*, Jan. 8, 1879.
39. (Washington) *Evening Star*, Nov. 12, 1864; (St. Louis) *Missouri Democrat*, Dec. 6, 1866.
40. *New Orleans Times-Picayune*, Feb. 5, 1867; *New Orleans Times-Democrat*, Feb. 8, 1867.
41. *Boston Traveller* [sic], Sept. 18, 20 and 28, 1867; *Missouri Democrat*, Sept. 24, 1867; *Cincinnati Daily Gazette*, Nov. 8, 1867.
42. *New York Tribune*, Apr. 4, 1867; *Boston Traveller* [sic], Apr. 30, 1867; *New York Sun*, Apr. 12, 1867; *Brooklyn Eagle*, Apr. 15, 1867.
43. *New Orleans Times-Democrat*, Feb. 10, 1867.

Chapter 8
"Maggie Mitchell stands unrivaled"

The trip Maggie took to Europe with Anna in the summer of 1867 was not the one they had planned. For several months, Charles C. Duncan, a dubious character trying to recover from bankruptcy, had advertised a cruise to Europe and the Holy Land on the steamer *Quaker City*, which he would captain. To attract paying passengers at $1,200 per head, he had signed up—and widely touted—such celebrities as Dr. Henry Ward Beecher, Mark Twain (who from the venture would craft *Innocents Abroad*), Generals William T. Sherman and Nathaniel Banks, and the celebrated Civil War "Drummer Boy of Rappahannock," Robert Henry Hendershott (to wed his Poughkeepsie fiancée of two years).

If Maggie would join their company, Duncan promised that her passage and Anna's would be gratis, so they signed on. By late May, however, some of the celebrities got cold feet. Beecher withdrew, saying he had to finish the novel he was working on. Sherman and Banks did likewise, professing military responsibilities. On May 30, Hendershott, too, fled the scene, eloping with his fiancée. Dozens of non-celebrities backed out as well, saying they had been tricked into believing they would travel with celebrities. Twain, still relatively unknown, gritted his teeth and stayed on, realizing what fodder Duncan and his cohorts would provide an author.

Maggie and Anna thought the matter through carefully, and then boarded at the last minute, taking the large stateroom vacated by Beecher. They prepared to depart along with (variously) 65–80 fellow travelers. Even before departure, they developed serious doubts about Duncan and consulted a respected Manhattan merchant. He advised Maggie that while the Quaker City *may* be seaworthy, Duncan was far from competent to helm it. On June 7, the day before departure, she and Anna abruptly disembarked—too late to avoid newspapers listing them among the participating passengers. Reporter Moses

Beach of the *New York Sun*, who also left the ill-fated expedition, related that "the excursionists were greatly disgusted that Miss Maggie Mitchell did not go with them."[1]

As it turns out, she escaped the *Quaker City*'s nightmare of "queer navigation, storms, and ludicrous contretemps," as described by the embedded reporter for the *New York Herald*. At any rate, she had not applied for a passport in time to have traveled, perhaps another reason for her disembarking. This she remedied on June 12 at the Broadway office of the clerk of the New York Supreme Court. Her application, her signature matching that of countless other documents she signed throughout her life, delineates her physical traits. She reported a height of 4'5" with a high forehead, dark eyes, straight nose, small mouth and chin, light hair, fair complexion, and an oval face. Disingenuously, but typical of many actresses of her day, she recorded her age as twenty-four instead of thirty-one.[2]

Passport in hand, having left instruction for all business to be handled by James Collier in New York, she and Anna and their maid, Maria, boarded the steamship *St. Laurent* on June 15, bound for Europe. Among their fellow passengers, presumably also in first class, were W. C. McCormack (of reaper fame) and artist Albert Bierstadt, on his honeymoon. A little over a week later they arrived in Le Havre, then continued to Paris, where Maggie's primary aim was perfecting her French (which according to Collier upon her return, she achieved), along with sightseeing. European newspapers failed to follow her comings and goings, perhaps because she had not established her celebrity on that continent.

In mid-July Anna left her in Paris and traveled to London to visit family. Maggie, after a brief illness, followed her, leaving Maria in Paris (Anna felt it would cost too much to bring her to England). Together they toured Scotland and on their return stopped in the Lomax ancestral village of Knaresborough, which Anna had not seen for nearly twenty years. They hoped to visit a respected relative, Joseph Dodson Greenhalgh, but he was not at home. Later, he gleaned from local gossips that Maggie "keeps a carriage, and servants to match, both black and white, in livery, [and] spent £1,000 in jewelry or trinkets whilst Paris."[3]

On October 19 Maggie, Anna, and the retrieved Maria boarded the steamer *Russia* at Liverpool and after an uneventful journey arrived in New York on the 30th, Maggie's 1867–68 repertoire all planned out. It would consist almost entirely of *Fanchon*, *Barefoot*, and *Pearl*, with the addition of one important new piece.

Meanwhile, Maggie imitators, especially Emilie Melville, were going full tilt. Fannie B. Price would play *Fanchon* on Broadway that fall, and Emma Maddern would bring her *Fanchon* to the Brooklyn Park Theatre. Some critics considered both equal to Maggie and in some ways superior. An early nemesis, Alice Kingsbury, had staked out Lotta's old territory, California, leading Maggie to place it on her shortlist of future destinations. Also touring with *Fanchon* was Louise Sylvester, a "young and talented artist of the Lotta and Maggie Mitchell school" who would be a thorn in Maggie's side for two decades. Alice Vane, playing *Fanchon* in the South, was deemed "fully the equal of the original Fanchon." Bella Golden, "of the Maggie Mitchell style," was touring in *Pearl of Savoy*. By 1869 these would be joined by Leona Cavender, a "charming and vivacious little sprite . . . of the Maggie Mitchell school." The next season would add Katie Putnam and Josie Booth, who tried to convey Maggie's mannerisms, voice, and laugh and drew moderate houses in smaller towns, but quickly faded. There would be no rest for the real Maggie.[4]

Within days she and Collier were in Baltimore, opening on November 4 at Ford's Holliday Street Theatre. Ford provided strong stock support as they drew dense crowds, even against *The Black Crook* at the nearby Front Street Theatre. (Ironically, the cast of that New York-based touring company included Maggie's nephew Julian, now sixteen.) Although Collier still played Landry in *Fanchon* and William Peace in *Barefoot*, he switched in *Pearl* to playing the comical Pierrot, a more challenging role than Arthur.[5]

Despite an early snowstorm, they drew moderate houses in Washington in mid-November at the National Theatre, now managed by W. E. Spalding and William H. Rapley, sometimes assisted by Ford. Still clinging to Shakespearean aspirations, Maggie played Juliet to the Romeo of aspiring, capable stock actor Charles Vandenhoff, 17, Collier being demoted to Mercutio. Reviewers found her "better than we were, on the whole, prepared to expect." In tender moments she was fine, but in scenes calling for intense emotion, she was in over her head.[6]

Effusive reviews greeted her and Collier at the National Theatre in Cincinnati, where they drew good houses despite "execrable" weather. Acting "with a truth and power which distinctly marks her as a great actress, . . . Maggie Mitchell stands unrivaled."[7]

She returned home to New York for the holidays. Mary and Albaugh were in the city, too, showing off their newborn son and performing at Banvard's Opera House. 1868 opened with longer engagements for Maggie and Collier: four weeks in Boston followed by five in New York, consistently drawing full houses, primarily with *Fanchon*.

In February they returned to the theater which had first introduced New Yorkers to it. Laura Keene's theater had passed through several hands since then and now, as the Olympic Theatre, was nominally controlled by Leonard Grover, but managed by actor/dancer/clown/stage manager George L. Fox and business manager Clifton Tayleure. Maggie's previous theatrical home in the city, the Broadway Theater, was filled nightly by Lotta's antics.

Newspapers delighted in comparing the two women performing only three blocks apart, competing for the same audiences. Fortunately for Maggie, Lotta had given up Fanchon but had latched onto *Pet*, one of Maggie's old standards. Ultimately, both actresses drew well.

Backed by Collier's Landry and Adeline Hind's Fadet, Maggie followed a 100-night run of a lavish production of *A Midsummer Night's Dream* on which the management had spared no expense, and for *Fanchon*, they created all new scenery, perhaps the best it had ever received. Maggie's elfin charm was inevitably compared to the fairies of *A Midsummer Night's Dream*. Shakespeare's had been replaced by "a real fairy with lithe and glowing limb and fresh young blood, graceful, gay, bounding, a fairy fawn, now brightly bold, now beautifully shy, the cricket who chirps near every heart."[8]

For three of her five weeks, Maggie captivated everyone. Even acerbic critic William Winter decreed that she performed *Fanchon* "better than she has ever acted it before. Her old fault—a tendency to continual giggle and sob—has been in a great measure corrected and so, though she is still somewhat over-demonstrative and still indulges now and then in an unpleasant nasal twang, her personation is nearer to nature and far more agreeable." However, as most critics acknowledged, Maggie had moved beyond their poor power to add or detract. "Her performance is so far above criticism that any attempt to criticize would prove a failure." Her fans "do not seem to care what they see, in so long as they see Maggie Mitchell. She has passed the time of criticism," having "done more in teaching a moral lesson in Fanchon's triumphs than in all the sermons preached for the last twenty years." When she switched to *Barefoot*, with Collier as William and the irresistibly funny Fox—at forty-two a bit long in the tooth—as the half-witted Jemmy, they packed the house. *Pearl* generated no less.[9]

But after three weeks Maggie had nothing new to offer and business fell off—her last two weeks being the least profitable segment of the Olympic's season. "The public has been satiated with *Fanchon, Pearl of Savoy* and *Little Barefoot*," observed one critic. *Barefoot*, said another, was "a foolish, nonsensical piece in which she runs around the stage like a spoiled child, without either shoes or stockings on her pedal extremities."[10]

With Collier, Maggie closed out March in Philadelphia and Washington, where *Fanchon* was enjoyed by Secretary of State William H. Seward, as recovered as he would ever be from grievous wounds inflicted on the night of President Lincoln's assassination. Spurred by increasing calls for her to try something new—a wealthy New Yorker had offered her $10,000 to never play *Fanchon* again—Maggie opened her second Washington week with a completely new work.

The melodramatic *Lorle, the Tiny Belle of the Canton* was another adaptation of an adaptation of a novel. Like *Pearl*, it chronicled the mismatch of an untutored peasant girl with an accomplished man of urban society. Lorle, the goodhearted daughter of a humble Swiss innkeeper, agrees to sit as the model for a Madonna being painted for the village church by a visiting court artist named Reinhardt (Collier). As he works, fascinated by her beauty, he proposes marriage, which she accepts. She sadly (with a song) leaves her village and accompanies him into society, from which he keeps her hidden, embarrassed by her rustic demeanor. Complicating things is the presence at the court of his former pupil, Countess Ida, who still carries a torch for him. Lorle's well-meaning faux pas weary then disgust him and he plans to desert her. Overhearing him speaking longingly of Ida and confessing his mortification at having a peasant wife, Lorle goes mad, flees to her village and kills herself, dying in her father's arms amid weeping friends (Maggie's yearning for recognition as a tragedienne still beat on). The remorseful Reinhardt reaches her too late.

Originally a novel by Berthold Auerbach, *Lorle* was adapted for the German stage by Charlotte Birch-Pfeiffer, also incorporating parts of Tom Taylor's *The Unequal Match*. In late 1866 it had received performances in New York in a German theater and now came to Maggie in an English translation by Baltimore conductor and sometime-playwright Jacob H. Rosewald. Maggie bought it, but altered its plot structure further, abetted by her friend Fred Maeder. Soon, little remained of the original story. Someone—Maggie or Rosewald or Maeder—added songs, two for Lorle (one with a dance) and two for a chorus of villagers. The titles of these mutated as well (e.g., "Must I Leave This Pretty Little Town?" became "On the Morrow, Must I Go?"). Maggie's scripts were often fluid as she discovered what worked and what did not. Despite her steady use of *Lorle* for the next twenty-three years, it was never printed or copyrighted.[11]

Its theme was universal: "woman's devotion contrasted with man's neglect." But in Washington, its tragic ending did not go down well, and Maggie set it aside. She spent her days observing the proceedings of Congress, where she could be seen almost daily, sometimes in the company of General Sherman. It may have been he who secured for her greatly-in-demand tickets for the opening arguments by the defense in President Andrew Johnson's impeachment trial. Occupying one of the front benches in the Senate visitors' gallery, "the charming actress seemed to be enjoying the scene with as much delight as when she is herself the point of attraction."[12]

She tried *Lorle* next in Chicago, back at McVicker's for the first time since war's end. Vast new audiences queued up to see her in this city whose population had doubled during the 1860s and would reach nearly 350,000 by 1870. They liked what they saw. With "hair, teeth, figure, and money all her own," Maggie cut a fashionable figure, "a fine specimen of a blonde [who] drives a neat and stylish equipage." She and Collier performed *Fanchon*, *Barefoot*, and

Pearl for over a week while rehearsing *Lorle*, yielding a smoother production than Washington's.[13]

Conscientiously nurturing her following, she returned for the first time in several years to the upper Midwest. Spending most of May in Indianapolis, Milwaukee, and Detroit, she also added the first of many small but fast-growing towns: Jackson, Michigan. Managing the theater in Indianapolis was her original 1861 Landry, Charles Pope. Managing in the other three towns was Bernard Macauley, whose empire would soon encompass Cincinnati and Louisville. He would host Maggie many times over the next twenty years.

She and Collier kept their engagements short—one night to one week— and performed only their basic three productions, uncertain of the strength of local stock companies or the abilities of technical crews. In Milwaukee, Maggie's "shadow dance" was ruined by a lack of "moonlight" from a follow spot, and an actress was injured by a falling drop curtain. Unsophisticated audiences, too, were a distraction, with loud talking and stampedes to and from the bar common occurrences. These engagements were only moderately profitable for the management, but Maggie, now a full-fledged star, was paid nevertheless.

By June she was ensconced in New York on 54th Street, planning future real estate ventures, among them a row of brownstones on 121st Street, a four-story apartment building on 126th, a theater of her own, and even a summer home on the New Jersey shore. She knew what she was doing: from 1860 to 1870 the value of Manhattan real estate doubled, with brownstones the hottest properties and newly fashionable apartment houses on the cusp of widespread popularity.[14]

For her coming season, she hired for the first time in her life a Broadway booking/business agency, that of Benjamin Franklin Lowell (whom she knew from Hartford) and Morris Simmonds. For the next few seasons, she would be assured of a relatively logical, remunerative touring schedule.

She also reconnected that summer with Hank Paddock, the Clevelander who had pursued her so assiduously in 1854 and—if rumors could be believed—off and on since then. The second child of six of Thomas and Mary Ann Paddock of Cleveland, at thirty-two he was tall, swarthy, and heavy-set, an enterprising, handsome, affable, glad-handing salesman with a pleasant, open face, a twinkle in his eyes and a bristling dark mustache, always ready with a joke and a willingness to cover the next round.

He had served the Union in the war as a private in the 83rd Regiment, New York Infantry, seeing action at Second Bull Run and Antietam. Wounded at Fredericksburg in December 1862, he was discharged in September 1863 and took over his father's Cleveland haberdashery. Differing accounts of his financial worth categorized it as considerable or nugatory, but in either case,

Maggie had sufficient income. Now, sometime in August, shortly before she began her 1868–69 season, she and Paddock conceived a child. For this, the coming season would be one of Maggie's happiest. It would also bring her a portion of mourning.

That summer she softened *Lorle*'s tragic ending, having its titular character not die, but instead be enfolded at play's end in the arms of a changed Reinhardt, who now accepts her as she is. She realized that *Lorle* had to clear the high bar of New York critics, and decided to begin her 1868–69 season as the Grand Opening star at Manhattan's Metropolitan Theatre and Museum managed by her friend George Wood. He had spent over $100,000 renovating the run-down building on the corner of Broadway and 30th Street into a combination of 1,400-seat theater and museum of oddities characteristic of its age. Intent on attracting former patrons of P. T. Barnum's old American Museum, which had burned in March, Wood had collected nearly seventy tons of freaks of nature, including Siamese twins, giants and dwarfs, exotic snakes, and an assortment of macabre wax figures.

Amid this odd environment, and competing with Lotta at Wallack's Theatre, Maggie took the stage at Wood's on August 31 with *Lorle* following a dedicatory address by Barnum himself. With Collier as Reinhardt and a solid supporting cast, *Lorle* earned underwhelming reviews. It was "in the same class of plays as *Fanchon* and *Little Barefoot*, but considerably duller." After three weeks, she switched to *Fanchon* with Collier as Landry and Mary Wells as Fadet.[15]

Despite—or as yet unaware of—or to cover up for—her impending motherhood, Maggie announced in late September that she would tour Europe in spring, including a March 1869 engagement in London during which she would play Juliet. It did not occur. For now, she embarked on a round of return visits to smaller New England towns, performing in Lowell and Simmonds' theaters. Along with Collier, she secured on short-term contract Adeline Hind for "old woman" roles. They played two or three nights each in Brooklyn, New Haven, Hartford, Providence, Lowell, and Springfield with *Fanchon* and *Lorle*, filling houses, with standees and chairs set up in aisles. In Providence, receipts averaged over $1,000 per night. Reviewers who had seen her before thought she had never played better.

Inexplicably, she reinserted the old, tragic end into *Lorle*, indulging again in her poignant death scene. It didn't work. Lorle's was "the most unexplainable suicide on record. . . . The testimony furnished Lorle of her husband's fondness for the Countess wouldn't stand in a full court; he himself hadn't shown the audience that he was anything more than annoyed at the country manners of his wife [and] his affection for the Countess . . . amounted to nothing more than chasing her out of a side door when she was a little tantalizing. . . . No woman ever died for less cause than Lorle."[16]

In mid-October, the trio swung into upstate New York. In Troy, a crowded house cheered them. Maggie's step-brother, Joseph D. Lomax, lived and practiced medicine in Troy, and provided the venue for the next milestone in Maggie's life. On Thursday, October 15, two months pregnant, she married Hank Paddock in Joseph's front parlor. They all agreed to keep the marriage under wraps, purportedly so the newlyweds could pursue their careers (and later muddy the date vis-à-vis their child's birth).[17]

Paddock discreetly retreated to New York and Maggie moved on to Albany, Utica, Rochester, Syracuse, Elmira, and Buffalo. In Buffalo, Maggie's first time there in over seven years, their local support was exceptional but one woe after another befell them. Again, a lighting operator failed to provide the requisite moonlight for Fanchon's shadow dance amid missing most of his other cues, another night a fire broke out nearby during the performance, and Maggie suffered from a bad cold. She exerted every shred of energy she could to compensate, but audiences failed to respond with any enthusiasm. (Unfortunately, her successor in Buffalo, Emma Maddern, triumphed in *Fanchon*, Buffalo critics pronouncing it every bit as good as Maggie's.)

In November Hind returned to New York and Maggie and Collier moved on to St. Louis, in her brother-in-law John Albaugh's theater, the Olympic, followed by Pittsburgh and Washington. In the capital, they enjoyed strong support from the stock company at the National Theatre, especially stalwart Helen Muzzy. On November 19 President Johnson attended *Pearl* on November 19 with his daughter, Martha Johnson Patterson, her children and Secretary of State Seward. It was Johnson's only known theatrical performance while in office. But *Lorle* again fell short. As "bewitching, . . . sprightly, piquant and fascinating" as Maggie was when she "attempts to overstep the bounds" of *Fanchon*, *Barefoot*, or *Pearl*, "she fails." Lorle was "a peasant girl with all the coquetry of an abandoned flirt." Maggie's performance "always appears like going to a circus. It is the same restless, nervous, fidgety little actress, with the same affected laugh." Of Collier, "we cannot say much save that he prevents the defects in Miss Mitchell's characters being seen, by not outshining her."[18]

From Washington, she took the National's company down to postwar Richmond, drawing inconsistent audiences. There, she let drop to a reporter that her benefit the following night would be her last before her retirement from the stage. This, of course, stoked rumors for the next two months until the truth of her marriage emerged. (It was still traditional for most actresses, to keep their reputations intact, to retire from the stage upon marrying, unless their new husband was also in the profession.)

Maggie and Collier, still under Lowell and Simmonds' management, then careened to Pittsburgh, back to New Haven and Hartford, down to Brooklyn, then back west to start 1869 in Louisville. In Memphis, her last performances before giving birth, Maggie filled fashionable houses every night. Reviewers were kind, even to *Lorle*, its upbeat ending restored. Having not visited Memphis for eight years, all of her material was fresh and attractive. So, too, was her jewelry. On January 25, while she performed, a thief entered her hotel room and stole all of it, valued at $1,000. The next day detectives made an arrest, but whether or not the jewelry was recovered is unknown. In Memphis, seeing the handwriting on the wall or the swelling on Maggie's petite frame, Collier renounced touring and returned to Manhattan, planning to open a saloon. Maggie retreated there as well.

In mid-February, she learned through John Ford that the body of her dear friend John Wilkes Booth was to be disinterred from its ignominious grave in a storeroom at the Washington Arsenal and returned to his family for burial. Maggie sent word that it would mean a great deal to her if she might obtain a lock of his hair. When Booth's remains were brought to the funeral home in Baltimore, Ford's daughter Annie complied. Upon receiving the lock, Maggie knew it was "his hair beyond a doubt. No one ever had more beautiful hair than he. It was the loveliest hair in the world." She remembered John as "very handsome and agreeable, . . . a delightful companion through his great attainments and intellectual superiority. He was a splendid horseman and rode with ease and grace. Being fond of the exercise myself, I was often out with him on horseback." Since the assassination, though, it was "as much as a woman's life was worth . . . to have had an intimate friendship and acquaintance with him." Ultimately, deeply touched by the grief of Booth's mother, Maggie returned the lock to her.[19]

About the same time, the news finally broke nationwide of Maggie's marriage to Paddock, variously reported as having occurred either four or seven months before, the latter date purposely leaked to legitimize their child's birth. The marriage had been kept secret, they told reporters, because of professional interests and obligations. The couple announced that Maggie had quit the stage and they would live in Toledo. Neither occurred. Within a month, rumors appeared that Maggie had already given birth.

That did not occur until May 16, 1869, Maggie delivering in her home on 54th Street a healthy, blue-eyed baby girl whom she named Fanchon Marie in recognition of the two roles which had brought her greatest fame. As Paddock explained, "Fanchon was not only a pretty but an eminently fitting name to give a child, who was expected to grow into modest womanhood."[20]

For two weeks Maggie lingered on the brink of death from complications from that birth. In the same house her mother, Anna, who had endured a partial paralysis (likely from a stroke) for several months, died on Sunday morning, June 6, aged 69. Widely known in the theatrical profession, Anna was mourned as "a most estimable lady, a true Christian woman, warm-hearted and charitable."[21]

It was not until mid-June that Maggie was out of danger. After a summer of rest, though, she was insistent about returning to the road and announced that she would do so by October. While still nominally under the management of Lowell and Simmonds, she decided that her husband would take control of her career, but would remain in New York.

It may have been his business acumen, Maggie's desire for tangible assets, or advice picked up from managers like McVicker, who had invested there, but in summer 1869 Maggie bought a five-acre parcel of land near the ocean in Long Branch, New Jersey, in an unincorporated section of over two hundred acres known as Elberon, morphed from the name of its 1860 developer, Lewis B. Brown. Drawn by its sea breezes, relaxed atmosphere and tranquil vistas from wide verandas, a growing number of financial, industrial and political figures enjoyed summers in Long Branch. Mary Lincoln had visited in 1861 with sons Willie and Tad, and Ulysses Grant had begun vacationing there in 1867 as a general and soon would as homeowner and president. "In all my travels," he said, I have never seen a better place suited for a summer residence than Long Branch." His sentiments would be echoed by Presidents Hayes, Garfield, Arthur, Harrison, McKinley, and Wilson.[22]

Hotels and amusement parks rose quickly, tycoons erected mansions, and by the time Ocean Avenue was laid out in 1867, lots were selling for $1,250 to $2,000 ($22,000–35,000 today). They appreciated rapidly, some going for $5,000–$10,000 within a year or two. Although some "cottages" (country manors, actually) were built for $20,000–30,000, Maggie began cautiously, erecting hers for $10,000 on her lot on the northwest corner of Cedar Avenue and Deal Turnpike (now Norwood Avenue, her land a part of Monmouth University). Realizing its value, she would soon buy other lots as investments. She had the money: as early as 1868, reports appeared that at this relatively young age she was already worth over $100,000. (By 1871 such reports would escalate to $300,000.)

Soon, Mary and John Albaugh would build a summer home across Cedar Avenue. Along with McVicker, Edwin Booth, Broadway theater owner William Henderson, actor-producer James W. Wallack, Jr. and wealthy actress Josephine Hoey, they became the vanguard of a large "summer theatrical colony" in Long Branch. Lotta, too, had a home there. On June 7, 1869, Booth married Mary McVicker in her stepfather's Long Branch cottage, "Meerschaum Villa." Over the next two decades, increasingly tiring of the rigors of touring, Maggie would appreciate ever more deeply the sentiments of the *Brooklyn Eagle*: "No class of people appreciates the word 'home' so much as the wandering players. Tossed from city to city for eight months out of twelve, they learn to estimate home life at its true value. A cottage at Long Branch just fills the bill."[23]

With Paddock remaining in New York—listed on census records as a gold broker—it is unclear whether or not Maggie took little Fanchon with her as she embarked on her 1869–70 tour. But no reporter mentions the presence of a child on the road, and there was ample family to care for the baby at home on 54th Street, including Maggie's widower father, 64, widowed half-sister Sophie, 42, and her four children (including Julian), and Maggie's sisters Emma, 28, and Sarah, 24.

For this tour, Maggie needed a dependable, competent replacement for Collier. She would spend the season cycling through several, all ultimately incompatible. Lowell and Simmonds provided her with a nucleus of competent supporting players, but she would still largely have to rely on local stock companies. To make it easier on everyone, she kept her repertoire small, with no new pieces. A typical week would consist of two or three *Fanchons*, one or two each of *Barefoot*, *Pearl*, and *Lorle*, and possibly a *Margot* and *Katty* together. *Fanchon* would comprise over a third of her performances.

Maggie opened on October 4 close to home, at the Academy of Music in Brooklyn with *Fanchon*. Her Landry was an actor she had relied on a few times before, James Duff, who like Collier also played Pierrot in *Pearl*. He remained with her through a fall tour of New England, which included two new towns, Newport, Rhode Island, and Portland, Maine, plus Hartford, Connecticut. Despite rudimentary facilities, she easily filled the limited capacities of these houses nightly. She would personally earn from these four weeks in New England about $8,000, noteworthy in light of the September 24 "Black Friday" collapse of the U.S. gold market, severely curtailing discretionary spending.

One night in Providence, just before the Act I curtain went up on *Pearl*, company member J. P. Sutton, who played Marie's father, from whom she must tearfully part, received a telegram informing him of the death of his mother. He shared the sad news with Maggie, still mourning the loss of Anna. The parting scene that night produced copious tears, but both performers stayed in character, creating a powerful moment for the audience, who had no idea how real the grief was that they were witnessing.

Critics' familiarity with Maggie's repertoire led to fewer reviews and nearly no mention of Duff except to acknowledge him as a worthy successor to Collier. A remarkably insightful review of her *Fanchon* emerged from the pen of the young men of Harvard:

> Maggie Mitchell . . . plays her few notes with a wonderful intensity that thrills the great heart of the public more than all the *technique* of more versatile artists. . . . The prevailing characteristic of her acting is intensity. . . . The child-nature which ripples through her laughing and weeping, the intensity of her scorn and wrath in the second act, the whole crushed desolation of her figure as

she lies sobbing on the ground after Landry's departure . . . can arise from no stage trickery. [Of her shadow dance] there is an elvish pathos about it which can only arise from intuition. . . . Maggie Mitchell is not a thorough artist. Her mannerisms are many and indefensible, and she has a tendency to prolong her acting until parts of it resemble the heads of a sermon. But, in spite of all these things, her rare genius shines forth and exerts a stronger popular influence than that of any performer on the American stage.[24]

Maggie and Duff then took the Lowell and Simmonds actors to the Boston Theatre, managed by Junius Brutus Booth, Jr., John and Edwin's eldest brother. At first, she filled the house with *Fanchon*, *Barefoot*, and *Pearl*, with Mrs. H. P. Grattan (Maggie's original New York Mother Barbeaud) competently filling old woman roles. But after the first week (with three more to go), attendance waned. Reviewers contended that "the public has tired of her limited range, pretty and pathetic as her performances are. . . . Her repertoire is not only very limited, but is worn threadbare." They hoped she would try a new role or two, perhaps "some character of a higher range," specifically Juliet.[25]

She did not oblige, except with *Lorle*, which met with even smaller audiences and mixed reviews. It was "incoherent," "feeble, tearful [and] overdone," the plot had huge holes (e.g., "Why Countess Ida should determine to ruin Lorle's happiness is not entirely clear"), Maggie's final [reinstalled] death scene was self-indulgent, Duff appeared moribund, and the chorus of villagers sang wretchedly. The only grace note was the orchestra under the leadership of Napier Lothian. Maggie would remember him and would continue to tinker with *Lorle*.[26]

Possibly related to Duff's lackluster performance, he and Maggie now parted ways, never again to act together. The Lowell-Simmonds actors also departed. Maggie closed out the year back at McVicker's in Chicago, relying entirely on his company. She opened with *Fanchon* but added a clever new bit. As she cavorted in Act I, one of her shoes would invariably fly off into the house, sometimes as high as the gallery. She would sing, "Where's my shoe-y, shoe-y," and in "a trick that never fails to captivate the house," someone would always toss it back to her on stage. "Ha, ha!" she would cry with a laugh, "I did that a-purpose [sic]." But now, knowing of the tremendous popularity of minstrel Dan Bryant's new number, "Shoo Fly," she ad-libbed, "Did you see that *shoe fly*!?" It brought down the house, so she kept it in for the rest of her career, changing its origin story to please local fans as if they were seeing it for the first time. When Maggie switched to *Pearl*, attendance surged, but *Barefoot* and *Lorle* were poorly received.[27]

To start 1870, Maggie hired a new tour manager. Her brother Charles, 30, had married Emily Wilton, 17, and with Emily's older brother George, had just formed a partnership to manage theaters and tours. George took over Maggie's spring schedule, sending her back to DeBar's in St. Louis, supported by a mediocre company. She opened with *Pearl* on January 10, followed by *Barefoot, Lorle*, and, of course, *Fanchon*, all of which drew full houses despite the weak economy. Only moderate houses attended her engagement in Cincinnati for Macauley. *Lorle*, despite its novelty, "has not taken hold upon the popular heart that *Fanchon* has so long held, and it probably never will. . . . Maggie Mitchell will never be able on the stage to divest herself of her identity with the poor, merry, brave little Cricket."[28]

In Pittsburgh, wartime transgressions forgiven, Maggie attracted large audiences despite bad weather. She was supported by a strong stock company, the nucleus of which was Samuel K. Chester, an erstwhile friend of John Wilkes Booth, as Landry, and his wife, Annie, as Madelon. Surprisingly well-received was *Lorle*, which inspired "a heartier appreciation of all that is good in the character of woman, and a Christian detestation of the pride, pomp, and conventionalism of a rotten and disgraceful fashionable society." It was thought perhaps her finest character.[29]

Back at the National Theatre in Washington, Maggie was again supported by its competent company. Helen Muzzy, in one of her final roles, enacted a superb Fadet. Maggie was still tinkering with the ending of *Lorle*, now prolonging her death scene in a "spirit tableau" (apparently an ascent of her character's spirit). However, it generated little interest. As Maggie toured to Baltimore, Albany, Troy and Buffalo, it was still *Fanchon* that drew the largest audiences. "Better than ever before," it allowed them "to enter with her in all her joys and sorrows. . . . Her impulses, her surprises, her fits of merriment, her overwhelming sorrows, her pride, her indignation" were conveyed "with electric rapidity and force. . . . Her ringing laughter might well be set to music, . . . her pathos is the very poetry of sorrow, and her quaint, girlish humor fairly sparkles with sunshine. In action she is as graceful and light as a fawn, and her free, wild energy gives one a sense of liberty which is absolutely exhilarating."[30]

Still, she wrestled with dependence on local companies. For the next month, Lowell and Simmonds again provided her with a viable stopgap as she completed a round of their New England theaters. Their leading man, Charles Vandenhoff, Maggie's Romeo in Washington in 1867, had matured into a capable leading man, deftly handling Landry, William, and Pierrot. (For now, there was no more *Lorle*.) In New Haven, Hartford, Springfield, Worcester, Lowell, Providence, Newport, Woonsocket, Brooklyn, Syracuse, and back to Hartford and New Haven, they drew sold-out, often overflowing houses, some nights bringing in $800–$1,000. But at season's end, Vandenhoff left for England, sending Maggie back to the drawing board for an acting partner.[31]

It had been a grueling season, or so Paddock believed. Simultaneously concerned for his wife's well-being and holding the opinion that a respectable married woman should quit the stage, he wrote on May 5 from New York to a Boston manager who offered an engagement for June, "Maggie desires me to say that she has had a very long and arduous season and had concluded not to play after the next week. She feels that the rest and quiet will be more valuable to her than any engagement." She would find this in Long Branch, where her new cottage had just been completed. In Cleveland, Paddock's home town, a newspaper announced—likely prompted by Paddock—that "Maggie Mitchell promises to quit the stage after the present season." Other papers across the country picked up the item, along with hints that Maggie might again be pregnant.[32]

These rumors proved unfounded and, contrary to Paddock's wishes, by October 3 she was back touring Lowell and Simmonds' New York–New England circuit. Each stop, only a few days each, consisted of the same repertoire: one night each of *Fanchon*, *Barefoot*, and/or *Pearl*, and sometimes *Lorle*, still with its tragic ending. Congruent with a widespread trend in American Theatre, Maggie no longer enacted a farce before or after her main pieces. Lowell and Simmonds this time provided her with a twenty-five-member supporting company, all generally well-received. Of course, in these towns, Maggie would be well received, as one newspaper pointed out, "whether she is supported by sticks or flesh and blood." More full-to-overflowing houses attended in Elmira, Rochester, Auburn, Syracuse, Utica, Springfield, Worcester, Lowell, Taunton, Newport, Providence, Hartford, and New Haven. There were no complaints of *Fanchon* being shopworn, but occasionally a reviewer wished *Lorle* had a happier ending. Of this Maggie took note.

By sending this company out with her, Lowell and Simmonds were at the forefront of another significant trend in American Theatre: the birth of "combination companies." These were pre-packaged touring productions with full casts, scenery, costumes, and props—the precursors of today's road companies of Broadway shows. Freeing touring stars from their dependence on local stock companies—which after the financial panic of 1873 would become too expensive to maintain—"combinations" proliferated along with the nation's burgeoning rail network. By the end of the decade, nearly no stock companies would exist, as hundreds of combination companies moved from town to town. This innovation had many putative fathers, among them Joseph Jefferson and Dion Boucicault, but Lowell and Simmonds can assert a rightful claim.

In Chicago, in early November Maggie enjoyed the excellent facility, stage equipment and supporting company afforded by McVicker's Theatre, tragically for the last time. In its fourteen-year existence, she was one of its most frequent stars (nine long engagements, four more than even Edwin Booth). One of the most generous, well-liked citizens of Chicago, McVicker invested considerable funds over the years to maintain his theater's reputation, only to lose it all in the Great Chicago Fire of October 1871.

But Maggie's final engagement there engendered one of the final workhorses of her career. Perhaps prompted by critics calling for her to try something new, on November 18 she brought out Clifton Tayleure's dramatization of Charlotte Brontë's *Jane Eyre*. He had submitted it to Maggie some months before, but she had set it aside, aware of poorly received productions of it under Hamblin at the Bowery in 1849 with Kate Wemyss in the title role and an attempt by Laura Keene to make a go of it at her theater seven years later. These had used an adaptation by John Brougham, which plodded along, telling nearly every twist of the complex, compelling story of a mistreated orphan who evolves into a poised, erudite governess for a Byronic squire named Rochester, with whom she becomes emotionally entangled.

In the interim, Tayleure had awarded temporary rights to his version to German tragedienne Marie Seebach, who would be performing it at Crosby's Opera House in Chicago the same week as Maggie's opening at McVicker's. Maggie had tried unsuccessfully to obtain a copy of Brougham's script and now took up Tayleure's anew. Although she had misgivings over the liberties he took with Brontë's beloved text, she secured rights from him and launched McVicker's company into a week of rehearsals, simultaneously re-reading Brontë's novel for insight to Jane.[33]

Tayleure's version compressed the novel's early narrative of Jane's misery at the hands of her aunt Mrs. Reed and cousin Georgiana into Act One. Her time as an orphan in the asylum of the sanctimonious Professor Blackhorst, and then as an assistant teacher there, comprise Act Two. Deprived by Blackhorst and Reed of her rightful inheritance, she is hired as a governess at Thornfield Hall in Act Three. She finds herself falling in love with its master, Rochester, in Act Four, which ends dramatically with her rescuing him from perishing in a fire set by a madwoman (changed for morality's sake from Rochester's wife to his sister-in-law). In Act Five, Jane is restored to her rightful inheritance and her place by Rochester's side.

Rochester in Tayleure's hands became less churlish. The sensational aspects of young Jane's suffering and Rochester's backstory, along with any expendable characters and subplots, were dispensed with. This, however, made for implausible moments and relationships: "The love passages between the faithful, clinging heart of the orphan girl and the grim misanthrope [Rochester] are intensely thrilling, but are not representative of anything we see in real life." Also, the exposition was awkwardly inserted: "The manner in which Rochester and Jane Eyre stop to talk over family secrets while the flames are bursting through the chamber door was a sad blow to dramatic [plausibility]." At bottom, though, Maggie hoped the script would allow her to escape the hoydenish roles she had trapped herself in.[34]

She achieved her goal. The new role "was a grand success," "characterized by much more dignity, . . . more dramatic power and effectiveness and less eccentricity" than her other parts. Finding Jane, she finally laid to rest her dreams of fame as Juliet. For the rest of the season and nearly a decade more, she would play *Jane Eyre* as often as *Fanchon*, *Barefoot*, or *Pearl*.[35]

Unwilling to chance a poorly prepared *Jane Eyre* at her next stop, Ben DeBar's Theatre in St. Louis, she rehearsed it thoroughly while performing her other mainstays, bringing it out only at her last matinee. She then took *Jane Eyre*, with DeBar's company, to his St. Charles Theatre in New Orleans. Major stars were inching back into the area, but there was little money to be made in the postwar South. Leading members of DeBar's company were Mary and John Albaugh, guaranteeing Maggie strong support when she opened on December 5 (e.g., enacting Fadet and Landry to her Fanchon, and Albaugh as Rochester to her Jane Eyre). Except for *Fanchon*, her repertoire was new to Crescent City theatergoers and reviewers, and most responded with fervor. She had "lost none of her winsome grace, and her fair face looks just as fresh and girlish as when she charmed us all five years ago," able to "make an audience for the time being forget that it is the unreal rather than the reality that is being presented."[36]

Through three weeks of evenings, matinees, and even a Sunday evening performance against Maggie's preference, *Fanchon*, *Barefoot*, *Pearl*, and *Jane Eyre* went down well, although audiences diminished as the days went on, due in part to wretched weather, in part to postwar poverty and part to her switch to other scripts. *Lorle* seemed fine—for four of its five acts. The problem, still, was that the title character was too well-loved and admired to meet a tragic end, and an audience which has empathized with her valiant attempts to fit into high society "sinks in sorrow when she is made to die from a broken heart." During Maggie's last week, she became "disheartened night after night by the silence of vacant chairs." She never returned to New Orleans, which had brought her such happiness and success before the war.[37]

She then detoured with DeBar's company to Montgomery, Alabama, like New Orleans her first return since the war. Keene had scheduled an engagement there, but running out of funds to pay her actors had abruptly terminated it after one night, Christmas Eve. So, either out of loyalty to Keene or the citizens of Montgomery, Maggie took her place for the holiday week. No paper reviewed her.

1871 began for her in St. Louis, followed by Wood's Theatre in Cincinnati and Ford's Holliday Street Theatre in Baltimore in February, all to sold-out houses. One matinee of *Fanchon* in Baltimore was so crowded that the orchestra had to relinquish their chairs and play from the wings. Even *Lorle* was well received, although *Jane Eyre* eclipsed everything else, eliciting wild, prolonged applause. It "ought to become as popular on the stage as the novel is with all who admire steadiness, devotion and solidity in feminine character, joined to the tenderest of womanly qualities."[38]

This paean to womanly virtues rebutted the sermon that winter in Baltimore by Baptist Rev. Dr. Richard Fuller, who decried "with horror and loathing" the evils of attending the theater, "the cheap resort of the low, the vicious and debauched, [which] ought to make any modest woman feel it impossible to be present." Its "snares . . . are most ruinous." The *Sun* rebutted him: "the most complete answer to Dr. Fuller's theatrical sermon would be Maggie Mitchell's *Fanchon*, . . . a young woman of spotless life" in a "drama of humanity with teachings of the purest practical Christianity." Another paper agreed; the play served not only to increase the public's admiration of Maggie's acting, "but to elevate her character publicly and privately." Equally ardent in defending actors was the Rev. J. F. W. Ware, whose brochure, "May I Go to the Theatre?" that year sold over 10,000 copies. Unbeknownst to him, when he spoke approvingly on that topic in Baltimore's Masonic Temple on February 7, extolling Maggie specifically as "one of the bright and pure lights of the dramatic profession," she was among the congregation.[39]

Out of respect for Ford, Maggie agreed to perform for one night a dramatization by his eldest daughter, Annie (who had clipped Booth's locks for her) of the English translation of a German novelette by Elsie Marlitt (pseudonym of Eugenie John). *Over Yonder* provided Maggie with nothing new. Her character was a precocious, prankish, inquisitive girl who, upon being told to remain inside the garden hedge and never go "over yonder" because the owner of the neighboring estate is engaged in a feud with the girl's aunt, promptly does just that. Her adventurous spirit leads her to meet the estate's squire, the notorious Blue Beard, who is intimidating but ultimately rather enchanting. No one reviewed the production, Ford never published it, and Maggie never repeated it.

Pocketing $5,000 from her Baltimore engagement, she returned in March to Troy. At Wilton and Mitchell's Opera house, *Fanchon* attracted full houses so attentive "that you could hear a pin drop." Her character "is always the child—at heart innocent, girlish, pure and strong." In Buffalo, it hardly mattered that her Jane Eyre was "scarcely the Jane of Charlotte Brontë." It was Maggie they loved and Maggie they flocked to see.[40]

She spent the final five weeks of her 1870–71 season touring New England with a combination combined company of twenty-four assembled by Lowell and Simmonds. Among them, she finally gained a competent, trusted leading man. Thirty-one-year-old William Harris was a New York native and former Union Army captain wounded in 1864 in West Virginia, who had been acting in Brooklyn with Albaugh, who may have recommended him now. Also among the company were Maggie's sisters Emma, 30, and Sarah, 26, both seemingly content to carry small roles. It had been some time since the sisters had acted together.

Dropping *Lorle*, the company performed *Fanchon*, *Barefoot*, *Pearl*, or *Jane Eyre* in Lowell and Simmonds' theaters in Rochester, Auburn, Syracuse, Utica, Albany, Springfield, Worcester, Lowell, Portland, Salem, Newport, Providence, and Hartford, plus three new towns in Connecticut: Ansonia, Waterbury, and Bridgeport. The house was always crowded and reviewers for the most part sympathetic except regarding the mediocrity of the supporting company. Sarah, in particular, seemed ill-suited to acting (Maggie's repeated sympathetic hiring of her and her never marrying suggest some deficiency of mind or talent, in addition to being the least attractive sibling).

It had been a grueling, yet lucrative, tour—Springfield and Worcester alone yielded Maggie $9,000—bringing to a close her twentieth year of performing. Now, four months pregnant, she retired for the summer to Long Branch.

NOTES

1. *Memphis Daily Appeal*, Sept. 27, 1867. Maggie also expressed concerns about her name being exploited. One or two newspapers reported erroneously that it was Maggie to whom Hendershott had been engaged.

2. Passport files, National Archives and Records Administration.

3. Joseph Dodson Greenhalgh, *Memoranda of the Greenhalgh Family*, Bolton, UK: T. Abbatt's Machine Printing Works, 1869, 27–28.

4. *The Capital* (Washington), Nov. 8, 1874; *Charleston Mercury*, Feb. 13, 1868; *New York Herald*, Jan. 26, 1868 and May 26, 1869.

5. It is unclear whether or not Anna traveled with Maggie this season; they may have depended on Collier for her protection.

6. (Washington) *National Intelligencer*, Nov. 30, 1867.

7. *Cincinnati Gazette*, Dec. 4, 1867.

8. *Turf, Field and Farm*, Feb. 1, 1868.

9. *Ibid.*; Winter for *New York Tribune* reprinted in *Sacramento Daily Union*, Feb. 25, 1868; "What the Theatres Are Doing," *Watson's Art Journal*, vol. 8 (Feb. 15, 1868): 230.

10. *New York Clipper*, June 13, 1868; New York correspondent for *Marysville (CA) Daily Appeal*, Mar. 15, 1868.

11. *Lorle* also became an 1891 opera by Alban Förster and Hans Heinrich Schefsky.

12. *Kansas City Times*, Jan. 22, 1886; *Baltimore Sun*, Apr. 10, 1868.

13. *Chicago Tribune*, Apr. 16, 1868; *Chicago Republican*, Apr. 14, 1868.

14. Esther Crain, *The Gilded Age in New York, 1870–1910*, New York: Black Dog & Levanthal, 2016, 35–44, 78–81.

15. *New York Post*, Sept. 1, 1868.

16. *Hartford Courant*, Oct. 5, 1868.

17. It would be another twenty years before Paddock learned of Maggie's momentary marriage during the war. He never spoke publicly about Maggie's close relationship with John Wilkes Booth.

18. (Washington) *The Critic*, Nov. 18, 1868; *Turf, Field and Farm*, Nov. 27, 1868.

19. MM interview with Cincinnati correspondent, *Louisville Courier-Journal*, Sept. 28, 1881.

20. Paddock interview, *Syracuse Standard*, May 22, 1887.

21. *New York Herald*, June 9, 1869.

22. Sharon Hazard, *Long Branch in the Golden Age*, Charleston, SC: The History Press, 2007, 25.

23. *Brooklyn Eagle*, July 10, 1881.

24. *Harvard Advocate*, Oct. 29, 1869.

25. *Boston Traveller* [sic], Nov. 30, 1869; *Boston Journal*, Nov. 22, 1869; *New York Tribune*, Dec. 11, 1869.

26. *Boston Advertiser*, Nov. 30, 1869.

27. MM interview, *Cincinnati Sun*, reprinted in *Boston Weekly Globe*, Jan. 8, 1879; *Oakland* (CA) *Tribune*, Mar. 21, 1885; *New York Sun*, Sept. 27, 1891.

28. *Cincinnati Gazette*, Feb. 3, 1870.

29. *Pittsburgh Weekly Gazette*, Feb. 9, 1870.

30. *Buffalo Courier*, Apr. 5, 1870.

31. *Ibid.*, Apr. 9, 1870.

32. HTP to R. M. Field, manager of the Boston Museum, HTP Papers, HTC; *Cleveland Plain Dealer*, July 12, 1870.

33. Seebach's repertoire also included an apparently unauthorized *Fanchon*.

34. Holden 317–18; *Fort Wayne (IN) Sentinel*, Nov. 25, 1874; *Hartford Courant*, Sept. 26, 1874; *New York Times*, Nov. 17, 1885.

35. *Chicago Tribune*, Nov. 19, 1870; *Chicago Journal*, reprinted in *New Orleans Times-Picayune*, Dec. 1, 1870.

36. *New Orleans Times-Picayune*, Dec. 7, 1870; *New Orleans Republican*, Dec. 17, 1870.

37. *New Orleans Republican*, Dec. 22, 1870 and Mar. 15, 1872.

38. *Baltimore Sun*, Feb. 17, 1871.

39. *Baltimore Sun*, Jan. 23 and Feb. 6 and 7, 1871; *New York Herald*, Mar. 10, 1871; Unidentified Baltimore clipping, Feb. 17, 1871, in Crawford Collection, Box 338, Yale University Library.

40. *Troy Whig*, Mar. 7, 1871; *Buffalo Courier*, Mar. 18, 1871.

Maggie Mitchell c. 1852
Credit line: Harvard Theatre Collection, Houghton Library

Anna Mitchell c. 1855 by Black and Case (Boston, MA)
Credit line: Museum of the City of New York, gift of Miss E. H. Fairman, 1933 33.152.2

Maggie Mitchell as Fanchon, by Gurney, c. 1861
Credit line: Author's collection

Maggie Mitchell c. 1868
Credit line: New York Public Library

Maggie Mitchell as Little Barefoot
Credit line: Harry Ransom Center, University of Texas at Austin

Maggie Mitchell as Pearl of Savoy
Credit line: Author's Collection

Maggie Mitchell c. 1875
Credit line: Author's Collection

Maggie Mitchell as Jane Eyre
Credit line: Harry Ransom Center, University of Texas at Austin

Maggie Mitchell by Sarony, c. 1885
Credit line: New York Public Library

St. Andoche Apartment Building, 855 West End Ave., New York City
Credit line: Photo by Author

Medallion of Fanchon/St. Andoche
Credit line: Photo by Caitlin Hawke

Headstone (sans birthdate) of Maggie Mitchell, Green-Wood Cemetery, Brooklyn
Credit line: **Photo by Author**

Chapter 9

California and "Cricket Lodge"

Finally, Maggie could afford to breathe, although her tireless work ethic would not allow it to be for long. From their cottage on Cedar Avenue that summer of 1871, the Paddock family—soon to be larger—rode out regularly in one of their four carriages, pulled by one of their three horses, up and down Ocean Drive, admiring the sumptuous hotels that had sprung up. If they needed to return to New York, they took the steamer from Sandy Hook.

Several offers arrived for the coming season. Edwin Booth proposed a run of eight weeks of *Jane Eyre* at his New York theater, which Maggie declined. John T. Ford had a more lucrative idea: he would pay Maggie $200 a night (about $4,000 today) to tour for one hundred nights to major northeast cities with a limited repertoire. She would be supported by a partial combination company drawn from his Baltimore stock company in a limited number of scripts: *Fanchon*, *Barefoot*, *Pearl*, and *Jane Eyre*, with *Jane Eyre* prominent. They would perform in theaters Ford had leased, and he would reap all box office funds and cover all costs. Maggie trusted him and so signed on for fall.

On October 4 in her Long Branch home, she delivered Henry M. Paddock (not Jr.), to be known as "Harry," this time experiencing an uncomplicated delivery. Within the week their joy was tempered by news from Chicago of the utter destruction of that city by fire, including the theater of their friend and Long Branch neighbor, James McVicker. Maggie immediately donated $500 to relieve sufferers in their profession there and followed it with $10,000 to help McVicker rebuild his theater.

Maggie's husband opposed her continuing to act, announcing that "Maggie thinks this is not just the kind of life now, and she sighs for the tranquility of domestic peace. She has been many years on the stage and she thinks our children ought to have more of her." But Maggie disagreed and motherhood never slowed her down.[1]

By the end of October, she was able to rehearse with Ford's new company. Playing romantic leads opposite her would be thirty-eight-year-old L. R. (Linington Roberts) Shewell, known as "Len." He was matinee-idol handsome long before that appellation was coined: tall, well-built, with thick dark hair topping a perfectly proportioned face with brooding dark eyes, a sensuous mouth, and full mustache. Her low comedian would be twenty-six-year-old Harry S. Murdoch, nephew of James Murdoch. Old women and men would be played by Lizzie Anderson and W. M. (William Melmoth) Ward. Important supporting roles would be covered by Mr. and Mrs. Fred Williams (he also as stage manager), Harry B. Hudson, Jane Germon, Effie Warren, and Jenny Anderson, who specialized in young, beautiful, scheming vixens who squared off against Maggie's characters.

They opened on November 6 in Philadelphia at the Academy of Music with *Jane Eyre*, with Shewell embodying Rochester better than anyone had so far. In *Fanchon*, he was rather mature for Landry but carried it off and good houses resulted. Next, they appeared in Ford's lavish new Grand Opera House in Baltimore.

Annie Ford had penned another dramatization, which Maggie's group performed for the first time anywhere on December 4. Annie based *Fay; or, the Old Mam'selle's Secret* on an 1868 translation by Annis Lee Wister from another novel by Elsie Marlitt. Original music was added by J. H. Rosewald, who had written *Lorle*. Maggie played the titular character, another orphan, and the offspring of an actress killed by an errant onstage gunshot. A kindly old man takes her in, then dies, leaving her to the care of his haughty scholar son, Professor Hellwig (Shewell), whose shrewish mother and cousin make Fay's life miserable (The parallels to *Jane Eyre* were inescapable). Cast out again, Fay is sheltered and nurtured by the religious "Old Mam'selle" (Fadet redux). When she, too, dies, Hellwig comes to repent of his neglect of Fay and longs for her affection. Meanwhile, Fay has discovered a secret trove of papers left by Old Mam'selle and obtains them via a harrowing rooftop crossing. These predictably expose the embezzlement practiced by generations of Hellwigs, for which the repentant professor atones, winning the heart of the now-mature Fay, another sophisticated young woman who never complained of her fate.

As critics noted, this was another "wretched child," another "forlorn orphan, . . . pure, pious and plucky, patient, persistent and indomitable, controlling the situation by sheer dint of her own virtuous desperation, butting against appalling calamities and wits-endy [sic] predicaments with the straightforward stubbornness of devoted destitution, and organizing victory [with] triumphant virtue." "Miss Maggie Fanchon Barefoot Mitchell" was thus the definitive stage orphan, "compared with which the afflictions of all other parentless waifs are positive comforts." This time, though, there was no

Fanchon-ish "run-mad hair, . . . no jigs nor romps nor lovely rowdiness, but grim purpose and tooth-and-nail fight from first to last."[2]

Maggie ended the year in Cincinnati at Ford's leased Pike's Opera House, where she exemplified "simplicity of innocence and domestic love." Her supporting company held its own, especially Shewell, and audiences were appreciative but disappointingly small, partly due to inclement weather and nearby competition from the effervescent Lotta. Comparisons of the two actresses were increasing in papers across the country, but Lotta laughed them off. Reporters, she scoffed, "say such queer things. One of them the other day gravely compared me to Maggie Mitchell. The idea! . . . There can be no comparison between us. Why, Maggie's an artist, and I—well, I am myself, that's all. Maggie does beautiful things beautifully, and I—well, if I'm in pretty good spirits I do funny things." Some critics were dismissive: "Lotta, with all her entertaining piquancy, knows as much of Maggie's characters as a ploughboy does of philosophy. . . . Maggie Mitchell has a theatrical realm of her own, and in it her right to reign supreme is undisputed." But at thirty-five Maggie was tiring more easily. She fainted backstage at the close of her December 29 performance, forcing the cancellation of the next night's *Fay*. One critic felt that her age was showing: "We used to love Maggie, but she is too old now."[3]

Ahead lay another five weeks of touring under Ford's aegis, beginning 1872 in Louisville followed by smaller towns, including Toledo and the oil boomtown of Titusville in northwest Pennsylvania. John Ellsler's new opera house in Pittsburgh yielded full houses and glowing reviews. Even *Pearl*, now played less often, drew praise for Maggie's mad scene. Her Jane Eyre, despite Tayleure's adaptation, was deemed the truest to Brontë. The engagement was a tremendous financial and artistic success. There was "a witchery about the little woman that set at naught all canons of criticism." She was never "stilted, stiff or constrained. She has no stage grimaces or attitudes. She never rants."[4]

Next came Williamsport, Pennsylvania, and Wilmington, Delaware, where she drew moderate houses but mixed reviews, for example, "She can hardly be called a great actress; her warmest admirers must admit that neither her voice nor her elocution qualify her for [that], but in her own charming style she reigns without a peer." Maggie closed the tour in Washington with standing room only at the National Theatre, the box office averaging $1,200 a night. On February 5, she gave her final performance of *Fay*; her obligation to Ford fulfilled.[5]

Ford's actors returned to Baltimore, prompting Maggie to turn to B. F. Lowell to furnish new venues and a small combination company, which included James Collier, whose saloon had never gotten off the ground. From mid-February to late April they toured Lowell's Upstate New York–New England circuit, playing one or two nights each in Elmira, Rochester, Auburn,

Syracuse, Utica, Springfield, Lowell, Salem, Woonsocket, Worcester, Hartford, Bridgeport, New Haven, Providence, Meriden, Waterbury, Middletown, New Britain, and Portland. They drew fine, and in some cases excellent, houses and reviews, mainly with *Fanchon* and *Jane Eyre*. But by any measure, this was a grueling route. When Lowell reclaimed his actors, Maggie hired Boston favorite Joseph F. Wheelock for leads for an engagement at the Boston Theatre. Otherwise, she relied on the local company of manager Junius Brutus Booth, Jr., although this required time-consuming rehearsals.

Repeated rounds of New England enabled her to remain close to her family in New York but were doing nothing to further her professional reputation. She needed to expand into new areas of the country and in one, specifically, she was far behind the curve. California had spawned two homegrown stars, the infamous Lola Montez and her protégée Lotta Crabtree, who had staked the state out as their territory. Since professional theater first came to California amid Gold Rush fever, nearly every major star had performed in San Francisco to acclaim, along with some of Maggie's most persistent imitators. By the time she decided in 1872 to perform there, it was clear she would be an alien invader who would have to prove herself.

A significant advantage for her, now that the transcontinental railroad had been completed in 1869, was no longer having to endure a long voyage by steamer from New York to Panama, then an arduous trek across the isthmus, followed by another steamer up to San Francisco. In the decade following the Civil War, rail's greatest growth in history was well underway, particularly in the North, with route mileage rapidly doubling. (The wretched state of the postwar Southern rail network may well have been the primary cause of Maggie's eschewing performing there with any regularity for years.) When she embarked for California on May 13, her comfort was enhanced by traveling in the Director's Car of the Union Pacific Railroad express train, also carrying T. E. Sickles, General Superintendent of the line. Theirs was one of the first Pullman sleeping cars, with amenities unavailable to the average traveler. Still, the journey would take seventeen days.

For nearly a decade, newspapers had been speculating about a Maggie Mitchell tour to California, usually hinting about a sizable quantity of gold being her enticement. In the two decades since gold was discovered, San Francisco's population had exploded from under 1,000 to over 150,000, far outpacing any other American metropolis. Dozens of theaters had come and gone, most going up in flames. Theatrical conditions had not kept up with Eastern trends, however. Mediocre stock companies, with actors trapped in "lines of business" whether their age was appropriate or not, still abounded, and a few rudimentary scenery pieces served to identify myriad locations.

Much of this would change during the 1870s due to the efforts of another of Maggie's train companions, Lawrence Barrett. He and John McCullough in

1869 had opened the magnificent, state-of-the-art California Theatre on Bush Street, regarded as one of the finest theaters in the Union. But while Barrett would be performing there, Maggie was booked for four weeks at the déclassé Metropolitan Theatre, located in a less-savory part of town, its glory days behind it.

However, Manager E. G. Bert had been confident enough in Maggie's drawing power to agree to pay her half the gross receipts, with a guarantee of $2,500 a week (over $50,000 today) in gold. At first, she appeared worth the investment, opening on June 3 to a full house in *Fanchon*, well supported by the stock company leads, particularly W. J. Cogswell, her wartime Washington Landry. She "took the house by storm," hailed by "deafening shouts" from its notoriously raucous audiences when called before the curtain after each act. Despite theatergoers' familiarity with *Fanchon* from Maggie's imitators, "Her wonderfully vivid impersonation made it seem a new character." "There is so little appearance of art in her acting that one forgets to be critical at all." *Jane Eyre*, with Cogswell as Rochester, also went down well. Despite some critical quibbling about Tayleure's script, Maggie's performance remained true to Brontë. *Barefoot* and *Pearl*, too, were well received, but as the weeks passed, business ebbed.[6]

But Maggie had contracted shrewdly. When she left San Francisco at the end of June for Long Branch, she carried enough gold to purchase outright for $15,000 McVicker's slate-colored Elberon cottage, "Meerschaum Villa" near the southwest corner of Park Avenue and Deal Turnpike (now Norwood Avenue) and rename it "Cricket Lodge." Erecting twin stone pillars at the estate's entrance with the word "Cricket" on one and "Lodge" on the other, she ordered additions and placed nearly all of its twenty acres under cultivation. She could be seen throughout July and August "sitting on the veranda with her quiet husband, baby Harry swinging in the hammock under the trees, and little Fanchon rollicking over the grass." She had not lost her love of horses and was a frequent sight on the beach driving a Shetland pony harnessed to a "basket" phaeton. The pony, observed a visitor, "sometimes follows her into the house and won't go out until he has been fed with cake." She also purchased the twelve-year-old turf champion Aldebaran, "and will amble him up and down the beach at Long Branch." It was a welcome, idyllic life compared to the rigors of touring.[7]

The 1872–73 season would be as rigorous as any. Again, she focused on New England and the Midwest. Lowell was now partnered with Mat Canning, the erstwhile Montgomery manager. With Maggie, they assembled a decent supporting company, whose centerpiece was again Shewell. Maggie's sister Sarah joined, playing minor roles. They would perform the same repertoire as that of the past two years. They opened on September 23 in New Haven to a box office of $1,500, with Maggie as celebrated as ever. Then it was on to Hartford, Providence, Manchester, Salem, Lowell, Worcester, Albany, Rochester, Auburn, finally disbanding in Syracuse.

But it was time for Maggie to re-cultivate her following in the Midwest. Bringing only Shewell, she headed for Chicago, where McVicker's Theatre had risen from the ashes. Except for the addition of a striking new chandelier and seating 1,800 instead of 1,400, it was essentially the same venue. McVicker's stock company, though, was weaker than those he had proudly assembled in previous seasons, which perturbed the perfectionist Maggie. To gain the necessary time to rehearse other pieces, she opened on October 28 with a solid week of *Jane Eyre*, with Shewell as Rochester. As much as Maggie would have liked her appearance to swell the coffers of her friend McVicker, their timing was bad. No sooner had she opened for him than a citywide outbreak of Equine Influenza sharply curtailed theater attendance. After a week of such houses, some of the worst of her career, she switched to *Pearl*, to no avail. Only in her final week did attendance pick up again, for *Jane Eyre* and *Barefoot*, but it was too late. McVicker lost $9,000 on the venture.

Maggie's husband began taking a more immediate interest in her career. He joined her and Shewell in Chicago as they headed for Louisville and then St. Joseph, Missouri, where on December 9 she inaugurated Milton Tootle's superb new $200,000 Grand Opera House with *Fanchon*. Paid $2,000 for one week by manager John A. Stevens, she played to full-to-overflowing, fashionable houses swelled by special trains from surrounding towns—a pleasant change from Chicago. For her benefit night's *Pearl*, 1,600 people crammed into the opera house's 1,500-seat capacity. The range of her acting impressed St. Joseph reviewers, admittedly not as cosmopolitan as those in large cities. In *Fanchon*, "it is almost impossible for one to believe that she is a grown woman, so perfectly does she play the mischievous hoyden." In *Jane Eyre*, she exhibited the "flashes of noble and womanly nature of Miss Bronte's heroine." Columnists treated her like a celebrity, reporting on her comings and goings, her appearance, even her shopping habits.[8]

Stevens, only 29, was the manager at her next two stops as well, having created the "Great Western Star Circuit" to bring stars like Maggie to St. Joseph, Kansas City, Leavenworth, and Omaha. Like Lowell in New England, he developed a hybrid stock-combination company, based in Kansas City, to tour the circuit in support of the stars performing in his theaters. His venue in Kansas City was the two-year-old Coates Opera House, where Maggie and Shewell opened with Stevens' company on December 16, with a one-night detour to Leavenworth. One of the best-equipped opera houses in the West, the Coates seated 1,200–1,600 depending on seating configuration. Although Kansas City had enjoyed rudimentary professional theater since 1858, it was only with the opening of the Coates, under its first manager, Charles E.

Pope—Maggie's original Landry—and now Stevens, that stars of the magnitude of Booth, Barrett, Forrest, and the irrepressible Lotta visited. (Lotta in March despite a massive snowstorm had broken all box office records for the city.) Maggie could well have heard of the money to make on this circuit from Pope or Booth or Barrett, or may simply have been motivated to top Lotta.[9]

Advance sales in Kansas City suggested she might: three hundred tickets were presold for her opening. There, and in Leavenworth, theatergoers and critics could not get enough of her. No one else "will be remembered longer, nor receive more praise." She conveyed "almost every phase of passion, and so successfully as to carry her audience by storm." Standouts among the company were Stevens himself in comic roles like Pierrot; Marion P. Clifton, 39, who would play old women roles for Maggie for another sixteen years; and Alice Gray, also 39, a Ford protégée still playing soubrettes. Offstage, Maggie and Gray may have shared memories of John Wilkes Booth, Gray having also been a warm personal friend of the actor-assassin.[10]

The next stage of Maggie's itinerary was atypical in its complexity. It took four days of travel, changing trains four times, waiting thirty hours in a freezing, barren train station (making a fire there and trying to sleep), and finally hiring a boat to cross the ice-congested Mississippi River, reaching Memphis just in time to perform *Jane Eyre* on December 26 in Stevens and DeBar's new opera house, supported by DeBar's St. Louis stock company, already there.

Shewell, though, had been gorging himself over the past few months. Obese and well on his way to his three hundred pounds at death, on the cusp of forty he was no longer suitable for any romantic leads except Rochester, and even that was a mismatch. Landry and William Peace were out of the question. Maggie demoted him to Father Barbeaud and Farmer Peace and in Memphis used William Harris, down from St. Louis, in his former leading roles.

Working against Maggie in Memphis was the recent engagement at the opera house of Charlotte Thompson in some of Maggie's roles, notably *Jane Eyre*. Suffering from a severe cold and still somewhat unnerved by her journey, with an inadequately rehearsed company, Maggie failed to please critics, who found her "snappish and exaggerated." They declared her untrue to Brontë, unable to step into Jane's adult elegance, having for "so long been identified with the lighter and more juvenile characters." Amid unseasonably cold weather, houses remained half empty. But *Fanchon*, *Barefoot*, and *Pearl* turned things around. In these Maggie exhibited a remarkable "freshness, beauty and naturalness." It was "impossible to resist the histrionic power of the fair actress."[11]

She was scheduled to open January 6, 1873, in St. Louis for DeBar, but was again beset by the curse of winter travel. She and DeBar's company were delayed five hours, the last hour of which the St. Louis audience patiently waited in their seats. With no rehearsal necessary, and the scenery hurriedly placed, the actors quickly donned costumes and plunged into *Fanchon*.

While in St. Louis Maggie found time to grant a lengthy interview to a reporter, who found her enchanting, her beauty "heightened by the great charm of more matured, graceful and easy manners." He admired her "beautiful and naturally blonde hair combed back [from a] face still youthful and remarkably pretty" and "her dress remarkable for the absence of a load of flashy jewelry." At this point in her career, she said, she strove to project a more settled image. As successful as *Fanchon* had been, she hoped with *Jane Eyre* "to achieve a lasting and enduring reputation [which rests] upon a surer foundation than a mere capacity to exhibit light, thoughtless and vivacious characters."[12]

Critics admired her evolution. Until now she had been perceived only as "a wild, elfish young girl [of] shadow dances, unlaced shoes and the like." But "the struggles of a girl, though often affecting, fail to excite the intense interest attendant upon the portrayal of a woman's wrongs." Her *Jane Eyre* "set all fears at rest and has established her in the higher ranks of her difficult profession. In that play she rises completely above her every other effort." "We see the self-disciplined, strong-willed woman, resolute in her duty, self-sacrificing, retiring, and with a world of tenderness and a love so strong in its devotion as to win the hardest of hearts." When Rochester proposes marriage, "she displays an emotion and quiet power rarely seen on the stage, the struggle between pride and love, the joyous cry of an overflowing heart."[13]

Some critics, though, thought Thompson, not yet thirty, ironically brought greater maturity to the role. Their two Janes "are poles apart in both conception and artistic merit." Maggie "presents a Jane Eyre of flighty, flippant emotions that seem to go up like a rocket and come down like a stick. Not a tone, a glance, a gesture, ever indicates that years of persecution have curbed the fresh and generous aspirations of a high and independent girlhood." Thompson, on the other hand, "indicates by the drooping of her head and constant timidity in the presence of Rochester that persecution has subdued much of her independence, and when some thrust made at her dignity and womanhood is haughtily resented, these outbursts seem like the sudden uprising of a noble nature."[14]

As she traveled, Maggie continually perused new plays offered to her, most of which she found disappointing. She wanted more inspiring material and regretted the deterioration of the moral tone of American theater. She understood that during the war people had sought diversion in lighthearted comedy and escapist spectacle, but it was time to move away from that. "I have always felt that the stage had a noble mission to accomplish," she said. While "managers are compelled to meet the requirements of the popular taste," she preferred to "appear in purely legitimate and moral plays." But "so long as the popular taste remains unchanged, actors are well-nigh, if not totally, powerless."[15]

Seeing herself as "a hard student both of authors and human nature," Maggie was "by no means satisfied with what I have yet accomplished." When "defects, or even blemishes, have been pointed out and made clear to my comprehension, I have earnestly striven to remove them. . . . I court criticism as an efficient aid to improvement, but I never seek for mere 'puffs.'" Acclamatory blurbs were appearing regularly, however, in cities in which Maggie would shortly appear, an indication that her new advance man, Thomas W. Brown, was doing his job.[16]

With Harris committed to DeBar, except for Shewell Maggie again had to rely on stock companies. John Ellsler managed her next two stops, Cleveland and Pittsburgh, rotating his actors between them. But lately, he had fallen on hard times, and attendance had dropped off despite such pandering productions as *Buffalo Bill, King of the Border Men*. For over a year rued the *Cleveland Plain Dealer*, managers of combination companies "tell us that this city is becoming the poorest 'show town' on their routes." Moreover, Ellsler had just lost to McVicker his most promising leading man, James O'Neill, with whom Maggie would act when she got to Chicago, and who would father arguably the greatest American playwright of the twentieth century.[17]

Back in Cleveland for the first time in over eight years, Maggie—likely holding her breath—gave leads, including Landry, back to Shewell and performed with Ellsler's company. They drew good houses, Shewell was well received, and reviewers, who considered Maggie something of an adopted Clevelander, favored her: "Time seems to have passed her by or at least to have touched her with a gentle hand." Her *Fanchon* "may be imitated but not equaled."[18]

She must have hoped that theatergoers shared that belief, for she was succeeded in Cleveland by Thompson, who in June would gain considerable recognition in New York for her *Jane Eyre*. Katie Putnam, too, was circling, her *Fanchon* often referred to as equaling or surpassing Maggie's (although Maggie consistently outdrew her by far). Only twenty years old, but with sixteen of them on stage, Putnam "reminds us of Maggie Mitchell years ago, but is more natural than Maggie Mitchell ever was." Soon the *New York Clipper* would be describing the "Maggie Mitchell, Lotta, Katie Putnam school of drama."[19]

When Maggie, Shewell, and parts of Ellsler's stock company moved on to Pittsburgh, Ellsler came along, leaving his wife in charge in Cleveland. Despite the relatively short distance, the troupe was stranded for hours by a train accident, keeping the audience on February 3 at Ellsler's Pittsburgh Opera House waiting for over an hour. But they enthusiastically received

Jane Eyre, then also *Pearl* and *Fanchon* (with Ellsler as Barbeaud). A good measure of Maggie's believability came at the close of one night's *Jane Eyre* when a trio of rubes complained they had been cheated, for they "came for nothing else but to see Miss Mitchell" and she never appeared. Informed of their error, they exclaimed, "What!? That little thing that had so much to say?"[20]

Maggie finished the winter in Baltimore at Ford's Grand Opera House and in Boston for Junius Booth. With Shewell in mature roles like Rochester, Lonstalot, and Barbeaud, she received strong support from both stock companies and drew well. In the latter venue, as many as 3,000 patrons attended nightly for *Fanchon*, *The Pearl of Savoy*, and *Little Barefoot*, with hundreds turned away at the door. This seemed "pretty good evidence that the public is not tired of witnessing these pieces." Box office receipts for her two weeks totaled $27,000 (four times that of any other Boston theater, $5,648 of it from three matinees), of which she brought away $5,000. Although Shewell would see the season out with her, he found his truer calling in management, agreeing to take over the Boston Theatre in fall when Booth went to New York to try to revive the failing fortunes of his brother Edwin's theater.[21]

Ending her season with a swing through New England, New York, and Pennsylvania, Maggie depended not on Lowell for arrangements, but on a little-known Hartford printer, Alexander L. Calhoun, previously a real estate agent, who in the future would graduate to managing the tours of Lawrence Barrett and various opera stars. Maggie entrusted the details to Calhoun and her husband, with unfortunate consequences by the end of the decade.

For six weeks, she appeared for a night or two each in second- and third-tier venues in a bewildering array of towns: Hartford, Providence, Salem, Lowell, Pittsfield, Troy, Syracuse, Auburn, Harrisburg, Scranton, Reading, Wilmington, Trenton, Middletown, Hartford again, New Haven, and Bridgeport. Six hundred dollars counted on some nights like a good house. She took with her a modest, competent company, buoyed by the return from DeBar of Harris in younger leads. At thirty-three, he remained boyish enough to pull these off, and Maggie's diminutive stature not only allowed her at thirty-six to do likewise but to continue doing so for another twenty years. A reviewer every now and then would question the appropriateness of this as she entered middle age, but no one much listened. Universally a favorite, she "seems to please everybody, and at a second appearance anywhere always attracts a larger audience than on a first visit."[22]

Exhausted, she retired in June to her Long Branch farm and drives with her husband and children along the beach in a carriage drawn now by two spirited chestnut horses. On July 12 the Paddocks hosted the first of many annual lawn parties, this time celebrating their fifth anniversary

For two years announcements had surfaced in New York papers of an impending Maggie Mitchell restaging of *Fanchon* at Booth's, none of which had come to fruition until now. But just as rehearsals got underway at the end of September 1873, the nation convulsed with a financial panic that would take nearly a decade to ease. Credit and discretionary funds evaporated and banks collapsed, taking countless businesses, including theaters, with them. Despite his brother's astute management as he frantically toured the country, Edwin Booth was about to lose his theater—the very one into which Maggie was booked. A half-million dollars in debt, he would soon be bankrupt.

Nevertheless, Maggie took the stage there on October 6, the night of a drenching rainstorm, as Fanchon in front of beautiful new scenery by T. B. Glessing and surrounded by a stock company that included several friends from her years of touring. As Landry, she brought in James Collier, pushing forty, for their last long engagement together, and added her old friend Sam Glenn as Father Caillard. Mary Wells returned to the role of Fadet. All seemed poised for popular and critical success. But cautious audiences stayed away, and critics pounced on Maggie's "maudlin juvenility." Her performance was marred by over repetition of "certain violent motions of her body, laughing and crying." "She is not a great actress by nature, nor is she a great artist by cultivation. She does not thrill by the power of her acting." "Less of giggle, less of sob, less of nasal whine, less of the cricket's hop, and a total avoidance of grunting, would be satisfactory to good taste."[23]

Fanchon was simply another of "the singularly feeble pieces to which Maggie Mitchell has devoted her life." The stock company was "not a strong one under the most favorable circumstances," but Collier came off the worst. A "dreadful" actor whom Maggie continued to use only because he danced so well, he "has the stiffest method of reading, and no more sentiment than a sardine box. When he exclaims, 'Oh, Heaven! I shall go mad with joy!', he says it exactly as though he were remarking that there had been a rise in the price of butter."[24]

Staying close to home, Maggie then switched over to Brooklyn's newly reopened Park Theatre under A. R. Samuel, whose minimal management experience in this wretched economy pushed him into bankruptcy at the end of the season. Maggie, though, proved a boon to him, and the small audiences he had been experiencing swelled for her week, albeit with prices sharply reduced. His company supported her ably, led by the Landry of W. E. Sheridan, who had played the role for her at Niblo's. There was "a charm and an abandon about her acting," admitted the *Brooklyn Eagle*, "a naturalness, a childishness, a prettiness and a pathos that wins the heart of the sternest critic." With Maggie, "sympathies are won in spite of one's better judgment. This is the secret of Miss Mitchell's success. She has overridden the rules of art and the critics' prejudices."[25]

Just before leaving New York for Ford's Opera House in Baltimore, Maggie was saddened by the death in New York of an old friend, poet and *Knickerbocker* columnist James Linen. A bookbinder like Maggie's father, he had known her since her youth and had recently penned an ode to her that opened with the lines,

> Bonnie Maggie, young and fair!/Little fairy! jewel rare!/
> Virtue on her spotless throne/Proudly claims thee as her own/ . . .
> With thy witching charms of art/Thou canst thrill the human heart/
> Tame the passions strong and wild/Nature's sweet and wondrous child![26]

After Baltimore came the National Theatre in Washington, newly reopened after a devastating fire. Its furnishings were sumptuous and its equipment ultra-modern (including the use of electricity to ignite the gaslighting). Manager J. G. Saville had assembled a good stock company, although Maggie had brought Sheridan with her as insurance. On opening night, December 1, with President Grant and civic leader Alexander Robey "Boss" Shepherd applauding from a prominent box, *Fanchon* was a roaring success before a full house. For the rest of the week, even as artists put finishing touches on theater décor and scenery, *Fanchon* reigned. The second week, Maggie switched to *Pearl*, bringing down from Brooklyn a promising young soubrette she had spotted named Katie Mayhew to play Chouchon. Mayhew would, like several others, closely observe Maggie and then tour, proclaimed "the Maggie Mitchell of the future." As aware as she must have been of such comparisons, Maggie was buoyed by others that fall which asserted that she "looks no older, and is as girlish in spirits, as when she first began to climb the ladder of fame." *Barefoot*, with Saville as William, and *Jane Eyre*, filled out the engagement before Maggie headed to Wilmington.[27]

There, for unknown reasons she replaced Sheridan with Harris as Landry, Pierrot, William, and Rochester. Wilmington theaters, like those elsewhere, struggled mightily. Yet despite a severe rainstorm, the Grand Opera House was jammed half an hour before the curtain rose on Maggie. "Applause commenced the moment her voice was heard behind the scenes, and as she came through the window in pursuit of her chicken, it burst into a perfect storm."[28]

She closed out 1873 in Albany, supported by an uneven stock company, then headed to Troy. On January 12, 1874, she opened at the Academy of Music in Cleveland for Effie Ellsler. For some time both Effie and her husband in Pittsburgh had also been struggling to stay afloat; citizens of both places were "tired of amusements and turn out very slowly." The only star who still pulled them in was Cleveland native and Ellsler discovery Clara Morris. A teenage dancer supporting Maggie less than ten years ago, Morris was now, at twenty-six, an international "sensation star" famed for her unbridled tragic acting. Unfortunately for Maggie in Cleveland now, Morris was billed as the upcoming attraction, and theatergoers held back their funds.[29]

Maggie's travel to Pittsburgh was another troublesome sojourn. With no passenger trains running on Sunday and the company needing to arrive by Monday, she decided to take a late freight train. She, Paddock, Harris, and her maid took its caboose, with the other actors huddled in a freight car, as they made their slow way in pouring rain all night and well into Monday. And yet Maggie appeared that night "gifted with perennial youth, . . . as young and full of vitality now as we remember her to have been" twenty years before. "You feel her as you feel the air; she eludes you when you undertake to fix and fasten her."[30]

In Pittsburgh, absent the lure of Morris, Maggie raked it in. With Ellsler himself acting with her, she drew capacity houses all week—one of the most successful engagements ever known at his theater. For her final matinee of *Barefoot*, over 2,600 people, mostly ladies, crammed in, nearly every seat having been sold by 10:00 that morning, with hundreds turned away at the door. Many were repeat attendees. Why? "For the same reason that you saunter into the woods in June, that you read again a beloved poem or go twice to hear a singer sing the same sweet song, or are drawn again and again by the same work of art." Across generations, Maggie's fans remained reliably loyal.[31]

In St. Louis at DeBar's Grand Opera House, she found herself competing directly against Morris at the nearby Olympic Theatre and only drew moderate audiences. Initially scheduled to depart on February 15, yielding her place to the next star, she remained in St. Louis, idle (and doubtless calling on friends, including DeBar) through the 21st to perform *Fanchon* in a special benefit for its author, August Waldauer. The *St. Louis Democrat* questioned whether "a woman of forty [sic: 37]" should continue to play Fanchon, a girl of sixteen, "but she does so acceptably" and audiences love it, so "nobody else has cause to complain."[32]

Harris now accepted an offer from Ford to become a leading man and stage manager in Washington and departed, leaving Maggie reliant on stock companies to finish out her season. Temporizing, she borrowed actors from the Olympic, since a minstrel troupe was installed there, and headed off on a one-week round of St. Joseph, Leavenworth, and Kansas City. Their critics still loved her acting, which was "more natural and life-like than is scarcely ever witnessed. Upon the stage, she does not appear to be beyond her teens." However, her borrowed leading men were merely tolerable.[33]

At Robinson's Opera House in Cincinnati, she utilized its company but ran into another snag. After three successful nights of *Pearl*, she was rehearsing *Fanchon* when its tall, handsome leading man and stage manager, forty-one-year-old Matt Lingham, refused to play the boyish part of Landry. He had similarly refused when Maggie had last played Cincinnati, at Pike's Opera House, and had been fired for it. Now, manager Robert E. J. Miles also fired him. Lingham refused to say whether it was the role or Maggie he disliked but considered himself suited only for nobler roles. Maggie made do with an adequate substitute.

She was assured of a competent supporting company next, at the Boston Theatre, where Shewell now managed and played older roles. Two other assets were a superb orchestra, led by Napier Lothian, 27, and new, lavish scenery by Charles S. Getz, previously the artist for Ford. Most memorable was the rustic exterior of Fadet's cottage, beside which ran a fully operational brook. Working against Maggie was harshly inclement weather, which left her with a severe cold and rasping voice.

Two lighthearted moments occurred during this engagement. On the night of Maggie's benefit in *Barefoot*, Lothian bet her that he could perform the role of William as well as anyone, and she accepted. He acquitted himself surprisingly well, and they agreed to make this an annual event. Four nights later, during *Fanchon*, comedian H. S. Murdoch as Didier had just begun his run across the long bridge spanning that operational brook when the seat of his baggy peasant trousers failed him. As he "ran up and along the bridge as fast as his legs could carry him," the "merciless" audience erupted in "a perfect howl" but awarded him good-natured applause at the close of the act. The lucrative engagement defied the current economic climate by yielding over $27,000, "more than double the amount received at any other place of amusement in the city." Maggie's three matinees alone realized nearly $6,000.[34]

To finish out her season in the upper Midwest and Chicago, McVicker loaned her a small combination company which included leading man and future star James O'Neill, 26, as Landry, Pierrot, and William, Maggie's only season acting with him. Still hoarse from a succession of colds, she slogged through Toledo, Detroit, and five new towns in Michigan: Jackson, Ann Arbor, Kalamazoo, Battle Creek, and Niles. Admittedly smaller venues, they nevertheless expanded her following. In Chicago, moderate houses at McVicker's applauded her *Jane Eyre* with O'Neill as Rochester, but reviews were mixed. Brontë's novel depicted "delicacies of feeling" and the "gradual growth toward each other of two natures [Jane and Rochester] widely and fundamentally different, if not mutually opposed." Clearly, Tayleure had written "for but one person—the star. . . . There is little of anything but Jane Eyre in [it, and] only Jane Eyre who is brilliant," crowding everybody else off the stage.[35]

Still, after three years, Maggie had perfected her ability to convey Jane's subtle transitions. Fanchon, Amry, Marie, and (very occasionally of late)

Lorle were still effective characters, but these remained variations on "a wild, elfish young girl." Jane transcended these, conveying "a womanly sweetness," an "aroma of womanly purity" in a performance "marked by evidences of deep study, thorough conviction as to the author's meaning, . . . 'a sermon without words.'"36

In Chicago Maggie's voice continued to fail her "as though she knew she had more than her share of the lines and hurried over them to conceal this inequality from the audience, just as a greedy schoolboy gobbles down the piece of pie he has purloined from his schoolfellow's satchel in order to escape detection." After a week she could barely be heard beyond the second row of the dress circle, her ailment "becoming more pronounced and disagreeable as time passes." To cover her vocal inadequacy, she overdid physical mannerisms, a tactic that became "strained beyond a possibility and very embarrassing." Again, a few critics proposed that *Fanchon* be put out to pasture. It "comes round to us year after year until we have all seen it and sympathized with it and pronounced it clever and forgotten all about it until it comes round next season as surely as the flies and new potatoes of early summer." Then, "we fidget and clear our throat and—well, yes, we say, we are getting a little tired of *Fanchon*. [It was] very popular in its day, but, well, its day has gone by." When McVicker stepped in (improbably at age fifty-two) to portray Jemmy to Maggie's Amry in *Barefoot*, attendance picked up some, but not much. Critics perceived Amry as merely "a species of Fanchon, or what Fanchon might have been if she was not the Cricket." Even their dances were similar, Fanchon's shadow dance recycled as Amry's beer-garden farewell waltz. In a thinly veiled insult, Maggie's Amry was "a mild form of Lottaism."37

Maggie must have been buoyed on May 17 by the words of Rev. N. F. Ravlin at Chicago's Temple Baptist Church. Attending with Paddock, she heard Ravlin decry those who denounced the theater: "Thousands of respectable people all over the land know the charge is false and unwarranted." Yes, there existed a "lower order of theatres," dance halls and such, but there was a difference, Ravlin preached, "between the shameless performance of one class, and the higher and purer and more distinguished order of talent in the other." Acknowledging her presence, he asked, "Who that knows Maggie Mitchell will say aught against her character, or question her womanly virtues? Those who know her best appreciate most the beautiful charity of her private life. A true wife, a loving and devoted mother, a genial friend, a generous almoner of the poor and needy, and yet a star of the first magnitude." With her "unselfish devotion to the happiness of others, she has done much to elevate the drama. . . . Who that has ever seen her [performances] can honestly say there is anything wicked, or any of evil tendency, in her peerless rendering of those stories?"38

Near the end of her third week in Chicago Maggie was distressed by news from Long Branch that two-and-a-half-year-old Harry had contracted pneumonia. A team of physicians had been called in, and his condition was dire. Maggie was about to cancel the rest of her performances but rallied when news of his improvement reached her. Still, she sleepwalked through the fourth week's *Pearl*, and the box office dropped off sharply. The end of the season could not come soon enough. McVicker, too, must have been glad to see it: only two stars had brought in enough money to keep the doors open, Adelaide Neilson and Maggie, just barely.

On Sunday, May 31, Maggie and Paddock headed straight for Long Branch and their children.

NOTES

1. Paddock, soon after Harry's birth, overheard in a hotel by a correspondent for the *Kansas City Times*, reprinted in *Eaton (OH) Democrat*, Apr. 14, 1881. Maggie likely entrusted Harry to her family as she toured, as she had with her daughter.

2. Unidentified clipping, Dec. 5, 1871, Crawford Collection IV:338, Yale University Library.

3. *Cincinnati Times and Chronicle*, Dec. 22, 1871; *New Orleans Republican*, Dec. 2, 1871; (Washington) *National Republican*, Jan. 30, 1872; *Cincinnati Enquirer*, Dec. 8, 1871.

4. *Pittsburgh Chronicle* quoted in *Wilmington News Journal*, Jan. 20, 1872.

5. *Wilmington Commercial*, Jan. 27, 1872.

6. *San Francisco Bulletin*, June 4, 1872.

7. *Cincinnati Times*, Aug. 9, 1872; *Cincinnati Commercial Tribune*, Sept. 7, 1872; *Sacramento Union*, Sept. 25, 1872; *St. Louis Post-Dispatch*, Oct. 9, 1887.

8. *St. Joseph Gazette*, Dec. 10, 1872.

9. Kansas City circuit context and theaters' operation herein derives from Felicia Hardison Londré's *The Enchanted Years of the Stage: Kansas City at the Crossroads of American Theater, 1870–1930*, Columbia: University of Missouri Press, 2007, passim.

10. *Leavenworth Times*, Dec. 20, 1872.

11. *Memphis Appeal*, Dec. 27 and 29, 1872, and Jan. 1, 1873; *Memphis Public Ledger*, Jan. 4, 1873.

12. *St. Louis Times* reprinted in *Cleveland Plain Dealer*, Jan. 22, 1873.

13. *St. Louis Democrat*, Jan. 16, 1873; *Albany Argus*, Sept. 21, 1876.

14. *Indianapolis Sentinel*, Mar. 31, 1875.

15. *Cleveland Plain Dealer*, Jan. 22, 1873.

16. *Ibid*.

17. *Cleveland Plain Dealer*, Dec. 7, 1871.

18. *Cleveland Leader* quoted in *Harrisburg (PA) Patriot*, Apr. 25, 1873.

19. *Richmond Whig*, Nov. 12, 1872; *New York Clipper*, Oct. 28, 1876.

20. *Pittsburgh Weekly Gazette*, Feb. 6, 1873.
21. *Boston Journal* quoted in *Luzerne Union* (Wilkes-Barre, PA), May 7, 1873.
22. *Hartford Courant*, Apr. 14, 1873.
23. *New York Herald*, Sept. 14, 1873; *New York Sun*, Oct. 7, 1873; *New York Tribune* quoted in *St. Louis Democrat*, Oct. 18, 1873.
24. *New York Herald*, Nov. 25, 1873; New York correspondent for *Baltimore Bulletin*, Oct. 18, 1873.
25. *Brooklyn Eagle*, Nov. 18 and 24, 1873.
26. James Linen, *The Later Poems and Songs of James Linen*, New York: W. J. Middleton, 1873, 49.
27. *Washington Evening Star*, Dec. 2, 1873; *St. Louis Democrat*, Aug. 9, 1874.
28. *Wilmington Every Evening* quoted in *Augusta (GA) Chronicle*, Feb. 23, 1876.
29. *Cleveland Plain Dealer*, May 28, 1870.
30. *Pittsburgh Commercial*, Jan. 20–21, 1874.
31. *Pittsburgh Dispatch* quoted in *St. Louis Democrat*, Feb. 9, 1874.
32. *St. Louis Democrat*, Apr. 26, 1874.
33. *St. Joseph Herald*, Feb. 24, 1874.
34. Boston correspondent for *Chicago Post and Mail* quoted in *St. Louis Post-Dispatch*, Apr. 16, 1874; *Washington Evening Star*, Oct. 24, 1874.
35. *Chicago Inter Ocean*, May 5, 1874; *Chicago Tribune*, May 5, 1874.
36. *Ibid.*; *Pittsburgh Commercial*, Jan. 23, 1874; *St. Louis Democrat* quoted in *Hartford (CT) Courant*, Sept. 22, 1874.
37. *Chicago Tribune*, May 5, 12 and 20, 1874.
38. *Chicago Tribune*, May 18, 1874.

Chapter 10

"she does not counterfeit it, but feels it"

As if to justify Rev. Ravlin's praise, the first thing Maggie did upon returning to Long Branch was donating $100 to help retire the debt of Sea-Shore Baptist Church. She put other funds to more practical use, purchasing stock in the Long Branch Banking Company and a six-acre plot of land near Edwin Booth's cottage for $65,000. Next to horses, real estate was her preferred investments. This would prove unwise in September when a fire destroyed several hundred wooded acres she owned six miles west of Long Branch.

Except for a June 4 matinee of *Barefoot* in Boston for Napier Lothian, he again as William and Len Shewell as Farmer Peace, she spent the summer lavishing care on little Harry, slowly recuperating. Of course, she could be seen most days driving along the beach behind a pair of jet-black ponies and like President Grant often appeared at the new Long Beach racetrack (observing, not betting—she was too frugal for that).

Professionally, she would spend the coming three seasons further experimenting with combinations, while continuing her search for a few good scripts. She had to have been aware that *Fanchon* was growing stale, but expanding her touring territory brought new fans for it and her. For the 1874–75 season, she decided she had relied long enough on local stock companies, and formed her partial combination. Having watched contemporaries—including Laura Keene, Mary Provost (Maggie's childhood inspiration), John E. Owens, and Edwin Booth—struggle with the management of physical theaters, she would channel her indefatigable energy and perfectionism into directing this ensemble.

Many of her actors, whom she signed to a sixteen-week contract, were a proven quantity. The centerpiece would again be William Harris, 34. For old men like Blackhorst in *Jane Eyre* and The Commander in *Pearl*, she chose George H. Griffiths, 52, whom she had known since her early Bowery days.

Old Women, including Fadet, would be covered by Marion Clifton. Soubrettes would be a newcomer from McVicker's, Phosa McAllister, 23. The others were comedian T. E. Jackson, Jennie Fisher, and Mr. and Mrs. George F. Carlisle. The diligent Thomas W. Brown would continue as advance agent.

Maggie's repertoire would remain limited. She dropped *Barefoot*, keeping *Fanchon*, *Pearl*, *Jane Eyre*, and reactivated *Lorle*, but with a new ending crafted by Fred Maeder that lessened its depressing, maudlin effect. In a timeworn device, the artist Reinhardt now falls asleep under a tree after his betrothal to Lorle at the end of Act I and merely *dreams* Acts II, III, and IV, in which Lorle tragically perishes. He then reawakens amid birdsong to a joyous reunion with her in Act V as the villagers dance around them. Most reviewers considered the alteration an improvement, even if it was a "trick of the dime novels." However, it confused some theatergoers who had previously seen it, causing them to exit after the Act IV death scene and needing to be herded back in by the manager for the new Act V.[1]

That season, Paddock took over his wife's touring schedule, traveling the whole route with her. Lacking big-city connections, he built it around small towns in the Northeast and upper Midwest, many of which she had visited recently, plus others which were entirely new or had not seen her for several years. The frenetic tour began on September 21 with *Fanchon* in New Haven, followed by one or two nights each in Hartford, Newport, Providence, Salem, Gloucester, Lawrence, Haverhill, Concord, Augusta, Bangor, Portland, Lewiston, Biddeford, Portsmouth, Lowell, Worcester, Springfield, Westfield, Pittsfield, North Adams, Rutland, Utica, Syracuse, Elmira, Lockport, oil boomtowns in northwest Pennsylvania, Akron, Canton, Toledo, Fort Wayne, Evansville, Bloomington, Vincennes, Indianapolis (a rare metropolis), Hamilton, Dayton, Columbus, Wheeling, Pittsburgh (a second metropolis), Williamsport, Reading, Lancaster, Harrisburg, Wilkes-Barre, and finally New Brunswick, New Jersey, on January 7, 1875.

In most of these, audiences were large and enthusiastic despite sometimes disagreeable weather, and reviews were laudatory if a bit jaded, especially where Maggie had performed recently: "There is too much of the . . . mother's blessing business, but that is what pleases the masses, and that is what Maggie is here for." Most found the poise and dignity of the womanly Jane Eyre (in the play's later scenes) a remarkable evolution from the "capricious child" they knew Maggie as. Many reviewers marveled that she "must have discovered the fountain of youth." "She comes again as fresh and apparently as young as when she first entered upon her wonderful career." "Time has passed her by, or at least touched her with a gentle hand." Her supporting players came in for consistent praise, especially Harris, Clifton, and Griffiths.[2]

Monitoring the competition, she detoured to Buffalo to catch a matinee of Lotta in her newest piece, *Musette*. Although comparisons of the two elfin actresses continued to appear in newspapers, Maggie left no record of her opinion of Lotta's performance. She did, however, begin to incorporate into her performances a unique "kickback" dance step perfected by Lotta.[3]

In Columbus, Ohio, Maggie's *Lorle* on December 11 inaugurated the Opera House's first use of electric stage lighting. The effect was "charming, fairly magnetizing the audience with quietude." At the close of the first act "Lorle, observed through a gauze-covered window to her bedroom, was arranging her hair to retire for the night. Rainhard [sic], her lover and artist, was lying on a lawn seat under stately and spreading trees by the house. The villagers had gone home and all the lights in the house were extinguished except those of the gallery circle and they were lowered to a deep twilight shade. Lorle, in a sweet and low voice, was singing a love song. . . . Before the attentive hearers were scarcely aware of the fact, the curtain had descended slowly and noiselessly to the floor. Instantly a flash of electric current lighted the whole house. The spell was broken."[4]

Not all technical conditions ran as smoothly, especially in smaller theaters. In Lowell, onstage candles ignited a lace curtain during *Jane Eyre*, but the fire was quickly extinguished by Jackson in character as Sam, the butler. In Fort Wayne, Indiana, a piece of scenery representing Fadet's cottage fell forward, narrowly missing Maggie. Also, religious opposition at times reared its head. While Maggie's troupe was performing in Evansville, Indiana, a local minister assailed the profession, leading Harris to publish an informed, reasoned rebuttal. (In 1877 the Methodist Church would formally ban theater-going among its members under threat of expulsion from the church.)

For unknown reasons—perhaps a joint Paddock decision—Maggie on January 8 dissolved her partial combination, keeping only Harris, and relied for the rest of the season on local stock companies. She stumbled along for a week with a mediocre company at the Park Theatre in Brooklyn in its final days under manager Edward Lamb before William E. Sinn converted it to a combination house. But at Shewell's Boston Theatre for three weeks the company was of a higher caliber. She had acted with them several times over the past three years and could count on their professionalism.

There, in *Jane Eyre*, with Shewell as Rochester; *Fanchon*, with Harris as Landry to Shewell's Father Barbeaud; and *Pearl* and *Lorle* (with the new ending, well-received), jammed houses applauded her. Lothian reprised William for one night of *Barefoot*. (With ludicrous results, Harris took Lothian's place conducting the orchestra during the last act, introducing musical commentary on stage events, engendering impromptu asides. Maggie openly shared in the fun.) For Shewell's benefit, he preferring tragedy, she took on the role of Parthenia to his *Ingomar*, which she had not played for almost ten years. Despite following Lotta, Maggie's three weeks set records for attendance at the Boston Theatre, with total receipts over $27,000, including three matinees which together generated around $6,000. Reviews seemed superfluous: Maggie was "too well known to need further description."[5]

At Albaugh's Opera House in Albany, she was reunited with family. Among the company was her sister Sarah, now 29, acting minor roles under the name of Constance Mitchell, and her half-sister Mary, 43, in leads. In a practice which would increasingly become the norm for Maggie, they gave eight performances that week, including matinees on Wednesday and Saturday.

After stops in Troy and Rochester, she opened with Harris at Effie Ellsler's Cleveland Academy of Music on March 1, where the company included John Ellsler, again successful as Barbeaud. In Pittsburgh, critics thought Tayleure's script for *Jane Eyre* was problematic, "a hybrid between sensational melodrama and the emotional society play of the cheap variety." Anyone who had read and loved Brontë's novel would have been "painfully jarred at the incongruity." Maggie's "impersonation of the wonderful little woman is the only redeeming feature in the fearful array of material."[6]

In Cincinnati, St. Louis, and Chicago, she continued to follow, precede, or compete head-on with Charlotte Thompson and Lotta. The latter was "the recognized peer of Miss Mitchell. . . . She appears in different plays entirely, but the character of her acting is substantially the same. She bubbles over with mirth, song and dancing." Thompson performed *Jane Eyre* "with less dramatic but far more natural effect" than Maggie. "She displays all the strength of character, all the smothered wrath, all the submission to unmerited wrong to which the orphan is subjected. . . . She evinces emotion without the aid of dramatic trick. She reveals a passion without sawing the air making an animated bellows of herself."[7]

In Cincinnati and St. Louis, Maggie and Harris filled houses, supported still by local actors. But in Chicago, attendance was only fair, and she appeared tired, as anyone near the end of such a touring schedule would be. Showing the wear most keenly was her voice, her hoarseness noticeable to all. Congressman James A. Garfield, who knew Maggie from Washington, caught her *Fanchon* in Chicago and recorded, "The little woman has a strong hold on her auditors, though I think her voice is losing something of its old sweetness."[8]

She finished her season in the welcoming environment of John Ford's Baltimore Opera House, supported by his always-competent company. Amid good houses, she seemed unable to let go of the last shards of her aspiration to play tragedy, and on her benefit night played Parthenia—for the last time. Still hoarse, she closed her season in Washington at Ford's Opera House on May 17, performing *Pearl* to a full house for a benefit for manager Harry Clay Ford. Playing Chouchon in her first performance since marrying Harry last June was soubrette Blanche Chapman Ford, 24. She, too, had been a friend of John Wilkes Booth and had been present with Harry when Annie Ford clipped the lock of hair for Maggie from Booth's disinterred body.

Then, it was back to a tranquil summer at Long Branch with husband and children, driving her ponies along Ocean Avenue and stopping by the Monmouth Park races. When she opened Cricket Lodge for a home show to benefit the local Catholic Church, hundreds of people trooped through, Maggie tirelessly greeting them in her parlor under a fine pen and ink sketch of the elder Booth. A year short of forty, she seemed still a teenager, "her long, graceful waist, her flowing golden hair [and] her Cinderella feet" as striking as ever.[9]

That summer she learned that her early manager, John G. Cartlitch, 81, was impoverished and incurably ill. She established him in a rest home in West Philadelphia, charging Paddock with his upkeep. When Cartlitch died, his last wish was that her letters to him be interred with him. Maggie paid for his funeral.

By 1875 the trials of depending on stock companies as she traveled had become too much, and she chose that summer to embrace the national trend of forming her own full combination company for the upcoming season. Between 1872 and 1880 the number of major stock companies in America would dwindle from fifty to eight, while the number of combinations grew from five to nearly a hundred. To form hers, Maggie and Paddock periodically ran up to New York to Union Square, whose east and south sides formed an annual "slave market" of actors and their agents haggling and striking deals with booking agents and managers. These new combinations could travel on an ever-expanding rail network, which since the Civil War had grown from 35,000 miles to nearly 80,000, opening up countless new towns to performers.[10]

The combination company Maggie formed for 1875–76 consisted of eighteen actors, most of whom she already knew. Harris at thirty-five was nearing the end of his time as Landry, but audiences loved his personable onstage demeanor, clear enunciation, and freedom from stagey mannerisms, and he had grown nicely into Rochester and Reinhardt. He could "make a score of lines go further than the majority of actors could do with a hundred." In *Pearl*, Maggie cast him as Lonstalot, the most demanding role.[11]

Comedian J. Edward "Ted" Irving would play Didier, Jemmy, and Pierrot. Edwin Varrey, a Shakespearean actor in his mid-fifties, would play crusty old men such as Blackhorst, Father Barbeaud, and the Commander. Other old men and women would be played by Albert G. Enos, Jennie Fisher, and Susan Flood Stoddard, the latter as Fadet. Soubrette Alice Wyndham would be fetching as Madelon, Chouchon and the Countess. Among those playing small roles were Maggie's still-unmarried sister Emma, 34, and her eighteen-year-old nephew Willie Mitchell (the son of her half-brother, John H. Lomax Mitchell). Paddock would serve as a company manager and Brown would continue as advance agent. The repertoire would consist of *Fanchon, Barefoot, Pearl, Lorle,* and *Jane Eyre.* No new works would be introduced until March.

Leaving Fanchon, 6, and Harry, 3, in New York with Sophia and her five children, Maggie and Paddock launched the company onto a circuit of New England towns, opening September 6 in Danbury, Connecticut. It was the first of seventeen new towns she would visit this season, all on convenient, sometimes new, railroad lines. These towns averaged about 10,000 inhabitants; a population figure Maggie and Paddock estimated was worth only one night each. Due to her novelty, nearly all of the towns provided effusive reviews.[12]

Playing one- and two-night stands, she went as far as St. John, New Brunswick—her first performances out of the country—then down into New York State. This included a week in Albany, while Albaugh's company—including Mary, Sarah Constance, and now Maggie's nephew Julian, 24—stepped aside. Moving west through New York in November they played Buffalo in early December, Maggie's first visit there in four years. She remained for a week and in Cleveland for another before hitting smaller towns in Ohio, then the holiday week in Cincinnati. Maggie's father joined them there and she hosted a formal dinner at the Grand Hotel to honor his seventy-first birthday on New Year's Day 1876. The honoree, "a very eccentric character of wonderful memory, who had committed Shakespeare so that he could repeat any portion of it, and who was excessively fond of the drama," cheerfully recited "The Bashful Man."[13]

January took the company to Louisville, back though Ohio to Wheeling and Pittsburgh, then Washington and Baltimore. In Washington, Congressman Garfield preferred her *Lorle* to *Fanchon,* considering it "a course [sic] but rather effective performance."[14]

Throughout the tour, sometimes despite harshly inclement weather, Maggie consistently drew immense houses, often so full that only standing room remained and patrons were turned away, matinees as well as evenings. Reviewers were uniformly positive, iterating the same key points of years past:

- Maggie remains youthful, vivacious and sprightly, having lost none of her powers to bewitch and to readily elicit tears and laughter. Whenever asked how long she had been acting, she would quip, "Ever since I can remember."[15]

- Her acting is heartfelt, natural, and believable, sinking her individuality into her characters: "There is no acting about it," "All traces of the artificial vanish, and the auditor feels almost as if he were a participant in a real life scene and not a mere beholder of fiction."[16]
- Her performances are a welcome relief from the barrage of classical tragedy and morbid domestic dramas. Such "stormier passions . . . leave ruin and disaster behind," but Maggie's are "sweet poetry," "gentle pastoral idylls of the stage," leading the audience "into romantic by-ways of which they could never dream."[17]
- But her rare tragic moments are still powerful: "We doubt if anyone at present on the stage can picture more perfectly abject despair and a heart almost broken by the sorrows unjustly heaped upon it."[18]
- She remains beyond criticism: "Certain masterpieces in art or literature are quite above criticism."[19]
- The quality of Maggie's support was a minor matter: "People go to see her and care but little for the company."[20]
- She remains unaffected in personal life, "a sweet, graceful little lady, without one bit of staginess in speech or manner," who "can curl herself up in any corner and stay there like a little pet kitten."[21]

When she headed south to some cities she had not visited since 1860, audiences dwindled. Money for entertainment was simply not there in Richmond, Wilmington, Charleston, Savannah, Augusta, Atlanta, Nashville, and Memphis. The last southern town was to be Little Rock, but Maggie uncharacteristically broke her engagement and returned north. In St. Louis in late March, reviewers were unsupportive. In DeBar's otherwise lavish staging of *Jane Eyre*, "there was a certain bizarre movement in Miss Mitchell's acting that at times grated somewhat harshly on critical ears, which had the effect of destroying the power of some of the intense passages."[22]

She did little to help her cause by choosing St. Louis to rehearse new material. Two years before, she had contacted novelist Marian Calhoun Legare Reeves to obtain the dramatic rights to Reeves' latest book, *Wearithorne*. She thought its central character, a Scottish lass named Nannette, might be perfect for her. Rather than turn to a professional like Tayleure, she asked Reeves to adapt it. Lacking experience as a dramatist, Reeves (with the help of Edward Spencer, author of one lugubrious period tragedy) eventually produced a work long on dialogue and short on action. Its plot consisted almost entirely of young Nannette's being deprived of her rightful inheritance but ultimately reclaiming it along with the hand of her dashing male cousin, Colonel Miles Lethwaite. Despite Reeves' inclusion of a Scottish ballad for Maggie and a song for a chorus of villagers, there was little for anyone else to do.

Retitled *Nannette o' Wearithorne*, it debuted on March 24 with Maggie as Nannette and Harris as Lethwaite. Unsatisfied with its reception, she pulled it after one night to rehearse it further and try it again in Chicago in May. She spent April touring with her other repertoire through Indiana, Illinois, Wisconsin, Minnesota, and Iowa. When she played *Fanchon* in Minneapolis, one rube, touched by "the way she pulled her hair and kicked off her shoe, twisted her body all out of shape and acted so she got all out of breath" pining for Landry, set out to "do something to help Maggie." He started to "go out to find her a husband" until his wife pulled him back by his coattails, reminding him it was only a play.[23]

Opening for McVicker on May 8, Maggie, unfortunately, followed the hugely popular Edwin Booth and met with small audiences. *Nannette* yielded blistering reviews. It was "crude, ill-digested, and clumsily arranged," "deplorable," "hopelessly dull and foolish," "a ridiculous drama" with "not one quality to recommend it to public favor." "The story is improbable and uninteresting, the action meager, and the dramatic movement almost incomprehensible." In a "frantic endeavor to keep it alive," Reeves had inserted "anything, bonfires, contra-dances, or an explosion of gunpowder barrels [for what purpose] nobody can tell. In the last act, Nannette's identity is revealed by an old woman, impulsively and accidentally. If the old woman had not happened to speak at that moment, there would have been nothing to prevent the play from running on forever." It left her audience "disappointed and puzzled." Minor characters, "who are introduced at odd moments," merely "come on the stage and relate the story. There is nothing dramatic in this. One might better buy the novel for 50 cents [second-hand] than pay $1 to hear a lame version of it in a theatre. . . . Miss Mitchell ought to have had better judgment." It was such a complete failure that Maggie never performed it again, and left Chicago with the *Tribune*'s final barb: "We will not bend down the knee and worship your Maggie Mitchells and Lottas."[24]

After a swing through Michigan and New York, she ended the season on June 10 with one night of *Fanchon* in Port Jervis, a coal-shipping port on the Delaware River with a population of less than 8,000. Few attended. Dispersing her company, Maggie gave each actor a train ticket to New York City. She was in poor health and had fainted on stage during the final act of *Pearl* one night in April in St. Paul. She had just turned forty, and rumors resurfaced that she would quit the stage.

Far from the nation's raucous, extravagant Centennial Exposition in Philadelphia that summer, she recovered amid family, home, and horses at Long Branch. A highlight was the August 5 annual picnic of theatrical residents, which Maggie and Paddock hosted. Their children joined those of Chanfrau, Collier, and others to present plays, including the farce *Married Life*. Maggie spent considerable time selecting new material for the 1876–77 season. She chose two from the pile submitted to her: journalist James B. Runnion's *Mignon* and Tayleure's *Becky Mix*. For better or worse, both featured intrepid central characters she could easily step into, closely resembling her other roles.

She declined to form another combination company, opting to rely again on local stock companies. Since her route this season would take her to established theaters with competent managers rather than the small-town venues of the previous season, she and Paddock may have figured she could get by. For insurance, though, she re-signed Harris for leads. Brown continued as advance agent, distributing glowing snippets from reviews to upcoming managers.

On September 18 Maggie opened her season as the first attraction at Albaugh's Leland Opera House in Albany, in *Fanchon*, with a stellar supporting company. Its soubrette, playing Madelon, was nineteen-year-old Ada Rehan, who had debuted three years ago in Louisville, toured for John Ford throughout the South, and would soon become an international star. Mainstays Mr. and Mrs. Eugene A. Eberle, 36 and 35, had Broadway experience and embodied Father Barbeaud and Fadet. Low comedian H. C. Curley was Didier, and of course, Harris was Landry. Their roles in *Jane Eyre* and *Barefoot* paralleled these.

Maggie began her second week with the premiere of *Mignon*. Loosely adapted from Goethe's *Wilhelm Meister*—with some new characters and a much happier ending—*Mignon* was a cut-and-paste amalgamation of Maggie's previous roles, a contrivance not lost on critics. Clearly, Runnion had observed her performances and molded the script to her needs. He also borrowed freely—one reviewer called it "literary larceny"—from two operas, Michael William Balfe's *The Bohemian Girl* and Ambroise Thomas' *Mignon*.[25]

Its plot was ridiculously convoluted. Maggie's titular character has been stolen by gypsies, deprived yet again of a noble heritage. Her mother has died of grief and her father, half-mad, perpetually searches for her (cf. Lonstalot in *Pearl*). The gypsy chief, Romaine, forces her to sing and dance for money (cf. Marie in *Pearl*). "There is a freshness and innocence in her rippling laugh . . . which only belong to the age of girlhood" (cf. *Fanchon*). But when she tires, Romaine beats her, and she becomes "almost a little savage, whose spirit has been crushed" (more *Fanchon*). Handsome young Wilhelm (cf. William and Arthur) observes one of the beatings and rescues her by buying her from the gypsies. Dressing in boy's clothes (cf. early breeches roles) to serve him as page, she becomes inordinately attached: "She becomes his slave, for she worships him. Her high spiritedness forsakes her and she becomes humble" (cf. Jane with Rochester).[26]

Enter a touring troupe of actors, featuring the alluring Philina (cf. The Countess in *Lorle*), who steals Wilhelm's heart. Sparati, a mad pilgrim, lurks nearby, strangely drawn to Mignon (heavy-handed foreshadowing). Mutual hatred and jealousy erupt between Philina and Mignon, the latter turning for solace to the old pilgrim, and "a strange sympathy springs up between them." Philina plots with Romaine to steal her again. To win back Wilhelm, Mignon sneaks into Philina's dressing room and dons her clothes, comically admiring herself in the mirror. Romaine steals in, and mistaking her for Philina, reveals the planned abduction.[27]

Wilhelm, "far from being pleased with her gay attire, reprimands her severely and finally sends her away," leading Mignon to consider suicide (cf. *Lorle*) by jumping in the river. The mad Sparati prevents this and out of misguided revenge sets fire (cue special effects) to the castle, which he inexplicably actually owns, where the actors are performing. But Mignon has snuck back inside. Wilhelm heroically rescues her, taking her to Sparati's previously unexplained manorial home on the shores of an Italian lake (exotic locale of lavishly painted backdrop). Traumatized from her burns, Mignon raves madly (cf. Marie), revealing a crucifix she carries (cf. the pendant touchstone in *Fanchon*) which proves to Sparati that she is his long-lost daughter! She announces her long-sublimated love for Wilhelm, winning him at the close (cf. *Barefoot*). "Wickedness is punished and virtue rewarded." The actors and gypsies are forgotten.[28]

Harris, now thirty-six, played Sparati. A new addition to the troupe, Richard ("Dick") Fulton Russell, barely thirty, beginning eight seasons of association with Maggie, enacted the heroic Wilhelm. The vixenish Philina was Russell's sister-in-law, Rehan. On the first night of *Mignon*, Maggie was hoarse and visibly nervous, but her subsequent performances went more smoothly and were moderately well received.

The next week in Providence with the Albany Company, Runnion personally supervised rehearsals with Maggie. Dubiously hailed as "a new creation, no touch of *Fanchon*, no sign of *Little Barefoot*, no remembrance of *Lorle*," *Mignon* drew mixed notices, with reviewers disagreeing over whether the role was a good fit for Maggie. Despite Runnion's polishing, the script remained seriously flawed and "a judicious purging of superfluous lines" was called for."[29]

Maggie quickly returned to other roles. She gained a measure of control over some through a letter from Waldauer in early October granting her exclusive rights to perform *Fanchon*, *Pearl*, and *Barefoot*. Imitators "had no right to do so," he assured Maggie. "They have sailed under false colors and their personations have resembled a bad counterfeit." She "deserves all the credit, fame and praise bestowed upon her" for bringing them to life. While this would lessen infractions, it had no effect on offenders like Emma

Maddern and Effie Ellsler (John and Effie's daughter, now twenty-one, whom Maggie had known since birth) who not only continued to tour in *Fanchon*, but earned notices as being superior to Maggie. Ellsler was deemed more powerful, more polished—resembling Maggie back "when Maggie was everybody's sweetheart."[30]

On October 12, following a week of rehearsals, Maggie debuted *Becky Mix*. This time she played a nineteen-year-old match girl struggling to survive on the streets of New York—not much different from *Mignon* or *Pearl*. Swindled out of her fortune this time by her nefarious father—who has also procured the murder of her mother—she is assisted in her efforts to reclaim it by her newfound brother (Russell), who discovers the treachery (as the *Clipper* put it) "by means of that always useful newspaper advertisement." Amid confusing and tedious plot complications, he and Becky and a friend (Harris) who coincidentally falls in love with her, unearth papers (when the father conveniently leaves the room for a few moments) which restore her fortune. The brother ends up with an attractive, similarly swindled heiress (Rehan).[31]

Tayleure like Runnion had shaped its central character for Maggie. Becky was "piquant, vivacious, brimming over with fun and merry antics, and deals out sharp sayings in prolific style." This "bright little waif and child of circumstance" applies her shrewd native intuition "to pilot her through many vicissitudes which would prove a slough of despond to commonplace girls" and conquer "the temptations and tribulations of life." But the script was problematic: unoriginal and poorly constructed, with pedestrian and somewhat offensive dialogue, of which there was far too much. The father was "exceedingly unpleasant," yet his sudden disappearance at play's end yielded no satisfaction via retribution for his evil deeds or reconciliation with a forgiving Becky. Although some thought it deserved an early death, Maggie persisted in performing it for over a year.[32]

In Washington and Baltimore in late October for Ford at his National Theatre and Grand Opera House, respectively, Maggie found herself supported by an uncharacteristically weak company, which included Maggie's nephew Julian in minor roles. In the capital, a large share of her sold-out audiences consisted of boisterous, appreciative veterans of the Army of Tennessee, celebrating their tenth reunion amid ceremonies for unveiling the statue of General James B. McPherson. Its president, U.S. Commanding General W. T. Sherman, a decided Maggie fan, attended her *Fanchon*. *Becky Mix* was considered unworthy of Maggie: "a rather poor piece of business, a dramatization of newspaper paragraphs, a mingled maze on the shape of an intricate plot and impossible situations" and "altogether too unnatural." Becky "is the sole character of any note in the drama, and it is by far too slangy." Baltimore was more receptive.[33]

For the first three weeks of November, perhaps due to illness, Maggie retreated to New York without performing. When she reemerged, it was in Buffalo with Harris in *Fanchon*, *Jane Eyre*, and *Becky Mix*, earning polite applause from small audiences. Managers Henry E. Abbey and John B. Schoeffel, with whom Maggie would contract for another decade in various cities, had agreed to pay her $800 but lost $500. She and Paddock generously repaid the loss.

Still lacking a company of her own, Maggie moved on in December to Pittsburgh. At its Grand Opera House, she drew inconsistently, playing on some nights to fewer than a hundred people. On December 11 she performed *Becky Mix* in a special benefit for victims of the horrific Brooklyn Theatre Fire of December 5 which killed nearly three hundred people. Among them was actor Harry Murdoch, with whom she had performed and for whose funeral she sent an elaborate floral arrangement. But the benefit's meager audience produced only $352. Times were still tough.

Maggie's sister Emma, who had grown close to Harris (they would soon wed), joined them in Cincinnati for the holidays but did not act (perhaps as a personal attendant on Maggie). Under the management of her friend Bob Miles, whom Maggie had known for nearly a decade, the stock company of the Grand Opera House was a strong one, albeit with a tendency to overact. *Mignon* and *Becky Mix*, along with the usual pieces, played well to capacity audiences in a holiday mood. *Becky Mix* was still flawed, though, with "some glaring anomalies" and minor characters who were not lifelike. "The play is constructed for Maggie Mitchell and hers is the only character that has a distinct outline." Her Becky, "a phenomenon of shrewdness and natural intelligence, develops under the care of kind friends into a very remarkable heroine." Her repartee was "brilliant" and her spunk "exuberant."[34]

To open 1877, Maggie took Miles' company on a quick tour of Ohio towns, including Dayton, Springfield, and Columbus, then headed for St. Louis with Harris. There, she provided DeBar with *Mignon* and *Becky Mix*, but audiences were again disappointing, as was the stock company—both anomalous for DeBar. Worse, one night a descending curtain tore loose the mooring of a massive chandelier which crashed to the stage, barely missing Maggie and jamming deeply into the floor.

Next, at McVicker's in Chicago, Maggie played only *Mignon*, attracting large, enthusiastic houses but a buzz saw of negative reviews: "Maggie Mitchell has grown passé, having long since worn out in her peculiar round of characters." "She is utterly mistaken in supposing that the same artifacts of theatric art can be employed in depicting the strange, unearthly passion of Mignon." "She is in everything she undertakes the same everlasting Fanchon and Little Barefoot. She can't leave off the hop, skip and jump jig, and she persists in that silly, country schoolgirl nasal twang in her attempts to be coaxing or affectionate." Such acting "is completely worn out and seems very flat and tiresome." "In olden times Miss Mitchell pleased by her kittenish ways and arch manner. But she is no longer a kitten, and her archness is no longer [enjoyable]." Perhaps the cruelest cut recalled her forgotten hopes for success as a tragic actress: "In emotional parts of any importance, Miss Mitchell imitates the Clara Morris [maudlin] style and is decidedly unequal to the attempt. Such passages in her hands are a little better than burlesque."[35]

Critics deplored the script's contrived, implausible, needlessly complex plot and trite dialogue (e.g., "We never know the value of a jewel till we have lost it"). Audiences should "dismiss at once any thought of Goethe." The *Chicago Tribune*, for whom Runnion served as an editor, defended his need to take liberties with Goethe's philosophical, didactic, lugubrious work: "Imagine the dense amazement . . . of the audience on being told by a lecturer stationed in the wings [about] the subjective character of Mignon." If that lecturer should (as Goethe did) "discourse upon her intuitive perceptions of right and wrong, there would probably be a demand for a return of money at the box office. . . . Psychology cannot be taught on the stage."[36]

Attendance dropped off, and Maggie switched to *Jane Eyre*, then *Becky Mix*. If Chicago critics had been caustic about *Mignon*, they were savage in dismissing *Becky Mix*. "A painful mixture of trash," it was "certainly the worst affair that we ever saw dignified with the name of a play," "the stupidest that has been seen here for months, and it is venturing nothing to say it will never be seen here again, nor often in any other part of the habitable world." Tayleure's "deficiency as shown in *Becky Mix* seems to be a total capacity to construct a plot."[37]

What there was merely "furnishes Becky with an excuse for coming on the stage and dancing around in her own elfin way." She was a disagreeable character whose "villain father has punishment severe enough in being obliged to take her to his heart." First seen selling matches on the streets of New York, "there is no explanation for her getting there nor is it explained why and how she has command of language of the most extraordinary character. The author makes her quote from every book in existence. . . . She talks bad grammar, too." She "acts like a rowdy and talks like a Christian father afflicted with the dyspepsia." Her character development consisted of "whacking visitors with a broom-handle" and knocking off men's hats."[38]

The play's dialogue was "stilted and unnatural, . . . abounding in claptrap effusions designed to catch the applause of the galleries." Sub-plots were thrown in for no purpose, and minor characters "unlike anything or anybody on earth are being continually lugged in without any reference or improvement to the story." They served "to raise a laugh, but have nothing whatever to do with the play or with anything else under the heavens." Attempts at comic relief were unoriginal (e.g., a corrupt, speculating congressman was a clone of *The Mighty Dollar*'s Bardwell Slote). The poor actors "had little or nothing to do and did that as well as they could."[39]

Maggie tried to save the rotten material, her personal vivacity "imparting to the text a liveliness which it did not inherently possess." But her methods were irritating: "Her mannish tones are distracting, her coyness ridiculous, and her roughness exaggerated." She had not helped McVicker, who would go bankrupt by the end of the next season despite a loan from Maggie (one of four actors to do so, the others being Edwin Booth, Joseph Jefferson III, and Lotta) of $20,000 which was never repaid. With a long haul ahead of her to Boston, Maggie left Chicago after her last Saturday matinee.[40]

At Shewell's Boston Theatre, *Mignon* failed to draw consistently, and reviews were equally caustic. *Mignon* "is in four acts, but the material would suffice for three. . . . Miss Mitchell as Mignon is Fanchon, Marie the Pearl, Little Barefoot, and Lorle over again. It seems impossible for her to separate these from any character that she may assume." Her acting was "the same infantile voice, kittenish in all her movement, same impetuosity and pathos, while her skipping and jumping is as lively and quick as when I first saw her in *Fanchon*." In *Jane Eyre*, *Pearl*, and *Barefoot* she fared no better. "Her fervor carries her away so that she rattles off her words, claps her hands together so often, and has many old stage tricks which . . . become wearisome. [She] does not realize the Jane Eyre of the novel." The other actors, including Shewell as Lonstalot and Farmer Peace and Lothian again as William, were merely adequate, and Harris was noticeably weak.[41]

Mignon and *Becky Mix* were more favorably received in smaller cities and towns as Maggie toured with Harris, supported by a nondescript, mediocre company her husband had hired, for ten weeks of mostly one-night stands through upstate New York and New England. These new characters "fit her as neatly as a glove." Admittedly, the scripts were weak, *Becky Mix* being "about as bad as can be, and is only redeemed from utter stupidity by its good fortune in having its principal role enacted by a woman of genius." "In other hands the character would have fallen very flat." That was precisely the attraction: people came "to see Miss Mitchell's wonderful impersonation of childhood, and expected and cared to see little else."[42]

She closed her season and disbanded the company in Binghamton, New York, on June 2, the eve of massive railroad strikes across the country. She had continued to accrue wealth, often clearing $1,500 a week and nearly always at least $1,000. So why, asked the *Dramatic News*, does someone "as enormously successful as she still continue to lead the arduous life [she does], living for nine months of the year on the railroad and the stage?" She had sadly "ceased to be the popular star she once was, not because her peculiar ability is any less, but by reason of the seeming antiquity of the plays which she presents. Her greatest successes are really played out."[43]

She was reportedly worth half a million dollars, primarily in real estate ($200,000), including ten lots near the ocean in North Long Branch, some rented out and some growing hay and corn. However, "while Maggie Mitchell is a very rich woman on paper, she is a very poor one in fact," needing to earn at least $18,000 a year to cover the interest on her mortgages. This debt was due to Paddock's risky speculation in real estate against the advice of others but with Maggie's acquiescence. She had trusted Paddock to control all of her funds, and by summer 1877 the value of the real estate had dropped to a third of its purchase price. So, "no thanks to her husband," Maggie worked just "to keep what she has got. . . . Not to work would mean ruin. She hopes, as do many others, that better times are coming. Then she will rest." That would not occur for another fifteen years.[44]

NOTES

1. *Indianapolis News*, Dec. 5, 1874.
2. *Hartford Courant*, Sept. 26, 1874; *Wheeling (WV) Register*, Dec. 15, 1874; *Pittsfield (MA) Sun*, Oct. 21, 1874; *Rutland (VT) Globe*, Oct. 27, 1874.
3. *Memphis Public Ledger*, Mar. 1876.
4. *Columbus Dispatch*, Dec. 12, 1874.
5. *Boston Post*, Jan. 19, 1875.
6. *Pittsburgh Commercial*, Mar. 10, 1875; *Pittsburgh Chronicle*, Mar. 10, 1875.
7. *Minneapolis Star Tribune*, Apr. 20, 1875; *Scranton (PA) Republican* quoted in *Newport (RI) News*, Mar. 20, 1876.
8. James A. Garfield, *The Diary of James A. Garfield*, ed. Harry James Brown and Frederick D. Williams, 4 vols., East Lansing: Michigan State University Press, 1967, 3:62.
9. Actress Olive Logan writing for *New York Graphic*, reprinted in *Wheeling (WV) Intelligencer*, Aug. 26, 1875.
10. "Theatre as Industry: From Stock to Combination," John Frick, *The Cambridge History of American Theatre*, ed. Don B. Wilmeth and Christopher Bigsby, 3 vols., Cambridge: Cambridge University Press, 2:201–4.
11. *The (Washington) Capital*, Oct. 22, 1876.
12. The new towns were (in order): Danbury, CT; Fall River, MA; Rockland, ME; Nashua, NH; Clinton, MA; Fitchburg, MA; Greenfield, MA; Cohoes, NY; Saratoga Springs, NY; Rome, NY; Tiffin, OH; Terre Haute, IN; Jacksonville, IL; Jollet, IL; Racine, WI; Rock Island, IL; and Point Jervis, NY.
13. *Summit County (Akron) Beacon*, Jan. 29, 1873.
14. Garfield 3:228.
15. *Wilmington (NC) Journal*, Feb. 18, 1876.

16. *Buffalo Evening Post*, Dec. 7, 1875; *Cincinnati Enquirer*, Dec. 31, 1875; *Augusta (GA) Chronicle*, Mar. 3, 1876; *Quad-City (Davenport, IA) Times*, Apr. 29, 1876.

17. *Wilmington (NC) Journal*, Feb. 18, 1876; *Buffalo Courier*, Dec. 6, 1875; *The (Washington) Capital*, Feb. 6, 1876.

18. *Rochester Democrat and Chronicle*, Dec. 3, 1875.

19. *Portland (ME) Press*, Oct. 27, 1875.

20. *Providence Press*, Oct. 27, 1875.

21. *Wilmington (NC) Journal*, Feb. 18, 1876.

22. *St. Louis Post-Dispatch*, Mar. 22, 1876.

23. *St. Cloud (MN) Journal*, May 4, 1876.

24. *Chicago Inter Ocean*, May 27, 1876; *Chicago Tribune*, May 23 and June 18, 1876.

25. *Albany Morning Express*, Sept. 27, 1876.

26. *Ibid.*; *Albany Argus*, Sept. 26, 1876.

27. *Ibid.*

28. *Ibid.*

29. *Boston Globe* quoted in *Cincinnati Enquirer*, Dec. 31, 1876; *Providence Evening Press*, Oct. 4, 1876; *New York Clipper*, Oct. 14, 1876.

30. Waldauer to MM reprinted in *Providence Evening Press*, Oct. 10, 1876; *Cleveland Plain Dealer*, Nov. 14, 1877. Waldauer's total compensation from transferring the rights to *Fanchon, Barefoot*, and *Pearl* to Maggie, according to his hometown *St. Louis Post-Dispatch*, Sept. 1, 1887, was a mere $600.

31. *New York Clipper*, Oct. 21, 1876.

32. *Providence Evening Press*, Oct. 13, 1876; *New York Dramatic News*, Oct. 21, 1876; *St. Louis Post-Dispatch*, Jan. 16, 1877.

33. *The (Washington) Capital*, Oct. 22, 1876; Washington correspondent for *New York Graphic*, Oct. 26, 1876.

34. *Cincinnati Gazette*, Dec. 26, 1876; *Cincinnati Times*, Dec. 26, 1876.

35. *Chicago Inter Ocean*, Jan. 30 and Feb. 3, 1877; *Chicago Tribune*, Jan. 30 and Feb. 4, 1877; *New York Dramatic News*, Feb. 10 and 17, 1877.

36. *Ibid.*

37. *Chicago Inter Ocean*, Feb. 17, 1877; *New York Dramatic News*, Feb. 24, 1877; *Chicago Tribune*, Feb. 18, 1877.

38. *Ibid.*

39. *Ibid.*

40. *Ibid.*

41. *New York Dramatic News*, Mar. 3 and 17, 1877.

42. *Albany Morning Express*, Mar. 13, 1877; *Portland (ME) Press*, Apr. 30, 1877; *Hartford Courant*, May 14, 1877; *Syracuse Daily Standard*, May 24, 1877.

43. *New York Dramatic News*, Mar. 24, 1877.

44. *Harrisburg (PA) Patriot*, Mar. 24, 1877; *Chicago Tribune*, Mar. 25, 1877; *Springfield (MA) Republican*, Sept. 1, 1877; *Cincinnati Gazette*, Feb. 28, 1878.

Chapter 11

"everything she attempts is Fanchon"

Regardless of her purported wealth, Maggie was unwilling or unable to fund a combination company for the 1877–78 season. Except for the loyal Harris, she would seek venues where stock companies would be fairly dependable. She entrusted business arrangements to her husband, who would travel with her.

She opened the season on October 1 in Brooklyn for New Park Theater manager William E. Sinn. *Jane Eyre* and *Mignon* drew fair houses and good reviews. In Albany at Maggie's brother-in-law's Leland Opera House, *Becky Mix* was so poorly received that she never played it again. A night of *Lorle* was ruined by actor E. A. Eberle, who forgot his first act lines as Lindenhost, tried to improvise, read from the script for two acts, and finally just collapsed. Albaugh loaned her other actors for a tour of upstate New York and New England.

Following two weeks for L. R. Shewell in Boston, she headed west, to Evansville, Indiana, Nashville, and Memphis, performing *Mignon*, *Fanchon*, and *Lorle* with mixed results. In Memphis, she likely stayed with her half-brother's family. John H. Lomax Mitchell, 44, was a Memphis builder and the father of four children, the eldest of whom, Willie, had briefly toured with Maggie. This visit, however, would be the last time Maggie saw her half-brother and his (second) wife alive.[1]

In Indianapolis, she developed a severe cold and sore throat. By the time she got to Detroit in mid-December her laryngitis had become so bad that she had to cancel performances and remain in her hotel under a physician's care. She recovered in time to play to good houses in Louisville, then open in Cincinnati on December 24, followed by a Christmas Day matinee and evening. She drew full houses despite poor weather, the matinee bringing in over $1,350 and that evening $500 over that. Reportedly the largest audiences ever for that opera house continued for two weeks, with a New Year's matinee of *Barefoot* yielding nearly $1,500.

In mid-January 1878, back in Brooklyn, Sinn provided her with a first-class supporting company. Several were standouts: H. B. Phillips, a Washington actor who had spent years with John Ford, as Father Barbeaud; and a vibrant, versatile twenty-four-year-old Kentuckian named Marie Prescott, quite credible as Fadet. In fact, Maggie was so impressed with Prescott—for the rest of her career considering her the definitive Fadet—that she offered her a salary higher than Sinn provided to join her for a March run of *Mignon* in Manhattan and a summer tour of California.

Seeking a viable new script to replace the disastrous *Becky Mix*, Maggie thought she had found it in a new translation by John Hollingshead of Henri Meilhac and Ludovic Halevy's recent Paris hit, *La Cigale*, rendered as *The Grasshopper*. But no sooner had she paid Hollingshead his $500 than she learned that Katie Putnam was already acting it and that Lotta was embarking on a tour with a different version penned by Olive Logan. So, Maggie dropped her plans and Lotta went on to showcase the piece for the rest of her career. Logan afterward told Maggie, "I would have strongly counseled you not to buy Hollingshead's *Grasshopper* had I known of it, for I saw at a glance the piece was no good for you. . . . The part is not in the least your style."[2]

At the Pittsburgh Opera House, Maggie ran up against hometown favorite Effie Ellsler, touring with *Fanchon* despite Waldauer's letter granting Maggie sole rights to it, at the rival Library Hall. Newspapers played up the actresses' mutual jealousy, misquoting and distorting the sentiments of both. Remarkably, several argued that Ellsler had a right to perform any scripts she chose. To make matters worse, Ellsler outdrew Maggie despite performing in a smaller venue.

Next came Cincinnati, where a full house yielded $1,500. En route to St. Louis in February, Maggie reacquired her cold and sore throat. By the time she got to Washington, they had become a bronchial infection which she fought bravely. Audiences and critics disregarded her hoarseness, though, and applauded her and the strong supporting company collected by Ford at his newly renovated National Theater. It included two of Maggie's nephews, aspiring actors both, in minor roles: Julian Mitchell, 26, brought in from Albany, and Walter Collier (James Walter Collier, Jr.), 22. This troupe supported her as well at Ford's Baltimore Grand Opera House.

For Maggie's *Mignon* debut on Broadway on March 18, Paddock had arranged for the Standard Theater, whose manager, William Henderson, was a Long Branch neighbor and friend, the ally who had defended Maggie against charges of southern sympathy in Pittsburgh. It would be her first return to Broadway in nearly six years except for scattered benefits. Henderson mounted the production well and provided good support to Maggie and

Harris (as Wilhelm), and *Mignon* had every chance to succeed. Nevertheless, it failed, playing to half-empty houses.

For one thing, *Mignon* was outdated. By the late 1870s, Broadway productions, chiefly those of Augustin Daly, were increasingly exploring challenging social issues, and *Mignon* was a throwback. To make matters worse, on March 22 Booth's Theater produced an opera of *Mignon* starring famed soprano Clara Louise Kellogg as Philina, which proved a complete triumph. Adding to Maggie's problems, her voice still had not healed. She spoke rapidly and breathlessly, fighting laryngitis.

Despite Mignon being a new character for Maggie, "it unmistakably was Fanchon who accompanied [her lines] with a hundred little movements and gestures which all the theatergoers in the city have laughed or cried over in years past." After a week she and Henderson acceded to popular demand and switched to *Fanchon*, and in its familiarity lay success. "We think of her far more frequently as Fanchon than by her name. She has made the part as wholly her own as Jefferson has that of Rip Van Winkle or Sothern that of Dundreary." "In exuberance, picturesqueness, pathos and an indefinable charm of personality, it is unchanging." Her "fantastic gambols," her "defiant mirth," her half-contemptuous, half-sympathetic attitude toward the 'handsome Landry,' her changes from the hoyden to the gentlewoman . . . cast a spell over every imaginative spectator." Her voice, though, remained noticeably strained. Midway through her fourth week at the Standard she switched to *Barefoot* and filled her fifth and final week with *Pearl*, with Harris as Lonstalot and Russell Bassett (who would stay with Maggie for five seasons) as the Commander.[3]

Then it was time for the annual cycle of one-night stands in New York and Pennsylvania towns, supported by Harris and a small company assembled by Paddock, almost all inexperienced unknowns except for Julian, still playing minor roles. In April they toured Poughkeepsie, Saratoga Springs, Syracuse, Lockport, Wilkes-Barre, Scranton, Easton, and Reading.

For the first time in over six years, Maggie went next to Philadelphia for a week in early May at the Walnut Street Theater, now another combination house. She had avoided the city, she said because during the war she had been branded a "Little Rebel" there and consistently met with the financial loss. But attendance remained good and reviewers kind, one focusing on the many moods of Fanchon: "fiercely defiant, then tenderly melting, one minute full of [deviltry], the next all gentle meekness, now merry as a cricket, again half heartbroken, at one time a bold, reckless tomboy and then again blushing, trembling maid with a heart brimful of love."[4]

Then came two nights in Wilmington, followed by one-nighters in Paterson, New Jersey; Bridgeport, Connecticut; Springfield, Worcester and Lowell, and Massachusetts. She closed her season in Newport and Providence, Rhode

Island, heading back to Long Branch to recuperate before an August tour to California.

Finances were still a problem, though. Falling behind on interest payments on some of her Long Branch properties, in July she signed over to the bank one hundred shares of capital stock in The Cincinnati Gaslight and Coke Co. in exchange for a loan of $10,000 at 6 percent interest. Unable by November even to meet that interest, she would lose the shares when the bank sold them for over $13,000 (the profit reverting to Maggie), but at least would get to keep her land. Ironically, some papers were reporting that summer that Maggie possessed a gem collection worth at least $20,000, buying "any rare and valuable stones that suit her fancy."[5]

With Paddock, Harris, Prescott, Bassett, and a few others, she left Long Branch on July 31 for California—her first return in six years—for an August 12 opening in San Francisco at the luxurious California Theater. Buoyed by a speculative wave of gold and silver mining, California had escaped the financial panic and bank failures of 1873–1877, until now. Several theaters had just gone under, leaving dozens of unemployed actors and stage technicians wandering the city. The California Theater had remained in operation under the astute management of Barton Hill after the departure a year ago of John McCullough. From the ranks of the unemployed Hill easily filled out the casts to support Maggie.

Granted, California was still Lotta's territory, and many of the greatest names in theatrical stardom had preceded Maggie, along with minstrel, burlesque and variety shows, but she was intent on providing San Franciscans not only her established repertoire but at least one new piece. She had purchased a new "comedy-drama" from playwright Louis Vider entitled *Birds of Passage*, rehearsing it on the train west. It would debut in two weeks. In the meantime, she readied *Mignon*, a dubious choice, for her opening, which was delayed a day to honor popular British light comedian H. J. Montague, who died in the city on August 11.

Situated on Bush Street in the heart of San Francisco's entertainment district, the mammoth California Theater threatened to engulf tiny Maggie. It could accommodate (tightly) up to 2,500, with a 77′×80′ stage lit by three rows of twenty-seven footlights and dozens of calcium limelights with parabolic reflectors. *Mignon* failed. It was "tedious" with "scenes being, to a certain extent, repetitions of each other, representing, as they do, Mignon's love and misery in one form or another." Maggie labored heroically, but Harris dropped the ball: "He merely walked through his part and spoke the lines in a matter-of-course sort of manner which betokened either an utter lack of interest or else a fear that any increased effort might betray him into a rant." Bassett as Sparati "had little to do but walk off and on in the most incomprehensible manner." The others fared little better, with Prescott—unhappy in her role—coming in for particularly harsh treatment.⁶

With Harris as Landry, Bassett as Father Barbeaud and Prescott as Fadet, Maggie offered *Fanchon* the following week but still drew disappointing audiences. By Friday she switched to *Pearl* and did slightly better. The actors she brought seemed competent, but some of the locals hired by Hill were woefully deficient, especially a wretched Madelon.

For her third week, Maggie brought out the melodramatic *Birds of Passage*. She and Harris played Rosetta and Lazaro, street singers (again) who wander Mexico City famished and penniless. The viceroy of Mexico (Bassett) hires them for a court banquet, where they become caught up in palace intrigue and accused of complicity in an incipient rebellion. Condemned to death, they are saved when Rosetta miraculously produces (yet another) locket which proves she is the rightful daughter of the viceroy. Lazaro, created a marquis, wins her hand. The play's only humor came in the banquet scene when Rosetta comically over imbibes wine.

But even Maggie could not rescue a script which was "weak, wishy-washy [and] intolerable. It is without grace, wit, force, or elegance of detail, . . . has not a shadow of originality [and] is amateurish and crude." After three nights she withdrew it. "Everyone saw it who wanted to, and no one who saw it ever wanted to see it again." It almost destroyed her engagement, rescued only by a benefit night of *Jane Eyre*, although Harris' Rochester was "wholly unlike the misanthropical Lord Rochester as lined by Charlotte Brontë. . . . We have witnessed none worse." It came as a welcome deliverance when actress Kate Claxton offered Maggie $1,000 over the cost she had paid for the rights to *Birds of Passage*.⁷

Maggie's San Francisco engagement "really should have proved to be more successful than it did. The grand mistake was in opening in *Mignon*, and insisting on its repetition for the livelong week, despite the earnest protests entered by the overwhelming vacancies in the auditorium. *Fanchon* and *Jane Eyre* would have been winning cards if they had been played at the beginning of the game." Concluded one reviewer, "California does not seem to hold luck for" Maggie Mitchell, who "has never been a California favorite."⁸

Hoping for better reception in Sacramento, she took her actors there for a week at the newly renovated Metropolitan Theater, opening on September 9 with *Fanchon*, which was deemed much better than that of the recently successful Kingsbury, still dogging Maggie in the role. *Jane Eyre* also proved a hit. It was "the realism of art, the emotions aroused through the imagination, acted upon and swayed by intellectual power, and held in check by heart heroism [sic]." Maggie's Jane "was the embodiment of Charlotte Bronte's heroine." She finished the week with large houses but would come away from California worse off financially.⁹

She then rushed to Memphis upon receiving news of the death there from yellow fever of her half-brother John H. Lomax Mitchell, along with his wife and three of their five children, including young Willie who had performed with Maggie. (Sixty-four deaths occurred in Memphis in twenty-four hours.) The remaining two, Dodson Lomax Mitchell, 10, and Johnny H. Mitchell, 4, were also ill. Maggie arranged for them to travel to Baltimore if they were well enough by November when she was scheduled to perform at the Holliday Street Theater and could care for them.

Her children, Fanchon, now 9, and Harry, 6, were still being cared for by Maggie's siblings Sophia, Charles, Emma, and Sarah, in New York. The letters Maggie exchanged with her children are warm and encouraging. She wrote Harry, "I *love* you and Fanchon so *dearly* that every word is dearly cherished," reminding him to obey his aunts and expressing her pride in his schoolwork and music and dancing lessons. In fall she would enroll him in the Flushing Institute on Long Island.[10]

She was able to spend time with them in New York during her next engagement, the week of October 7 back at Sinn's in Brooklyn. There, with Harris, she ran through her repertoire supported by its indifferent company, which included a familiar face who became a stalwart for the remainder of her career: Robert F. McClannin, 44. Except for the first night, when a rainstorm depleted their audience, they drew decent audiences. The *Brooklyn Eagle*, though, panned her characters "which, while they unquestionably exist in real life, are not quite the sort of persons we desire to see upon the stage, and certain suggestions in the course of the play offend good taste and more than verge upon impropriety"—an unusual rebuke for this moral woman. Harris presented a "large, robust figure" which lent "dignity to age and sorrow, and his firm voice gives full expression to distress."[11]

In Manhattan, Maggie opened for three weeks on October 14 at the Grand Opera House, which managers John F. Poole and Thomas L. Donnelly publicized as being safe and attractive to families. This delineation was increasingly necessary because of the practice of prostitutes getting minimal acting training and then performing on stage for no salary to snare wealthy men, all with the winking complicity of some managers. Decent women were urged to avoid contact with these depraved females and corrupt managers. Maggie, an "irreproachable wife and mother," naturally did so.[12]

Mignon having tanked at the Standard in March, she stuck this go-round with *Fanchon* (and shelved *Mignon* for almost a year). The result was full houses nightly, with standing room and seats in the aisles. In her first week, she played to an unprecedented 26,000 people. Poole and Donnelly provided her and Harris with a strong supporting company which included two actors she knew well, playing old men: H. B. Phillips, up from Washington, and

Albert G. Enos, who would tour with Maggie off and on for another five years. Olivia Rand, Shewell's wife, shone as Chouchon in *Pearl*.

John Albaugh had taken over Baltimore's Holliday Street Theater from Ford and next hosted Maggie, who brought Harris and Rand with her, opening on November 4 with *Pearl*. Four days later her two orphaned nephews arrived from Memphis, and Maggie took them under her wing at Guy's Hotel. When she played *Fanchon* the following week, she installed them in box seats. "They leaned forward as eager to drink in to the full every word that fell from the lips of the 'Cricket,' and they laughed and cried and crowed and wept, as one emotion succeeded another, and their heartstrings were touched one by one." But this escapism was momentary. "The stories they tell of the dreadful plague that deprived them of their father and mother, brother and sister are touching in the extreme."[13]

Not wishing to subject them to the rigors of the road, when Maggie closed in Baltimore she took them to New York to be cared for by her sisters until she could take them with her to Long Branch in summer. Then, with Harris, Rand, and part of the Holliday Street Company, she played a few nights in nearby Wilmington and Newark en route to an opening on November 25 at Albaugh's home base in Albany.

There, this mini-combination performed five different plays in six nights, then headed to one-night stands in Troy, Utica, Watertown, Oswego, Syracuse, and Rochester. Audiences were large and reviews mixed, the supporting company bearing the brunt of the criticism. Harris' days with Maggie appeared numbered as he drew increasingly acerbic notices. ("Not much can be said" for "the same leading man who has dragged through her plays for several years.")[14]

Still temporizing for support, Maggie sent Albaugh's actors back to Albany, then headed west with Harris to meet the St. Louis-based Olympic Theater company in Indianapolis for two nights, then returned with them to St. Louis for two weeks of *Fanchon*, which drew only meager houses. One critic attributed this to Maggie's having "being too well known and having been too frequently seen in the characters she presents."[15]

For the third year, she played Cincinnati over the holidays. For two weeks at the Grand Opera House with the Olympic company, she provided "the strongest and most perfect characterizations ever seen on the American boards." Reviewing her would be "like gilding gold or painting the lily. . . . She never grows old and she weaves her enchanting spell, compelling laughter or beguiling tears as no other enchantress of the stage."[16]

"Escorted by her popular husband," she received a reporter at breakfast at the Grand Hotel, her "quaint, piquant face" with "its mobile features . . . set in a frame of goldish hair gleaming like an aureole about her forehead and breaking out in sunshiny tresses from the ribbon confining it." She claimed

Fanchon as her favorite role but admitted sometimes tiring of it. "But, of course, after I am on the stage, I enter into it as heartily as ever." Asked how many times she had played it, Paddock, still functioning as her manager, provided an inflated estimate, which got picked up by newspapers across the country, of over 3,300 times. Such estimates had circulated for years, but this was the highest yet. This, of course, was impossible, as it would have meant her performing the role 183 times in each of its eighteen seasons, each of which averaged forty-two weeks of six or seven (with matinee) performances, meaning she would have played *Fanchon* two-thirds of the time, with all other roles crammed into the remaining third. But puffery reigned, and such inflated figures—stoked by Maggie's claims in 1880 that she had played the role nearly 4,000 times—were eventually included in her obituaries.[17]

It had been "a hard season," she acknowledged, and a western engagement remained before she could return east for a week in February 1879 at the Park in Brooklyn. But upon receiving news of the death in New York of her littlest nephew, Johnny, not yet five, she canceled the western booking, dismissed the Olympic company, and rushed home to bury him.

In Brooklyn with Sinn, her vetting of new scripts proved as misguided and ill-fated as it had been for *Becky Mix*. Shewell, not content to act and manage in Boston, had written a "new emotional play" (melodrama) expressly for Maggie, which she now debuted. *Flotsam and Jetsam*, based on a French tale, recycled the woeful fate that befalls a young maiden named Marguerite (Maggie) who rejects the true love of a young sailor and marries a man (Harris) who repulses and subsequently abuses her, to save her father's (Shewell himself) farm.

It was an unqualified failure. Trite, melodramatic moments abounded, the "absurdly feeble" plot contained gaping holes and improbabilities, and the dialog and characters were contrived and boring. Her character was "so small as to leave hardly any impression but that of a graceful, charming little lady without any will of her own." In a decade when other playwrights were producing serious, realistic problem dramas about marital inequality and divorce, it was "neither new nor emotional, and its French origin sticks out as emphatically as a wart in every scene and almost every sentence. . . . There is nothing in the piece that should commend itself to Miss Mitchell and nothing which should commend it to an audience." Sinn, who had interrupted a highly successful run of Gilbert and Sullivan's *H.M.S Pinafore* to accommodate Maggie, insisted she return to *Fanchon*, and audiences returned. Maggie never touched *Flotsam and Jetsam* again.[18]

The *Pinafore* juggernaut was threatening to derail her and other stars and would careen further out of control with countless productions of *The Pirates of Penzance*, *Patience*, *Iolanthe*, and *The Mikado* in the early 1880s. Their escapist stories, beguiling melodies, and clever lyrics cut deeply into

Maggie's territory. Over the next decade, she would find herself fending off not only competitors like Lotta and the growing threat from Buffalo Bill's Wild West shows, but also ubiquitous Gilbert and Sullivan comic operas performed by amateur and professional companies. Even her friend John T. Ford had assembled one. There was some speculation that Maggie herself would assemble a combination company of *Pinafore* and play Josephine, but that never came to fruition. She insisted repeatedly that she had no intention of playing any Gilbert and Sullivan character.

To reassert her preeminence, she now formed a full combination company for her most energetic and expansive tour to date, four months of travel from New Jersey to Nebraska and back to New England. *Fanchon* and *Lorle*, with an occasional *Pearl*, would predominate until May, when she added *Jane Eyre* and *Barefoot*. She drew from a body of actors she knew and trusted, many of whom already knew her repertoire. Despite his increasing age and girth, Harris would anchor the group of twenty-two, along with McClannin and Enos (old men), Nellie Whiting from the Olympic company (soubrettes), Maurice Bertram "M. B." Curtis (low comedy), and Marion Clifton and Mrs. J. H. Rowe (née Georgie Dickson) (old women, the latter as the vital Fadet). Maggie's nephew Julian, now 27, would join her tour for the first time, but only in minor roles. Utility players auditioned in New York would take the rest. Maggie also hired a new advance man, former Wilmington manager W. T. Elliott.

Paddock, traveling with her, booked the tour into combination houses—those intentionally lacking stock companies—for one-, two-, or three-night stands. They began February 18 and 19 in Newark and Trenton amid snowstorms, followed by Harrisburg, Wheeling, Steubenville, Youngstown, Akron, Toledo, and Detroit. For the most part, she drew large audiences, including many ladies, but the upper gallery tended to remain "comparatively bare, as is generally the case when the stage is occupied by any other than a blood-and-thunder play [melodrama]." The general verdict was that "she has lost none of her magnetic power." Almost forty-three, "Her fresh and youthful appearance and rounded figure she retains perfectly, and sings and dances with the graceful abandon of a girl of sixteen."[19]

From mid-March through late April she and her company conducted a frenetic swing through Ohio, Indiana, Illinois, Missouri, Kansas, Nebraska, Iowa, and Minnesota. Thanks to the growing rail network, she visited nineteen towns for the first time in her career (Ohio: Sandusky, Wooster, Newark, Chillicothe, Xenia; Indiana: Richmond, Logansport, Lafayette; Illinois: Danville, Rockford; Missouri: Jefferson City; Kansas: Lawrence, Topeka, Atchison; Nebraska: Omaha; Iowa: Council Bluffs, Des Moines, Keokuk, Cedar Rapids). This was a shrewd tactic, as these averaged nearly 13,000 citizens and most sported a new "opera house." For two weeks in early May in Chicago at Hooley's Theater, built soon after the Great Fire, they attracted only light houses and apathetic critics. The only acts drawing large houses were Lotta and the comedy duo of Stuart Robson and William H. Crane.

Still, at it, Maggie began advertising for a new script, "a purely American play containing a character suited to her style of acting and with all the other characters subordinate to it." She bemoaned to Logan that *Flotsam and Jetsam* had failed and the tour was exhausting. Logan, in London (her husband was U.S. consul in Cardiff, Wales), understood. "It is really because your standard is so high and your style so peculiar that you are more difficult to 'fit' than an ordinary artist." But not to worry, she had an idea "to get you *L'Ami Fritz* from the French authors [Émile Erckmann and Alexandre Chatrian] and myself write up the part as I know it might be able to suit you." The Comedie Francaise was bringing it to London in June when Logan would assess its appropriateness for Maggie. She enclosed "a resumé of the plot, which I am pretty sure will strike you, as it does me, as quite promising." Logan would handle negotiations with the French agent and did not doubt that permission would be granted. However, nothing came of this.[20]

Playing *Fanchon* and *Lorle* almost exclusively, Maggie and company continued their tour for another month up into Michigan, then across Canada and down into New England. She played many towns—about the same size or larger—for the first time (Michigan: Kalamazoo, Grand Rapids, East Saginaw, Port Huron; Ontario: London, Hamilton, Toronto, Kingston; Québec: Montreal; Massachusetts: Holyoke). In these, she and the company were generously applauded and critically praised. In Hamilton, she and Paddock took time to assist in the wedding of two of the company's young utility players, Marie Henley and Rufus Scott. In Montreal, the Governor-General Marquis of Lorne and Princess Louise (Queen Victoria's daughter) attended *Fanchon*.

Paddock erred in setting ticket prices too high in the houses he had booked in Maine (50¢ admission, $1 for a reserved seat). This, combined with bad weather and a political convention in Portland, kept audiences small. When she closed her season on June 14 in Springfield, Massachusetts, seven men of her company presented her with a symbolic gift, a bronze ornament depicting a stag at bay, worth $100, along with a silver medal engraved with their names.

With no evidentiary trail, it is difficult to assess the financial success of this combination tour. But multi-script combinations like Maggie's were generally more successful than those with only one. Numerous newspapers that spring speculated on the wealth and earnings of various stars, including Maggie, John F. Owens, Edwin Booth, E. A. Sothern, and of course Lotta. Maggie, it was claimed, netted $30,000–50,000 a year. The *New York Herald* bewailed that this handful of stars unfairly "have the cream of the [theatrical] business, leaving the skim milk for managers and pretty hard tack for the minor people." But the *New York Dramatic News* asserted that these stars' earnings were overstated: "'Maggie Mitchell makes $30,000–50,000 a year with ease.' She does, does she? Miss Mitchell would be happy to know where."[21]

That summer she suffered two financial setbacks, one of staggering proportion. In June Paddock's sloppy and/or unethical management led to a suit by Hartford manager-printer Alexander Calhoun over unpaid tour profits from Spring 1873. He alleged that Paddock had padded accounts of expenses to deprive him of $1,380. The Connecticut Superior Court decided against Paddock, who was ordered to pay Calhoun, with compounded interest back to 1873, over $2,000. Calhoun would not be through with Paddock, though.

The second setback was worse. Self-admittedly "in no sense a businesswoman," Maggie still trusted her husband with all of her finances, investments and real estate transactions. Several years ago, before the financial panic hit, he had purchased some adjacent wooded lots at Long Branch for $75,000, putting down $40,000 (over $1 million today) of Maggie's money and signing a note for the rest. Unable to meet the mortgage payments, the Paddocks lost all of the lots to foreclosure, netting not one cent. Since Maggie remained the sole "carry-all for her entire family, . . . feeds them, lodges them, and clothes them," she forsook any plans of retirement. To assuage her losses, she rented out her older Long Branch cottage that summer to actress Mary Anderson, who would purchase it outright the following year and become a close friend.[22]

By 1880, touring with a combined company had become *de rigueur*. Maggie and Paddock spent much of the summer assembling theirs for the 1879–80 season, one of a reported forty going out. It would consist of only sixteen actors: Harris, McClannin, Enos, Clifton, Julian (promoted now to comic roles like Didier, Jemmy, and Pierrot), newlyweds Marie and Rufus Scott, George F. Carlisle, J. H. Redding (acquired in Montreal, to stay with Maggie for five years), Annie Mortimer (for old women, specifically Fadet, also for five years), Lettie Allen (acquired in Chicago, having acted since infancy, to stay with Maggie for two years playing soubrettes like Madelon and Chouchon), and a few utility players. Maggie's brother Charles would serve as advance agent. Except for one ill-fated new script, her repertoire would remain *Fanchon, Barefoot, Pearl, Lorle,* and *Jane Eyre*.

With Paddock as manager, the tour began auspiciously on August 25 at the rebuilt Grand Opera House in Columbus with *Jane Eyre*, attended by Treasury Secretary John Sherman. By the end of the week, Maggie had brought in over $4,000, "proof that the popularity of the little lady is not on the decline." The second week, six one-night stands in smaller Ohio towns, yielded over $1,000. In Louisville, even "Maggie Mitchell's poorest of acting could be classed among the average star actress' best."[23]

A week in Cincinnati followed by two in Pittsburgh produced houses crammed "from pit to dome," with hundreds of extra chairs and campstools placed in aisles and the orchestra forced to give up their seats, with other patrons left standing. Almost unheard of, in Pittsburgh (far past her Civil War–era opprobrium) "hundreds of ladies took seats in the gallery." "Who is there," asked one critic, "that can imitate the gifts that nature has lavished upon this sunny little actress—her winsome manner, the ever-flitting modes, the lights and shades, the almost girlish prattle, the womanly indignation? It is hers alone."[24]

In October it was back to one-night stands through Pennsylvania, New Jersey, Connecticut, and Rhode Island. Crowds were good but reviews rare: "Maggie Mitchell is so well known here as to make a criticism on her performance unnecessary." Struggling to understand the decades-long allure of this "spoiled child-wife that holds the stage and the attention and sympathy of the audience" was the *New Haven Register*:

> She defies all the rules of the art. . . . She is always the same. . . . Her presentation of one character is like another as two peas. She is always Maggie Mitchell. . . . She is not an actress. She is always the same thoroughly spoiled child pouring forth a torrent of maudlin sentimentalism which would not be tolerated for an instant in any other actress, and which for that matter no other actress would dare attempt, for it would be fatal. . . . She is thoroughly unnatural and unreal . . . and yet this very unnaturalness seems to add to her popularity. Although now nearly fifty years of age [sic], she retains her youth wonderfully and still skips about the stage like a girl in pinafores. . . . There is no music in her voice, . . . which is a cross between a groan, a whinny, and a screech and would ruin any other actress. The constant use of the rising inflection in the conversational parts is absolutely painful and monotonous, but no one thinks of complaining. The action, too, is too childish, not natural nor artistic. To counterbalance these defects, she has a petite and pretty figure, some pert ways, and does her "asides" occasionally in a very charming manner and dances very prettily at times. [Her] faults of voice, the over-buoyancy of manner and the whining, crying tone of a petted child asking a favor are forgotten, particularly by the ladies of the audience, who are always in sympathy with her. . . . Ask a lady the reason for her admiration of Maggie Mitchell and the answer will be, "Oh, she is so cunning." Ask her if the acting be art-like or natural and she will at first be dumbfounded [then reply,] "Well, she's too sweet for anything, and there isn't anybody like her." And so the people throng to see her, and hear her and are amused.

They also shed copious tears: "The clotheslines all about the city today are full of handkerchiefs drying. Maggie Mitchell was here last night."[25]

Brooklyn's Park Theater was a haven, though, and Maggie settled in with her company for a week of *Lorle* (its first time there) and *Fanchon* in late October. Houses were filled to standing room, and reviews effusive. "Whether as the village belle, who is not shy because she knows no better than to be natural, as the nervous little bride, conscious of her solecisms only through the disgusted expression of her husband's face, as the outraged and indignant discoverer of her husband's perfidy, or as the suffering little victim of masculine infidelity, she is entirely truthful to nature.... There is no artist on the stage today who has so firm a hold upon the affections of the Brooklyn public as this amiable little lady and most accomplished actress."[26]

By the end of October Maggie had reportedly personally cleared over $24,000. Her good fortune continued during a week each at Ford's National Theater in Washington and Louisa Lane Drew's Arch Street Theater in Philadelphia. At Albaugh's Holliday Street Theater in Baltimore, "her spirited grace" and "airiness of a fairy" elicited raves. "One might imagine she had explored the springs of all human feeling and surprised the secret of every heart." Her "transitions from gaiety to sadness or from sorrow to a smile were so sharp at times that ... the spectator was in danger of swallowing a tear hot from his eyelids.... The immortal verse of Shakespeare never commanded more rapt attention."[27]

Confident among such accolades, in Baltimore she tried out yet another new role. On Thanksgiving Day, both matinee and evening, she performed the title role in *Trix*, the rights to which she had purchased for $3,000 from journalist-critic-playwright Archibald Gordon. He originally wrote it for another actress who rejected it, then claimed it had been written exclusively for Maggie. It never seemed quite whole. She played another indigent strolling singer-dancer who has been cheated out of her rightful inheritance, who travels under the protection of a broken-down old actor (McClannin). Wealthy young men (Harris chief among them) pursue her, but her cunning, spunk and wryly apropos witticisms fend them off. Comic relief is provided by a bumbling caretaker and a "stupid servant" (Julian and Henley). In the last act, through the revelation of yet another secret of birth, she is restored to her proper station. Audiences enjoyed *Trix*—5,000 attended these first four performances—but Maggie remained unsatisfied and set it aside for three years.

Tending her territory, she returned in December to the Deep South for the first time in nearly four years. In Richmond, Charleston, Savannah, Augusta, Atlanta and Montgomery, houses and reviews were good. She was called the opposite of Rip Van Winkle, remaining the same while everyone and everything around her aged. "Maggie Mitchell does not simulate.... She looks the character, she feels the character, and she is the character." Some critics ranked her fame with that of Edwin Forrest and Joseph Jefferson III.[28]

Heading west into Texas for the first time, she stopped in New Orleans to catch a Sunday performance of Tony Denier's Humpty Dumpty Pantomime

Troupe, whose antics matched her own. In Galveston for Christmas week, she drew modest but appreciative houses while fighting another sore throat. *Jane Eyre* drew the warmest reviews, especially for her transitions, as her subservience evolved to admiration for Rochester, finally "blossoming into a burning and ill-concealed passion."[29]

She rang out 1879 in Austin and opened the new decade in Marshall, Texas, where *Pearl* drew sharply divided criticism. One reviewer derided such "sentimental dramas that are not to be commended for their delicacy or propriety.... It is a travesty in emotional exhibitions and a burlesque upon comedy. Some of the scenes were very gross and the play itself a confusion." But another was deeply moved by Marie's final scenes when first "the light of reason departs from her and an idiotic stare, a maniacal laugh, and wild wandering talk proclaim that she is mad" and her subsequent return home. "There was not a dry eye in the house, as footsore and weary, deaf only to the sound of her mother's voice [she] returns to reason during her mother's prayer."[30]

Maggie next played Little Rock (first time), then Terre Haute, Crawfordsville (first time), Lafayette, and Indianapolis, Indiana, followed by Bloomington and Springfield, Illinois. In Indianapolis and other cities, she began to attract hints, some not so subtle, about her age: "Maggie Mitchell seems to be losing her attractiveness as a star. Can she be growing old?" At one time her "girlishness was much appreciated by playgoers, but it is so no longer." "The little lady is beginning to outgrow her characters. Age never stales genius, but physical changes necessitate a change in her characters, not right now, but in a short time." "She should abandon these girlish characters entirely, or try another line of characters." *Jane Eyre* was the most often-cited alternative. She "has played *Fanchon* till everything she attempts is *Fanchon*." Plus, her mature voice was no longer appropriate for her roles: "She ought to replace the songs with others better suited to her voice." Some company members came to her defense, including McClannin: "She's just as lively a cricket now as she was when she first hopped on the stage"—and there were times when she attended late-night post-show events, some involving dancing.[31]

Still, that winter she toyed with the idea of retiring at the end of the season, to "settle down to home life. The frequent complaints about her voice are causing her to lose prestige." The time was right, she said, as this had been her best season since 1872.[32]

She abandoned all plans to perform in England, too, despite urging from Charlotte Cushman, Henry Wadsworth Longfellow, and James Collier, among others. "Her style would set them wild," Collier believed, "but she set herself resolutely against it. 'Why should I go to England to play,' said she; 'I am popular in my own country, and can fill any house I play in. If I should go to England and be successful, I could do no more when I returned, and it would cost me a season's savings to make the trip and do the honors properly. Besides, the very mannerisms that here are half the cause of my popularity might there be a source of criticism and rebuke. No, Jim: America is good enough for me.'" When reporters pressed, she demurred: "I had better let well enough alone.... A great many worthy people as good as I am have attempted to please the English, who have peculiar views and hard to suit, and I do not care to make the adventure." As she told Logan, "What is the use of my going? I don't need the prestige in case of success, failure would annoy me, and under any circumstances the money they offer is nothing."[33]

She spent February touring the Midwest: Missouri (St. Louis, Kansas City, St. Joseph); Kansas (Leavenworth and Atchison); Nebraska (Omaha); Iowa (Davenport, Clinton [first time]); Illinois (Rock Island, Freeport); Wisconsin (LaCrosse, Eau Claire [first time], Beloit [first time]); and Minnesota (St. Paul and Minneapolis). In one-nighters in smaller towns (and their surrounding burgs) she sold out "opera houses" and in larger cities drew the largest crowds of their seasons.

During a week of sold-out houses in Chicago in early March, she and Paddock received word that his hat store in Cleveland had first been burglarized of over $1,500 in goods, and within a few days destroyed by fire. He rushed there to assess damages. There is no record of its being rebuilt or the extent to which he recovered any insurance money, but he returned to Maggie's side by the following week as she played a week in Detroit.

Backstage after her Saturday matinee of *Fanchon* there, she welcomed a reporter "in the childish yet earnest tones that have come to be inseparably associated with the character." He marveled at her endurance, considering the demands of that script. "It is talk, act, sing, and dance all the time," she reminded him. "Fanchon opens every act and is on stage most of the time during the piece. I tell you it is hard work." Was she losing her affection for the character? "No, I cannot say that such is the case. I like the part and never go to act it that I do not feel some new love for it. Often, before going to the theater, I feel tired and have a thought that I would like to be excused from the task for just one night. [However,] the instant that I reach the theater— and the ladies and gentlemen who are acting with me can tell you the same thing—my nerves are at their very greatest tension. I am all excitement all interest in my work ... and I do not think it egotism that when I am on the stage as Fanchon, I feel every word. In fact, I *am* Fanchon."[34]

After a few nights playing Michigan towns, among them for the first time Lansing and Adrian, she dipped into Ohio, to Toledo, Sandusky, and a week in Cleveland, followed by another in Buffalo, Dunkirk (first time), Syracuse and Utica, New York. In these, as had been the case all season, the same five supporting actors consistently drew praise: Harris, McClannin, Julian, Clifton, and Allen.

Then it was back to Broadway, opening for Poole and Donnelly at the Grand Opera House on April 5. Maggie intended to perform *Fanchon* for only a week, followed by *Barefoot*, but popular demand drove her to extend *Fanchon* into a second week. Everyone wanted "the same *Fanchon* as of old, with the rippling laugh and pleasant voice, the inexhaustible flow of spirits and love of mischief, with a maidenly purity showing through it all, a picture of innocent girlhood run wild." Mid-week she switched to *Barefoot*, then to *Jane Eyre*, in which her "girlishness, tempered by maidenly dignity and a touch of sadness . . . swayed the audience, as it were, as completely as though she were pulling the strings [of] marionettes."[35]

Following a week for Albaugh in Albany, Maggie played one night in Troy, New York, filling out two more in Massachusetts. In Holyoke, on May 10 the Calhoun legal judgment from the previous summer, which Paddock had never paid, caught up with him. He was arrested that evening at the opera house and remanded before a hearing on May 12. With no alternative, Maggie went on to Taunton and Fall River. Claiming no assets, his Cleveland store having burned and all property in Maggie's name, Paddock took the "poor debtor's oath" and was released. To prevent Maggie's property in New York—her house on 54th Street and two lots on 126th Street—from being attached, Paddock claimed that their primary residence was the former and had the latter transferred for one dollar into the name of her brother Charles. No attempt was made to attach either of their properties in Long Branch, and Maggie later quietly bought the New York property back from Charles. The court decided that Paddock, who had made the contract with Calhoun, could not claim his wife's earnings.

However, news of his evasion "virtually shut out the Maggie Mitchell combination from playing in New England," and she was forced to truncate her tour on May 15 in Brockton, Massachusetts, after which she visited friends in Boston. Contumely was heaped on Paddock's head: "It would seem to the average citizen that he could better afford to pay the judgment than to try and secure release on such a plea." "Paddock's attempt to escape by taking the poor debtor's oath while wearing diamonds and other valuables" was laughable. By July, newspapers across the country were deriding his willingness to live off his wife's earnings, calling it strange and selfish. Some men would do anything to chase a dollar, "as Hank Paddock will swear on a stack of Bibles as colossal as his cheek when he is full of gin at his wife's expense and rattles her money in his pocket with his back against a bar, while she is earning his living and his luxuries for him on the stage."[36]

Ironically, it had been Maggie's most profitable season yet, yielding her over $35,000. At forty-five she was still at the height of her popularity, "just as sprightly and sweet and charming as when long ago—and yet it seems but yesterday—we laughed and cried and cried and laughed at her cunning little antics and delightful touches of pathos. Maggie Mitchell has lost none of her beauty—a beauty of simplicity, artlessness, and vivacity combined, . . . like the recurrence of a sweet dream of which one never wearies and of which one only complains that it is all too short." But more Maggie clones were waiting in the wings.[37]

As assiduously as she worked to maintain the exclusivity of *Fanchon* and critics pronounced her beyond imitation, imitators abounded. The latest was pixyish, sixteen-year-old Anna Boyle, touring with yet another unsanctioned *Fanchon*. "There was a time," wrote one smitten Boyle adherent, when Maggie "held, as if by the divine right of genius, the supreme place in the delineation of this delicate and difficult character, but that time has passed, never to return. Age and ugliness, those twin faces of dramatic queens, have set their seal upon her face and form and the roses have been driven out by the wrinkles. . . . Miss Anna Boyle now wears the crown, for today she reigns supreme in the glorious Cricket." By next season Boyle would be performing *Fanchon* on Broadway.[38]

Thirty-something Nellie Boyd, too, had been playing an unauthorized *Fanchon* in smaller venues in the Midwest for ten years and would continue to do so with a combination for another decade. Another comer whose style imitated Maggie's was twenty-two-year-old Annie Pixley, a chubby soubrette who had been performing on the west coast and Australia since age nine and married at fourteen. Her current vehicles, *H.M.S. Pinafore* and an adaptation of Bret Harte's "Luck of Roaring Camp" called *M'Liss* would bring her considerable New York success.

But Maggie shrugged them off and prepared another tour, thoughts of retirement dismissed.

NOTES

1. John had remarried a few years after the death of his first wife, Willie's mother, in 1860.

2. Olive Logan Sikes to MM, May 4, 1879, MM Papers, MS Collection 4552, NYPL.

3. *New York Graphic*, Mar. 26, 1878; *New York Evening Telegram*, Mar. 26, 1878; *New York Tribune*, Mar. 19, 1878; *Spirit of the Times*, Mar. 30, 1878.

4. *Philadelphia Inquirer*, May 7, 1878.

5. Promissory note, MM Papers, MS 4552, NYPL; *St. Louis Post-Dispatch*, Sept. 7, 1878.

6. *Alta California*, Aug. 18, 1878; MM interview with *Cincinnati Sun* reprinted in *Boston Weekly Globe*, Jan. 8, 1879.

7. *Alta California*, Aug. 27 and 31, 1878; *Chicago Tribune*, Sept. 8, 1878; *New York Times*, Sept. 15, 1878.

8. *Alta California*, Sept. 1, 1878; San Francisco correspondent for *Chicago Tribune*, Aug. 25, 1878.
9. *Sacramento Union*, Sept. 10–11, 1878.
10. MM to Harry from Harrisburg, PA, Mar. 9, 1879, MM Papers, MS 4552, NYPL.
11. *Brooklyn Eagle*, Oct. 8, 1878.
12. *New York Dramatic News*, Dec. 14, 1878.
13. *Pittsburgh Post-Gazette*, Nov. 12, 1878; *Los Angeles Herald*, Dec. 12, 1878.
14. *New York Dramatic News*, Dec. 7, 1878.
15. *St. Louis Post-Dispatch*, Dec. 21, 1878.
16. *Cincinnati Enquirer*, Dec. 31, 1878; *New York Dramatic News*, Jan. 4 and 11, 1879.
17. MM interviews, *Cincinnati Sun* reprinted in *Boston Weekly Globe*, Jan. 8, 1879, and *St. Louis Post-Dispatch*, Jan. 28, 1880.
18. *Brooklyn Eagle*, Feb. 11, 1879; *New York Dramatic News*, Feb. 15, 1879.
19. *Wheeling Register*, Feb. 27, 1879; *Wheeling Intelligencer*, Feb. 27, 1879.
20. *Brooklyn Eagle*, Feb. 3, 1879; Logan, *op cit*.
21. *New York Dramatic News*, Feb. 15, 1879; *New York Herald*, Feb. 10, 1879.
22. *New Haven Evening Register*, Sept. 4, 1879; *Washington Post*, Nov. 21, 1880.
23. *St. Paul (MN) Globe*, Sept. 15, 1879; *Louisville Commercial* reprinted (doubtless circulated by Maggie's brother) in *Harrisburg (PA) Patriot*, Nov. 5, 1880.
24. *Pittsburgh Post*, Sept. 29, 1879; *Pittsburgh Leader*, Oct. 5, 1879;
25. *Harrisburg Patriot*, Oct. 7, 1879; *New Haven Register*, Oct. 23–24, 1879.
26. *New York Herald*, Oct. 28, 1879; *Brooklyn Eagle*, Oct. 28, 1879.
27. *St. Paul (MN) Globe*, Nov. 2, 1879; Unidentified Baltimore paper (also likely provided by Maggie's brother) quoted in *Richmond Daily Dispatch*, Dec. 1, 1879.
28. *Atlanta Constitution*, Dec. 16, 1879.
29. *Galveston News*, Dec. 27, 1879.
30. *Marshall Tri-Weekly Herald*, Jan. 8, 1880; *Marshall Messenger*, Jan. 9, 1880.
31. *Chicago Inter Ocean*, Apr. 29, 1879; *Chicago Tribune*, May 19, 1878 and Apr. 29, May 8, 1879; *Cleveland Plain Dealer*, May 17, 1879; *New York Sun*, July 13, 1879; *Indianapolis Sentinel*, Jan. 17, 1880; (Bloomington IL) *The Pantagraph*, Jan. 20, 1880.
32. *Leavenworth (KS) Times*, Feb. 6, 1880.
33. *St. Louis Post-Dispatch*, Jan. 28, 1880; *St. Joseph (MO) Gazette*, Feb. 7, 1880; Logan, dateline London, Mar. 20, 1880, for *Cincinnati Enquirer*, reprinted in *Washington Sunday Herald*, Apr. 11, 1880; *Cincinnati Enquirer*, July 31, 1881.
34. *Detroit Free Press*, Mar. 14, 1880.
35. *New York Tribune*, Apr. 10, 1880; *New York Herald*, Apr. 17 and 19, 1880.
36. *Hartford Courant*, May 12 and 22, 1880; *National Police Gazette*, Oct. 21, 1882.
37. 1880 review of MM by Eugene Field of *Kansas City Star*, reprinted Mar. 29, 1918.
38. *New York Herald*, Nov. 30, 1880; Cincinnati correspondent for *Denver Tribune* quoted in *Washington Evening Star*, Nov. 6, 1880; *Macon (GA) Weekly Telegraph*, Oct. 14, 1879; Odell XI:282.

Chapter 12

"bathed in the fountain of perennial youth"

For 1880–81 Maggie and Paddock re-signed nearly all the same actors as last season except for Harris. On August 5, Harris married Maggie's sister Emma in New York, and then signed on with Mary Anderson. Maggie replaced him with Dick Russell, 34, the workmanlike actor who had briefly supported her four years ago. He would stay with her for three seasons but not receive the star billing that Collier and Harris had. Paddock would travel along as manager, and Charles Mitchell would continue as advance agent, a role in which he was skilled, with ever more gushing blurbs appearing in newspapers just before Maggie's arrival in a given town.

Before setting out, the Paddocks hosted at Long Branch a massive anniversary party for themselves attended by nearly a hundred noteworthy theatrical professionals, many giving recitations. One of the liveliest guests was Maggie's erudite father, at seventy-eight still slender and hearty from his daily, brisk eight- to ten-mile walks. He divided his year among his offspring at Long Branch, New York City, and Troy.

Maggie's combination, its repertoire unchanged except for one short-lived new piece, was only one of many setting out from New York that fall. What had been estimated as forty of them a year ago had become 120 by the close of last season, and would swell to 160 during the coming one. But the system had its drawbacks. As the *Mirror* would soon rue, "Esprit de corps, artistic progress, pecuniary advantage—these things are difficult under the tramping system."[1]

Maggie's combination opened the season on August 30 in Columbus, Ohio, followed by Chicago, drawing only fair houses. In what was becoming a frequent refrain, reviewers found themselves unable "to find a new thing to say of the *Fanchon* or the *Pearl of Savoy* of Maggie Mitchell. For twenty consecutive years critics have puzzled their brains to find something to add to the praises of Maggie's *Fanchon*, and they now give it up in despair. . . . Her plays—never worth much as plays—have long ceased to interest the older habitues of the theater, but the younger generation seems to find a never-ending fund of enjoyment in them."[2]

A week through Illinois and Indiana brought good houses, but reviewers noticed a touch of age in Maggie's voice. During two weeks in Cincinnati, her Jane drew the most praise, with Russell considered a better Rochester than Harris. The two weeks brought in over $13,000, including $1,100 from one Wednesday matinee. Buoyed by her success, she took time on her last Sunday afternoon there to drive a trotter sulky around the track at Chester Park, through the suburbs and surrounding hills, and back to the city.

October took her to Pittsburgh for John Ellsler, then Washington and Baltimore. In Pittsburgh, she drew "the largest audience ever gathered at a dramatic performance at the Opera House." In the capital, she was still "the unshaken favorite." Through a week of packed houses in Pennsylvania and New Jersey towns, she battled another severe cold that especially hindered her singing. From there the company settled into Mrs. Drew's Arch Street Theatre in Philadelphia, competing with Annie Pixley at Walnut Street. Maggie and Pixley did collaborate, though, in a Friday matinee benefit for the Order of the Elks (until about 1900 predominantly a theatrical charity).[3]

For Thanksgiving week in Brooklyn, Maggie gave nine performances in six days to consistently good business, notably attracting a multi-generational following. Then it was back to Broadway, to Poole and Donnelly's magnificent white marble, 2,000-seat Grand Opera House on 23rd Street, three blocks off the newly electrified Great White Way. Maggie's *Jane Eyre* earned praise for avoiding emotional sensationalism (the province of Clara Morris), achieving a total immersion in her character.

She closed out the year at the Park in Boston where she drew well despite intense competition from Sarah Bernhardt at the nearby Globe. It "was like a gathering of *Little Barefoot*'s old friends, and a more enthusiastic and responsive body of auditors is seldom seen." In Boston she began rehearsing a new script, *The Little Mother*, predictably taking the diminutive title role. She had known its author, George F. Fuller, the New York correspondent for the *Louisville Courier-Journal*, since his managerial days in Louisville during the war.[4]

She inaugurated 1881 with a five-week tour of New England and upstate New York. In Rochester, despite a driving snowstorm and almost impassable streets, she filled the house and won over critics. Like *Jane Eyre*, she blended "force and feeling in repose and with genuine grace and dignity."[5]

Jane Eyre drew the largest houses in Chicago in mid-February at Hooleys. More often, now, Maggie chose it to open an engagement, admired for its "sweetness of nature, the dignity of character, the delicate susceptibility, and the romance found in the life of the plain little governess. . . . Her child-like little figure excellently suits the character, whether as the young girl in her coarse pinafore, mutinous under injustice, or shooting courteous scorn at her exceedingly unpleasant relatives, or as the womanly little governess in her scenes with Rochester."[6]

Snow hurt attendance in Chicago, then attacked in force once the company headed west. The winter of 1880–81 went down in history as one of the most severe ever recorded, with the Midwest hit especially hard. Blizzards delivered nearly three feet of snow in some cities. Maggie ran into it when she tried to leave Davenport, Iowa, on March 3 after playing to a small audience and a caustic critic (*Jane Eyre* was "a travesty of the novel," its fire scene "laughable." Russell as Rochester "rolls his R's and prolongs his inflections disagreeably," making him not worthy of Jane).[7]

At 3:00 that afternoon they left Davenport on a special train with five engines, intending to perform in Iowa City on the 4th. The train fought deepening snow for hours until becoming snowbound for the night at a tiny depot at Walcott. Paddock groused, but Maggie kept calm and led the company in song and chat (and perhaps rehearsed *Little Mother*), then slept as best she could. After breakfast delivered from town and the efforts of a hundred volunteers from Davenport, the train was freed, retreating there by 9:00 p.m., after which a grateful Maggie performed *Fanchon*. After one night in Iowa City (curtailed from three) and canceling Minneapolis, she opened with *Jane Eyre* in St. Paul on March 10 to a large, cheering audience. On March 12, she debuted *Little Mother*. No one reviewed it, and over the next three weeks, Maggie only performed it twice before abandoning it entirely.

She was scheduled to open in Omaha on March 14 followed by Lincoln, Nebraska, on March 17, but again became snowbound upon leaving St. Paul. She made it to Omaha by the 18th, performing *Fanchon* to a surprisingly packed house, but skipped Lincoln, prompting its manager to threaten a lawsuit. After more cancellations in a swing through Kansas, she greeted the spring thaw in Kansas City and St. Louis.

Despite the travails of rail travel and poor hotels, Maggie continued to be "a vision of brightness and as bewitching as a fairy" once on stage. And the practice was perfecting the company, at least in the eyes of Midwestern reviewers. As the irascible Mrs. Reed in *Jane Eyre*, Marion Clifton avoided stereotype; as the scornful Georgina, Lettie Allen took her rejection by Rochester with grace; and Russell and McClannin gave polished performances. Local musicians, though, were disappointing. In Kansas City the orchestra "was simply awful, the players themselves bowing their heads in shame."[8]

In a grueling endgame, April and May took the company through Kentucky, Indiana, Ohio, and West Virginia to Wilmington, Delaware, then up into

Pennsylvania, upstate New York, Massachusetts, New Hampshire, and Maine, to close the season in Newport, Rhode Island, on May 28. Only a handful of towns en route were new. Audiences were generally large and appreciative, and reviews, while few, were enthusiastic, most commenting on her perpetual youth and vivacity.

It had been Maggie's most profitable season yet, bringing her almost $60,000, enough to pay off the last of her mortgages. Dispersing her company, she and Paddock retreated to Long Branch. There, former President Grant could be seen strolling along Ocean Avenue with Maggie or with Mary Anderson, who that summer was embellishing the grounds of the cottage she would buy from Maggie. President James Garfield came down for a restful stay at the Elberon Hotel in June. Some of the resort's original summer residents had died, notably the elder Wallacks, but the air in Long Branch remained festive, especially for the Paddocks' annual lawn party.

The atmosphere darkened in early September, just as Maggie was preparing her fall tour. On July 2 Garfield had been shot in the nation's capital but was expected to live. However, as his health worsened during August, his doctors believed he might recuperate better in the fresh sea air of Long Branch, and on September 6 he was brought there by special train, with tracks laid to the door of his cottage. By the 13th he seemed to rally, and Maggie finalized plans to open on the 19th in Cincinnati.

She had assembled a new combination company, again to be managed by Paddock, which contained some new faces. Gone were Russell, McClannin, and Clifton. Most male leads would be carried by newcomer Will A. Sands, 38, whose wife, Laura Le Claire, 43, would play old women. Other, more distinguished male leads like Rochester would be played by Maggie's old friend Len Shewell, 48. Retained were her nephew Julian and J. H. Redding for comic roles, the recently married Rufus Scott and Marie Henley, along with George Carlisle, Lettie Allen, and Annie Mortimer. Added were Mrs. D. B. Van Deeren (whom Maggie had known from Troy for over a decade and who would play Fadet for her for six seasons), British actor James Taylor, a new ingenue named Carrie Wyatt, 26, and a few utility players.

In Cincinnati, at 10:30 p.m. on September 19, their opening night *Fanchon* nearly done at the Grand Opera House, cast and audience heard bells slowly tolling outside. Maggie left the stage to learn the cause as dread mounted. She deputized Shewell to break the sad news to everyone that Garfield had died at Long Branch. The weeping capacity crowd dispersed, and all performances were canceled for the following night. More than a few onstage and out front were reminded of the tragic events of April 14, 1865. Maggie, moved by this association, recalled for an interviewer at her hotel her strange dream of that night, and the subsequent clipping of a lock of hair from the head of her dearest John Wilkes Booth.

Performances resumed on the afternoon of September 21—Maggie was performing Wednesday matinees more frequently—and on the 30th she debuted to a packed house *The Little Savage*, a new three-act comedy by George F. Fuller with many familiar elements. She played Cora, "the self-willed daughter of a wealthy planter and a creole, who delights in all sorts of mischief, and turns the heads of all who come under the influence of her witcheries." Act I is set in Guadeloupe, incorporating its exotic scenery and festive melodies, and establishes seventeen-year-old Cora's loss of her rightful wealth and the recall to France of her true love, a young officer named Leon (Sands). Brought in Act II to France as the ward of Leon's uncle, the crusty old Commandant (Shewell), Cora is led to believe that Leon has married the flirtatious Clairette (Wyatt) and fathered two children, which sends Cora into a jealous rage. But it is all a ruse to satisfy the Commandant, whom Cora bewitches. Confined to his chair by gout, he rages in confusion as he "is teased by Cora with all the mischief [sic] pranks that her fertile imagination can suggest. She dances war dances about him, has a tipsy reel, the effect of a glass of sherry, and cuts up such pranks that the stranded commandant believes that she is possessed by a demon, or is perhaps a 'changeling.'" Two comic notaries (Julian and Redding) pretend to be doctors and pronounce the Commandant ill to further confuse him. Finally, Cora conspires with the others to badger him into allowing Leon to marry her. The play "misses being a farce by a hairbreadth and no more."[9]

Confused Cincinnati audiences and critics did not appreciate Cora's cavorting, which had no "real bearing whatever upon the development of the story, which is altogether one of the queerest bits of dramatic abortiveness we have ever seen." Her antics were tedious and "would mean nothing at all if they did not mean that the 'star' wished to appear in many costumes, sing a variety of songs and go through a great deal of what is happily called 'business.'" Her jealousy "more like a friend than a savage" and her tipsiness in Act III played "with disagreeable verisimilitude. The script was "often dull and seldom brilliant." The characters were "without exception familiar and conventional stage types, except the twin notaries, who are quite beyond our ken." The scenery provided by manager Bob Miles was exquisite and appropriate, but the costumes, drawn from the stock of the traveling company, were a jumble of Spanish, Italian, African, and English cultures of the uncertain period. On its first night, the cast dropped some lines and Maggie appeared uncharacteristically nervous. Yet, despite this first "sad failure," *The Little Savage* improved under Fuller's revisions, allowing Maggie to perform it for four more years.[10]

From this Cincinnati engagement, if Paddock can be believed, Maggie took away almost $5,000. For two months she toured Pittsburgh, Wheeling, and Columbus; various towns in Indiana, Illinois, and Iowa, then St. Louis. *Little Savage* was still less than a complete success. Reviewers acknowledged its possibilities, but disdained its wordiness, its superfluous incidents, and its cardboard characters, except for Maggie's, which was "admirably adapted to display her peculiar excellencies." Cora was "little else than Fanchon in a new guise—Fanchon as the petted, indulged, spoiled child of wealth instead of Fanchon the beggar child! Cora has all Fanchon's sweetness, sharpness, agility, and mischief in her composition, and is up to just as many tricks, impudences, and harmless plots for the overthrow of her enemies and the triumph of love." The supporting company was generally acceptable but "not remarkable for excellence." They "did not have much to do and did not do much with what they had to do."[11]

But no one who saw Maggie onstage would have guessed she was forty-five. She "more than any actress now on the stage retains to a remarkable degree those youthful movements and girlish use of her voice which made her famous twenty years ago. She seems to have bathed in the fountain of perennial youth, and there was not the slightest action or expression . . . which showed the sluggishness of declining powers or the stiffness of aging bones. In her dancing . . . there were grace and vigor."[12]

Now in her eighteenth year of playing Marie in *Pearl*, she had refined the role's tragic dimensions, which by today's standards seem mawkish. Marie's descent into insanity was "not the ravings of madness, the rant, and the shriek. It was a much higher bit of artistic work. It was the Ophelia madness, in which some strange, sweet spirit of unrest seizes possession of her. She sees the home of her childhood, and in the tones of an organ she hears her mother's voice calling to her broken heart, and the pathos with which she bids her lover, who in her imagination is by her side, a fond goodbye and waves a sad adieu as she follows the voice of her mother [was] powerful and sweet and moved [one] to tears as naught but genuine genius can do."[13]

By late November, playing Hooley's in Chicago, Will Sands was not working out and left by mutual agreement. Maggie replaced him with Dick Russell, who had been performing in Philadelphia, who stepped easily into the role of Leon in *Little Savage*. Sands' wife, Laura Le Claire, remained in the company, though. Chicago critics were relentless and cracks were beginning to show in Maggie's voice and façade of youth by persisting in playing child-like roles. She was also growing a bit stout. "Maggie Mitchell is a cheerful, clever little lady, but she is a woman who has outgrown her child's clothes, and the parts she plays are no longer suited to her." They yield "comparisons which, however odorous, are unavoidable. . . . To listen to her attempt to sing when the voice refuses to respond, to see her seeking to win favor by kittenish actions when the grace and ease of youth have long since left her, is neither pleasant nor profitable." Her acting was "more artful and less spontaneous. . . . As a piece of machinery, it moves with mathematical precision. There is not a cog out of place. But it does not breathe. It is manufacture, not a creation."[14]

Chicago critics condemned *Little Savage* for its hackneyed plot, stale dialog, and shallow characterization, obviously contrived purely as a showcase for its star. Cora's " 'savagery' is chiefly manifested by her constant iteration of the fact that she *is* a 'little savage.' " Moreover, "the sobriquet 'Little Savage,' applied to the creole in the play, is as foreign and inappropriate as it would be if applied to one of the well-reared, patrician belles of modern New Orleans." Only with revision could this "crude" play be salvaged. Just as bad, in an age that had long demanded verisimilitude on the American stage, its characters were clothed "without any regard to the historical accuracy of their costumes." As for the supporting company, Shewell was monotonous and distracted, Julian's comedy was forced, and William H. Burton, playing old men, was "painfully absurd." Scott was ridiculous as a lover: "If he were to take upon himself in actual life the part of an honest wooer, heaven only knows where could be found the girl who would listen to his addresses."[15]

But as Maggie moved north and east, she read rebuttals (possibly planted by her brother Charles or Paddock) to any assertions that she "is getting to be too old to play juvenile parts. She never was more sprightly, vivacious or full of mischief than now." "There is no sign about her of advancing years. We see the same neat, muscular figure." "We detect no lessening of the old elasticity, no want of the kittenish grace that was one of her earliest charms. The closest scrutiny of her face reveals no inroads of time. . . . She might pass for 18 on the stage."[16]

She spent December touring Michigan, Ohio, Pennsylvania and New York State. By the time she hit Rochester on December 23, her voice was nearly gone from another persistent cold and sore throat. She nursed it along under a doctor's care, seriously considering canceling a week of performances. But as usual, she toughed it out and continued, omitting some songs and asking the audience's indulgence. There was no visible diminishing of her energy.

Celebrating the holidays in Syracuse, she arranged for her children to attend her Christmas matinee. Fanchon, now 12, and Harry, 10, watched, "leaning over the velvet-covered rail of the lower right-hand proscenium box." Both "watched their mother with intent interest, now and then getting a covert recognition from the stage. . . . They very seldom see their mother on the stage, and are therefore afforded unusual pleasure whenever there is an opportunity." Fanchon was "marvelously like her mother in looks. Harry, who was more wrapt up in the play than his sister, is a cheery faced little man with fair hair and bright eyes."[17]

Financially, Maggie ended the year in fine shape. She estimated her current personal worth, including real estate and cash, at $500,000, and various newspapers, doubtless fueled by Paddock, asserted that she was earning $300,000 per season, although the truth appears to lie somewhere between $30,000 and $40,000, reported in larger cities. In the context of that pre-income tax era, it is difficult to assess her true worth until it was spelled out when her will was probated. She owned (in her name, not Paddock's) the two cottages at Long Branch (one soon to be sold to Anderson), plus thirty acres of land. In Manhattan, having sold the brownstone on 54th Street at a considerable profit, she held the deeds of five houses on 126th Street and eight lots on 124th Street—on one of which she built, for a reported $30,000 ($750,000 today), a large frame "cottage" which she maintained year-round as a primary residence—and a prime lot on 86th Street near Central Park.

In acquiring and developing these, as prescient as she had been in 1863 when she moved uptown to 54th Street, she anticipated the boom in Harlem real estate that would occur in the 1880s. True, Harlem retained "the character of a frontier town," but Maggie had seen what the infamously corrupt William "Boss" Tweed had accomplished in the past decade in building construction and the extension of roads and sewer lines north of Central Park, and she realized the potential for growth that the new (1879) Third Avenue elevated line represented. Given her penchant for enjoying thoroughbred horses, she likely also found attractive the racing at Harlem Speedway.[18]

Furthermore, tributes and royalties flowed in from such disparate entities as "Maggie Mitchell Company's" silver mine in Colorado, racehorses named "Maggie Mitchell," similarly named yachts, chewing tobacco, and continued endorsements for skin cream. The obscure, hand-to-mouth existence of Fulton Street was far behind her.

1882 began with a few days in Albany and Buffalo, then east into Massachusetts. In small towns, Maggie was well received, but Boston reviewers had tired of her repertoire, except for the eternal *Fanchon*. *Jane Eyre* was "strained and stilted," conveying a "morbid and monotonous theme" so unlike *Fanchon*. "For pure human interest, homely joy and pathos, deep emotion and light mirth," *Fanchon* was preferred. "Few can go away from the theater where it is played without having been inspired to a deeper purpose of kindliness and virtue."[19]

Little Savage was as much a failure in Boston as it had been in Chicago, condemned for its "woeful" improbabilities of the plot. It was "tediously dull and utterly weak and meaningless, . . . one of the most dismal and oppressive compositions through which an audience ever yawned. It is unrelieved by a touch of real humor or accented by a shadow of genuine pathos, although there are numerous ghastly attempts at both, and all sorts of extravagant incidents are dragged in, in the vain effort to keep up the pretense of interest."

"The attempts at humor are dismal failures." The characters were "old acquaintances masquerading under new names." This was "wholly unworthy of the powers of Maggie Mitchell." Enacting this "heedless, noisy, saucy, 'cheeky' hoyden, . . . she labors hard and unceasingly—sings, dances, romps, and frolics with unflagging spirits in the endeavor, . . . but gains only a partial success." Finally, "the curtain comes down and much to the relief of the audience too, who had feared it never would do so." They "received the play coldly and were very much bored." Still Maggie stubbornly stuck with it for an entire week and featured it prominently in her repertoire for the rest of the season.[20]

It remained a centerpiece of her engagements in late February in New York after two more weeks in New England. At Sinn's Park Theater in Brooklyn and the Grand Opera House in Manhattan, she drew full houses and prolonged applause upon her first entrance. Reviewers had little new to say, even about *Little Savage*, except to note that her voice was beginning to show a little wear. The same held true through March in towns across Delaware and Pennsylvania. *Little Savage*'s weaknesses were rationalized by its being a star vehicle for Maggie, who gave it her charming all, and audiences loved her for it. In Wilmington she thrilled the members of the amateur Maggie Mitchell Dramatic Association who visited her in her hotel, receiving an inscribed portrait in a gilt frame.

Four major cities followed, for a week each: Baltimore, Washington, back in New York, then Philadelphia. Fuller may have further revised *Little Savage* in New York, for it seemed more acceptable—or critics were simply becoming inured to it. In Baltimore, it was considered the best play in her repertoire, and in Philadelphia, she felt confident enough to run it all week, including matinees. While in Washington on Easter Sunday, she visited the imprisoned Charles Guiteau, Garfield's assassin who had been sentenced to hang. Amid a media circus, Guiteau was peddling from his cell autographed photographs and loose-leaf copies of a defense he had penned of his mad act. Maggie, knowing the value of fame, purchased five photographs for five dollars and briefly conversed with him. Shortly before his execution he sent her at her request the first copy of his book, bound in Morocco and gilt, inscribed "To my Friend, Miss Maggie Mitchell. Love God and do right and we will meet in Heaven. Yours sincerely, Charles Guiteau."[21]

In mid-April Maggie returned for the first time in thirty years to the neighborhood of her youth, performing at the Windsor Theater on the Bowery below Canal Street, across the street from where she had begun her career with Thomas Hamblin. She had steadfastly refused to return there, either due to bad memories or disdain for its notoriously ill-mannered audiences. Early May took her through New England, where *Little Savage*, if not celebrated, was tolerated, for "Maggie always draws, whatever the play, and is likely to for a long time to come." She closed her season in Lynn, Massachusetts, on May 13, again providing her company tickets back to New York and accompanying them there.[22]

While in the city, she took in on May 15 the premiere of *Fogg's Ferry* starring her newest competitor, Minnie Maddern, at seventeen on her third Broadway production. Also in attendance that night were three almost-as-young Maggie clones: Annie Pixley, 24; "Little Nell, the California Diamond" (Helen Dauvray), 22, who had acted since childhood; and Minnie Palmer, 25. Maddern, it seemed, "is already treading on their toes."[23]

Maddern was Maggie's biggest threat yet, as big as Lotta. She was "pretty, bright, vivacious and clever, [with] a way of saying cute things cutely, and makes friends with an audience at short notice," precisely like the Maggie of the 1850s. Reviewers predicted that she would soon eclipse Maggie, whom she resembled (pointedly) *at that age*, and in some ways was already superior. "Long years ago," Maggie had been "the herald of novelty upon the American stage, and her fine rendition of *Fanchon* covered a multitude of sins in other parts. She became the pet of the old-fashion people." But now it was Maddern's turn.[24]

And there was still Charlotte Thompson, her Jane Eyre favorably compared to Maggie's: "In no sense are Maggie and Charlotte to be regarded as rivals in this character. Maggie romped and danced and wiggled the girl into an impossible being. Charlotte gives it not only possibility but actualness [sic]. One is ridiculously ideal, the other is absorbingly real." Unlike Maggie, Thompson conveyed "an emotion with fierce intensity and with the least display of physical exertion." Worse, even more newcomers were now performing *Fanchon* or *Jane Eyre*: Florence Herbert, with her own combination company; Katharina Schratt, in German at the Thalia (formerly Maggie's Bowery); and Ida Lewis, 26, who like Thompson was said to surpass Maggie. Also compared favorably to Maggie, there were Belle Archer, 23, a John Ford protégée, starring on Broadway in *Hazel Kirke*, and Marion Elmore, 23, in *Chispa*. Canadian actress Margaret Mather, also 23, "in the voice is so like Maggie Mitchell that, close the eyes and one would certainly suppose that superannuated star was speaking, with less harshness and jerkiness." But Maggie was a keen competitor and self-promoter, with definite ideas about maintaining her following. For the coming tour, she planned to give away 15,000 photographs of herself.[25]

In a summer of self-renewal at Long Branch among the "actors' colony," she swam, sailed, drove her black ponies, and hosted another lavish lawn party in mid-August. Again, she welcomed theatrical personalities and her extended family, including Sophia's sons Julian, now 29, who would go off this season to perform on his own, and Joseph, 30, who soon would take his place in Maggie's company, but only as utility. Circulating among these thriving young people, she appeared "more captivating, if that be possible," recorded Fuller. This "graceful, pretty little woman" remained "a bright little creature of winning ways, [with] sunny-smile laughter like rippling water." Russell, who would again play leads opposite Maggie in fall, spent the summer as the Paddocks' guest. Len Shewell was there, too, but quite ill and unable to rejoin Maggie on tour.[26]

For 1882–83, in addition to Russell, she hired Russell Bassett, W. H. Burton, Albert Enos, Mrs. Van Deeren, Carrie Wyatt, Welsh Edwards (a known drunk who was supposedly reformed), Louisa (Mrs. James J.) Prior (for older women), Mr. and Mrs. James T. Galloway (he as a low comedian), and Charles Lothian (son of Maggie's Boston colleague Napier Lothian).

Looking for new material, her judgment again failed her. *Elsa* was a ludicrous paint-by-number translation by Charles Turner Dazey of a German adaptation of *Die Geier Wally* (*The Vulture Maiden*), a German dime novel by Wilhelmine von Hillern. Maggie played the titular sixteen-year-old "hawk-maiden, wild as the wind and as full of mischief," so named for rescuing—stealing, actually—a young hawk from its precarious nest. This free spirit is in love with a poor peasant, Joseph (Russell), "the best shot, the bravest, most handsome fellow in the whole Tyrol," who makes his first entrance wearing the skin of a ferocious bear he has just slain. Elsa's love is both unrequited and contrary to the wishes of her rich, irrational uncle, Strominger (Edwards), who disowns her and casts her into the winter wilderness. In retaliation, she sets a barn afire and retreats to an icy mountain, where she dreams that the mountain tries to adopt her and taunts her with ice fairies with whom she wrestles. She awakens on a barren rock in an icy gale (cue the elaborate scenery and special effects) and returns to her village to find her uncle dead and she the wealthiest maiden around. To win over Joseph, she wrestles him for a kiss, but when he wins he declares he wants nothing to do with such a wild creature. Out of spite, she announces her love for a viscount whom she convinces to kill Joseph, who is flung over a cliff. A remorseful Elsa has herself lowered over the precipice (as she had done for the hawk) to rescue Joseph, then retreats to her hovel and vows celibacy and starvation. Only when Joseph comes to her abjectly does she relent, whereupon they proclaim their mutual love as the curtain descends.[27]

On September 2, 1882, Maggie debuted *Elsa* at Henry E. Abbey's Park Theater at Broadway and 22nd Street, planning to run it every night and matinee, indefinitely. The critics pounced. As bad as the reviews had been for *Becky Mix*, *Nannette o' Wearithorne*, and *Little Savage*, those for *Elsa* were far worse. The only aspect of the "unpleasantly bad performance" to escape castigation was the scenery, and that was awkwardly handled, evoking laughter. Dazey "has marred and broken the simple charm of *Geier Wally*." His play "is duller than ditchwater and clumsier than a cow, . . . so transparent that it is an insult to our intelligence. . . . It is all the old, old stuff patched up, revamped, turned and used again in the old cut and dried fashion." The dream sequence was "introduced solely to show a pretty nice scene," and "the dialog is carved out of the novel with scissors. . . . All of the characters, except the heroine, are as conventional as the wooden soldiers in a toy shop. . . . Characters there are none, except Elsa herself. All the other parts are mere sketches, and the actors were not competent to fill them up and give them vitality." Russell's Joseph was "lumpish and monotonous" to the point where "the audience lost all interest in him."[28]

Maggie herself, uncharacteristically "hesitant and blundering," appeared to be

> . . . a nervous amateur and her attempts to sing were simply preposterous. Her idea of Elsa, like her Fanchon, and all her other parts, is that of an oppressed and persecuted girl who bullies everybody. Her idea of acting is to take the center of the stage, with the company arranged in lines on either side of her, and say her insulting speeches in a very tame way, without the slightest demonstration of interest in what she is saying, except a nervous movement of her hands. . . . She burns a barn and climbs down a precipice with the same placidity with which she makes love and incites one of her lovers to commit murder. . . . She was Fanchon as Little Barefoot; Fanchon as The Pearl of Savoy, and now she is Fanchon as Elsa. If anybody writes or adapts a different character for her, she quietly changes it back to Fanchon, . . . for Fanchon marks the limits of Miss Mitchell's powers. . . . She never looked young; she was never pretty; she is not a singer; she is not a dancer; she has no fire nor force as an actress; and yet for many years she has been a popular favorite, has drawn very large audiences, has accumulated a handsome fortune, and, although rather passé in New York, is sure of a warm welcome in the provinces. . . . Stick to Fanchon, by all means, Miss Mitchell, and make money, and let art and nature and the critics go hang.[29]

Even her die-hard fans were scandalized when, improbably, tiny Elsa readied herself to grapple with bear-slayer Joseph: "As Miss Mitchell undid her bodice and displayed her bare shoulders and her chemise, to give free play to her muscles in the wrestle, a shudder ran through the house. The Maggie Mitchell audience were not accustomed to this sort of realism in their favorite. It created the sensation that a teacher might cause by wearing a ball-dress, with bare bust and arms, in a Sunday school. So, the only bit of real acting which Miss Mitchell did pleased her followers less than any other part of the play. She was a poor, oppressed peasant girl, and yet wore diamond rings; but the audience didn't mind that. She wore a summer dress in a snow-storm on the Alps, but the audience didn't mind that. . . . When, however, she acted like a true Tyrolese, they disapproved of her. What are you to say to an audience like that?" They were also shocked when Elsa's rival for Joseph's affection,

Afra (Wyatt), turned out to be his sister, hinting mildly at incest. "There was a conspicuous lack of applause throughout the evening." *Elsa* was "one of the most complete failures we have ever witnessed in New York."[30]

Maggie felt violated. "This is abuse," she cried, "and not criticism. If it were criticism, I would accept it gladly. As it is mere abuse, I ignore it." The question again arose of her continuing to tour. Here was "a woman long past middle age [sic], rich, with a clever fellow for a husband, a delightful home, and every reason for desiring a future of ease and comfort! What does she do? Work! Where? On the cramped stage of the interior, breathing dust, stared out of countenance by gleaming lights, succeeding here, failing there—for what? More money? I think not. She may want more money, but the inside reason is a liking for the fuss and feathers, the glare and glitter. . . . There she is, pulling away in her harness just as she did thirty years and more ago when she had to work for her bread and butter."[31]

For a week she nailed the colors of *Elsa* to the mast, furiously calling rehearsals and slashing and rewriting portions of the script—largely those of other characters—to no avail. On its third night, she had had to replace Edwards, who "went on the stage maudlin drunk, insulting his audience by his condition, and ruining the effects of the piece, such as they were, by his vinous imbecility. He was very properly fired by the angry Maggie who lassoed a wild fake of the square to fill his place, and who did it at short notice and without a rehearsal, in a commendable manner."[32]

But even Maggie had her limits. After a week of declining revenue, she threw in the towel and abandoned *Elsa* for good, substituting *Jane Eyre*, with Russell again as Rochester. Its larger cast required additional hires and rehearsal, both inadequate. One critic urged her "to shelve *Jane Eyre* alongside the Geier Wally, and give the public the *Fanchon* for which they crave."[33]

By September 23 she did just that. Into her new *Fanchon* cast, now the "Maggie Mitchell Combination," went her nephew Joseph, along with eleven other new actors, some from her previous companies. Inept performers from *Elsa* were summarily dismissed. Wyatt left on her own, signing with the respected Madison Square Theater Company—a significant loss for Maggie, who replaced her with two new ingenues, the petite Jennie Kennark, who two seasons later would follow Wyatt, and Lavinia Shannon, "a young lady of rare beauty" who was "graceful, forcible, and effective." Maggie's husband and her brother resumed their managerial duties.[34]

When the new company left New York, embarking on Maggie's thirtieth consecutive season on the road, they would tour, eat and sleep (and presumably, with this group, rehearse) in a "special palace [rail] car." Onboard would be all of their scenery and trunks of costumes and props—a true combination. Other stars, including Helena Modjeska, Edwin Booth, Lotta, and Mary Anderson, already had these, and their routes often intersected Maggie's. Slow, circuitous, grueling rail travel was becoming a thing of their past.

On October 2 Maggie opened at Abbey and Schoeffel's Park Theater in Boston, where she "has lost none of her gaiety and vivaciousness" and "appeared not a day older than 16 years." Next came Providence and Brooklyn, then Manhattan at Niblo's Garden, followed by a week of one-night stands in New England and a week in Albany, all of which drew large, enthusiastic audiences.[35]

On November 26 she took her company to Syracuse for Thanksgiving week, to include a night of *Trix*, which Maggie had not performed for three years and would rarely perform again. That evening her husband encountered Miss Minnie E. Moore, who lived with her mother, and went home with her. The next afternoon he called on Minnie twice and on the second visit paid her $12 for sex, plus an extra dollar for a ticket to Maggie's show (a complimentary ticket might have raised suspicions). For unknown reasons, possibly to finance such dalliances, he was also quietly borrowing money from Edwin Booth and soon fell behind on its interest.

Paddock exhibited to the world the image of "a bright, kindly, genial, enterprising gentleman who has merged himself so thoroughly in the personality of his wife that nobody outside of the profession knows him. Mr. Paddock is a handsome man and a quick-witted one. . . . Better educated than most commercial men, with unusual good humor, a ready wit, and a comely face and figure, he might and no doubt would have achieved fame and fortune on his account." Perhaps resentfully or opportunistically, when he married Maggie "his entity completely disappeared in that of the charming and clever little actress." His children "regard him perforce as their mother's husband." He toils "to do homage to his wife as the bread-winner, forgetting his arduous responsibilities and the zeal and intelligence with which he promotes her personal and professional fortunes." For now, over the Mitchells' marriage "no cloud of disagreement, no breath of scandal, has risen to cast a shade upon their domestic life. He has proved to her that she made no error of judgment in her selection of a mate, proved it by the integrity of his character, his devotion to her interests, his respect for her position, and his loyalty to the home in which she presides over the welfare of the younger Mitchells." However, he confessed to a reporter that he was "thoroughly tired of *Fanchon*, but the managers want it, and she will continue to appear in it as long as it pays. . . . In spite of the fact that she is tired of it."[36]

Unaware of any clouds on the horizon, by December Maggie felt secure enough in her career to impart some insights to young women seeking a career in the theater. Her tips for "Success on the Stage" in the *North*

American Review included the necessities of an attractive appearance, sincerity, keen observation, a resonant voice, and clear articulation, a good sense of humor, pride in her work, and "docility" (presumably to her profession). Eighteen, she thought, was the optimum age to begin. She advised, as she had done, joining a stock company (although those were waning), and disdained private lessons. While she recommended a thorough study of the French language and English literature, she recognized that Shakespeare's plays were being performed far less often. There were faults to be avoided, she cautioned: envy and jealousy, frivolity and carelessness, and exhibiting anything less than ladylike behavior, for "mere weaknesses are magnified into flagrant immorality." "It is a lottery, this profession," she concluded, with prizes which are "not very considerable," a very public life of travel and hotels with long absences from home and family, "with brief intervals for rest and food and little sleep." At times, life on the stage could become "a torment and a burden," with each season "harder and drearier." Yet she remained "the eager, yet weary slave of my profession." This eagerness would ebb the nearer she got to her fifties.[37]

Such travails were echoed by Maggie's contemporaries, who often emphasized the moral challenges inherent in a life on the stage. Lester Wallack asserted that "absolutely the stage is no place for a woman and more particularly when the woman happens to be a lady." Practice at playing love scenes on stage did not necessarily translate into discernment off of it. Temptation abounded, explained one actress: "Right and wrong merge easily, and unless one is an expert in moral latitude, it is not always easy to discern the dividing line." All the more impressive in this context was Maggie's sterling reputation.[38]

For two months, well into 1883, she toured the Great Lakes area, encountering dreadful weather and a few snags. In several cities, icy weather and snowstorms kept theatergoers away and left those who did attend less than enthusiastic. In Rochester the management publicized *Pearl* while Maggie and the company prepared *Fanchon*, leading to some frantic backstage rearranging and a long-delayed opening curtain. In Buffalo, an inept stagehand rang down the final curtain before Maggie had finished her big dramatic scene. Renowned for her scene-ending tableaux, she was furious and let everyone know it.

But the company was traveling in style, even leaving their parlor car for occasional stays in upscale hotels. In Pittsburgh, Maggie and Paddock stayed with Mr. and Mrs. George N. Mashey, a wealthy liquor merchant who operated the saloon in the Opera House. Their twenty-four-year-old son Harry would later become a part of the family. Two high points for Maggie were a visit backstage in Buffalo by touring performers Tom Thumb (his 1860 slur forgotten) and his wife Lavinia Warren, both shorter even than she, and finding lavish *Fanchon*-themed Christmas decorations in her hotel room in Cincinnati. Her Christmas matinee of *Barefoot* and evening of *Lorle* drew the most crowded houses she had seen yet that season, bringing in nearly $3,500. (On a good night in a large city, she could be counted on to generate $800–1,200.)

After a week in Indiana, where countless citizens of outlying villages who rarely attended the theater came in to see Maggie, she once more faced the stern critics of Chicago, who handled her supporting company harshly. They were "commonplace and feeble" (Enos), "lackluster" (Galloway), "more suited for the role of a fishwife than of a Marchioness" (Van Deeren), and "insufferably vulgar and offensive" (Shannon).[39]

To outrun an approaching snowstorm, Maggie boarded her company on a fast train to their next stop, one night with *Little Savage* in Rockford, Illinois, leaving local stagehands to load their scenery, costumes, wigs, and props into a second, slower train. Unsurprisingly, the latter derailed into a snowdrift, forcing Maggie and her actors to improvise a bare-bones performance of *Jane Eyre* in their traveling attire. A "moderate audience" derived "a reasonable amount of enjoyment out of the time-worn play." When the slow train arrived at 2:00 a.m., Maggie simply redirected it to their next stop, Janesville, Wisconsin, yet another new town for her.[40]

For three weeks they slogged through frozen Wisconsin and Minnesota towns, *Little Savage* predominating, providing audiences with a vicarious Caribbean escape. Maggie might have avoided the inconvenience of snowstorms and ice had she toured in winter into the South, but she still neglected the region almost entirely. The climate was no better in February when she moved down into Iowa, Missouri, and Kansas, where massive flooding caused train delays, keeping her from arriving in St. Joseph one evening until 8:00, with the curtain going up much later. At least they had power: other theaters in the region had been deprived of gas, using jury-rigged electric lights that cast ghostly shadows. Predictably, these audiences—full houses in almost every case—preferred Maggie's older repertoire. *Trix* and *Savage* "met with a cold reception," the former being "simply a concatenation of conventional scenes, very absurd."[41]

While her support was considered excellent (outside of Chicago), it was Maggie who was "always fresh, always bewitching, always herself. Time takes nothing from the poetry of her every motion or the fascination of her airy grace." Her "perennial youth," "vivacity and girlish eccentricity" and "jaunty, saucy, bright acting" were remarkable. When asked how she managed to stay looking so young at forty-six, she replied, "I never dissipate [sic]. I take long walks every day, bathe a good deal in saltwater during the summer, and keep peace in the family."[42]

At her physician's insistence, she also maintained her youthful glow by taking nightly sponge baths at the theater with rum, which she carried on her train in a five-gallon demijohn, transferred to her dressing room by each theater's property man. Toward the end of this season, though, she felt its effect waning and consulted her physician. He proposed adding an emetic to the rum, which he said did not affect the bathing, but "hurts pretty badly for drinking." Soon after, several stagehands became violently ill. Her rum "thenceforth resumed its pristine strength."[43]

She battled her way through another severe cold in March touring Michigan towns, but remained the eternal enchanter from her first entrance: "A graceful curtsy, a smile, and the radiant Maggie speaks. Instantly the charm is complete, the spell reigns, and the audience settle comfortably in their seats and draw a sigh of relief: 'It's all right, it's the same little Maggie Mitchell.' . . . She seems to be imbued with a new life every time she appears on the stage."[44]

April took her east to Brooklyn—gearing up for the inauguration of its eponymous bridge—and to Washington and Baltimore for a week each, including matinee benefits for the Actors Fund and the Elks. At the close of the latter, five men of her company, including her nephew Joseph, presented her with eleven painted photographs they had created depicting her in various roles, matted together in crimson velvet in a large bronze frame selected by Paddock, along with a dedicatory poem. Maggie was visibly touched and grateful. After a quick round of Pennsylvania and New Jersey towns, she closed her season at the Grand Opera House in Manhattan, heading on May 13 for Long Branch.

She needed the rest. Her age was starting to show and talk of retirement was again in the air. "There is no doubt of the fact that the freshness of her style is more or less impaired by the weight of advancing years." Yet she insisted she had "no idea of abandoning the stage at present, no, or for some time to come, unless I am not needed, and from my past successes I am vain enough to believe that my career is comparatively young. I continue to draw well, make money and please the people. Under these circumstances, I would be foolish to think of withdrawing."[45]

Another decade of performing lay ahead of her.

NOTES

1. *New York Dramatic Mirror*, Sept. 26, 1891.
2. *Chicago Tribune*, Sept. 9, 1880; *Chicago Inter Ocean*, Sept. 11, 1880.
3. *Pittsburgh Post-Gazette*, Oct. 9, 1880; *Washington Sunday Herald*, Oct. 24, 1880.

4. *Boston Journal*, Jan. 1, 1881.
5. *Buffalo Courier*, Feb. 1, 1881.
6. *Chicago Tribune*, Feb. 15, 1881.
7. *Quad-City (Davenport) Times*, Mar. 3, 1881.
8. *Kansas City Mail*, Mar. 25–26, 1881.
9. *Cincinnati Gazette*, Sept. 17, 1881; *Boston Herald*, Jan. 29, 1882; *Louisville Courier-Journal*, Jan. 20, 1884. *The Little Savage* is not to be confused with the identically titled farce of 1859, in which she played Kate Dalrymple.
10. Unidentified Chicago newspaper clipping from late November 1881, MM file, HTC; *Cincinnati Gazette*, Dec. 31, 1881.
11. *Indianapolis News*, Oct. 24, 1881; *Quad-City (Davenport) Times*, Nov. 3, 1881; *Rockford (IL) Register*, Nov. 21, 1881.
12. *Rockford (IL) Register*, Nov. 21, 1881.
13. *Ibid.*
14. *Chicago Tribune*, Nov. 23–24, 1881.
15. *Ibid.*; Chicago correspondent for *St. Paul (MN) Globe*, Nov. 27, 1881; *Chicago Inter Ocean* quoted in *Indianapolis News*, Nov. 30, 1881.
16. *Rochester Democrat and Chronicle*, Nov. 28, 1881; *Detroit Free Press*, Dec. 10, 1881; *Syracuse Standard*, Dec. 27, 1881.
17. *Syracuse Standard*, Dec. 27, 1881.
18. Jonathan Gill, *Harlem*, New York: Grove Press, 2011, 118.
19. *Boston Journal*, Jan. 17 and 20, 1882.
20. *Boston Herald*, Jan. 31, 1882; *Boston Journal*, Jan. 31, 1882.
21. *Baltimore Sun*, Apr. 10, 1882.
22. *Hartford Courant*, May 5, 1882.
23. *New Orleans Times-Democrat*, May 28, 1882.
24. *Memphis Appeal*, Oct. 15, 1882; *Hartford Courant*, Dec. 26, 1882.
25. *Wilkes-Barre (PA) Record*, Feb. 11, 1884; *Music and Drama*, Dec. 23, 1882, 12.
26. *Louisville Courier-Journal*, Aug. 27, 1882.
27. *Spirit of the Times*, Sept. 9, 1882. Von Hillern was the daughter of Charlotte Birch-Pfeiffer, the original source for *Fanchon*.
28. *Ibid.*; *New York Times*, Sept. 3, 1882; *Music and Drama*, vol. 2 (1882), 7; "The Drama," *The Critic*, Sept. 9, 1882; *National Police Gazette*, Sept. 16 and 23, 1882.
29. *Ibid.*
30. *Ibid.*
31. *Spirit of the Times*, Sept. 16, 1882; New York correspondent for *Philadelphia Times*, Sept. 17, 1882.
32. *National Police Gazette*, Sept. 28, 1882.
33. *Spirit of the Times*, Sept. 16, 1882.
34. *The (Washington) Critic*, Mar. 23, 1883.
35. *Boston Herald*, Oct. 3, 1882.
36. *New York World*, July 26, 1883; *Wheeling (WV) Intelligencer*, Sept. 29, 1883; *Detroit Free Press*, Sept. 30, 1883; *Indianapolis Sentinel*, Dec. 1, 1881.
37. Original, handwritten version in MM files, NYPL MS 4552, published in *North American Review*, Dec. 1882.

38. Margaret Townshend, *Theatrical Sketches*, New York: Merriam, 1894, 12; Elsie Ferguson, "Do You Yearn to Go on the Stage?" *Green Book Magazine*, vol. 9 (Aug. 1908), 602.

39. *Chicago Tribune*, Jan. 16, 1883; *Chicago Inter Ocean*, Jan. 16, 1883.

40. *Rockford (IL) Register*, Jan. 23, 1883.

41. *St. Joseph (MO) Herald*, Feb. 18, 1883; *Kansas City Times*, Feb. 23, 1880.

42. *St. Paul (MN) Globe*, Feb. 9, 1883; *Oshkosh Northwestern*, Jan. 31, 1883; *St. Joseph (MO) Gazette-Herald*, Feb. 17, 1883; (Lansing, MI) *Mower County Transcript*, Feb. 21, 1883; *Kansas City Journal*, Feb. 23, 1883.

43. *Denver Republican*, July 15, 1883.

44. *Detroit Free Press*, Mar. 23, 1883; *Brooklyn Eagle*, May 13, 1883.

45. *Topeka Capital*, Feb. 25, 1883; *Augusta (GA) Chronicle*, July 14, 1883.

Chapter 13

"she can't quit the stage"

By the summer of 1883 Maggie was reportedly one of the four richest actresses in America, along with Lotta, Mary Anderson, and Fanny Davenport, and one of the four largest landholders in Long Branch. There, she enjoyed having Fanchon and Harry near her, at fourteen and eleven old enough to enjoy the parties and athletic contests on the Paddock lawn. Even Maggie herself was known to enter into a lacrosse match.

She batted away rumors about Fanchon following in her footsteps, telling a reporter, "My daughter is still a child, and . . . not even dreaming, I trust, as yet, of a professional career." At any rate, noted a reporter who knew the family, "the girl, though companionable, pretty and bright, lacks the volatile temperament of the stage soubrette and, indeed, seems to have no special desire for footlight fame."[1]

Maggie and her husband made periodic trips into New York on the Long Branch steamboat to recruit actors in Union Square for her fall tour. Most of her combination would be returning, but a few required replacements. Dick Russell had signed on with an Augustin Daly combination and Maggie replaced him with a young actor with New York and Boston experience named Benjamin R. Graham. Lavinia Shannon left for Philadelphia, replaced by the very pretty Lizzie Goode, still in her teens. Thankfully, Robert McClannin returned to play distinguished older men, replacing W. H. Burton, and Sidney R. Ellis came on to play "heavies." Harry E. Sanford joined Charles Mitchell as combined advance/business manager.

Maggie's repertoire for the 1883–84 season would consist of *Fanchon, Barefoot, Pearl, Jane Eyre, Mignon, Lorle,* and *Savage,* anomalous among the one-show combinations proliferating across America. And she had learned her lesson: this season she would introduce no new works. She began on September 17 in Cincinnati with *Mignon,* attracting an over-capacity crowd of fashionable people, drawn by the fact that she "never allows a taint of suggestiveness" (ignoring her bare shoulders in *Savage*). She drew raves, as did Graham, McClannin, and Louisa Prior. After the first night, though, attendance fell off.[2]

A tragedy befell Prior in Cincinnati. At dinner following her performance on September 27, she ingested a chicken bone that lodged in her throat. Medical assistance availed nothing and she took to bed. On Sunday night, September 30, she traveled east with the company but became sicker. Between Buffalo and Rochester forceful coughing dislodged the bone, but violent vomiting and hemorrhaging ensued. In Boston, she still could not perform, but by October 8 seemed better and resumed the role of Mrs. Reed in *Jane Eyre*. The next morning she relapsed and her doctors said there was no hope. She died the afternoon of the next day, age 53. She had toured with Maggie for two years and been on the stage for forty.

Maggie sadly replaced her as Fadet with another experienced actress, Annie Locke, as the troupe toured New England and then settled into Sinn's Brooklyn Park Theatre. There, including matinees, Maggie changed her bill a remarkable seven times in six days, keeping her company on its toes. After a few nights in Poughkeepsie, Wilmington, and Trenton, she headed into Pennsylvania, where a bizarre event occurred.

In Easton, a woman appeared at the theater claiming to be Maggie's long-lost sister. Mrs. John Able, née Baker, 38, a poorly dressed, brawny, swarthy woman from Bloomsbury, New Jersey, bore little resemblance to Maggie. Able claimed that when their parents had died, they and their brother "William Baker" had been placed in an orphanage, from which Maggie "Baker" had been given to Charles and Anna Mitchell, some "theater people." "William Baker" had for years been pestering Maggie with letters and personal visits as she toured, once accosting her as far west as Denver. Each time Paddock had kept him away. He did so again with Able at the theater and their hotel. But Able was insistent: Did Maggie not remember another orphan named "little Mollie," and the little cottage in which Maggie had been born? Able had even named one of her eight children, a twelve-year-old daughter, for Maggie. Turned away, Able went to the press "to compel the actress to acknowledge me as her sister."[3]

Maggie found the claim more curious than frightening. "I am constantly learning something new," she quipped. "I was not prepared to learn . . . that my name is Baker." She supposed that the woman was earnest but delusional. Such had been the case, she said, with others claiming over the years to be relatives: "There are hosts of people in New York who know my entire family history." Others leapt to her defense, among them actors who had known Maggie since adolescence. "It is all bosh," they stated. "The woman must be a crank. . . . The whole thing is absurd. . . . There is not a word of truth in her story or assertions." Of course, there was the record of Maggie's christening at St. Paul's in October 1836, showing Charles and Anna Mitchell as her parents, but no one wanted to bother Maggie's elderly father about such nonsense. The woman and her claims soon faded away.[4]

After more eastern Pennsylvania towns, November took Maggie and her combination back into Brooklyn, Manhattan, and Providence. Then it was down to Baltimore and Washington and a swing through western Pennsylvania, ending for the holidays in Pittsburgh, where Ellsler still managed. Attendance sometimes proved disappointing due to the 1882–85 Depression settling over the nation. When banks began to fail in 1884, belts and purses would tighten further. But those who did attend were enthusiastic, and reviewers continued to marvel that a woman of Maggie's age—the true number a closely guarded secret—could still believably play teenagers. The words "sprightly," "graceful," "vivacious," and "exuberant" still predominated. "Maggie Mitchell has been 24 for the past thirty years." "Her step is as elastic, her movements as quick, her arm as round, her voice as full as the youngest soubrette of her company."[5]

She forced her way past any warning signs of age. Early in 1883, reported the *New York Sun*, "a sudden paralysis of her left leg confounded her doctors and resisted all treatment, including electrical stimulation, but she remained determined to go on that night in *Fanchon*, using crutches. When the time came for her first entrance," she told the reporter, "with a supreme effort I threw the crutches aside and sprang through the window with the chicken in my arms, and went on with my part as naturally as ever. From that day to this I have never had a recurrence of the trouble."[6]

She rang in 1884 in Wheeling, West Virginia, then Ohio and Indiana towns, facing cold weather and more reduced houses. In Louisville, crowds were better despite rotten weather, partly to see Louisville native Jennie Kennark. *Jane Eyre*, though, was "a dead waste of dreariness." At the Grand Opera House in St. Louis, Maggie competed with the nearby engagement of renowned tragedians Henry Irving and Ellen Terry. On Terry's one evening off, she attended Maggie's *Fanchon*, greeting her warmly and sending flowers and, like so many others, urging Maggie to perform in London.[7]

But this she would not do. Some of her imitators, including Annie Pixley, had already done so, but it took all of Maggie's energy and focus to maintain her following in the United States. There was always another, younger competitor gaining on her. That spring it was nineteen-year-old Lizzie Evans, heralded as "aiming to eclipse or at least equal the disciples of the Lotta, Maggie Mitchell, Annie Pixley and Minnie Palmer school of acting." Still, "Maggie Mitchell is in really a class to herself."[8]

Business picked up when she hit St. Joseph and Kansas City, Missouri. For her sole night in the former, where she contributed a piece of one of her dresses for a charity quilt, over 2,000 people bought advance tickets. In the latter, she performed at the glowing new Gilliss Opera House. Located near the city's metropolitan center, it seated 1,700 and featured a tastefully furnished interior and the latest stage equipment and conveniences. Business was excellent, with audiences hungrier for Maggie's style of entertainment than for Irving and Terry's: "Kansas City can not always be depended upon to boom the legitimate drama, but when it comes to spectacle, she looms up strong; our wild western appetite craves something bracing in the theatrical line."[9]

She also outdrew competition in Topeka, Lincoln, Omaha, and Chicago in February, with standing room only almost every night. March took her into Michigan and Ohio, where she remained "as pert, as active and as graceful as ever, the same old infectious wrigglings of an outré nature." The novelty of *Savage* proved attractive, especially her "errant fancy and fleeting moods, in which laughter and tears chase one another like the sun and shadows of an April day. She storms, she dances, feigns tipsiness, sings, boils over with anger or bubbles over with merriment."[10]

The rest of March took her through her usual Pennsylvania and New York towns, ending in Syracuse, where Paddock again sought out Minnie Moore. Although grown portly, he presented to her the image of wealth and accomplishment. Again, he went to Moore's home and paid her $6 for sex plus $1 for a ticket to Maggie's show. He also began to correspond with Moore, which would initiate his downfall.

For six more weeks, Maggie took her combination through New England, for the most part enjoying large audiences, closing her season on May 10 in Pawtucket, Rhode Island. Long Branch beckoned.

Untouched by the Depression, she invested $10,000 (over $250,000 today) in improving Cricket Lodge, with Paddock overseeing the work. Previously "a cheap old-fashioned farmhouse," it would become airier, three stories topped with a cupola and with sprawling piazzas along its sides, and decorated more lavishly, with costly works of art adorning its walls. It perched atop twenty acres of broad lawns enclosed with hedges. Massive granite vases filled with blooming plants flanked the entrance gate, and marble and bronze statues dotted the grounds.[11]

When the work was completed, the Paddocks hosted in mid-August another gala garden party for their extended family and Long Branch neighbors, with games on the lawns and dancing in the enlarged drawing-room, followed by a sumptuous supper at midnight. Maggie presided throughout, "in white silken train and point lace. Diamonds flashed on her fingers, at her throat, in her ears, and her hair." (By that time she possessed "the choicest collection of gems of any woman on the American boards, and her diamond necklace is reported worth treble the cost of

[Sarah] Bernhardt's baubles.") By her side stood timid Fanchon, home for the summer from Mount St. Vincent Academy in New York. It was an idyllic life and Maggie at forty-eight was as happy as she would ever be. Unaware of her husband's hours with Minnie Moore, she told a reporter, "This is what it is to have a useful husband. . . . He is a dear good fellow." The reporter came away convinced that "no more loving couple" existed in Long Branch.[12]

Soon it was time to embark on the 1884–85 season, for which Maggie formed a largely new combination. With her repertoire remaining the same, at least for the first three months, it is unclear why she continually lost about half of her company from year to year. There are few comparisons since most other combinations were formed for, and dictated by the casting needs of, one specific production. Maggie's contracts with these actors have not survived, nor did the actors speak on the record of their reasons for moving on or of any alienation from her.

The most significant changes were her leading man and her soubrette. Over the summer Graham and Goode had joined other combinations. Maggie replaced Graham with Charles Abbott (real surname Mace), 32, a large, muscular, handsome, wavy-haired South Bostonian who had been acting for over a decade but "not evincing any great talent as an actor." Outwardly genial, he was known to be something of a brawler—a wonderful physical specimen, but a man to be wary of. A bit strapping for the youthful Landry and somewhat stiff on stage, he would nevertheless make an impressive Reinhardt and William. In Goode's place, Maggie hired Lillian Andrews, a comely young Australian with considerable experience in the United States. For old character women, notably Fadet, she took a chance on Eliza S. Hudson, with whom she had acted in Washington in the early 1870s, but who carried no New York experience.[13]

Eight new additional actors came on board, prominent among them George Parkhurst, 44, a veteran Washington actor, to play old men, and Mary (Mrs. Eugene A.) Eberle, 44, for maternal roles. Maggie could count on the returning McClannin, Galloways, and an intact management team. Having experienced some woefully unprepared orchestras on the road the past two seasons, she now added a musical director, Otto Vogler.

In scheduling Maggie's season, Paddock had received considerable pressure from theater managers for her to perform on Sundays, by then common practice on the American stage. One even offered a guaranteed $2,000 for two Sunday evenings. She continued to refuse, though, channeling "the rigid Puritanism of the old Bostonians, who would not even permit a Saturday night performance." Even though, as she acknowledged, it cost her an average of $500 for each Sunday night, this determination remained unchanged to the end of her career.[14]

Now, as she hit the road for her thirty-fourth year of performing, she would be cultivating a new generation of audiences, as noted by Chicago humorist Eugene Field. In his ode to Maggie published in the *Chicago News* to coincide with her season-opener in that city on September 29, he recalled that his grandfather "years and years ago/ In Round old English used to praise/ Sweet Maggie Mitchell's pretty ways/ And her fair face that charmed him so." Then, "in time my father felt the force/ Of cunning Maggie Mitchell's smiles/ And, dazzled by her thousand wiles,/ He sang her glories too, of course./ Quite natural, then, it was that I/ Of such a sire and grandsire too/ When this dear sprite first met my view/ Should learn to rhapsodize and sigh./ And now my boy, of tender age/ Indites a sonnet to the curl/ Of this most fascinating girl/ That ever romped the mimic stage!"[15]

A more cynical view was that of British theater critic Alan Dale (Alfred J. Cohen), who seems to have had Maggie and her imitators in mind: "Every month you may see some enterprising 'soubrette' come forward in a play specially written for herself, in which she is everything, and everybody else nothing. Behold her, as she approaches in a ragged dress and a pinafore, eating an apple, and endeavoring to look exceedingly infantine [sic]. You will at once see what you have to expect, and if you are sensible you will leave the theatre. [Those] in America are endowed with perpetual youth."[16]

Good houses held for Maggie and her company in Chicago and around Illinois, Wisconsin, and Minnesota. St. Paul, where she bought a sealskin coat for $375, was undergoing one of the most rapid population explosions in the Midwest and large, fashionable audiences flocked to its Grand Opera House every night and for "ladies matinees." There, she drew some of her best reviews: "It would seem almost as easy to describe to a deaf man the song of the lark or to convey to one devoid of sight the beauties of a spring landscape as to adequately transcribe one's impression of . . . the bright and winsome Maggie Mitchell." Her "gay and blithesome laugh" and "light and fairy footstep" were as "indescribable and effervescent as the sparkle of the morning dewdrop or the aroma of the rose." Every member of the company was deemed excellent.[17]

Minneapolis was as enthusiastic as St. Paul, marred only by a brawl on the afternoon of their departure setting Paddock, Abbott, and Charles Mitchell against a local editor. The editor, who had slighted Maggie, afterward claimed nothing had occurred and did not press charges. Abbott had been in previous physical confrontations, such as one in an Alabama town in 1876 when its mayor allowed "a squad of boys and negroes" to attend a reading by Abbott and his wife Nellie Taylor over Abbott's violent objections (he prevailed). Last spring he had thrashed a visiting Englishman who called American actors "ham-fatters."[18]

As the company traveled, they rehearsed a new work Maggie hoped to unveil by Thanksgiving. Numerous new scripts were urged upon her each summer, but she had learned that most were worthless. Still, she bought them by the dozen and stashed them in her garret at Long Branch. "I've done an incalculable amount of good in that way," she quipped. "When you buy it, you don't have to read it!" Now, though, she found two that held potential. The first, an inchoate dramatization by Blanche Willis Howard of her latest novel, *Guenn: A Wave on the Breton Coast*, Maggie ultimately discarded. The second one she kept and reworked as no other script she had encountered was as blatantly tailored to her character, her personality, her talents, and her style.[19]

It was *Maggie the Midget*, by Frederick Williams, with songs by David Braham, an old friend. In it, almost every cliché of Maggie's previous scripts found iteration. She played the diminutive (of course), young (again) Margaret (conveniently) "Maggie the Midget" St. George, an English girl disinherited (again) when her father dies, leaving everything to her selfish but beautiful stepsister, Claire (Andrews), and domineering stepmother (Hudson), another of each type. Sent to school, she evolves (yet again) from a hoyden to a lady, poised but feisty, a tennis player "proficient in the use of slang in four languages," and (as always) pretty enough to attract the interest of all men. Her clothing stretches the bounds of modesty, from peasant blouses and flared skirts to a tight-fitting riding habit.[20]

She is cast-off (again) to the (typically exotic) Basque countryside and poverty, where she devolves into a heathen (again), only to be befriended by local gypsies (again). They teach her joyful ethnic songs and dances (to exhibit Maggie's skills and provide light entertainment). These included a fandango, a bolero, a tarantella, and a "bull fighter's dance," which she performs with her closest gypsy friend, Ishmael (Fred Queen, a lithe, graceful utility player who helped her choreograph).

Stepmother and stepsister arrive unexpectedly and are appalled and embarrassed by Maggie's slovenliness, lack of erudition (again) and low company. They are accompanied by the gallant, virile Capt. Falconer (Abbott), up to that moment affianced to Claire, but who instantly falls for Maggie. She is unceremoniously hauled back to England, where the two rivals for Falconer's love exchange spite, jealousy, and anger (again). Claire tries to arrange Maggie's death from an untamed horse, but Maggie's robust prowess (again) and riding skill (Mitchell's own) allow her to thwart Claire. Protectively, Ishmael has followed her to England and, having witnessed the preceding, out of revenge strangles Claire with Maggie's scarf. Suspicion thus falls on Maggie, who is pronounced guilty at the coroner's inquest, whereupon (typical lastmoment twists of fate), Ishmael reappears to confess, just as Claire reawakens from her dead faint (no one checked for breathing). Maggie is restored to her rightful inheritance (again) which the stepmother had withheld, and marries Falconer, which Claire seems not to mind. Low comedy is provided by a foolish guardian hopelessly in love with all the girls in the village, a blustering magistrate (McClannin) (a Commandant clone), his addled wife, and a pretentious coroner. Requiring a cast of 22, *Maggie the Midget* meant the hiring of a few locals for minor roles, primarily gypsies.

Late each morning, after a night sleeping aboard the train—Maggie and Paddock in their own "palace car"—arriving in their next town around dawn, the company rehearsed *Maggie the Midget*. Maggie intended to have the piece ready for Thanksgiving in Kansas City, but postponed its premiere to December 3 in Omaha, about as far out of town as any New York tryout could be.

Heading into Iowa, Missouri, and Kansas, the company played one-nighters, and then entered new territory. Colorado, a state for only eight years, beckoned with ornate new opera houses built by silver magnate Horace A. W. Tabor. Having given the silver boomtown of Leadville a $65,000 opera house in 1879, he had outdone that by developing another in Denver in 1881 at a cost of over $750,000. It was one of the most magnificent, best-equipped opera houses in North America, a far cry from the "opera houses" which had hosted Maggie in so many Midwestern towns. Denver, whose population had more than doubled in the past decade, making it the largest city in the West after San Francisco, filled 1,500 seats for Maggie every night for the week of November 10. The next week she drew capacity houses and rave reviews in Colorado Springs, Leadville (at Tabor's Opera House) and Pueblo. *Fanchon*, being a novelty, predominated.

Maggie finished November with a week of full houses in Kansas City, and then moved into Nebraska. After a night of *Fanchon* in Lincoln and Omaha, she finally brought out *Maggie the Midget*. She performed it that winter in almost every town she visited through Iowa, Illinois, and Indiana, even if just for one night, tinkering with it as she went (The original version, for example, had Claire dying, which was not well received). Advance men Mitchell and Sanford did their best to promote it, placing notices a few days ahead of each performance disingenuously informing the public that "*Maggie the Midget* was produced for the first time last week and at once scored a hit."[21]

In Louisville in mid-December, *Fanchon* was welcomed like "a little spring flower that modestly puts its head above the snow and smiles kindly on a cold world." But *Midget* failed. A capacity audience "was decidedly bored" for this "very far inferior" script "in which nothing happens on the stage except two Spanish dances." Occasional "hints that a plot might be forthcoming" do not bear fruit. Each time, "it is dragged out by more talk, while the audience grows impatient to leave the theater. The characters themselves, except for 'Maggie,' are uninteresting, and the plot, when it does arrive, is unpleasant. . . . One fails to see the dramatic necessity for the fright about the supposed murder," which "one rather regrets, . . . since, after all, nothing has happened in the whole course of the play."[22]

Reviews of *Maggie the Midget* from this point forward were more positive, perhaps attributable to less acerbic critics, more rehearsal, and/or more easily pleased audiences. It was well-received over the holidays in Cincinnati. There, on her final Sunday, she went with Paddock and Charles to the Chester Park track to see champion trotter "Maud S.," its owner being a Long Branch neighbor, followed by an evening production of the touring melodrama *Youth*, the saga of a soldier misled by a treacherous wife amid abundant military spectacle.

Maggie began 1885 with a tour of Ohio towns, followed by Pittsburgh, with *Midget* playing to full houses almost every night. Maggie also reactivated *Jane Eyre*, which for unknown reasons had sat on the shelf for almost a year. To ready *Midget* for performances in major east coast cities, she brought in a more experienced choreographer, Arthur Novissimo, to retool the dances. She ran it for at least a night or two during three weeks in Washington, Baltimore, and Pennsylvania towns, drawing large houses and generally good reviews (with some quibbling about its sameness and its darker aspects), but then dropped it again for months.

In Harrisburg, Pennsylvania, she had to step out of character as Maggie the Midget to confront a "loud-mouthed brawler" in the gallery who was determined to keep the issue of her Civil War disloyalty alive. Striding to the edge of the stage, she announced, "Unless such conduct ceases, I shall leave the stage. I cannot play while it is continued." The offender and his "hoodlum" friends were ejected, and the performance resumed, but the incident did nothing to alleviate Maggie's dread of that town, shared by some other actresses. She vowed never to return to Harrisburg until such disruptions ceased.[23]

On February 16 she returned to Broadway but kept to *Fanchon* and *Barefoot*. In the former, she had to remove the "painfully flat" Eliza Hudson from the vital role of Fadet, demoting her to lesser roles. Paddock found a replacement, who would play Fadet, the stepmother in *Midget*, and similar roles for the remainder of this season: Maggie Harold, 32, who had extensive New York and touring experience in comedy and serious drama.[24]

During this New York engagement, a reporter asked Maggie how she managed to keep *Fanchon* so fresh. For longer than Joseph Jefferson had famously been performing *Rip Van Winkle* and James O'Neill *The Count of Monte Cristo*, Maggie was by now well into her third decade with it. She had even stopped posting its (questionable) number of past performances on playbills, as doing so "might set people to ciphering on the problem of my age." Yet she never shirked the requirements of the demanding role, and reviewers continued to extol her energy and spontaneity. Whenever she found herself tempted to let up, she said, she turned her attention to the audience. Sometimes she admittedly found herself performing "absent-mindedly, scarcely aware of the familiar task [of performing] until some pathetic point fails to excite the accustomed rustle of interest, or a sentence or skip doesn't produce the usual laughter." Then, "I know that I am getting careless, and I at once put more vim into my work. If they laugh heartily when I ought to be funny, and are perfectly silent during my pathetic passages, then I feel that I am up to my average—that, no matter how much I might otherwise be bored, I am not boring [them]." There is no evidence that with *Fanchon* she ever did.[25]

She also worked tirelessly to expand her following. From Manhattan she moved for the first time up into Harlem, playing the last week in February at the Mount Morris Theatre on 130th Street. It was a less-than-attractive venue, on the third floor above stables, odors from which wafted up into the theater, but it was the best Harlem had. That would change over the next fifteen years. Harlem was increasingly accessible, at least to middle-class theatergoers who could afford a few pennies for the horse cars and omnibuses up from lower Manhattan. As Mount Morris lay only five blocks from Maggie's real estate investments, it was possible now that the idea came to her to utilize one or more of her lots for the construction of a first-class theater in the area.

During her next week, in Brooklyn, she performed *Mignon* for the last time, exchanging it—gypsies for gypsies—with *Maggie the Midget*. Then it was on to the discerning audiences and critics of Boston. After a week of older repertoire, she brought out *Midget* and, as she had done with *Elsa*, nailed it to the mast for a week, with mixed results. Attendance dropped and critical knives came out. Most of the fault fell to Williams, whose script was "utterly lacking in originality." It was "disagreeably mechanical and moves along as though someone behind the scenes was continually pulling the strings or turning the crank which caused the people on the stage to be in just such a place at just such a moment in just such a manner as was to be expected." Maggie's eponymous character was correctly seen as nothing but a mashup of all of her others. The only real enjoyment came from its dances.[26]

Predictably, a week in smaller New England towns generated more heartening reviews and attendance. After taking off Holy Week, she sprinted for the finish line of Long Branch through six weeks in New England, New York State, and Pennsylvania to close the season on May 16 in Newark, New Jersey. Audiences varied, some being barely half full and others the largest of the season. In tiny Bradford, Pennsylvania, *Midget* drew a large house despite a blinding late-season snowstorm. In Buffalo it was "unique in plot, interesting in dialogue and thrilling in climax [and] probably is the best of Maggie Mitchell's repertoire."[27]

As usual, rivals had multiplied during the season. Three more young Fanchons and Amrys had emerged—Maude Atkinson, Lillie Hinton, and

Jennie Calef—all compared favorably to Maggie. Plus, Minnie Maddern was still going strong, increasingly well-reviewed. But Maggie was the perennial yardstick, each newcomer being "as good as," "as pretty as," or "as vivacious as" she. Sometimes along with Lotta, but as often alone, she was cited as the progenitor of a unique school of performance. A Syracuse reviewer tried mightily to comprehend her enduring popularity:

> I had seen Maggie Mitchell dozens of times before, but I strolled into the opera house yesterday afternoon [and] determined—vain fool, I—to get at the root of the sprightly actress' popularity with her audiences. First, I strove to make an inventory of her resources as a performer with the intention of fixing a theatrical value on each sly wink of the eye, pas of the toe, toss of the curls, inflection of the voice and shrug of the shoulder. There is not much else in her armory of resources. As the little scullery maid of the play [*Barefoot*] made her entrances and exits I found it a comparatively easy task to take note of the dainty artifices she employs in winning attention, but to divine just where they touched the human heart, or account for their potent charm, was, I am free to confess, beyond my analytical power. She is the veriest vandal in the world, a destroying angel, when she is judged as an exponent of elocution, for nobody ever took such license with the commonest rules of that art and survived a week on the stage. Nevertheless, she quite overthrows the senses with those quaint and plaintive tones. Maggie Mitchell always had tears in her voice. There is something in the way she says "O, dear, O, dear," which will open "the fruitful river of the eye." One of the most captivating of her blandishments is the cute way she takes her audience into her confidence, a flirtation over the footlights as it were, carried on with incessant glances, ever so furtive, between the people on the stage and off it. She seems to be prodding you in the ribs with a merry chuckle. Anyone else doing the same thing would be leering, or insincere, but to her this little byplay is as spontaneous and innocent as the gambols of a lamb. She always kneels in prayer more or less in the course of a scene. It is no wonder. There is a devotional spirit in the act which relieves it of mawkishness and sacrilege. One of her most effective gestures is made by lifting her fingers to her mouth, its suggestion of coy deviltry . . . being irresistible. . . . The opening and closing her eyes is another snare of the fairy. In one act yesterday I was able to count her repetition of it eighty-one times, the thing being premeditated and with design. Most of those choice inflections of hers, as for instance in her love making when she archly says, "O, you're joking with me," are inspiration—that is, they are spoken as she inhales breath into her body, a trick, I flatter myself, I discovered yesterday. But that is about as far as I got in trying to make out the secret of her witchcraft. Before the play was half done I gave it up as a bad job.[28]

Talk of retirement in this, her fiftieth year kept popping up, sometimes even voiced by Maggie herself, and then just as quickly shot down, by her or her husband. "She can't quit the stage," he said (sidestepping his financial dependence on her). "Acting is a part of her nature. The stage is her home and she would be lonely away from it. . . . It makes no difference to her whether there is only one person in the audience or whether she is playing to a $10,000 house."[29]

But she was tiring, expressing a more jaded view of the profession at season's end than she had conveyed in her *North American Review* article three years before. She would no longer encourage any young woman to become an actress: "The profession is already crowded, and very little room is left." And while salaries may seem higher in these days of combination companies, and she had enjoyed receiving many valuable gifts, the cost of lavish wardrobes and months of travel were steep. When would-be actresses asked her for advice, she hesitated to give it: "If a young girl has very strong dramatic ability, she will, as a rule, sooner or later find her way to the stage without advice from anyone." Actors, she asserted, "are born, not made" and must possess "an absolutely retentive memory, a good voice, common sense, and an irresistible inclination toward the stage." If so, the best opportunities lay in burlesque and frothy comedies, which were on the rise. Tragedy—Booth and Irving and Terry aside—was on the decline, for "the public much prefer laughter to tears." When asked to compare herself to any of her peers, she demurred: she hardly ever got a chance to see them perform. Unaware of her husband's infidelity, she dismissed any talk of domestic conflict arising from theatrical careers; such was a result of "vulgar curiosity." Actors were "kindly, generous, charitable, and forgiving. . . . There are no people who possess happier firesides." Unfortunately, for her, that would change.[30]

On the positive side, she was rich despite the Depression which had forced the sale (many at auction) of the majority of Long Branch summer homes which comprised "the actors' colony." Her property had significantly increased in value over the past decade, representing at least half of her total worth, estimates of which varied from $250,000 to $500,000. She rode as usual with her family down Ocean Avenue that summer resplendent in "a landau drawn by two handsome bays, driven by a coachman in a blue and gold livery." Her "teams are the most stunning and showy at the shore, changing every year to be in accord with the newest 'fads.'"[31]

By 1885, with her wealth stabilized and the economy soured, Maggie no longer performed Friday evening benefits for herself. She did, though, contribute her time and talent that spring for two for others. The first was a matinee of *Barefoot* at the Boston Theatre for conductor Napier Lothian, who once again played William opposite Maggie, supported by her company, kept intact for that performance. The second benefited James Collier, now the manager of New York City's Union Square Theatre, who had fallen on hard times. A highlight was *Fanchon*, he and Maggie in their old roles.

By now she was stretching her summer breaks from twenty weeks to thirty while auditioning replacements for the 1885–86 season. She planned to play *Maggie the Midget* at least half of the nights and thus hired a company of twenty-three. Added to stalwarts Abbott, McClannin, the Galloways, Parkhurst, Queen, Andrews, Hudson (demoted to minor roles), Mrs. Eberle, and a returning Van Deeren (for old women, especially Fadet) were nearly a dozen new actors. These included Andrews' husband, Fred Doud, 30, and, close to Maggie's heart, Dodson Mitchell, 17, the sole survivor of her brother's family felled by yellow fever. "Dod," playing small parts, would be making his debut on the American stage, where he would eventually rise to some prominence, like his cousin Julian. The rest of the additions were utility players, primarily for gypsies in *Midget*. The company's management remained intact.

Maggie adjusted casting a bit, too. In *Pearl*, for instance, as her leading men had aged out of the romantic lead, Arthur, she had had them play the larger, more challenging role of Marie's father, Lonstalot. Now, the younger Abbott would play Arthur, and the capable, older Parkhurst would be Lonstalot. Otherwise, Andrews would remain the flirtatious Chouchon, McClannin the Commander, Galloway the antic Pierrot, and Van Deeren the imperious Marchioness.

Following her annual summer's-end reception at Long Branch for family and fellow professionals, Maggie devoted all of September to rigorous rehearsal in New York. She arranged for sumptuous new scenery for *Midget* and costly new costumes, to be carried on the road. Along with her omnipresent live chicken used in her first entrance in *Fanchon*, her baggage now included two dogs—a St. Bernard to enhance the character of the alpine Marie in *Pearl* and a Newfoundland for *Midget*—miscellaneous poultry, including several pigeons and an obstreperous gander, and calves, for barnyard ambiance in *Barefoot*. (She left one more dog, which she had taught clever tricks, with her cousin in New York.) This menagerie sometimes proved problematic. One night during *Barefoot* the gander wandered too close to the gas jets and got its bill nipped, sending it squawking into the air and out among the audience, convulsing them with laughter.

Maggie opened the season with *Midget* on October 5 in Bridgeport, Connecticut, working her way with it through a week of New England towns to Boston. There, for the first of two weeks at the Park Theatre, *Midget* held sway, received warmly by critics and large audiences. With Williams' and Braham's acquiescence and assistance, she had made changes to the script to lighten some moments, changing, for instance, her jealous fury with Claire to a quarrel (which illogically minimized Claire's murderous retaliation). She darkened others melodramatically. A new second act picnic scene featured a chorus of happy villagers (the *Fanchon* villagers'

Maypole festivities redux) who suddenly arise in fear and gather up their belongings to escape a sudden storm: "The shadows grew dark in the wood, the rumble of thunder grows louder, vivid electric flashes light the scene, when suddenly the murder [of Claire] is discovered, and as the frightened group stand with blanched faces, the inanimate form of the murdered girl is borne by upon a litter, made ghastly by fitful flashes of lighting." She also gave herself a new plaintive song in the third act, accompanying herself on the guitar.[32]

After two more weeks in New England, primarily of *Midget*, Maggie took the company back to Broadway for a week, opening November 16 at the Grand Opera House with *Jane Eyre*, holding *Midget* in abeyance. Having now played Jane for fifteen years, it had become her favorite role. Still, she added diplomatically, "The part I like best is the one upon which the curtain has just fallen; tonight one, tomorrow night another." While performing, she said, "I do not see my audiences at all. For the time being, I am the character I appear to be, and it is only when the curtain falls that I become again Maggie Mitchell." Her continued support of the Elks was evident in her participation in a matinee to benefit them, joined by Lotta and Mary Anderson. (In Boston, accompanied by Paddock, she was the first woman to set foot in the new clubhouse of the Boston Elks Lodge.)[33]

Midget predominated that fall in New England, in Brooklyn, Baltimore, Washington (at Albaugh's new Grand Opera House), Pittsburgh and Cincinnati (again, for the holidays). Her loyal following, sizable but no longer overflowing, still loved her as "she romped about the stage as though it were a playground." At Albaugh's as the audience took their intermission refreshments in his lavish lounge, they could gaze upon "a bewitching full-length portrait in oils of Maggie Mitchell, the evergreen little sprite, standing in a familiar attitude, with arms crossed in a girlish way," hanging among portraits of immortal actors John McCullough and Edwin Forrest.[34]

Starting the new year in Louisville and St. Louis, "she looked no older than eighteen, and her dancing was as sprightly as ever, even including high kicks in *Midget* that knocked off Ishmael's hat (given her height, a considerable feat). Doing the fandango, "the little heroine displays her well-shaped limbs with grace and amazing activity." Executing the "bullfighter's dance," "she pounds the paint off the stairs with her heels." She maintained her modesty during this by wearing "bicycle pants" (bloomers) under her childish short skirts. Sporadic comments about her declining voice, evident crows-feet, and increasing plumpness—while retaining "all the cuteness and kittenishness" of her youth—indicated how near her fiftieth birthday was. But such shortcomings were almost immediately qualified by statements of their needing to be overlooked given the energy, fame, and popularity of such a star.[35]

After a one-nighter in a new town, Sedalia, Missouri, Maggie opened January 21 in Kansas City, not in the Gilliss, but back in the Coates, to which the city's commercial center and fashionable society had migrated. She played *Lorle* to a full house and supportive reviews, but the following night as the curtain went up on *Pearl*, a massive blizzard swept in across the plains. Remarkably, the full house remained, cheering her and calling her before the curtain several times (January 1886 was a notorious month for snowstorms across the country).

By morning she and her company were trapped in Kansas City, with rail travel impossible. So, on the spot, she contracted with manager Mel Hudson to perform into the next week while Paddock telegraphed ahead (where possible, with many lines down) to rearrange her schedule. By January 28 she was able to get to Atchison, Kansas, for a night of *Midget*, which on one day's notice nearly filled the house despite the snow. The same thing happened the following night in Topeka, so Maggie stayed one more day, doing a matinee of *Fanchon* and *Lorle* that night. Sunday the company celebrated with a sleigh ride before trying again to travel west.

On Monday, February 1, the tracks opened enough to get them to Denver for a week at the Tabor, then on to Nebraska towns, two of them new (North Platte and Hastings). In Lincoln, defying another snowstorm, an immense throng at the Funke Opera House, many from surrounding farms and ranches, cheered *Midget*, calling for encores for Maggie's dances.

In Atchison, Topeka, Lawrence, and Leavenworth, many rural, first-time theatergoers attended. Maggie's "mad scene" in *Pearl* brought men and women alike to tears, and the farcical scenes on *Midget* threw them "into convulsions." She felt so welcome in Lawrence, her third time there, that she granted an expansive interview, expressing her regard for "all the people of the west. There is a freedom from restraint out here, coupled with a graceful sense of propriety, which makes me feel at home. The newspapers always give me such nice notices, not stiff and formal like those of the big cities." A pet peeve was anyone who asked, or speculated, about her age. "One paper said I was seventy-two years old! And another that I was fifty-three [not far off]. But come over to the opera house and see me dance, and you'll think I am not much beyond twenty." Her husband attributed such speculation to her having begun starring at a relatively early age, but in reality, it was her tiny frame and electric energy that allowed her to play child-like roles this late in life.[36]

Frigid weather continued as she pressed on into Kansas, Nebraska, and Missouri, then north into Iowa and Minnesota. Due to the weather, audiences were only fair to good, but criticism remained unnecessary. Whether in Omaha or St. Paul or anywhere else, "To attempt criticism of Maggie Mitchell would be something like sitting in judgment on the merits of the Songs of Solomon or debating the artistic points of a Raphael masterpiece. . . . Her hold on the public is just as strong today as it ever was. And what is more, no one ever saw a Maggie Mitchell play that did not feel the better for it."[37]

Yet criticism is exactly what Chicago papers undertook in mid-March, especially of *Midget*. Again, they were incisive. Williams' adaptation was fine for three and a half of its four acts. However, the doctored ending gave the lie to all preceding dramatic value. How could such early promise "come to so lame and juggling a conclusion in order that there may be a happy outcome?" Williams "stripped his play of a strong dramatic climax in pitiable deference to an absurd sentiment. After leading the audience to a high pitch of interest by forcible, rational work, [he] whistles at the old humbug of happy adjustment, resuscitates a murdered girl, annuls the heroism of his most manly character, cheapens the tragic romanticism of his unique gypsy boy, and complacently turns his heroine over to the fellow who has really forfeited the right to her love, and drops the curtain on an ending that disappoints the audience." It would have been far better "to let Ishmael fade away with the compassionating sympathy of the audience" and have Falconer "reap the reward of unmanly, vacillating character." Maggie's vitality alone saved *Midget*: "The spectator would grow weary at intervals were it not that her interest in the piece was so evident and her earnestness so pronounced."[38]

The play disappointed patrons of smaller towns of the Midwest. Since *Midget* was "made to order" for Maggie, its other characters faded to a bland dimness "that the star may shine more brightly by contrast." Yet even this "heroine has not the same dramatic traits which the heroines of other plays of this actress have." The plot was "absurd" and its "denouement is unfortunate and absolutely distasteful." Maggie's two advance men, Charles and Sanford, relentlessly flogged a handful of positive reviews that *Midget* had received in New England, but it seemed destined to be short-lived.[39]

In these smaller towns, Maggie was "the same spirited little actress she has been for years, retaining all of her old powers to please. She is alternatively vehement, passionate, indignant, vengeful, pathetic, lighthearted, gay, yet always supple, agile and quick as a panther." But one critic after another remarked that her voice was not what it used to be, whether speaking or (especially) singing. Some were blunt: "She will soon be compelled to renounce the stage or at least the delineation of youthful characters." Most criticism, though, she just sloughed off. She was, after all, "a tough little woman" who was "still piling up the ducats."[40]

Arriving in Akron on April 20, she received word of the death in Troy of her father at eighty-one. He had been a patient for some time at Marshall's Infirmary there, where Maggie's half-brother Joseph D. Lomax practiced, and had been unconscious for a week. She soldiered on with *Midget* that night but fainted twice backstage. The next day, her depression over missing her father's funeral in Troy caused her to move lethargically through her performance in Youngstown, and much the same on the 22nd in Meadville, Pennsylvania. She was able to attend his interment beside Anna at Brooklyn's Green-Wood cemetery on the 23rd, and by the next evening was back in Elmira. She continued to be visibly depressed, almost to the point of illness, for the rest of the season, but nearly always rallied to give her all to her audiences across Pennsylvania, Delaware, and New Jersey, with *Midget* still predominating.

On May 10 she returned to Harlem for a week, this time at impresario Josh Hart's Theatre Comique on 125th Street between Lexington and Third Avenue. It stood to the east of one of the most fashionable neighborhoods in Harlem, with homes built for $15,000–40,000 ($400,000 to $1.6 million today). Surrounding the Comique was a commercial district which included Maggie's brother Charles' new hotel, along with upscale department stores and, soon, other theaters, crowned in 1889–90 by the West End Theatre (which Maggie would originate), Oscar Hammerstein's magnificent Grand Opera House, and the Columbus Theatre. Soon, predicted the *New York Sun*, "125th Street will rival Broadway."[41]

At the Comique, Maggie closed her season, retiring for the summer to Long Branch in time to celebrate her fiftieth birthday on June 2. Enthused one newspaper, "If any lady now upon the stage can look and act in a more juvenile manner at 50 than Maggie Mitchell, the world knows her not. At 100 Maggie Mitchell will still be inquiring for Farmer Barbeaud."[42]

NOTES

1. *Chicago Tribune*, Jan. 14, 1883; *Philadelphia Times*, Mar. 3, 1889.
2. *Cincinnati Commercial Tribune*, Sept. 18, 1883.
3. *New York Sun*, Nov. 14–15, 1883; *New York Tribune*, Nov. 17, 1883.
4. *Ibid.*; *Trenton (NJ) Times*, Nov. 20, 1883; *New York Tribune*, Nov. 28, 1883.
5. *Cleveland Plain Dealer*, Jan. 11, 1884; *Pittsburgh Post-Gazette*, Dec. 25, 1883.
6. *New York Sun*, July 12, 1883.
7. *Louisville Courier-Journal*, Jan. 17, 1884.
8. *New York Clipper*, May 24, 1884; *St. Paul (MN) Globe*, Oct. 12, 1884.
9. *Kansas City Evening Star*, Dec. 15, 1883, quoted in frontispiece, Londré. Note Londré's (p. xv) spelling of Gilliss.
10. *Detroit Free Press*, Mar. 11, 1884; *Toledo (OH) Journal* quoted in *Dunkirk (NY) Evening Observer*, May 9, 1885.
11. *Indianapolis News*, June 7, 1884.
12. *St. Paul (MN) Globe*, Dec. 2, 1883; *Philadelphia Times*, Aug. 17, 1884; "Long Branch Letter," *Clay Center (KS) Times*, Sept. 10, 1885; *Detroit Free Press*, July 28, 1887; Carboy.

13. Unidentified clipping c. 1890, MM Papers, HTC.
14. *Brooklyn Magazine*, April 1885 (II:1), 8.
15. Eugene Field, *Sharps and Flats*, ed. Slason Thompson. New York: Scribner, 1900, I:243–44.
16. Alan Dale, *Jonathan's Home*, Boston: Doyle & Whittle, 1885, 150–51.
17. *St. Paul Globe*, Oct. 15, 1884.
18. *St. Paul Globe*, Oct. 12, 1884; *Opelika (AL) Times*, Apr. 15, 1876.
19. *Salt Lake Tribune*, Oct. 22, 1881; MM correspondence with Howard in MM Papers, MS Collection 4552, NYPL.
20. *Chicago Tribune*, Mar. 10, 1886.
21. *Louisville Courier-Journal*, Dec. 12, 1884.
22. *Louisville Courier-Journal*, Dec. 17 and 20, 1884.
23. *Harrisburg Telegraph*, Feb. 6, 1885 and Feb. 9, 1888; *Harrisburg Independent*, Jan. 24, 1888.
24. *Minneapolis Star Tribune*, Oct. 21, 1884.
25. New York correspondent for *Chicago Journal* reprinted in *Lincoln (NE) Journal Star*, Mar. 12, 1885; Maggie quoted by Henry "Kit" Chanfrau, a Long Branch neighbor and friend, in *New York Star* interview, reprinted in *Kansas City (MO) Star*, Oct. 3, 1885.
26. *Boston Journal*, Mar. 17, 1885.
27. *Buffalo Evening News*, May 13, 1885.
28. *Syracuse Standard*, May 3, 1885.
29. *St. Paul Globe*, Mar. 7, 1886.
30. *Brooklyn Magazine*, April 1885 (II:1), 8.
31. "Long Branch Letter" in *Clay Center (KS) Times*, Sept. 10, 1885; *Wilmington (DE) News Journal*, Nov. 19, 1886.
32. (Davenport, IA) *Quad-City Times*, Mar. 18, 1886.
33. *Brooklyn Magazine*, April 1885 (II:1:8)
34. *Baltimore Sun*, Dec. 8, 1885; *Cincinnati Commercial Tribune*, Dec. 29, 1885; Washington correspondent for *Kansas City Times*, Mar. 6, 1887.
35. *Louisville Courier-Journal* quoted in *Michigan Argonaut*, vol. VI (1887–88), 81; *St. Louis Globe Democrat*, Jan. 12, 1886; *St. Paul Globe*, Feb. 26 and Mar. 2, 1886.
36. *Topeka Commonwealth*, Feb. 17, 1886; *Lawrence (KS) Herald-Tribune* reprinted in *Osage County (Burlingame, KS) Chronicle*, Feb. 25, 1886.
37. *Omaha Bee*, Feb. 23, 1886; *St. Paul Globe*, Mar. 4, 1886.
38. *Chicago Inter Ocean*, Mar. 10, 1886; *Chicago Tribune*, Mar. 10, 1886.
39. *Decatur (IL) Herald*, Mar. 24, 1886; *Jackson (MI) Citizen Patriot*, Apr. 7, 1886; *Fort Wayne (IN) Sentinel*, Apr. 1, 1886;
40. (Davenport, IA) *Quad-City Times*, Mar. 18, 1886; *St. Paul Globe*, Apr. 18, 1886.
41. *New York Sun*, Apr. 7, 1889.
42. *Jackson (MI) Citizen Patriot*, June 26, 1886.

Chapter 14

"completely under his influence"

Throughout the 1880s Paddock continued to manipulate Maggie's finances, not all of it done aboveboard. He attempted to sell an already-mortgaged Long Branch property to meet a note owed to Edwin Booth and was paying hundreds of dollars of interest to Booth on notes borrowed in Maggie's name. She may or may not have been aware of these loans, and would seem to have had no need for them herself, but held onto the evidence of them to the end of her life.

He also grew sloppy about theatrical management. One company member remembered him as "a happy-go-lucky fellow who gave scant attention to the business. One night he never came near the theater until everything was over. Then he appeared at his wife's dressing room. He wished to impress her with his vigilance, however, and so he said—we were doing *Fanchon* that night—'My dear, I think you had better call a rehearsal of the girls in the chorus about the Maypole [dance]. It went very badly tonight.' 'Henry,' said Maggie Mitchell, 'I cut it out tonight. It wasn't done at all.'"[1]

The couple began to fight about Charles Abbott. Despite his being married to actress Nellie Taylor, his senior by more than a decade and currently touring elsewhere, Abbott was in Paddock's eyes far too attentive to Maggie and her business affairs. He demanded that Maggie fire Abbott. She, in turn, harbored suspicions about her husband's fidelity, but as yet had no proof.

Soon, word of the Paddocks' marital conflict leaked to the press, and it became an open scandal, with journalists and the public taking sides: "Miss Mitchell's friends charge Mr. Paddock with dissipation, neglect of his wife, and extravagance in the management of her affairs. Mr. Paddock's friends tell all sorts of stories as to indignities put upon him by his wife, and say that he is a very patient and forbearing man that he did not long ago take extreme measures to rid her of the influence of one Charles Abbott." Some "acquaintances" "knew that her mimic lover of the stage had become her real lover, and would be glad to become her husband."[2]

By mutual agreement Paddock resigned as Maggie's manager, remaining in Manhattan to pursue a career in real estate. She replaced him with Harry Sanford, hiring a new advance man, Will S. Lykens, formerly a manager in St. Joseph, Missouri. Lykens soon proved himself highly capable, churning out advance notices all season. Only a handful of actors left that summer for other combinations. The biggest loss was Fred Queen, who had complemented Maggie so well in *Midget*. She replaced him with dancer Walter Perkins, and Marion Clifton returned for maternal roles.[3]

The 1886–87 season began on October 4 in Bridgeport, Connecticut, followed by other New England towns and then Boston. Perkins quickly distinguished himself as Ishmael but was otherwise relegated to minor roles. Abbott, "one of the cleverest and handsomest leading men now before the public," claimed the leads; Robert McClannin, grown portly, would enact older men along with Parkhurst; and James Galloway would handle comic roles. This company was thoroughly rehearsed, had perfected their roles, and functioned as a smooth ensemble. On this tour, *Midget* was rotated evenly as one piece among equals, not predominant as last season. In Boston, audiences were smaller than previously, but they picked up as she toured New England and then mid-Atlantic towns.[4]

At least at the start of the season, Maggie at fifty appeared "almost as chipper and vivacious, spirited and sparkling as she was years and years ago." She remained "the embodiment of youth." A reporter passing her on the street one afternoon was struck by her "quick, springy walk and hearty, merry laugh, as musical as that of a schoolgirl of 15." On the stage, "there is a charm about seeing such an old lady prance around, dance, etc., in a manner to make a young actress envious."[5]

When Maggie squared off during a week in Washington in late November against twenty-year-old Minnie Maddern in *Caprice* at the nearby National Theatre, reviewers inevitably drew parallels. They were in many respects "singularly and charmingly alike. Both have discarded from the outset the conventional, if indeed either was ever capable of it. Both act from the heart and to the heart. Both, defying all rules . . . by some sudden touch of nature bring tears to eyes yet wreathed with the wrinkles of laughter." If Maggie had established the school, Maddern was its most apt pupil. Maggie may have "many imitators, but no one has approached her." She remained the definitive Fanchon, to the point that "it is difficult to say whether Maggie Mitchell is Fanchon or Fanchon is Maggie Mitchell," an oft-repeated sentiment.[6]

After appearing at Albaugh's Holliday Street Theatre in Baltimore, she returned to New York, to Sinn's Brooklyn Park Theatre for the twelfth year, then Harlem's Theatre Comique, then on to Pittsburgh for the holidays. Her actors surprised her in her dressing room on Christmas with a large lithograph of her surrounded by a seasonal wreath, and a pair of elegant Dresden vases. She closed out 1886 and welcomed 1887 in familiar Cincinnati.

For the next five weeks, she trekked through small towns of Ohio, Indiana, and Illinois, some for the first time in years, into the frozen upper Midwest. In St. Paul and Minneapolis she was a universal favorite, "the sunbeam of the stage, sparkling and glistening and dancing on forever." She fully entered in the spirit of their winter carnivals, going out despite her age on toboggan rides some nights after performances. By comparison, actress Clara Morris had merely looked at the "ice palace one afternoon and pronounced it to be very beautiful." She lacked "the buoyant spirits" that Maggie exhibited so freely.[7]

In this devout heart of America, Maggie deserved to be "admired for her part in raising the standard of stage morality." Her uplifting scripts, especially "the thread of delicate Christian sentiment that runs throughout," were "as effective as sermons." "As Fanchon, the despised of the village youths and maidens, she puts them to shame by her reverence for her mother's prayer, as Barefoot, she recalls to wayward Jem[my] their Christian mother's prayers.... Lorle's faith and the Savoyard girl's [Marie's] prayer to heaven for strength in temptation are touching, and one can feel that the faith, the reverence... are not simply lines to be repeated, but the outgrowth of deeply-rooted Christian sentiment."[8]

Several hundred members of local snowshoe and toboggan clubs swelled her record-breaking, overflowing houses. They cheered her soundly between acts and made her an honorary member. Among their floral tributes was a toboggan with a prominent M on its upper curve, which Maggie integrated into the alpine scenery of *Lorle*. She appeared rejuvenated by the attention: "It seemed that never before had there been such a ringing quality in her gay and blithesome laugh, such an infection about her light and airy footstep. Her spirit was as effervescent as the sparkle of the morning dewdrop." The entire company was pronounced superior in all respects, especially Abbott, Galloway, and Andrews.[9]

Through Nebraska, Kansas, and Missouri in February, Maggie drew phenomenal houses despite severely inclement weather. She was irresistible, "a bright, bouncing young woman not yet far enough out of her teens to restrain a natural romping disposition. Every movement seems to be born of overflowing and uncontrollable animal spirits." "The thousands of times she has danced this [shadow] dance have not taken away from its attractiveness nor made it less popular." Although her voice showed occasional hoarseness, "her dancing is as light, her ridicule as keen, and her vigor as unflagging as they used to be." Her ability to "put tears in the eyes or lines of laughter in the faces" of her audience remained undiminished. The suave, handsome Abbott caused female hearts to flutter, but always "with care and taste."[10]

There were, of course, occasional sour notes: "Her voice is but a ghost of a voice and her dancing is but a succession of crinkles and reminds one of an antiquated stage horse which is so sore in all his legs that he cannot limp upon any particular one." "She has gained flesh surprisingly, and it is a roly-poly Maggie Mitchell that flits and dances and plays grotesquerie for us now.... Her cheeks are plump [and] her figure is rounded."[11]

After performing in Chicago in early March she headed into Michigan, and then toured Ohio towns. April took her into West Virginia, Pennsylvania, back into Ohio, then into New York State and New Jersey. She continued to draw excellent crowds, except when she followed Lotta. In these smaller towns where her following was most loyal, she utilized Sanford and Lykens to cultivate local goodwill, but not as unctuously as her husband had: "The genial face of her old manager, Mr. Paddock, is missed at the door, and the one who tries to fill it, H. E. Sanford, is better fitted to drive street cars than look after the interests of so brilliant a little actress as Mrs. Mitchell." Still, Maggie reflected her satisfaction with Sanford by renewing his contract for next season. "Under his management this year," asserted a St. Louis paper, she "has coined money."[12]

In light of that, more and more newspapers that season questioned Maggie's need to continue working. She was still estimated to be worth between $400,000 and $500,000, primarily in Long Branch and New York real estate, and still bringing in $30,000–40,000 a season. Moreover, she had accumulated "one of the choicest collections of gems of any American woman" and "a substantial library," having paid $1,250 for a set of Shakespeare's works. One paper speculated that she continues to perform only because "all her friends and acquaintances being in the profession, she has no other life, and wants no other." Another reported that she "declares her intention to go on acting just as long as the public will have her and her powers remain."[13]

Although her husband that season remained reliant on that "very large revenue which the actress brings into the family," he exerted considerable effort to not just be known as "the husband of Maggie Mitchell." Lionized and glad-handed on the road, he struck a reporter now as "a trifle fearful ... that the supreme favorite of the national stage would soon be unable to defy her advancing years" and keep supporting him. Yet, ironically, he denigrated her ability, attributing her protracted popularity "to the prevailing rage for the antique."[14]

Closing her season in Amsterdam, New York, on May 14, she dispersed her company and headed for Long Branch, picking up Fanchon and Harry on the way. Her children had grown into splendid young adults. At eighteen, Fanchon had blossomed into a charming, intelligent, yet still timid girl who at 5'5" stood head and shoulders over her mother. Although "not in any sense a beauty, she is very chic and has a host of admirers.... Her hair is brushed closely to her small head, [and] her bright eyes peep demurely from under her smooth bangs." Asked again whether Fanchon might join her mother on the stage following her graduation next summer, Maggie was adamant: "Never with my consent. She has displayed considerable histrionic ability, but I don't want her to appear before the footlights, and she never will if she listens to her mother, and I know she will." Harry, "the man of the family, grows like a weed every day that is added to his fifteen years." In the near future, Maggie planned to take him on tour with her and engaged a private tutor for him.[15]

Gossip spread that summer that Maggie's "life is anything but a bed of roses and that she may be placed on the list of unhappy women." She kept to herself, "seldom going anywhere, always studiously at work on new parts and refraining from meeting the company her husband, Hank Paddock, entertains." When she did venture out, it was in the company of her children, swimming in the ocean late each afternoon in a modest black bathing suit, her hair up in a fashionable turban. She hid any unhappiness. "Her step was as light, her voice as musical, her manner regal and as loyal as the sunflower to the sun."[16]

She took on a new wariness of the press, fearing they would cobble together an article "made up of scraps of incidental off-hand conversation and enough imagination to make it spicy." But she accommodated two reporters that summer, expressing her relief to be off the road: "This is my home. I yearn to come here and I hate to go away. You don't know how wearisome it grows to travel round and round for months at a time." She still regretted somewhat that her career had never turned to tragedy: "If I were commencing again, I should certainly work in that line. Many of my professional friends who know me well believe I would have been very successful in tragedy." During interviews, Paddock hovered, his "shaggy eyebrows, sandy moustache, square, determined chin and pleasant manners" providing the false impression that he must have been "an excellent manager for this little actress and, I believe, a good husband."[17]

Two of the new parts Maggie studied that summer held promise: Ruby Beach in Howard P. Taylor's *The Little Sinner*, and Ray Golden in *Ray*, written expressly for her by Philadelphia playwright and journalist Wallace Clifton. She certainly needed new material. No other star had performed a limited repertoire so consistently for so long. *Fanchon* was entering its twenty-seventh consecutive season, *Barefoot* and *Pearl* their twenty-fifth, and *Lorle* its twentieth.[18]

By the end of the summer she and Paddock grew further estranged, her suspicions growing and their arguments, especially over Abbott, increasingly acrimonious. He moved out, taking a room on Seventh Street just off Bowery. Maggie threw her energy into assembling her company for the 1887–88 season. Perkins having left, her new dancing partner as Ishmael would be Earle

Stirling. Lillian Andrews, having aged out of ingenues, was supplanted by young Almira Strong but remained in the company, promoted to older roles, including Fadet. Abbott would keep his romantic leads and McClannin, who had secretively yet unsuccessfully sent out letters that spring seeking employment elsewhere, returned to carry demanding mature roles. The management team remained the same.

Stirling and Strong proved themselves from the start when Maggie opened her season on September 22 in Duluth, Minnesota, followed by St. Paul and Minneapolis, her toboggan and snowshoe revelry from last winter fondly recalled. But audiences were slightly down due to theatergoers saving their money for the highly anticipated upcoming tour of Edwin Booth and Lawrence Barrett. That season, they outpaced even Maggie, playing 258 performances in 72 towns. Still, she soldiered on in October through Iowa, Nebraska, and Colorado, playing the Tabor Opera Houses in Denver and Leadville. In Kansas, in November she added to Wichita, Lawrence, Topeka, Leavenworth, and Atchison three new towns: Newton, Fort Scott, and Ottawa.

In Kansas City, a confrontation arose between Abbott and Sanford. Previously friends, the two men fell out on Thanksgiving Day over Sanford's belief, like Paddock's, that Maggie had become smitten with Abbott, entrusting him with too much of the combination's operations. Abbott, in turn, accused Sanford of embezzling money and failing to repay a sizable loan. Maggie, automatically siding with Abbott, forced Sanford to resign before she fired him. To replace him, she recalled Lykens from the field, rewarding him with a credit line on playbills as director. For a new advance agent, she turned to an old friend, Baltimorean John M. Barron, a former member of McVicker's company in Chicago who first met her—and John Wilkes Booth—thirty years before. They trusted each other, having formed back then what Barron termed "friendship of the heart."[19]

He got right to work ahead of her November 25 opening of *The Little Sinner* at the Coates Opera House in Kansas City. Citing his long connection with Maggie, he crafted for managers and newspapers a fulsome endorsement of her, citing her nobility, purity, integrity, and charity. "The life and career of this little lady are in themselves a wondrous sermon to those unthinking people that say the stage is degrading," he declared. Maggie stood as "the embodiment of all that women may be proud of, the pride of a thousand of pious hearts and the idol of the public."[20]

Such a testimonial counted for much in Kansas, which was experiencing a groundswell temperance movement (with Carrie Nation's ax hovering), on top of an existing religious conservatism. Maggie carefully nurtured her image of personal purity as well as that of her scripts. But as her popularity grew in the heartland, it was beginning to shrink in New York. Among

Manhattan photograph sellers, Lillie Langtry was the most in-demand actress, with only occasional requests for Maggie. Booth was tops for men, with Barrett and Lester Wallack close seconds.

Langtry, the beautiful, extravagant "Jersey Lily," represented Maggie's moral opposite, having conducted numerous, scandalous extramarital affairs with men in England—including the Prince of Wales—before her acting debut there at 28 in 1881. Now on her third American tour, she one night insulted Maggie, albeit indirectly. Infamous for her imperious manner and quick temper, Langtry had become irate upon hearing several men in her company singing backstage. One received a shove from her that sent him sprawling. They were not, she scolded, "playing in a variety show" (a genre of entertainment several notches below Broadway in talent, taste and, often, morality). "You are not," Langtry admonished, "with a variety actress like Maggie Mitchell." When the actor reported her remarks to the press, she promptly fired him.[21]

Maggie downplayed the slight: "I know of no reason why Mrs. Langtry should have picked me out, nor do I care," she stated. "It is a matter of utter indifference to me what she says. My reputation cannot be tarnished by her opinion or increased by her praise. . . . I am so far above anyone of the Mrs. Langtry kind that it would be unbecoming to engage in any controversy over what she says." "I will say," she concluded, "that there are some variety people for whom I have greater respect than [for] Mrs. Langtry, . . . of whom the public has long ago formed its opinion."[22]

She attributed the slur to Langtry's having been snubbed that summer by polite society in Long Branch, which Langtry denied: "Positively no effort was made by me to meet Mrs. Mitchell, and I didn't hear of any social overtures on her part." But a summer visitor who had been present reported that the married Langtry's current boyfriend, Freddy Gebhardt, in a hotel ballroom had waltzed with Maggie's daughter, Fanchon, "with Mrs. Langtry looking on." This would certainly not have gone down well with Maggie, maintaining her image of rectitude. New York journalistic "judges unanimously awarded the palm of victory to the American. If Maggie Mitchell is a variety actress, who, oh what, is Mrs. Langtry!"[23]

The Little Sinner debuted in Kansas City on November 21, with stereotypical roles for everyone. Maggie's Ruby Beach was yet another rural lass whose head is turned by the wealth and manners of high society. Engaged to a boyish mason, she nevertheless flirts with a gentleman of higher station, who escorts her to a fancy-dress ball (another opportunity for Maggie's fine costumes and agile footwork). When the day of her wedding arrives, the gentleman calls her away to give her a wedding present of diamonds. She tarries and returns to find the wedding guests departed. Her father and fiancé cast her into the street. In tears, she returns to the gentleman for protection and they plan by default to marry. A jealous local girl contrives to steal the mason's affections, but he realizes his true love for Ruby and appears at her wedding, whereupon the gentleman improbably but graciously cedes his place at the altar to the mason.

Reviewers were not kind. *Little Sinner* was condemned as lachrymose, and "Maggie Mitchell in tears is not 'America's Favorite.' It is like trying to cast Lotta as Desdemona." It was just another vehicle for Maggie. "Whatever the role she plays it is always Maggie Mitchell," although "her audiences would be disappointed were it otherwise." Furthermore, *Little Sinner* ran well past 11:00, eliciting calls for pruning if it indeed was worth repeating: "There never was a play with less interest about it or a poorer excuse for its existence." It was simply "worthless."[24]

Audiences quickly lost interest. Maggie's week in Kansas City "hardly paid for having the house open, the attendance being the lightest of any week this season." Determined, she announced *Little Sinner* for her next stop, in St. Louis, but at the last minute changed it to *Midget*. Thinking it might fare better in a cosmopolitan setting, she brought it out for three nights the week after that in Chicago (where she also inexplicably resumed *Jane Eyre*), with mixed results. She shelved *Little Sinner* for the rest of December as she toured towns in Illinois, Michigan, Kentucky, Ohio, and West Virginia, tried it for one final time in Pittsburgh in early 1888 then abandoned it for good.[25]

After playing Pennsylvania and Maryland towns and then Washington, she headed with some trepidation to Harrisburg on January 24, three years after her disruptive performance there. Although a brief newspaper item alluded to that occurrence, she received a warm welcome in *Midget*, with no untoward moments. In her first visit to Philadelphia in six years, she announced a solid week of *Midget* but changed it after two nights to *Lorle* and *Fanchon*. Combating extremely cold weather and an ongoing strike by railroad workers, she defused the latter by performing a benefit on their behalf, but the former rendered her voice weak and raspy. But again, she was forgiven: "Miss Mitchell hasn't the voice she once had, but her vivacious manner makes her songs hardly less charming."[26]

Her vocal problems continued through Pennsylvania, New Jersey, and New York towns but improved somewhat by mid-February in Brooklyn. There, on February 13, 1888, she gave her final performance (of nearly 500) of *Pearl of Savoy*. Next came Henry Miner's People's Theatre in the Bowery, a combination house near Delancey Street a half mile further into the "East Side" from her 1882 Bowery visit, which attracted a decidedly rowdier crowd. Maggie's performances were too tame for them, for while she earned enthusiastic applause from the higher-priced seats, "the gallery gods showed plainly that a clog or a shuffle with some novelty of step would have suited their fancy much better." It all must have reminded Maggie why she had been happy to leave the Bowery behind her.[27]

A troubling incident occurred one night at the People's Theatre. A tipsy young woman carrying a revolver showed up in the lobby demanding to see Lykens, claiming he had been stringing her along for two years since meeting her in Pittsburgh, promising he would make her a famous actress if she paid him enough. Money soon turned to diamonds, until she caught him bragging to male friends that she was "mashed on me." She determined to get revenge and her money returned. Fortunately, a detective in the lobby arrested her.[28]

A far more serious challenge confronted Maggie when she headed in early March to Rochester. Whatever suspicions she may have harbored about her husband's infidelity were cruelly confirmed one morning at the opera house as she prepared for the night's performance. A letter in an unfamiliar hand arrived for him and she, thinking it related to business matters, opened it only to read a love letter to him from Minnie Moore, unquestionably confirming their affair. Maggie immediately went to Moore's home and confronted her. Moore admitted everything and agreed to testify in Maggie's intended divorce.

It remains unknown if there was any connection to this discovery, but within days Maggie sold a stone house and a 20' lot on Summit Street in Toledo, Ohio, to real estate capitalists for $22,000. Whether this had been another of her shrewd investments or an intended home with Paddock near his native Cleveland, she was now rid of any tangible (or emotional) connection to Ohio. According to her friend John Carboy, as soon as Maggie was free of Paddock and his financial mismanagement, she proved a shrewd businesswoman: "no dealer in the Strand is sharper at a bargain than she." She now "understood financial matters as well as she did the steps of the shadow dance. . . . There was no nonsense about her."[29]

She returned to New York and announced the premiere of *Midget* on Broadway on March 12 at the Fourteenth Street Theatre, an aging combination house. But the massive Blizzard of '88 prevented any performance until the following night. Even then, only a few hardy souls attended. Meeting discouraging reviews, she continued to perform *Midget* but added matinees of *Fanchon* and *Jane Eyre*, which proved popular.

During this engagement, the simmering Abbott-Sanford quarrel erupted. On the morning of March 15, the brawny Abbott confronted Sanford in a printing office and accused him of spreading scandalous stories coupling his name to Maggie's. Although Sanford tried to defuse the situation, Abbott cursed and spat at him, then slugged him, bloodying his nose and blackening both eyes. Sanford pressed charges of assault, and on the night of March 20, just as the curtain was going up on *Midget*, police arrived backstage to arrest Abbott. Maggie intervened and guaranteed Abbott would show up the following morning in police court. He did, but when Sanford did not appear within ten minutes for the 10:00 arraignment, the judge dismissed the case.

Only moments later, as Abbott and several actors from the company—Maggie not included—jubilantly exited the courtroom, Sanford rushed in, having misjudged the time. Abbott and Sanford rushed to tell their sides to reporters. Abbott claimed he had "merely pulled him out of his chair by the nose," and Sanford argued that Abbott's original accusation was false, "but Miss Mitchell is so completely under his influence that, by his machinations and through no fault of mine, I was discharged from the company. I have a contract with Miss Mitchell and so I brought suit against her in the Supreme [Superior] Court for my salary for the balance of the season [$1,950]. . . . She alleges that I was not discharged but resigned, which is not at all likely when the facts are considered. Mr. Abbott is much larger than I am and is a regular slugger." Maggie's countersuit, doubtless urged by Abbott, claimed Sanford was incompetent and owed the company money which had been advanced to him in the execution of his duties, which he failed to fulfill. It was another embarrassment for this most moral of performers.[30]

As she had done so many times before in her long career, she kept her head down and focused on performing. But touring New England towns in April, she appeared distracted and suddenly old, and audiences responded poorly. One reviewer took her to task: "A woman possessing the fortune that Maggie Mitchell does should not destroy a reputation by continuing as a star. . . . Her age is against her. Her voice is against her and all the cosmetics that can be applied cannot make her face a girlish one."[31]

Abbott, too, was "careless and listless" and the rest of the company seemed to take their cue from him. Ironically, when Maggie was asked what she thought were weaknesses of combination companies, she cited a lack of adequate rehearsal time on the road and an abdication of oversight of production standards by stage managers: "The young actor or actress in a combination is rarely any better at the end than at the beginning of a season, and often considerably worse." She did acknowledge that the quality of stage furnishings had improved.[32]

As if hearing her own words, she announced a two-day hiatus for rehearsal before resuming this New England tour. She intended to polish everyone's performances, including her own, which must have worked because her return to the stage—more New England towns—yielded effusive reviews. A reviewer who had seen Maggie in *Barefoot* twenty-five years before wrote, "When Maggie Mitchell came upon the stage, I looked in wonder and astonishment. The same winsome, witching Maggie, looking younger than she did then. The same merry laugh and waltzing, as though for the very love of it, possessing a foot and ankle that would drive some of our burlesque [dancers] wild with envy." (Throughout her career, Maggie's shoe size grew only from a dainty one to a two-and-a-half.)[33]

In these closing years of the 1880s, she was competing not only with hundreds of other combinations but with such novelties as Buffalo Bill's Wild West Show, a box office juggernaut, and she needed an edge. Thinking *Ray* would provide it, she devoted considerable time to rehearsing it. This "comedy drama" carried a minor theme of labor unrest, especially relevant since the Haymarket Square bombing in May 1886, presaging a decade of violent labor conflict in the United States.

Once again, she played "a very waify waif, who does the usual cute, uncouth things," the titular orphaned child of the son of the owner of a mill in a western town and the village beauty who worked there. Entrusted to the care of the eccentric Simeon Stea (McClannin), an earnest, goodhearted labor reformer who endlessly spouts anti-capitalist rhetoric (but who is made to appear foolish, blunting the play's social criticism), the pretty but uneducated Ray is now sixteen. She has attracted the eye of the wealthy Percy Vorell (Galloway), the son of the woman (Clifton) who now owns the mill. Their courtship includes two comic scenes, one a messy shared lunch on the factory floor, and the other an interlude of kissing hidden under an umbrella, the bobbing up and down of which suggests the ardor of their passion.[34]

However, Percy's friend, the villainous Mark Walworth (played by a young newcomer, Harold Hartsell), convinces him to throw Ray over as being beneath him (providing Maggie another weepy jilting scene). Ray's pure heart leads her to shelter an escaped prisoner, Gabe Wilden (Abbott), whom she believes has been wrongfully convicted. (He was being chased by two live bloodhounds—further additions to Maggie's traveling menagerie, a gift from heiress Lucy Hamilton Hooper which included their stage training.) Gabe, however, turns out to be (in Maggie and Abbott's case, chronologically implausible) her still-living father. Cheated out of his mill, he was sent up the river through the treachery of Walworth, who is ultimately killed by strikers. When Gabe's mill, and thus Ray's wealth, is restored, Percy repents his misjudgment and he and Ray joyfully unite amid romantic special-effects snow. A few laborers and heiresses make brief appearances to provide context, but with only about a dozen roles, *Ray* would allow Maggie to cut costs as she toured with it for the remainder of her career. Significantly, the script no longer required her to sing or dance.

To ready *Ray* for its April 19 debut in Providence, increasingly serving as a Broadway tryout town, Maggie hired twenty-eight-year-old aspiring playwright Benjamin F. Teal, who for six years had been managing other tours. Since Barron was now traveling ahead of Maggie and would be gone by summer, Teal's expertise in staging and in eliciting strong performances from actors would prove invaluable. With his help, *Ray* was successful, but only to a point. After calling Maggie before the curtain for three acts, at the end of the fourth "the curtain fell without a hand, and a disappointed crowd silently left the theatre." The issue was Ray's acceptance of a man who had treated her so cruelly. Realizing the play was not ready for Broadway, Maggie and Teal continued to make adjustments—as Maggie always did—heightening Percy's repentance and atonement. (Well into 1889, playwright Clifton remained unsatisfied with the fourth act and continued to tinker with it himself.) Maggie resumed touring with it, playing to moderate audiences and modest reviews for another six weeks through New England towns, interspersed only with an occasional *Fanchon*.[35]

But after twenty-seven years of *Fanchon*, she had finally grown to dread performing it. She hated seeing advertising for herself in the part, forbade any mention of it by company members or even the humming of a tune from it in her hearing, and generally tried not to think about it. On days when she had to perform it, "before she goes on her loathing of the part really makes her ill, and it increases with each successive performance." But it remained a cash cow in a way none of her other scripts did.[36]

When she closed her season in Danbury, Connecticut, on June 2 and retreated to Long Branch, it was without Paddock, a fact that newspapers made much of. She announced, and then recanted, her intention to retire. She began, too, to cultivate a more maternal image. She dressed over-modestly when she went out and wore her hair, now tinged with gray, in a severe bun. She looked, said one observer, "more like a Quakeress than an actress."[37]

When Fanchon, newly graduated from St. Vincent's, left on June 20 for Hamburg, Germany to study music and German for two years, Maggie announced plans to travel there with Harry, but for now, did not leave. She dropped hints that she might tour next season to California and Australia, a plan espoused by Lykens. This may have emerged from reading raves flowing out of California for the *Fanchon* of Kate Mayhew, formerly a member of Maggie's company, now said to be her equal. But Maggie did not go there, either. By early August she was reportedly quite ill, secluded at Cricket Lodge, but her presence was reported at the July 31 wedding of her nephew John Albaugh, Jr. (whose engagement over the past year Maggie had helped to arrange and conceal from the bride's parents, who disapproved of the stage, John's chosen profession).[38]

She had no intention of moving back into the house on 124th Street that she had shared with Paddock and announced abruptly in mid-August that it would be torn down and a theater built on the site, encompassing all seven lots she owned, through to 125th Street. The grandiose theater, she stated, would be modeled after the Paris Opera House, would front on Seventh Avenue, and would seat 2,000 patrons under Lykens' management. At first, she planned to finance its construction from proceeds from her investments in the Chicago wheat market, which had brought her nearly $10,000. However, upon learning that a theatrical syndicate had raised $250,000 for building a new theater on 125th Street to compete with Hammerstein, she sold them her seven lots for $110,000 and relinquished control of the project in favor of the syndicate's appointed supervisor, Allen H. Wood. The edifice, to be designed by architect George H. Griebel "in the Byzantine style, with a warm Oriental tinge," and costing an estimated $300,000, was slated for completion by October 1889 as the West End Theatre.[39]

Before embarking on her 1888–89 touring season, Maggie instructed her lawyer, John E. Lanning, to file for divorce, citing her husband's dissolution, dependence on her earnings, and repeated infidelity, specifically with Minnie Moore, who would testify on Maggie's behalf. This Lanning accomplished on September 19, and notice was duly served on Paddock. His response, received well after Maggie had embarked on her fall tour, was predictable: her charges were "wholly untrue and a most unfounded and cruel imputation." He had not committed adultery with Minnie Moore at any time and place. Furthermore, he argued, Maggie owed him back pay for managing her tour, but he would settle for $25,000.[40]

Her tour would consist primarily of *Ray*. Lykens would arrange the itinerary and supervise the construction and painting of all new scenery. With Maggie's consent, he sent actor Earle Stirling ahead in a new capacity as advance man. While Abbott, McClannin, Marion Clifton, and Eliza Hudson returned, the new, smaller company included a few replacements. Playing Ray's love interest, Percy would be boyish Boston actor C. E. Boardman (who could also fill comic roles like Jemmy in *Barefoot*), the villainous Mark would be George W. Deyo (with seven years of touring experience), and the new ingenue would be Miss Virginia Nelson. Sheridan Tupper would act and function as stage manager.

Maggie opened her *Ray*-centric season on September 27 in Milwaukee and for three nights drew enthusiastic applause before moving on to Fond du Lac, Oshkosh, and Eau Claire. The following weekend brought Lykens his first frantic challenge, an ironic pursuit of Maggie's bloodhounds, which he had shipped ahead for her week in Minneapolis, followed by a week in St. Paul. A railroad express worker, allegedly drunk, misdirected them to *Indian*apolis, with Lykens only succeeding in the final moments through urgent telegrams, quipping that he would take the bloodhounds' place if they did not arrive on time. *Ray* was deemed "a rather gushy production abounding in cheap sentiment and unnecessarily replete with flapdoodle," whose plot and characters seemed lifted from Dickens. The decades, too, were beginning to take their toll: Maggie this fall appeared "fleshier and ruddier," clearly "getting stout."[41]

Following a series of one-night stands in Iowa and Nebraska, Maggie took *Ray* in November through Colorado, Kansas, Missouri, Iowa, and Illinois towns, opening in Chicago on December 3 for a week. She encountered only fair houses and jaded reviewers. Closing 1888 with brief engagements in Michigan and Ohio, she drew better audiences and reviews. While *Ray* admittedly contained stock characters and a predictable plot, Maggie acted "all the way from madcap mirth to genuine tear-compelling pathos," exhibiting "the same merry twinkle in her little dark eyes and the same cricket-like chirp which she mingles with her laughter. The simple word 'soubrette' has many sins to answer for and it is supposed to be descriptive of every actress who can skip about in short clothes, sing a song, dance a jig, simper and look 'cute,' but there are few soubrettes on the stage today who besides possessing the faculty of producing laughter can in the next moment cause the tears to flow. Such an actress is Maggie Mitchell."[42]

She began 1889 in Pittsburgh, where all echoes of her Civil War conduct had faded. Her engagement "was one of those phenomenal occurrences that seldom happen twice in the history of a theatre," with standing room only and chairs in the aisles all week. Hundreds were turned away from the box office. Still, reviewers were skeptical, believing the "offensive vulgarity" of *Ray* unworthy of Maggie.[43]

Through other Pennsylvania towns, then Washington at her brother-in-law's opera house, and Philadelphia, *Ray* drew good crowds but dismissive reviewers. Ray simply "laughs, quarrels, says sharp things, and behaves herself generally so that her blood relationship to Fanchon and many other stage children dear to the popular heart is unmistakable." Audiences missed her songs and dances.[44]

February took her to Boston, where *The Theatre* decided that *Ray* was "merely a conglomeration of weak sentimentality and dime novel situations." At least when Maggie was onstage, "and the clever dramatist kept her there all the time, the audience did not feel the play drag. . . . She has the smartness to keep doing something all the time, to act whether the play calls for it or not, to make a grimace whether it is natural or no. . . . She does as much acting with her elbow as most women do with the hands." The rest of the characters fade into the background. "They lack moral stamina. Their bravery is ostentatious, their pathos not genuine, their humor not healthy, their villainy purposeless, their actions not consistent. There was no moral in the play at all." Percy "showed a sad lack of manliness but he wins the girl in the end all the same. The pseudo labor reformer [Simeon Stea] is one of the most worthless persons in the piece."[45]

When Maggie debuted *Ray* on Broadway on February 11 at the Fourteenth Street Theatre, she drew adoring crowds but even more caustic critics. A play "of the machine-made kind, in which virtue is duly triumphant and the polished villain meets with his proper deserts," it was "evidently constructed to cover up Miss Mitchell's lack of voice and former ability to dance, and although her figure is matronly, her manners are still kittenish and her fun mischievous." Her character was "barbaric. Ray does not talk. She either yells or chuckles. She does not sit. She flops. She does not walk. She struts. Her voice had the melodious sweetness of the sawmill. Her movements are harmonious as a German street band." Her attempt to play a young girl "is perfect [only] from the rear of the house." The supposedly humorous umbrella scene was merely "vulgar." True, "those who have liked her in other plays will like her in *Ray*," but "the memory of her triumphs in *Fanchon, Little Barefoot* and others of her former plays is too strong, and the comparison necessarily detracts from her present performance." Except for McClannin and Clifton, Maggie was "surrounded by one of the worst companies that money can buy." Abbott as a leading man was "not an actor worthy of that position."[46]

Maggie finished February with two weeks of *Ray* in Brooklyn, one at the Lee Avenue Theatre and the second inexplicably at the Grand Opera House. She sold out both despite inclement weather, drawing mixed reviews along with regrets that she was not performing more of her old, familiar repertoire. She was again reportedly quite ill but kept performing.

She was weighed down, too, by immediate, personal anguish.

NOTES

1. Owen Fawcett, "Recollections of an Old Actor," *San Jose (CA) Mercury News*, Nov. 1, 1903.

2. *New York Times*, Mar. 4, 1889; *New York World*, Aug. 10, 1889.

3. Paperwork documenting Paddock's payments to Edwin Booth, MM Papers, MS Collection 4552, NYPL.

4. (Washington) *National Republican*, Nov. 18, 1886.

5. *Wilmington News Journal*, Nov. 19, 1886; *Ft. Wayne (IN) News*, Jan. 7, 1887; *Brooklyn Eagle*, Dec. 12, 1886; *St. Louis Globe Democrat*, Nov. 29, 1887.

6. *The Critic* (Washington), Nov. 23, 1886; *Washington Sunday Herald*, Nov. 28, 1886.

7. *St. Paul Globe*, Jan. 23–Feb. 5, 1887; *Minneapolis Star Tribune*, Feb. 2, 1887.

8. *Minneapolis Star Tribune*, Feb. 6, 1887.

9. *St. Paul Globe*, Jan. 23–Feb. 5, 1887; *Minneapolis Star Tribune*, Feb. 2, 1887.

10. (Lincoln) *Nebraska State Journal*, Feb. 10, 1887; *Topeka Daily Capital*, Feb. 15, 1887; *St. Joseph (MO) Weekly Herald*, Feb. 17, 1887.

11. St. Louis correspondent for the *Salt Lake City Tribune*, Mar. 3, 1887; *Detroit Free Press*, Mar. 25, 1887.

12. *Kalamazoo Gazette*, Mar. 16, 1887; *St. Louis Post-Dispatch*, Mar. 26, 1887.

13. New York correspondent for *Wheeling (WV) Register*, Oct. 9, 1886; *Chicago Inter Ocean*, Aug. 7, 1887; *Kalamazoo Gazette*, Aug. 21, 1887; *The Theatre* vol. 3 (Mar. 21, 1887–Jan. 23, 1888), 382.

14. *Syracuse Standard*, May 22 and Sept. 11, 1887.
15. *St. Paul (MN) Globe*, Sept. 6, 1884; *Pittsburgh Post*, Jan. 7, 1888; Unidentified clipping, MM Papers, HTC.
16. *Fort Wayne (IN) Journal-Gazette*, July 17, 1887; "Long Branch Letter," *Kansas City (MO) Times*, Aug. 14 and 21, 1887.
17. *Macon (GA) Telegraph*, Aug. 7, 1885; New York correspondent for *Buffalo Morning Express*, July 24, 1887; *St. Louis Dispatch*, Aug. 7, 1887.
18. Clifton was also known as C. Wallace Walters and Col. Cal Wallace.
19. Barron, "Actors of Days Gone By."
20. *Topeka Capital*, Nov. 16, 1887.
21. *New York Sun*, Nov. 17, 1887.
22. *Kansas City Times*, Nov. 22, 1887.
23. *Syracuse Standard*, Dec. 4, 1887; *Rochester Democrat and Chronicle*, Dec. 3, 1887.
24. *Kansas City Journal*, Nov. 26, 1887; *Kansas City Times*; Nov. 26, 1887; *Kansas City Star*, Nov. 26, 1887; *Racine (WI) Journal-Times*, Dec. 3, 1887.
25. *New York Clipper*, Nov. 26, 1887.
26. *Philadelphia Inquirer*, Jan. 31, 1888.
27. *New York Sun*, Feb. 26, 1888.
28. *New York World* reprinted in *Cincinnati Commercial Tribune*, Mar. 3, 1888.
29. Carboy.
30. *New York Herald*, Mar. 22, 1888; *Buffalo Evening News*, Mar. 26, 1888.
31. *Waterbury (CT) Evening Democrat*, Apr. 5, 1888.
32. *New Haven Morning Journal and Courier*, Apr. 3, 1888; *Chicago Inter Ocean*, Apr. 4, 1888.
33. *The Theatre*, May 7, 1888. The writer of this review, identified only as "L.H.," could very well, given its effusive tone, have been Maggie's close friend Luther Holden, dramatic editor of *The Journal*.
34. *New York Evening World*, Feb. 12, 1889.
35. *The Theatre*, May 7, 1888.
36. *New York Graphic* interview reprinted in *Trenton (NJ) Evening Times*, May 20, 1888; *Macon (GA) Telegraph*, Nov. 4, 1888.
37. *Buffalo Evening News*, Apr. 28, 1888.
38. It was only an hour before the ceremony that the bride's parents relented.
39. *New York Clipper*, Mar. 16, 1889.
40. Defendant's response to petition, filed Dec. 31, 1888, *Paddock v. Paddock* (13-300-1888, V-25-418), Chancery Court of New Jersey.
41. *Minneapolis Star Tribune*, Oct. 2, 1888; *St. Paul Globe*, Oct. 13-14, 1888.
42. *Detroit Free Press*, Dec. 14, 1888; *Cleveland Plain Dealer*, Dec. 21, 1888.
43. *Pittsburgh Dispatch*, Jan. 1, 1889.
44. *Washington Evening Star*, Jan. 22, 1889.
45. *The Theatre*, v. 5 (Dec. 29, 1888–Oct. 26, 1889), 150.
46. *New York Press*, Feb. 11, 1889; *New York Times*, Feb. 12, 1889; *New York Post*, Feb. 12, 1889; *New York Sun*, Feb. 13, 1889; New York correspondent for the *Cincinnati Enquirer*, Feb. 17, 1889; *New York Herald*, Feb. 17, 1889; *National Police Gazette*, Mar. 2, 1889.

Chapter 15

"dissipated and untrue"

The wheels of divorce spun slowly. At the urging of friends and, reportedly, her children, Maggie made a few anguished and ultimately unsuccessful attempts to reconcile with Paddock. At one point she instructed Lanning to withdraw her petition for divorce, and a New York newspaper reported (without attribution) that the Paddocks had briefly resumed living together. But by February 1889 it was clear that their marriage was at an end.

Maggie was outraged by Paddock's demand for money, which she had no intention of paying. When close friends broached the topic, she bristled. Her husband, they learned, "had got in trouble with the Tweed ring in New York and had been induced to invest largely in unproductive and depreciating property [the ruinous Long Branch venture]. At one time, but for the clemency of creditors, she would have been bankrupted." He had "mismanaged her affairs generally, was dissipated and untrue" to her, leaving her no recourse but the divorce court.[1]

Lanning re-filed her petition for divorce and depositions began. On February 25, at the order of New Jersey Chancellor Alexander T. McGill, Lanning deposed Minnie E. Moore (now Havens, having married in June 1888) and her mother, Ovanda E. Moore, at their new home in Rochester. Neither Paddock nor his attorney appeared. Minnie was fully forthcoming, admitting her involvement with Paddock. He had at first told her he was single, then, after their 1884 tryst, had admitted he was married to Maggie. Minnie corroborated having had intercourse with him and his paying her. Ovanda graphically corroborated his comings and goings to their house. Following Minnie's intercepted love letter to Paddock and Maggie's visit, Minnie avowed she was "reformed and married and leading a reputable life."[2]

Two days later, Maggie granted a rare interview on the subject of her pending divorce. Dressed demurely in black satin trimmed with lace, her curls up beneath a modest bonnet, and looking "not a whit more than the proverbial 'sweet sixteen,'" she received a *New York Sun* reporter backstage at the Grand Opera House in Manhattan following a matinee. At first reticent, she warmed under his gentle questioning to divulge that she had agreed to one final meeting with Paddock late that night or the following morning to try to effect a rapprochement. Still, she was resolved not to pay him the $25,000, as he had already wasted well over $100,000 of her money. She held out little hope for any settlement.[3]

Such was the case, and on February 28 she provided a deposition in Jersey City, New Jersey, expressing her early doubts of Paddock's rumored infidelity, only to have them confirmed by Moore's letter and personal corroboration. Since that discovery, she had refused to support him or recognize him as her husband. In fact, "I have always provided for him instead of his providing for me." She had remained a true wife to Paddock until October 1, 1887, when they separated. As with the Moores' depositions, neither Paddock nor his attorney attended Maggie's.[4]

When the *Sun* reporter returned for an update, he was rebuffed by Abbott, quite "combative in his manners." (Abbott had also "more than once made himself obnoxiously officious in her affairs" to a different reporter.) Asserting that he was protecting Maggie as "her manager," Abbott appeared "very much distressed lest Miss Mitchell 'say too much.'" There would be no interview if the topic was divorce. The reporter shifted gears and inquired about Maggie's children, a topic she embraced. She also expressed her relief over no longer being involved with the construction of the West End Theatre in Harlem, happy that the syndicate had taken it over and that she had prospered from the sale of the land.[5]

The reporter then sought out members of Maggie's company, all choosing anonymity, who disabused him of the notion that Abbott was Maggie's manager. Asked why Abbott was then so protective, the members "wore a knowing look and begged to be excused from answering." Abbott did not "seem to enjoy the friendship of all his associates in Miss Mitchell's support," one of whom revealed Abbott's involvement in the breakup of a different man's marriage. This "wasn't the first case of the kind in which he had figured." Some members of the company expressed their willingness to testify on Paddock's behalf concerning Maggie's estrangement of affection.[6]

Paddock steadfastly refused all comment. Such was not the case among family members. In Cleveland, Paddock's parents were not surprised: "We have known that there is trouble between them, but thought the trouble was merely of a business nature. We are on good terms with Maggie and of course our son." They did think it odd that Maggie uncharacteristically failed to visit them on her visit to Cleveland in December. Paddock's brother Charles revealed that when Paddock and Maggie had first separated,

Paddock had come to Cleveland with a trunk of belongings, saying he intended to leave her permanently. "But after having been here four weeks he received a letter from Maggie asking him to return to Long Branch," and it was supposed that they reconciled. When Charles later visited his brother in New York he was startled to find him and Maggie living apart. Paddock had "complained bitterly of his wife's actions with reference to her leading man, Charles Abbott, [saying] that his wife was thoroughly infatuated with her leading man and all his pleadings could not induce her to send him away, so he left her again."[7]

Gossip about the Paddocks had long circulated among actors and managers, especially after Paddock no longer accompanied Maggie on tour. It was thought among some that the "rupture between Maggie and her husband was on account of the latter's jealousy of her leading man, with whom, the story went, Miss Mitchell had fallen in love." But Maggie had "strong grounds for believing that the charges she makes against Paddock in her petition are absolutely true." His freewheeling lifestyle and profligate spending of her money were legendary: "It is no exaggeration to say that he has expended three or four fortunes [of hers]. He could get drunk, buy all the wine in town, half the carriages, and finally wind up by breaking all the mirrors and plate-glass windows he could get a shot at. The next day, of course, the bill would be to pay, and probably it would take $300 or $400 to settle. Those sprees were sometimes of frequent occurrence and long duration. Miss Mitchell probably got tired of such carryings on and means to end them."[8]

The press was divided in its loyalties. Some doubted that Maggie could win her case since her husband "has borne himself in the most manly and praiseworthy manner." Others trumpeted, "Give Miss Mitchell a Chance," castigating journalists who had treated her "cruelly and heartlessly in [their] flippant remarks about her divorce suit." "Maggie Mitchell, worth a half a million in money, too, has a right to ask for a divorce if she thinks she needs it in her business and her manager [Abbott] advises it." A rural Missouri paper struck a rueful tone: "Until yesterday," the Paddocks had served nobly "as a refutation of all the slurs and slanders hurled against the immorality of the stage." Now "they were just like the rest. More's the pity!" One cynical outlier even accused Maggie of staging the divorce action as an advertising gimmick, "to be in fashion and for the new experience it affords."[9]

Most embarrassing to her was the exposure on March 4 by an anonymous Chicago source of her abortive marriage in 1862 and its subsequent dissolution and cover-up. But as no concrete proof of it remained, due to the Chicago Fire of 1871, details of it were often erroneous, such as placing it in Richmond in the 1850s. Reached in Binghamton, New York, on her *Ray* tour, Maggie refused to comment. Paddock, though, tersely broke his silence: "You may say this, and nothing more—that I know all about my wife."

Maggie's brother Charles professed ignorance of this early marriage, as did Paddock's parents, but the latter admitted that they had not known of their son's marriage to Maggie for over a year.[10]

At trial, Paddock failed to appear and mounted no defense. On the recommendation of the domestic master who had deposed Maggie and collected all relevant evidence, McGill on March 26 granted Maggie's petition, formally ending the Paddocks' marriage. Touring New England towns, she issued only a brief statement reasserting her practice of not publicly discussing her private affairs. (Given her otherwise stainless reputation and the frequency of divorce among actors at the time—over 30 percent for men and over 45 percent for women—such discretion is understandable.)[11]

She continued to tour New England to good business, resting over the long Easter weekend. By April 12 newspapers were reporting that upon ending her season she would travel to Europe to see her daughter and possibly perform an engagement that could bring her over $60,000. (Despite years of such rumors, she never performed there.) While overseas, several reports ran, she and Abbott would wed. After a benefit on May 9 in New York for destitute, widowed actress Elizabeth (Mrs. David P.) Bowers, for which she and her company performed Act II of *Ray*, Maggie closed her season on May 11 in Jersey City.

Retreating to Long Branch, she and Abbott were quietly married in the front parlor of Cricket Lodge. (No records survive of Abbott's first marriage to, or divorce from, actress Nellie Taylor.) The only attendees were Maggie's son, Harry, and Mrs. Luther Holden, wife of Maggie's close friend, the long-time dramatic editor of *The Journal*. Private, even secretive marriages were commonplace among actresses, explained Clara Morris. For anyone else, a wedding can be her day in the spotlight; an actress often preferred a day out of it.[12]

On June 15, Maggie departed with Harry for Hamburg. Abbott stayed behind in Cricket Lodge to manage her financial affairs, which proved prescient. On July 21, the bubble that was the West End Theatre burst. Despite its cornerstone having been laid on June 10 and the walls under construction, the syndicate represented by Allen H. Wood had never completed payments to Maggie for her seven lots. Having received only $20,000, she retained the mortgage (and deed) for the remainder. Wood, it turned out, was, in reality, con artist Charles W. Hahr, 23. He had spent over $70,000 of the savings of his gullible, weak-minded father-in-law not on the theater's construction but richly appointed offices, personal amenities, and generous compensation of actor Tommy Russell, also 23. Contractors, the project's business manager, and architect George Griebel remained unpaid. Wood or Hahr, who was also wanted in New Jersey for forgery and whose brother was blackmailing him over his schemes, was nowhere to be found.[13]

On August 2, while Maggie and her children toured Switzerland, the sheriff took possession of the theater's site, and a judge subsequently restored the lots to Maggie. (When she returned, she rented the seven lots with their incomplete walls out for $7,000 per year, 5 percent of their estimated $140,000 value. The site housed a marketplace until she sold it at a handsome profit to a developer who built a new music hall.)

Meanwhile, Abbott auditioned and hired replacements for the 1889–90 season, which would consist only of *Ray*, *Fanchon*, and *Barefoot*. On his forays into the city, he cut quite a hale, stout, handsome figure, always dressed in the height of fashion. One observer in August watched this "notably good-looking man" as he "sauntered past a bevy of giddy girls in upper Broadway [who] turned to look after him. . . . The fluttering five girls, in costumes bright and breezy enough for a summer resort" and all notably a third to a half of Maggie's age, were hoping to be auditioned by him as soubrettes.[14]

But Virginia Nelson returned as the soubrette of Maggie's company, so there was no need. Abbott did hire replacements for C. E. Boardman, Clifton, and a few minor players. The new juvenile—for Percy, Didier, and Jemmy—would be William Wilson, and the new maternal figure would be Nellie Mortimer (Mrs. George F.) De Vere. Reverting to Elizabethan convention, one of the new minor actors, Stephen Wright, would play the crone, Fadet. Most of these new performers would be gone at season's end. Abbott also hired his good friend Frank Gerth as company treasurer and retained company manager (and still an advance man) Will Lykens and conductor Otto Vogler.

Maggie and her children arrived back in New York on September 18, heading to Cricket Lodge for two weeks to gather her strength. Then, sending Harry off to his college and private tutor, she hit the road, taking Fanchon with her (in an unknown capacity, but likely as dresser and confidante) along with widowed, retired actress Jean Davenport Lander to chaperone Fanchon on social occasions. These may have been somewhat awkward, as Fanchon, already timid, had grown into "a tall and somewhat heavy young lady—at least the double of her mother in bulk and weight."[15]

Maggie and her combination opened in Providence on October 3 with three nights of *Ray*, followed by a week in Boston. *Ray* was dismissed by critics as indistinguishable from countless melodramas peddled by Lotta and Pixley, "a mixture of absurd situations, heart-appealing sacrifices, hair-raising villainies and commonplacisms [sic], sure of applause from an average audience." But Maggie was markedly "different from other little ladies who strive to kick and giggle themselves into favor, as is Miss Lotta," and appeared revitalized.[16]

Throughout July, August, and September, unconfirmed rumors had trickled out about Maggie's secretive marriage to Abbott. But it was not until mid-October in New England, when they impulsively registered as Mr. and Mrs. Charles Abbott at their hotel in Brockton, Massachusetts, that Maggie admitted it to a close friend, an unidentified local actress, and the news broke nationwide. Maggie confessed, grateful that newspapers had kept quiet until then and relieved now that the secret was out. Beyond this, she had no further comment, and Abbott had not a word to say. Hank Paddock, interviewed in New York, expressed no surprise.

"Maggie Is No Better Than the Rest of Them" chided a Midwest paper, mocking accounts of her noble image. It just proved "no actress is so old and none so staid or so much divorced that she will not take another husband." When Maggie played a week of *Ray* in the Bowery, back at the Windsor (not the rowdy People's), one journalist quipped that Abbott "now also does the leading business at the fair actress' hearthstone." But the ever-loyal *Daily Saratogian* reminded readers that "although Maggie Mitchell's relations with Mr. Abbott have been friends for a long time, they never approached their present degree of intimacy until after she was divorced from Henry Paddock."[17]

That fall, critics were divided about the appropriateness of Maggie's continuing to play waifs. Some insisted she had "discovered the secret of perpetual youth," appearing ever "more youthful, more brimful of spirits, more light and gay in her movement, more sweet and tender in the simulation of emotion." Others were blunt. Off the stage, "Maggie Mitchell in a flare hat, her own fuzzy, wiggy hair, her cast-iron but intelligent countenance, her own eyes close together, looking askant at times across a high-bridged nose, is a picture. Who can remember Maggie's youth?" A few were downright snide, calling her "that sixty-year-old [sic: 53] impersonator of giggling young girls." While "in her tones and her outlines she remains a girl of fifteen, . . . it is only in her face, which she keeps adroitly shaded by overhanging hair while acting, that her sixty years are visible."[18]

A week of *Ray* in Baltimore was followed by another in Philadelphia, where Lykens fell dangerously ill, requiring hospitalization. Abbott, with Maggie's acquiescence, promoted Gerth to the position of company manager. The company moved on to Brooklyn, Buffalo (Maggie's first visit there in nearly five years), through a series of Pennsylvania towns to the nation's capital. There, on December 9, Abbott inexplicably pushed Maggie to fire both Lykens and Gerth. Iago-like, he told her that rumors were circulating that Lykens had been a rival for her hand.

For now, she took no action, but a determined Abbott had his understudy cover his roles and on the morning of December 13 headed to Philadelphia. There, on December 16, Maggie was to open in a lavish revival of *Fanchon* at the new Park Theatre. Lykens, recovered, was still there, working with Gerth to finalize arrangements for the revival. But Abbott intended to control all aspects of the company's management himself, and quickly hired Charles T. Atwood as the new advance manager, sending him on to Pittsburgh.

In the lobby of the Park, Abbott confronted Lykens and Gerth and hurled nasty accusations at Lykens. A row ensued, Abbott striking Lykens across the head with his cane. This degenerated into a brawl with the two men trading punches, then rolling in a clinch on the marble floor as a crowd of bootblacks jeered. Gerth tried vainly to separate the combatants, and only when the box office manager summoned the corner policeman did Abbott and Lykens flee, the former considerably bloodied. Both Lykens and Gerth vowed to seek restitution in court, as they had valid, signed contracts they believed to be still in effect.

Abbott spent Monday regaling hotel employees with the details of his thrashing of Lykens. By all accounts, he appeared at his virile best on Monday night as Landry opposite Maggie in *Fanchon* but was still upstaged by the extravagant scenery, including a real waterfall. Maggie, of course, shone and reaped the lioness' share of plaudits. On her closing night, esteemed Broadway producer Daniel Frohman came down from New York and applauded her work.

In Pittsburgh, despite following the phenomenally successful tour of *Count of Monte Cristo* starring Maggie's former company member James O'Neill, she drew immense crowds. Some nights the house was so packed that the orchestra was compelled to play from the stage. But when she began 1890 with a week in Cincinnati, previously one of her most loyal cities, especially around the holidays, the same was far from true. *Ray* was accepted by small, cold audiences, acceptable only "as a medium for the ever-youthful and kittenish Maggie to say sweet nothings and do all sorts of heroic things in her strange way, it is about as good as anything she plays. . . . She is not the same powerful attraction as of old."[19]

Such engagements sparked rumors anew of Maggie's retirement, but she emphatically denied any plans to do so, telling a friend, "I believe it would kill me to quit the stage. I have known no other life and would not know how to live one." More than a few journalists agreed: "She must play until she can play no more. We cannot write of retirement of her. . . . We know not that it will ever come."[20]

Abbott increasingly spoke and acted on Maggie's behalf. Still steamed from his encounter with Lykens, he warned managers across the country not to extend any credit to Lykens, and arbitrarily canceled contracts previously made with Lykens. This triggered a lawsuit in January when Maggie toured through Ohio—including her last visit to Cleveland—and Indiana, down to Kansas City. There, Lykens had arranged for Maggie to perform for a week at the Midland Theatre and its manager, David T. Keiller, had expended several thousand dollars in new scenery for *Ray*. Instead, Abbott booked Maggie into the rival Coates Opera House. Keiller, arguing that his contract with Lykens remained valid and was thus violated, filed suit against Maggie and

Abbott for $5,000. Lykens and Gerth (for $1,380 and $800, respectively) also sued them for unpaid salary and commission, arguing that their contracts ran through May 2, 1890. No record remains of the disposition of either of these lawsuits, suggesting both may have been settled out of court.

At the Coates, *Ray, Fanchon,* and *Barefoot* drew fair-to-good houses, but jaded critics: "There is nothing new to say about Maggie Mitchell." "Any criticism of her individual performance is superfluous." Her acting "was all that could have been expected." *Fanchon* was "too well known for comment or criticism." Attendance waned, and did likewise in Chicago, as Abbott scrambled to add new towns to his wife's itinerary. Some, such as tiny Piqua, Ohio, and Ottumwa, Iowa, she never returned to. She also carved out a swathe of new territory, heading into the northwestern United States. In February she played Laramie, Wyoming Territory, and Salt Lake City, Utah Territory, for the first (and only) times.[21]

In the latter, she performed in founder Brigham Young's new Salt Lake Theatre, erected with the express purpose of creating a place where his Saints "can meet together and have all the fun they desire." Nicknaming it "Fun Hall," he preached that no one "shall ever desecrate its sacred stage with the tragedies. It is built exclusively for the use of ourselves and our own holy fun." Maggie certainly filled the bill, and families attended together. The more melodramatic *Ray*, though, was not well received.[22]

Maggie missed her scheduled February 17 opening at the New Bush Street Theatre in San Francisco due to snow-blocked tracks in the Sierras. The worst storm of the season left drifts up to 18', stranding her train overnight at Emigrant Gap before the company arrived in San Francisco in the early morning hours of February 18. That night, *Ray* was not received as well as *Fanchon*. The same held true in Los Angeles (her first and only time there) and Sacramento (her first visit since 1878). But Maggie herself was incomparable: "She knows every trick of the stage, and uses it with natural ease and effect." *Fanchon* imitators such as Alice Kingsbury and Minnie Maddern "failed to grasp [its] wealth of tenderness, the deep sense of human justice" which Maggie effortlessly conveyed.[23]

For the first (and only) time, she ventured into far northwestern states, two of which—Washington and Montana—had only gained statehood in November. The steamboat taking her north was behind schedule, delaying her first night of *Fanchon* in Portland, Oregon, but a capacity audience waited patiently. Maggie and her cast applied makeup and costumes on board and the minute the boat docked, a slew of gallery boys rushed their trunks and scenery to the theater, and the curtain went up at 9:45. Maggie, though, had fallen ill and pushed herself to perform.

Through a few nights each in Portland, Seattle, Tacoma, Helena, Butte, and Anaconda (a silver boomtown), she drew large, enthusiastic audiences as she slowly recovered. From the similar wording in newspaper blurbs hyping each appearance, it was clear that Atwood was earning his pay. Maggie was hailed as "one of America's most brilliant artists," a "genius" who "skillfully, naturally and easily" transitioned from rough-hewn hoyden to polished womanhood in *Ray* and *Fanchon*, readily portraying "scorn, indignation, and melting tenderness." Her acting was "so coquettish, her laugh so infectious, her manner so chic that she carries the whole audience into willing captivity from her first appearance." After rushing through Minnesota, Iowa, Nebraska, and Colorado with *Ray* generally well-received, Maggie closed her season on May 10 in St. Louis and headed for Long Branch.[24]

That summer, as crow's feet emerged more prominently on her face and her once-golden hair turned a crinkly reddish-brown (dyed to hide the gray crowding her temples), more articles appeared focusing on her age and her marriage to the virile, opportunistic Abbott. She "might have been his mother." After playing her stage lover, "when the place of spouse became vacant, he secured it." "It was realism to the extent of not less than a quarter of a million dollars. . . . Acquaintances are watching to see how fast and how much Abbott will get control of the fortune." Speculation of her worth in real estate continued to vary between $100,000 and $350,000. She was "constantly seeking through her agent new channels of investment."[25]

Abbott was eager to provide those channels. He steered Maggie toward the purchase of a matched pair of handsome, well-trained Kentucky saddle horses, a coal-black and a chestnut, for over $1,000 each, shipped east to Long Branch. While in California, she purchased five acres of land in Peralta Park, Berkeley, for $14,000, where she planned to build them a villa as a second summer home, perhaps to rival Lillie Langtry's California ranch (neither actress ever lived in hers).

Abbott foresaw in the 1890s large combination companies with expensive production values playing major cities, rather than "the conventional peregrinations on the circuits," as Maggie had been doing. He began by forming a producing partnership with Ben Teal, the playwright-director who had readied *Ray* for Broadway. Abbott intended to "figure hereafter as a capitalist," and laid plans to hire actors and playwrights and build theaters. However, their first venture, "a local drama, domestic in theme, by Dion Boucicault and Mr. Teal," never came to fruition.[26]

To free up time for this, Abbott told Maggie he would perform only intermittently and only as Rochester, otherwise remaining in eastern cities to manage other productions, and hired a new leading man to replace him. The inexperienced (and non-threatening) Howard Gould, 17, was only one of eleven new, mostly forgettable company members he hired, lacking the touch and contacts of his predecessor. Major roles would be filled by George Deyo's wife, soubrette Ida Burroughs, low comedian Edward Poland, and

Jennie Carroll in maternal roles, with returning actor Sheridan Tupper to cover Fadet. The top tiers of actors were gone, lured to the tours of more prominent stars. At least Maggie could rely on McClannin and Deyo for continuity and experience, the former consistently praised.

Sending Harry off to Columbia Law School and leaving Fanchon this time in Long Branch, Maggie opened the 1890–91 season in Boston on October 6, prominently "under the management of Mr. Charles Abbott." Two nights later the cast did not know its lines for *Jane Eyre*, undoubtedly to the irritation of Maggie and Abbott. Clearly, they corrected this matter in rehearsal, for from that night on, the company earned good notices. But the attention, and responsibility, always lay with Maggie.

For a month, through various New York and Pennsylvania cities, she rotated *Ray* equally with *Fanchon, Barefoot, Jane Eyre*, and *Lorle*, drawing good houses. But critics had grown bored: "Regarding Maggie's acting—if it can be called acting—nothing new can now be written. The public long ago found a warm corner in its heart for the plump little woman whose utter defiance of stage canons was refreshing after the stereotyped delineators of hoydens and romps. Time has dealt kindly with her, and . . . no one would be ungallant enough to recommend retirement."[27]

By now, most of her imitators had faded from the scene. Even Lotta, Kingsbury, Maddern, and Putnam were deemed inferior in emotional range. In fact, when Maggie played Baltimore during Thanksgiving week, she competed directly with Lotta at a nearby venue and outdrew her. There was "no one now on the stage quite the equal of Maggie Mitchell."[28]

Either Atwood was not as effective as Lykens had been drumming up advance notices, or Maggie's star was fading, but Washington, Wheeling, and smaller Pennsylvania towns in December yielded only fair audiences. Although *Ray* was still new to most of them, Maggie decided to add another new script to the mix, acquiring the rights to a four-act comedy by Charles T. Vincent entitled *Lady Tom*, which she planned to rehearse as she traveled. It harkened back to her early "protean" roles as it required her to enact five different characters.

Attendance picked up as she played a week of one-night stands in small Ohio towns and Christmas week in Pittsburgh. There, she shopped for gifts for all of her company members, and upon arriving at her dressing room for the Christmas matinee was delighted by their gift to her: a monogrammed ivory-handled silver service, accompanied by an ode to her by Poland, with the walls and mirror decorated with copious holly wreaths. She closed the year in Toronto, where she dedicated the new Clark's Grand Opera House.

1891 began with a close-to-sold-out week and good reviews in Chicago, followed by six weeks of the same touring Wisconsin, Minnesota, Illinois,

Iowa, Nebraska, and Missouri. Many were one-nighters—another winter in the frozen upper Midwest. Constantly battling a cold and hoarseness, she still pleased her following. "If anything, she is quicker in her steps and throws her skirts higher." "As plump as a quail and as lively as a monkey," she looked "about 12 years of age, with ten times the activity and head for mischief that the ordinary little minx of that age possesses who has grown up from the cradle badly spoiled." *Fanchon* seemed "built for the sole purpose of giving the soubrette opportunity to kick and sing and chuckle, and the audience asks nothing more."[29]

A few critics muttered about *Ray*'s inadequacies but fiercely loyal old-timers showered her with affection and applause. One long-time theatergoer in Omaha explained the appeal. It wasn't Maggie's scripts; *Fanchon* "wasn't worth a tinker's darn. It had whiskers growing on it." It was her: "The play with Maggie Mitchell out would be something like *Hamlet* with the mad prince omitted. [Actually,] you may have *Hamlet* with the crank [Hamlet] omitted, sermons without a preacher, orations without an orator, but when the people come to see a play with Maggie Mitchell, the world would cease to move if Maggie should get sick. When the little woman came tripping out on the stage, I felt just like I do when I hear "Yankee Doodle" played with fife and drums. . . . I used to lie in the cradle and nurse a bottle and listen to the old women in the neighborhood telling about Maggie Mitchell." Some folks now brought their grandchildren. She was family: "Every old codger there seemed to feel like a brother-in-law to Maggie."[30]

A man in Lincoln, Nebraska, kept attending her performances for years "because I was under the impression that it would be my last chance to see her." Of course, "she may be playing for ten years yet, and as her voice can't get much worse and as her false hair and teeth and other personal charms will last forever, the people will probably get to see her hop around the stage and squeak until she is ready to die of old age."[31]

The road brought some fraught moments. In Winona, Minnesota, no sooner had she finished playing *Ray* to a packed house and left with her company, and the porters had carried the last trunks and scenery to the train, the entire opera house burned to the ground, ignited by smoldering drapes. In Lincoln, she auditioned, but fortunately did not hire, a replacement actor who turned out to be newly paroled from a murder conviction, having stabbed his girlfriend to death in a jealous rage.

When Abbott rejoined the company in St. Louis in March, she briefly reinstated *Jane Eyre*. His collaboration with Boucicault having gone nowhere, the next venture of "Abbott & Teal, Managers, Broadway" was *Niobe*, which they cast in Philadelphia, to open in May. Abbott brought Teal with him to St. Louis to helm another new Maggie project, *The Little Maverick*, by Charles T. Dazey, which she was enthusiastic about. They began rehearsals, but almost immediately postponed it until next season, and Teal and Abbott returned to Philadelphia to work on *Niobe*.[32]

A week touring Indiana brought Maggie up short. In Richmond, a town of 16,000, the audience received her coldly and the *Richmond Item* delivered one of the harshest reviews of her later career: "Maggie should drop out; her time to vanish has come, and she doesn't seem to know it. [She has been] keeping it up too long. The glamour is off, . . . there is no tinsel about her any more. It is a pitiful thing, this struggle of an old favorite to keep her place in the public esteem, but there is no reason why she . . . should be forever attempting to stay clever." Both *Barefoot*, which she had played there, and Maggie herself "are now threadbare." Moreover, the company supporting her was poor.[33]

But Maggie characteristically shook it off, embarking on a seven-week, 2,500-mile peregrination of one- and two-night stands around the Midwest, including a foray into the deep South for the first time in eleven years (to Tennessee, Alabama, and Arkansas, with a few towns for the first time), playing to generally good houses. Reviews were scarce, except for *Ray*, and those were mixed.

Abbott rejoined the company for a long Easter weekend in Topeka, taking over the young romantic lead in *Ray*, Percy. A few nights later he reclaimed Rochester. Maggie's Jane, especially as an orphan in the early acts, was considered far inferior to Brontë's, which "Miss Mitchell often seems to disregard openly and substitute her mannerisms." Given Maggie's interpretation of the character, "the book could be read with much better interest after, rather than before, one sees it upon the stage."[34]

That spring she moved on through Kansas, Missouri, and Iowa, again adding several new small towns. She often closeted herself in her hotel room—no longer was mention made of her special train—working on her lines for *Lady Tom*. She was also learning German, having hired and brought along a German woman named Maria Krampa as tutor and maid. (Maggie's previous maid had gone home following her mother's death, for which Maggie paid travel costs.) But Maggie was too demanding, and Krampa broke down under the strain, diagnosed "with nervous prostration" by a physician in Burlington, Iowa. Maggie, in turn, accused her of "shamming illness." On April 11 Krampa quit and with the help of a Burlington aid society made it to Chicago, where she spread her story. She had become "sick and was unable to do her work," whereupon "Miss Mitchell abandoned her without money." Whether any was forthcoming remains unknown, but one reporter decided that "the veteran soubrette is becoming hardened in her old age."[35]

After more one-nighters in Illinois towns, Maggie hit Chicago for a week in late April, taking advantage of Abbott's presence to enact her last performance (of about 300) of *Jane Eyre*. Then it was back to one-nighters in

Indiana and Ohio, mostly towns of 10,000 people or less, several for the first time. Audiences varied in size, and reviewers' knives again came out: "Thirty or forty years ago, Maggie might have been able to take the part of a fifteen-year-old girl, but she was not 'in it' last evening." She may have been a great actress, but "what constitutes greatness in this case must be a question, unless it is reputation." Her supporting company "seemed to be greatly amused at something not in the play and they divided their time between amusing the audience and themselves."[36]

During a week in Cincinnati, Maggie brought to a close three decades of repertoire. On May 7 she played *Lorle* for the final time (of about 325), the next night *Fanchon* for the final time (nearly 1,500 times over three decades), and the night after that *Barefoot* for the final time (almost 550). After a few Ohio towns, she closed her 1890–91 season, her fortieth on the professional stage, in Erie, Pennsylvania, on May 12.[37]

She headed with Abbott and her company to Philadelphia, where Teal had opened *Niobe* on May 3 to instantaneous acclaim. Hoping lightning would strike a second time with *Lady Tom*, with Abbott and Teal producing and Maggie as a star, they began intense rehearsals immediately, using the same actors who had toured with her. On June 8, a week after she turned fifty-five, they showcased it at the Academy of Music, a vaudeville house, in Newburgh, New York.

If ever there was a cut-and-paste assemblage of shards of Maggie's prior scripts, this was it. She played Lady Tom (a full name never revealed), a rough-around-the-edges American who has inherited wealth from her uncle on the condition that she marry the stuffy Sir Arthur Radcliffe (Deyo), who is engaged to an English heiress (Burroughs). Amid comical scenes in Venice during Carnival (cue the masks and colorful costumes) which satirized American tourists, Lady Tom alarmingly disappears with her true love, Archie (a new actor, Charles Coote). When all reassemble at the Radcliffe estate, Arthur's starchy mother, Lady Radcliffe (Carroll) detests Lady Tom on sight. Suddenly the undead uncle reappears but is attacked for unknown reasons by two conspirators and again left for dead. Lady Tom, of course, comes to his rescue just as Arthur receives orders to report to his regiment in the West Indies, where he is killed, leaving Lady Tom to marry her true love with the rich uncle's blessing. Minimal comic relief is provided by an Italian count who is repeatedly thwarted in his search for a wife. The play's reception in Newburgh was so poor that even though it had been announced on fall schedules in Philadelphia, Pittsburgh and New York, Maggie decided it was unsalvageable and permanently shelved it.

By mid-June, she and Abbott were on their way to Long Branch. Waiting at Cricket Lodge were Maggie's (now) eight horses. Around the twenty-acre grounds roamed her innumerable cats and dogs, including St. Bernards,

English Mastiffs, and Dachshunds. In the "cottage"—more of a mansion—resided her pet rats and mice and a monkey named "Mav" (whom she bathed each day, ornamenting him with scents and an engraved locket as he reclined on a satin cushion). Each morning she rose early, attired in a close-fitting riding habit, and was off beside Abbott—also an accomplished equestrian—on a jaunt along Ocean Avenue atop Cricket, her favorite, seemingly without a care in the world, "happier than she has ever been in all her life." She was reportedly worth a million dollars "and next to Lotta is without question the richest lady in American dramatic ranks." (Lotta, who had just retired, constrained by rheumatism, would leave an estate of $4 million when she died in 1924.)[38]

While Abbott auditioned and hired actors in New York for the coming season, Maggie stretched her summer well into October. On September 12 she hosted her annual summer's-end gala for over a hundred family members and theatrical associates, with hours of dancing culminating in a midnight supper.

After three weeks of rehearsal under Teal's direction, she opened the final season of her long career on October 12 with the postponed *Little Maverick* at the Amphion Theatre in Brooklyn. She played May Percy, the titular rough-edged, orphaned waif in Texas. Struggling through a hardscrabble life, she improbably discovers she is a lost heir to an Irish lord, and then falls in love in Ireland with a titled Englishman, whose life she saves, and acquires culture. Her superb Texan riding skills bring her first prize in a hotly contested fox hunt. Treacherously deceived into believing that her lover has jilted her, she gives away her fortune to the mother of her beloved and returns to Texas, but he pursues her to America and wedding bells chime. Predictably, at nearly every turn May dances, from an Irish jig in a low-cut peasant blouse to a "Texas dance" in an elegant ball gown with a full train. Comic relief is injected by a fortune-hunting Frenchman, an overly stiff butler, and a passel of Irish yokels.[39]

Its highly improbable plot was typical of Dazey, who in this instance "picks up a hoydenish tatterdemalion found on a Texas cattle ranch and installs her as the hereditary mistress of an ancient Irish estate supplemented by a vast unencumbered fortune, . . . passing from tatters and a cowboy swagger to silks and the graces of conventional society with incredible swiftness." The other characters "are simply hauled in by the heels whenever the somewhat remarkable heroine is really obliged to have somebody to 'sass back.'" Still, Maggie pronounced herself "more than delighted" with her newest role, and reviewers were kind. She showed "less of her mannerisms than usual," and May was a welcome relief after years of Maggie "representing good-goody girls of Alpine or Rhenish origin."[40]

As *Maverick* would predominate this season, a smaller company (nine other actors and a crew of six) would suffice. Most were holdovers, including the faithful McClannin as May's rawboned Texan uncle, the successful rancher who adopts her and sends her to New York and Europe to acquire culture. Maggie's new leading man was Virginian Harry A. Smith, 34, who was "slightly amateurish," but "an improvement upon the style of leading man the public has been accustomed to receiving from her."[41]

She then launched a two-month tour of New England, New York State, Brooklyn, New Jersey, and Pennsylvania, ending in Philadelphia. While *Maverick* was "not intellectual food of the highest order, there can be no doubt that it serves its purpose well enough." "Replete with good lessons [and] American to the core," it contained "the same cut-and-dried characters, the impossible hero, the very villainous villain, the missing heiress, and all the other old friends. All these people are like the little girl in the story, either 'very, very good,' or 'horrid.'" Overall, it was "neither better nor worse than the other plays Miss Mitchell has been presenting." She was "as irresistible as ever." "Like a sunbeam she flitted around the stage, carrying happiness in her wake." "She twinkles and glows, bringing light and gladness into the hearts" of everyone." Her effervescence once again redeemed a mediocre script.[42]

Reviewers in Washington, Baltimore, Pittsburgh, and St. Louis that winter voiced similar sentiments: "She is as ever our own particular dear Maggie" and seeing her perform "has become a custom which many people would sorely regret to be forced to forego. It little matters what the play may be." After all, "Maggie Mitchell would be out of her element if she was not seen in the first act in tattered costume, which she afterward exchanges for the train and short sleeves of the fashionable lady."[43]

From there she headed down into Tennessee, Arkansas, and Texas—including some small towns for the first time—to audiences ranging from capacity to sadly disappointing. Further west, in Salt Lake City, "beggarly," "woefully small" audiences met her engagement, "one of the few losing attractions of the season." Her final night there "did not bring in money enough to pay the janitor." Fighting another severe cold, Maggie was her usual engaging self, but reviews were harsh. *Maverick* was "probably as poor a play as any in which she has appeared in a quarter of a century," "a threadbare, uninteresting patchwork" the incidents of which "have been worked, kneaded, rolled and baked until it is as uninviting a doughnut as the theatergoer ever has served to him." When Maggie was not speaking or dancing, the audience was "decidedly bored." Her male support either "did not rise above mediocrity" or were "horrid," and the ladies were all "irredeemably bad."[44]

Poor attendance and harsh reviews continued in Nebraska. In Lincoln, people saved their money for the following attraction, boxer John L.

Sullivan. Maggie's "abilities and peculiarities are too well known already." Her popularity, her stage persona, and her voice diminished, "Maggie Mitchell shows the undoubted ravages of age." "There is nothing in Maggie Mitchell's acting now excepting the exhibition of a woman sixty-five [sic: 55] trying to appear a girl of sixteen. No one can say she is natural. Her voice and manner seem the epitome of affectation. Her walk is awkward, not to say coarse. There are a dozen young soubrettes who dance, sing and act better than she."[45]

She tried beefing up the show's singing, adding a "Texan quartette" while confining her own singing to a semi-harmonious alto, but "she isn't even equal to a small, weakly pipe." A reporter overheard a woman decline to buy tickets, saying, "If I was sure Maggie wouldn't sing, I would go to hear her, but I'm afraid to risk it." Under an assault like this, Maggie withdrew to her hotel room, having her meals sent to her room and coming and going with her face muffled. "The old lady is so fearfully passé that she religiously refrains from exposing time's ravages to a scoffing public."[46]

But she rallied, and all that fell behind as she toured Iowa, Wisconsin, Illinois, and Minnesota towns in early March: "She brings her old gurgle, her old purr, and the same old antics to which her audiences have become accustomed and which make her popular." The seclusion in Nebraska had yielded introspection, for in each of these towns she announced to the audience at the close of each night's performance that she was retiring at the close of the season. She was smart to do so, thought most critics: "There are few actresses who have the good sense to retire before they have lost their fame and popularity." The truth was, "Maggie Mitchell is too large to be taken for a child." "The make-up needs to be a little thicker" now, and her voice "has lost its youthful sweetness and now has a metallic and at times harsh tone that grates upon the sensitive ear."[47]

Spring 1892 brought her unprecedented ease, coasting to retirement, with Abbott, Fanchon, and Harry joining her. As she moved through Indiana and Ohio, then on to Detroit and Chicago, she played to full houses at inflated prices, word of her decision having preceded her. Reviewers competed with encomia. At the end, she remained "the free, uncouth child of nature," "the youngest, jolliest and cleverest of the soubrette comediennes before the public today." She personified "the vivacity, elasticity, gayety, and spring of jocund youth." For this "marvelous little woman, in whose veins is the sap of perennial verdure, the wonder is that she should think of retiring."[48]

When she ended her career at the venerable Hooley's Theatre in Chicago on April 30, a reporter asked her how she would fill the time. She would rest in Chicago for a few days, she replied, then gratefully return to Long Branch where "I can keep my house running properly, and I can ride and walk and swim and read." She would have many years to do so.[49]

NOTES

1. Interview with J. H. McVicker and Louis Sharpe of Chicago, in *Philadelphia Item*, Mar. 10, 1889.
2. Transcript of deposition, Feb. 25, 1889, *Paddock v. Paddock* (13-300-1888, V-25-418), Chancery Court of New Jersey.
3. *New York Sun*, Mar. 3, 1889.
4. Plaintiff's deposition, Feb. 28, 1889, *Paddock v. Paddock*.
5. *New York Sun*, Mar. 3, 1889; *Philadelphia Times*, Mar. 3, 1889; *New York Times*, Mar. 4, 1889.
6. *Ibid.*
7. *Cleveland Plain Dealer*, Mar. 4 and 6, 1889.
8. *St. Louis Republic*, Mar. 4, 1889.
9. *St. Paul Globe*, Mar. 9, 1889; *Lexington (MO) Intelligencer*, Mar. 9, 1889; *St. Joseph (MO) Herald*, Mar. 10, 1889; *Minneapolis Star Tribune*, Mar. 14, 1889.
10. *New York Evening World*, Mar. 6, 1889. A reporter sent to Richmond to verify the Richmond connection concluded that "the marriage register here and in other cities hereabout shows no record of such a marriage between the years of 1854 to 1858." *Baltimore Sun*, Mar. 11, 1889.
11. Benjamin McArthur, *Actors and American Culture, 1880-1920*, Iowa City: University of Iowa Press, 2000, 70.
12. McArthur 69.
13. Wood/Hahr, if either was his real name, then disappears from history.
14. *New York Evening World*, Aug. 10, 1889.
15. *Pittsburgh Post*, Oct. 26, 1889.
16. *Boston Globe*, Oct. 8, 1889.
17. *(NY) Saratogian*, July 26, 1889; *Indianapolis Journal* reprinted in *Cincinnati Enquirer*, Aug. 4, 1889; *New York Herald*, Oct. 22, 1889.
18. *New York Evening Telegram*, Oct. 19, 1889; *Pittsburgh Post*, Oct. 26, 1889; *Philadelphia Inquirer*, Nov. 12, 1889; *New York Press* quoted in *Kansas City Star*, Nov. 20, 1889; *Buffalo Courier*, Dec. 3, 1889.
19. *New York Clipper*, Jan. 11, 1890; *Cincinnati Commercial Tribune*, Jan. 2, 1890; *Cincinnati Enquirer*, Dec. 31, 1889.
20. *Salt Lake City Herald*, Feb. 9, 1890; *Jackson (MI) Citizen Patriot*, Feb. 15, 1890.
21. *Kansas City Journal*, Jan. 21, 1890; *Kansas City Evening News*, Jan. 21-22, 1890; *Kansas City Star*, Jan. 22, 1890.
22. Walter Gore Marshall, *Through America; or, Nine Months in the United States*, London, n.p., 1881, 396-97.
23. *Los Angeles Herald*, Mar. 4, 1890; *Sacramento Record-Union*, Mar. 8, 1890; (Sacramento) *Themis*, Mar. 8, 1890; *San Francisco Examiner* quoted in *Portland Oregonian*, Mar 8, 1890.
24. *Seattle Post-Intelligencer*, Mar. 17, 1890; *Tacoma Globe* reprinted in *St. Paul (MN) Globe*, Apr. 6, 1890.
25. *Kansas City Star*, June 28, 1890; *New York Press*, Nov. 7, 1890.
26. *Ibid.*; *Portland Oregonian*, Jan. 5, 1890.

27. *Albany Morning Express*, Oct. 21, 1890.
28. *Watertown (NY) Times*, Oct. 29, 1890.
29. *St. Louis Globe Democrat*, Feb. 17, 1891.
30. *Omaha World-Herald*, Feb. 15, 1891.
31. *Nebraska State Journal*, Feb. 17, 1891.
32. Abbott & Teal letterhead, HTC.
33. *Richmond Item*, Feb. 28, 1891.
34. *Kansas City (MO) Times*, Apr. 4, 1891.
35. *Chicago Herald*, Apr. 15, 1891; *Los Angeles Times* (AP), Apr. 15, 1891; *Omaha Bee*, Apr. 18, 1891; *St. Paul (MN) Globe*, Apr. 26, 1891.
36. *Huntington Daily Democrat*, Apr. 30, 1891.
37. Perhaps the oddest legacy of *Fanchon* was the appropriation of her Shadow Dance in the mid-1890s by vaudeville and burlesque dancers who turned it into the sinuous "serpentine dance."
38. *Ravenna (OH) Democratic Press*, May 6, 1891; *Cleveland Plain Dealer*, Nov. 29, 1891; Londré 80.
39. *New York Clipper*, Oct. 17, 1891.
40. *St. Paul Globe*, Mar. 22, 1892; *Chicago Inter Ocean*, Apr. 26, 1892; *Philadelphia Inquirer*, Sept. 28, 1891; *New York Herald*, Oct. 13, 1891.
41. *St. Paul Globe*, Mar. 15, 1892.
42. *Springfield (MA) Republican*, Oct. 21, 1891; *Philadelphia Inquirer*, Nov. 10, 1891; *Albany Morning Express*, Nov. 17, 1891; *Wilkes-Barre Record*, Nov. 26, 1891.
43. *Washington Sunday Herald*, Dec. 6, 1891; *Pittsburgh Dispatch*, Dec. 22, 1891; *St. Louis Globe Democrat*, Dec. 29, 1891.
44. *Salt Lake Tribune*, Feb. 2–4, 1892; *Salt Lake Herald*, Feb. 2 and 7, 1892; *Nebraska State Journal* (Lincoln), Feb. 17, 1892.
45. *Nebraska State Journal* (Lincoln), Feb. 17–21, 1892; *Lincoln Journal Star*, Feb. 17–18, 1892.
46. *Ibid.*
47. *Oshkosh Northwestern*, Mar. 8, 1892; *Duluth News*, Mar. 13, 1892; *St. Paul Globe*, Mar. 22, 1892.
48. *Portsmouth (OH) Times*, Apr. 16, 1892; *Chicago Inter Ocean*, Apr. 26, 1892.
49. *Chicago Inter Ocean*, May 3, 1892; *New York Evening Journal*, Mar. 23, 1918.

Chapter 16

"it is the music of the heart"

Rumors failed to stop with Maggie's retirement. For three years reports surfaced that she was contemplating a comeback with a series of farewell performances, but nothing ever came of it. Abbott was away much of the time, producing shows on his own, leaving her to relax at Long Branch, one of the few theatrical people there who had survived unwise investments and a fickle economy. Grateful to be rid of the rigors of the road, she admitted to a reporter that "she never knew just how much she needed a rest." Over a decade ago she had admitted that she "has never had a year's vacation since I can remember. It has been work, work, work and lots of it, always."[1]

She sometimes accompanied her husband to rehearsals or Broadway productions, especially if they were benefits or testimonials for former colleagues, but she did her best to stay out of the limelight. A backstage reporter found that "Maggie Mitchell 'off' is the same as Maggie Mitchell 'on.' Short-skirted and most bizarre as to frocks, she flits among the scenes, restless and untiring, forever on the jump. It is impossible to sit down for a quiet chat with her." All one heard was "a catching little laugh in which you always recognize Fanchon." She even tried her hand at writing plays, and attempted a memoir, but never published them.[2]

For all her stardom, in retirement she remained unaffected, a "little fat soubrette" reclining on her front porch, "looking as domestic as though she had been making butter and gathering eggs all her life." "Enjoying life to her utmost capacity," she rode daily, sometimes for hours. True, she "shows wrinkles, crows' feet and other evidence of old age, but has an elastic step still." Even if she could not cook or sew, she asserted, "I can keep my house running properly." Helping with this, all fifteen rooms plus (a slightly reduced) twelve acres of stables, orchards, and gardens, was Fanchon, back from Germany.[3]

It was just as well that Maggie had retired. The soubrette had become déclassé, pronounced the *New York Times*. Its "potency is growing less. The theatrical public is growing more refined and discriminating. A taste for the natural is rapidly developing." An ingenue was no longer "a puppet . . . but a real human being" who demonstrates a "fearless assertion of her vigorous and unconventional individuality." Actresses of the 1890s "would never dare have a twang like poor old Maggie Mitchell."⁴

No longer would the public buy the escapist tales of *Little Barefoot*, *Pearl of Savoy*, or *Fanchon*. The American stage was consumed with the grimly realistic social problem dramas of Augustin Daly, Steele Mackay, David Belasco, and James A. Herne, with George Bernard Shaw, Henrik Ibsen, Eugene O'Neill, and Sidney Kingsley on the horizon. Acted realistically within a detailed, realistic setting, these productions required skills and training beyond those Maggie had possessed.

Less realistic shows, including emerging vaudeville, were going in the opposite direction, with whimsey and pulchritude on display to an extent that would have offended Maggie and her following. Ironically, her nephew, Julian Mitchell, would soon become a highly sought-after director-choreographer for producer Florenz Ziegfeld, who epitomized lavish, scandalous extravaganzas (Maggie helped comfort Julian through a wrenching divorce in 1893 after his dancer wife ran off with her married manager). The long-limbed chorine of these productions supplanted the spunky, rustic beauty, which Maggie and Lotta had represented. Maggie imitators no longer emerged, prompting journalist Rebecca Harding Davis in 1902 to rue the "troop of poor incompetents" who had sought to emulate Maggie's *Fanchon*: "How soon their little penny lights flickered and went out in darkness!" Only one, in a clear stylistic lineage from Maggie, succeeded mightily: Maude Adams, who enacted similarly elfin characters, one of whom, Peter Pan, asked audiences to relive their childhoods as vividly as had Maggie.⁵

In retirement, Maggie served as a referent of longevity. Periodically an actress would relate that it was seeing Maggie on the stage decades before that inspired her to take up a career on the stage, or a joke would be made of someone's age and Maggie's name would arise. A faux interview with Christopher Columbus had him inquire about modern events. Told that Maggie might again enact *Fanchon*, he quipped, "Why, she toured Europe with that when I was a boy." A spoof of yearbook epigrams supposedly penned by prominent Romans included, "In memory of our school-life together. Maggie Mitchell, Rome, June 11, 481." But by the end of the century, newspapers needed to remind readers that Maggie Mitchell "used to be a very popular soubrette in the old, old days, and made lots of money."⁶

She could not have been thrilled to see her name slandered in March 1894 by Willa Cather. Not yet a renowned novelist but only a twenty-year-old theater columnist for the *Nebraska State Journal*, Cather complained of the poor theatrical season in the Midwest: "We have had most of the seven plagues of Egypt poured upon us, but we have hoped the Lord would spare us Maggie, and it almost seems that he is going to. We have seen her pictures [sic] yearly ever since we were little, and we have grown unspeakably weary of them and her. Fifty years ago, when Maggie was young, she had nothing but a laugh with mirth in it and a face with a moderate allowance of beauty. But how any actress can be so behind as to imagine that she is beautiful after she is seventy [sic] remains unexplained. . . . To see a woman of seventy, old and shrunken and 'wrinkled deep in time,' painted and padded and schottishing about the stage is more than most of us can stand with comfort."[7]

That fall, Abbott's partnership with Teal dissolved and he returned to acting, which he would continue to do as long as Maggie was alive. Having become "too stout to play juvenile business," he began by enacting the villainous gypsy Miles McKenna on Broadway in Lester Wallack's *Rosedale*. On September 3 Maggie was on familiar ground for his opening night events at Col. Sinn's Park Theatre in Brooklyn. But her husband caused her embarrassment once again a few weeks later when he drunkenly insulted and assaulted a reporter who asked about rumors that he was quitting the show before it went on tour (he did). Arrested, he paid a $10 fine and was released, apparently unchastened.[8]

After the turn of the century, Maggie's name appeared in the news only for predictable reasons: in connection with Julian's accomplishments; the recollection of old folks who saw her perform long ago; recalling the early days and performances of a given theater or "opera house," especially if it was being torn town; some young actress hailed as "the new Maggie Mitchell"; or merely to remind readers that she was still alive. She became "a forgotten stage figure, . . . one of the great stars that dazzled the older generation. . . . Soon it will be necessary to tell who she is and what she has done." "No one of this generation under forty years old is likely to have any personal recollections of Maggie Mitchell." A Cleveland paper identified Abbott, when he performed there, as the husband of a star "in the last generation." When rare revivals occurred of *Fanchon*, *Barefoot*, or *Pearl*, they were usually touted as "made famous by Maggie Mitchell." When a silent film version of *Fanchon* opened in 1915 starring Mary Pickford, Maggie was described as "the Mary Pickford of her day."[9]

Sometimes her name surfaced in news items about professional associates, such as her former co-star and brother-in-law James Collier being reduced by financial reverses to working as a prison warden on Randall's Island in 1893, and again at his death in May 1898, or the obituaries of Marie Prescott in 1893, John T. Ford in 1894, Robert McClannin in 1899, August Waldauer in 1900, John Ellsler in 1903, and Len Shewell in 1904. It even made the papers when the schooner "Maggie Mitchell" of Provincetown wrecked on a bar off the Boston coast in heavy winds.

In retirement, Maggie delved further into Manhattan's real estate. In February 1895 she bought two brownstones, one at 120 W. 80th Street for $38,500 (about $1.1 million today) and another at 41 West 68th Street for $32,000 which she transferred for $1 to philanthropist Winfield Tucker. In October 1896 she invested in a lot on the northwest corner of Grand Boulevard and 104th Street for $22,323. A few years later she purchased a four-story "flat house" and its lot on the northwest corner of 27th Street and Lexington Ave. Most of these investments doubled in value over the next decade as the city's population expanded uptown.

Her most lasting real estate legacy she conceived in October 1895. Anticipating the arrival over the next decade of trolley lines and the Interborough Rapid Transit Subway System which would link the opulent mansions on Riverside Drive and Bloomingdale Road, as well as the middle-class commuters of Harlem, to lower Manhattan, she bought two lots on the southwest corner of 102nd Street and West End Avenue. On these she contracted to build an eight-story apartment building of white marble and brick, construction of which commenced in December.

Completed by the end of 1896 at a cost of over $200,000, the building was named at Maggie's direction the St. Andoche, after the pivotal festival in *Fanchon* when her character is mocked by the villagers. A small figure of Maggie as Fanchon or of St. Andoche (it is impossible to tell which) was incorporated into a medallion above the entrance, a symbolic allusion to Fanchon's sacred medallion locket. The residents of its eight apartments, each occupying an entire floor with ten rooms and three baths, would enjoy electric lighting, a billiard room, a bowling alley, and elevator access to a roof garden for summer concerts, with storage for bicycles (a current fad) and horse stables in the rear. Her apartment there became her winter home with Abbott and Fanchon (Harry was in Boston beginning a mercantile career). By then Maggie was said "to have more property, real estate and personal, in her name than any other actress on the English-speaking stage." By 1898, her total worth was estimated at $2.5 million.[10]

One day in summer 1904 in Long Branch, Harry Paddock Mashey, the scion of the Pittsburgh liquor merchant with whom Maggie had stayed in 1882, approached Fanchon Paddock to inquire about their similar names. (They found they were in no way related.) Now forty-six and the owner of Pittsburgh's Hotel Dorset, he was staying in his parents' Long Branch cottage. Affection warmed into love, yielding the announcement in October 1907 that they would wed. As timid as Fanchon still was at thirty-eight, she insisted that Mashey first divest himself of the hotel, as it contained a saloon, which she could not abide, and that they would live in New Jersey, near her mother.

He agreed to both conditions, and they were married in Long Branch that November. Maggie's son Harry, now thirty-five, would soon acquire a wife, Elin. Neither couple had children.

But death was diminishing Maggie's family faster than marriage could expand it. Her half-sister Sophia, Julian's mother, passed away in November 1894, nine months after her son Alfred, her late husband's namesake. The following year Hank Paddock was discovered in dire distress, destitute, starving, blind, and paraplegic and was hospitalized. His condition was reported to his daughter, but Fanchon refused to come to his aid before he died on January 2, 1896. Maggie's half-brother Dr. Joseph D. Lomax died in 1899, her half-sister Mary in 1908, Mary's husband, John Albaugh, nine months later, and Maggie's brother Charles a month after that. By age seventy-two, Maggie had lost her parents, her former husband, and (counting the yellow fever victims of 1878) five of her seven siblings. Only Emma, 67, and Sarah Constance, 63, remained, and Emma, too, would pass away in February 1917.

Maggie could take enormous pride in the theatrical accomplishments of the new generations of her family. Not only was Julian successful on Broadway, but his sister, Julia, and two of his brothers, Joseph and Charles were acting there. Both sons of Emma and her actor-husband William Harris (Maggie's former co-star), William Averell Harris and Charles Mitchell Harris were active on stage and would soon act on the silent screen. Mary's son with Collier, James Walter Collier, had become an actor, as had Collier's nephew, Edmund, and three of *his* children, Helena, Catherine, and William. Mary's son with Albaugh, John Jr., was acting and managing in Baltimore, sometimes casting his sisters, Dottie and Sadie. The sole survivor of 1878's epidemic, Dodson Lomax Mitchell, became a respected actor and playwright. But it gave Maggie special pride in Fall 1911 to coach her grand-niece, fifteen-year-old Sophia D. Mitchell, in the role of Amry, *Little Barefoot*, at the Lyceum Dramatic Club in Long Branch.

Maggie lived quietly and modestly, eschewing high living and the trappings of wealth. "She objects to notoriety," noted the *New York Times* "and keeps her identity from the public as much as possible. The name of Maggie Mitchell was a household word for so long that many persons have an idea that Mrs. Abbott—Maggie Mitchell's name in private life—must be old and decrepit by this time. 'She went on the stage so young and played for so many years that people seem to think that she is a regular Methuselah,' her daughter says, in almost indignant tones."[11]

She attended the theater often, "usually veiled and rarely recognized," telling a reporter, "it is my favorite interest to watch what the others are doing." Observed one night in a box "applauding energetically the effective acting of Miss Julia Marlowe," she prompted the thought: "As she looked upon a newer star, did she recall her own past glories or is she content to be simply Mrs. Abbott, owner of Harlem real estate?"[12]

She still looked younger than her age, her figure still "trim and neat as a well-made girl's, and she is as quick on her feet as any miss of 16. With the exception of a slight streak of gray on each temple, her hair is as golden brown as it ever was." Asked about her youthful complexion, she admitted that her experience with stage makeup enabled her to look sweet 16 at the age of 64." As late as 1914, when she was nearly eighty, a contemporary maintained she had "retained her youthful figure and winsome ways."[13]

One incident at the theater in her final years revealed Maggie's generous nature. A special matinee of *The Harp of Life*, starring Laurette Taylor, took place on Broadway on December 15, 1916, to accommodate Sarah Bernhardt (all of its scenery, costumes, and actors had been moved over to the theater where Bernhardt was performing). Maggie, who had undergone a bad fall riding at Long Branch and had been recuperating at the Actors' Home on Staten Island, managed to arrive at the matinee on time and was ceremoniously shown to a prominent box. The curtain was held for nearly an hour for Bernhardt, who made a grand entrance. Shown to a different box which she deemed unworthy of her, she spent the first act loudly complaining. At intermission, she decamped to a seat in the wings until Maggie sent word backstage of her willingness to switch places.

As well as can be determined, this was Maggie's final theater performance. Her health began to deteriorate in August 1917 and she made out her will, dividing her belongings very specifically among Abbott, Fanchon, Harry, and a few relatives (curiously omitting Julian). She named as executor the United States Trust Company of New York, to administer and/or dispose of her extensive real estate holdings as they saw fit.

A month later she suffered a serious fall at Cricket Lodge and arranged to be transported to her apartment at the St. Andoche. Except for rare forays outside, she rarely left her room, where she suffered a stroke on March 18, 1918, and slipped into a coma from which she never emerged. At 3:15 a.m. on Friday, March 22, with her husband and children by her side, Maggie Mitchell peacefully passed away. Two days later, amid banks of floral arrangements, her private funeral was conducted in her apartment by Rev. H. P. Nichols, pastor of Holy Trinity Episcopal Church, Harlem, with over a hundred relatives and personal and professional guests in attendance. The next morning she was laid to rest beside her parents in Green-Wood Cemetery in Brooklyn.[14]

Understandably, her obituaries eschewed any mention of her antebellum enthusiasm for the secessionist cause or her close friendship with John Wilkes Booth. Several—perhaps prompted by Abbott—attempted to rewrite history, asserting that she had been among the first to celebrate the Union victory in April 1865, waving the Stars and Stripes while performing in Mobile, Alabama, when in fact she had remained in the upper Midwest and New York that spring.

Maggie's heirs and executors efficiently liquidated her estate. In the last week of 1918, the St. Andoche was sold to developer Daniel H. Jackson for $200,000. In March 1919, her collective holdings in Manhattan, including three other apartment buildings, were leased for twenty years to another developer for $400,000. In Long Branch, a seventeen-acre tract of land along Ocean Avenue in Long Branch went in February 1919 to yet another developer who planned to build a series of bungalows. That July, Cricket Lodge, too, went on the market, gone by December. Within three years, its land and buildings had lost considerable value, down to $25,000. The buildings were torn down for new homes, and the land is now part of Monmouth University.

With Maggie's passing, the last, definitive, soubrette was gone. Now, "the soubrette *non est*. Like the dodo, the auk, and the pterodactyl, she was too ethereal for this wicked world. . . . A fearsome thing was the soubrette. A being unlike anything above or in the waters under the earth. A creature of very short skirts, gold-plated curls, of kittenish propensities, who always sat on a table in preference to a chair, and who burst forth into song and dance with little or no provocation. Like the phoenix, the soubrette was immortal, age could not wither her, and she went on and on perennial and ever green. Lotta and Maggie Mitchell were the kingpins. Lotta was magnetic, a veritable sunbeam, and Maggie Mitchell an artist to her fingertips."[15]

Countless actresses had started as soubrettes and gone on to play mature leads and then old women. Maggie instead transformed the soubrette into something more, rising "above the ephemeral popularity which is obtained by a new kind of smirk, or a cute kick, or a bewitching make-up, or an arch manner, and has taken her place in a sphere where genuine art, genius, and abounding merit are made the qualifications." "An elfin little body, she had the charm of youth, comeliness, and phenomenal activity," eulogized the *New York Evening Post*. "A graceful and agile dancer, she could sing a little and act with pleasing vivacity. She had archness, humor, and a vein of somewhat dry and hard pathos. . . . There was a constant charm in her effervescent spirits and vitality."[16]

Her death "stirred up many of the veterans [of] a generation ago. . . . In their day Maggie Mitchell was a name to conjure with." Although first and foremost a New Yorker, "it is in the smaller cities all over the land that her death will be more sincerely regretted. When she was playing, the people of the towns and cities . . . waited for Maggie Mitchell. Mothers and grandmothers, fathers and grandfathers held the date to be observed as a duty. Not so much what she played, as how, was what satisfied. . . . It is doubtful if any of [her] plays will ever be put on the stage again—they don't synchronize with today's productions—but the chief reason is that there is no one who can do what the actress did in her inimitable way. And Miss Mitchell was inimitable in *Fanchon*. She was true to her art. She always seemed to be trying to do a little better every time she played." When she retired, "she left a niche which has never been filled and possibly never will be."[17]

The overarching theme of Maggie Mitchell's life is not the tragically effusive emotionality and struggle with drug addiction of Clara Morris, nor the grace under the terrible pressure of Laura Keene. Rather, it is the persistent vision of energetically performing endearingly elfin characters for four decades, rising from poverty to landed wealth.

Her acting style epitomized the Personality School, which Garff Wilson has defined as "the substitution of the performer's personality for the dramatic character, or the portrayal of dramatic characters which fit the performer's personality so exactly that performer and character are practically identical." He summarized the elements of Maggie's success: "her elfin, roguish appeal—an appeal that was always presented in a wholesome, uplifting fashion," enacting characters "which suited her wholesome vivacity and hoydenish charm."[18]

Her performances were a virtual Procrustean Bed, stretching or compressing any script to fit her idiosyncratic personality. Early in her career, critics realized this: "Miss Mitchell cannot divest herself of her own identity—particularly in female characters—and see her where we may—she always wears the air and face of 'charming Maggie.'" At its end, they reiterated it: "She has been playing the same role all her life; she couldn't play any other if she tried, and no one wants her to make a change. What that role is, every playgoer knows. First there is a waif, romping, wholesome and slangy. Secondly, the waif falls in love and gets woefully mixed up. Thirdly, she saves the pretty young man's life, thwarts the villain, or does something equally fine, and fourthly, she comes up in the last act a brilliant young woman."[19]

Maggie did not *perform Fanchon*, she *became* "the strange little being herself, who moves a whole house to laughter by her saucy impetuosity while in pursuit of her vagrant chicken, or by her exuberant mirth in her elf-like dance and anon to tears as she is forced to withstand the bitter taunts of the ignorant rabble." That scene, when "she bids defiance to the cruel mob who tear her mother's prayer from her neck is made positively thrilling by her terrible earnestness." Then, Maggie rose "to as great a height as anything we may see in the finest tragedy."[20]

Untrained beyond rudimentary stagecraft by Hamblin and Burton, she played "from her own impulses and conceptions, never mistaking her characters, being taught by nature and not by the stage manager." By trial and error, she taught herself gimmicks to win over an audience. Whenever her character was about to enter a fray, she would push her hat up determinedly. When bashful, she would kick one leg back and do a half-step back. When coy, she would put the end of her bonnet string in her mouth. One of her most effective tricks was having "a little catch in her voice that could be brimful of tears or mischief, just as she desired."[21]

Influenced at the start of her career by the pantomimic cavorting of Céline Céleste and the sprightliness of Clara Fisher, Maggie transcended their performances by adding a layer of pathos. Hoping for added height with age, which never came, and initially aiming for a career in tragedy, she yearned to "one day astonish the world with her Lady Macbeth, Bianca, and a new revelation of Juliet. She was emotional, but then she couldn't bring her bright, cheery features into the proper expression for a burst of grief." Smiling came more easily to her, and "her smile meant fun, jollity, and a benison of laughter. Mirth and good nature radiated from her like rays of light from a star, and then there was a ray for everybody within sound of her voice." Her comedic roles generated empathetic moments when "the audience laughed when she laughed, and wept when she wept. Not infrequently, the smiles shone through tears."[22]

"If Maggie was not actually born an orphan," observed one reviewer, "it is not difficult to imagine" her being so. She epitomized grace and goodness triumphant over rejection and deprivation—Cordelia to the world's Regans and Gonerils, especially as Fanchon and Jane Eyre, roles which embody a core of faith, trust, and love. In these roles, "she was acting with unfailing certainty, skill and delicacy."[23]

Regardless of critical response, regardless of how often she was assailed for performing nearly identical caricatures, Maggie's popular following rarely deserted her. There was "something about her so original and captivating that her audiences abandon all attempts at criticism and accept her as a piquant, delightfully saucy, ever welcome little being." She was, admitted the *New York Times* in 1862, "one of those bright little sympathetic actresses that somehow insinuate themselves into the affections of the public before the public has time to make up its mind on the subject of criticism." There was "a charming freshness and originality about her that forestalls without defying criticism, and that makes you feel at once she is not to be carped and caviled at, but to be studied and appreciatively understood. Her *Fanchon* is a performance of so much intelligence of conception and such exquisite neatness in execution, as to put fault-finding out of the question."[24]

She remained "Our Maggie," a dear, dear old friend. "There is," mused one reviewer, "a graveyard filled with the blasted hopes of fine actors of whom managers have undertaken to make stars, but whose playing left the audiences cold." But Maggie was "that *rara avis* on the stage, a child-woman who creeps into the affections of playgoers of all ages and comes to stay. . . .

When you are seeing her, you wish you could drop the bigness and the formality of the theatre . . . and just have her in some good, large, cozy home, where you could group the little folk all about you, hold their hands, and look into their eyes, and feel their pulses jump and hear their wonder words [sic] of delight."[25]

Through an ever-shifting array of leading men and supporting companies, she instilled in her characters "the sweetest and noblest virtues, and appeals directly to the hearts of the spectators." She possessed in spades "the *sine qua non* of all successful players or actors—magnetism. . . . There is probably not another actress living who could play the characters that she does with the same effect." "We have all seen the beautiful play of the lightning along the horizon of a sultry summer night," rhapsodized one journalist trying to limn the essence of Maggie Mitchell. "How it shifts and quivers. Sometimes only a pale glimmer is discernible, then brightens and faints again, but never dies. Ever and anon a blinding flash envelops every object in a flood of light. Thus it is with the play of emotions in *Fanchon*."[26]

But it fell to two poets to capture best Maggie's allure. Her performances, wrote Eugene Field, were "the tenderest bits of pastoral poesy imaginable, fresh as a June morning, pure as a mountain brook, and as full of the smell of daisies and rosebuds as the breezes that blow fresh from the flowery meads. [Their] moral is so pure and the sentiment so exquisite that to hear Miss Mitchell is not only to be pleased, but to be bettered."[27]

"What is it, Maggie," asked Benjamin F. Taylor, "that makes us go back again and again to you? Why does the old charm never fade? Why is the old story ever new? [Because] Fanchon is not a representation but an actual presence. From the first moment of her entrance the pure light of truth shines around her. The time, the place, ourselves are lost in the joys and sorrows of the peasant girl. Catching inspiration from the stars, the rocks, the sea, you play mightily on the harp of the affections, when lo! there bursts into sound a strange, wild, thrilling music, far reaching even to that depth of pathos, the font of tears. We hold our breath and listen. It is the music of the heart."[28]

What finer epitaph could any actress wish for?

NOTES

1. *Rochester (NY) Democrat and Chronicle*, Dec. 25, 1881; *Minneapolis Star Tribune*, Feb. 18, 1894.

2. *Boston Post*, Jan. 28, 1894; New York correspondent for (Boise) *Idaho Daily Statesman*, Mar. 15, 1894. None of Maggie's writing, except letters, has survived.

3. John Joseph Jennings, *Theatrical and Circus Life*, Chicago: Laird & Lee, 1893, 319; *Philadelphia Times*, July 2, 1893; *Buffalo Evening News*, July 21, 1893; *Cleveland Plain Dealer*, Aug. 26, 1894; *New York Sun*, Mar. 23, 1918.

4. *New York Times*, Sept. 17, 1893; *Omaha World Herald*, Apr. 14, 1893.

5. Rebecca Harding Davis, "Country Girls in Town," *The Independent*, vol. 54 (1902), 1691.

6. *Harrisburg (PA) Patriot*, Feb. 19; *Munsey's Magazine*, vol. 7 (Feb.–Aug. 1887), 84; Unidentified clipping from late 1890s in Crawford Theatrical Collection IV, 338, Yale University Library.

7. *Nebraska State Journal*, Mar. 13, 1894, 13.

8. *Boston Herald*, July 8, 1894.

9. *Boston Herald*, Jan. 25, 1907; *Philadelphia Inquirer*, Mar. 26, 1914; *Boston Journal*, May 1, 1916; *Washington Evening Star*, June 19, 1921.

10. *St. Louis Republic*, Jan. 22, 1897.

11. *New York Times*, July 3, 1898.

12. *Brooklyn Eagle*, Jan. 14, 1900; *New York Times*, Jan. 24 and Feb. 17, 1907.

13. *Philadelphia Times*, July 11, 1897; *Chicago Inter Ocean*, Dec. 3, 1893; Pitou 15.

14. Section 169, lot 12500.

15. *New York Sun*, Mar. 23, 1918; *New York Clipper*, Mar. 27, 1918; *New York Times*, Feb. 13, 1921.

16. *Ft. Wayne (IN) News*, Jan. 7, 1887; *New York Evening Post*, Mar. 23, 1918.

17. *New York Clipper*, Mar. 27, 1918; *Pittsburgh Post-Gazette*, Apr. 3, 1918; *New York Dramatic Mirror*, Apr. 6, 1918.

18. Garff B. Wilson, *A History of American Acting*, Bloomington: Indiana University Press, 1966, 140–44.

19. *Augusta (GA) Evening Dispatch*, Jan. 15, 1859; *Springfield (MA) Republican*, Oct. 21, 1891.

20. *Boston Journal*, Apr. 30, 1872.

21. *Cleveland Plain Dealer*, July 7, 1854; E. T. Harvey, *Recollections of a Scene Painter*, Cincinnati: E. T. Harvey, 1916, 8.

22. Holden 319; Carboy.

23. *Brooklyn Eagle*, Mar. 23, 1918.

24. *New York Times*, June 17, 1862.

25. *Brooklyn Eagle*, Nov. 7, 1886; Unidentified clipping, Crawford Collection Series IV, Box 338, Yale University Library; *Detroit Free Press*, Dec. 13, 1877; *Brooklyn Eagle*, Mar. 23, 1918.

26. *Lincoln (NE) Capital City Courier*, Feb. 21, 1891; *Quad-City (Davenport, IA) Times*, Apr. 29, 1876.

27. Eugene Field quoted in *Kansas City Star*, Mar. 29, 1918.

28. Unidentified clipping c. 1890, MM Papers, HTC.

Acknowledgments

I am grateful for the consistent encouragement on this work from historian Terry Alford, who early saw its relevance. As always, the staffs at various archival institutions are patient, persevering professionals, especially those at the Harvard Theatre Collection, the Yale University Libraries, the Library of Congress, the New York Public Library, the Missouri State Historical Society, and the New-York Historical Society. Inside the St. Andoche, which Maggie built and where she spent her final years, Caitlin Hawke and other residents graciously guided me around. Jon Sisk and the staff at Rowman & Littlefield have been supportive from the start. Most importantly, I am deeply grateful for the loving support of my wife, Gail, who lived more closely with Maggie than she anticipated.

Index

Abbey, Henry E., 178, 211, 214
Abbott, Charles (Mace), 225–27, 233, 239–44, 247–53, 256–68, 270, 273, 275–76, 278
Able, Mrs. John (Baker), 222
Academy of Music, Brooklyn, 97, 121–22, 126, 139
Academy of Music, Cleveland, 160, 170
Academy of Music, Milwaukee, 72
Academy of Music, Newburgh, NY, 267
Academy of Music, Philadelphia, 150
Actors' Fund of America, 32
Adams, Edwin, 37
Adams, Maude, 3, 274
Addams, Augustus, 10
Albany Museum, Albany, 14, 21
Albany Theatre, Albany, 22
Albaugh, John W., 10, 37, 59, 61, 69–71, 79, 111, 115, 122, 131, 136, 138, 144–45, 172, 175, 183, 189, 195, 198, 240, 277
Albaugh, John W., Jr., 250, 277
Albaugh's Opera House, Albany, 170, 234
Alfriend, Edward, 46
Allen, J. R., 104
Allen, Lettie, 193, 197, 203–4
All That Glitters Is Not Gold, 28
American Dramatic Fund Association, 32

Amherst, J. H., 31
Amphion Theatre, Brooklyn, NY, 268
Anderson, Jenny, 150
Anderson, Lizzie, 150
Anderson, Mary, 193, 201, 204, 208, 214, 221, 234
Andrews, Lillian, 225, 233, 241, 244
Antony and Cleopatra (burletta), 34, 37–38, 41, 50, 61
Archer, Belle, 210
Archer, Thomas, 17
Arch Street Theatre, Philadelphia, 88, 195, 202
Arnold, George Joseph, 15, 29
Arnold's Olympic Theatre, Baltimore, 15
Ash, David, 34, 38
Asmodeus, 17
As You Like It, 23, 32, 41, 71
Atkins, Brown, 123
Atkinson, Maude, 230
Atwood, Charles T., 260, 263–64
Auerbach, Berthold, 108n10, 133
Ayton, Richard, 90

Balfe, Michael William, 175
Banks, Nathaniel, 129
Banvard's Opera House, New York, NY, 131
Barnes, David M., 22

Barnett, Charles Zachary, 98
Barnum, Phineas T., 16, 56, 116, 135
Barnum's Museum, New York, NY, 13, 23, 84
Barrett, Lawrence, 72, 152–53, 155, 158, 244–45
Barron, John M., 3, 11, 37, 49, 244, 249
Bartlett, Truman H., 121
Barton, Clara, 123
Bassett, Russell, 185–87, 211
Bateman, Kate, 59, 120–21
Bates, John, 54
Beach, Moses, 130
Beauty and the Beast, 14, 51
Becks, George, 112, 119–20, 123–24
Becky Mix, 175, 177–80, 183–84, 190, 211
Beecher, Henry Ward, 129
Belasco, David, 274
Belle of the Season, 83
Bennett, Julia (Barrow), 18
Bernard, William Bayle, 12, 27, 35
Bernhardt, Sarah, 202, 225, 278
Berrian, Rev. William, 9
Bert, E. G., 153
Bierstadt, Albert, 130
Birds of Passage, 186–87
The Black Crook, 122, 131
Blaisdell, John W., 117–18
Blanchard, Kitty. *See* Rankin, Kitty Blanchard
Bland, Humphrey, 89
Boardman, C. E., 251, 259
The Bohemian Girl, 175
The Bonnie Fish Wife, 54, 64, 78, 80, 83
Booth, Clementine DeBar, 92
Booth, Edwin, 4, 41, 97–98, 101, 103, 113, 125, 138, 140, 143, 149, 155, 158–59, 167, 174, 180, 182, 192, 213–14, 232, 239, 244–45
Booth, John Wilkes, 45–46, 50, 79–80, 82, 84, 91n7, 92n16, 96, 101, 105, 113, 137; assassination of Abraham Lincoln, 1, 115; and Maggie Mitchell, 1, 41, 46, 48, 50–51, 59–60, 62, 82–83, 90, 92n14, 107, 109n31, 113, 116, 147n17, 155, 204–5
Booth, Josie, 131
Booth, Junius, Jr., 113, 140, 152, 158
Booth, Mary Ann, 137
Booth, Mary Devlin, 97–98
Booth, Mary McVicker, 138
Booth's Theatre, 185
Boston Museum, Boston, 73, 107
Boston Theatre, Boston, 103, 106, 109n33, 119, 121, 140, 152, 158, 162, 169–70, 180, 232
Boucicault, Dion, 21, 23, 28, 39, 83, 121, 142, 263, 265
Bowers, Elizabeth (Mrs. David P.), 107, 258
Bowery Theatre, New York, NY, 5, 11–13, 15, 18, 24n10, 29, 37, 41, 47, 50, 84, 143, 210
Boyd, Nellie, 199
Boyle, Anna, 199
Brady, Mathew, 52, 88
Braham, David, 227, 233
Broadway Theatre, New York, NY, 116, 122, 125, 131
Brontë, Charlotte, 122, 143, 145, 151, 153–55, 162, 170, 187, 266
Brooklyn Academy of Music, Brooklyn, NY, 97, 122, 126
Brooklyn Theatre Fire, Brooklyn, NY, 178
Brough, William F., 88, 91, 97, 99, 101
Brougham, John, 143
Brown, Lewis B., 138
Brown, Thomas W., 157, 168, 172, 175
Bruce, Amy, 121
Bryant, Dan, 140
Buckstone, J. B., 13–14, 17, 20–21, 33, 37
Buffalo Bill (William F. Cody), 191, 249
Buffalo Bill, King of the Border Men, 157
Bulwer-Lytton, Edward, 12, 121
Burke, Charles, 15

Burnett, J. G., 119–20
Burnham, T. R., 103
Burroughs, Ida (Mrs. George Deyo), 263, 267
Burton, William E., 10, 36, 280
Burton, William H., 207, 211, 221
Burton's New Theatre, New York, NY, 36
Byers, Samuel H. M., 114

Calef, Jennie, 231
Calhoun, Alexander L., 158, 193, 198
California Theatre, San Francisco, 153, 186
Canning, Matthew W., 47, 52, 59–61, 69–71, 79, 91n7, 153
Captain Charlotte, 17, 28
Carboy, John (John A. Harrington), 247
Carlisle, Mr. and Mrs. George F., 168, 193, 204
The Carpenter of Rouen, 11
Carroll, Jennie, 264, 267
Cartlitch, John G., 16, 18–20, 47, 171
Cartlitch's Atheneum, Cleveland, 18
Castle Garden, New York, NY, 11
Cather, Willa, 274–75
Cavender, Leona, 124, 131
Céleste, Céline, 28, 32, 35–37, 46, 56, 63, 281
Centennial Exposition, Philadelphia, 174
Chambers Street Theatre, New York, NY, 10, 36
Chanfrau, Frank, 107, 174
Chapman, Blanche. *See* Ford, Blanche Chapman
Charlotte Temple, 14
Chase, Kate, 103
Chatrian, Alexandre, 192
Cherry, Andrew, 10
Chesnut, Mary, 70
Chester, Samuel K., 59, 61, 141
Chestnut Street Theatre, Philadelphia, 16, 20, 51, 121
Chicago Fire, 143, 257

Chicago Theatre, Chicago, 21, 34, 49, 54
The Child of the Regiment, 21
La Cigale. *See The Grasshopper*
Cincinnati Gaslight and Coke Company, 186
Clarke, N. N. Belden, 11
Claxton, Kate, 187
Clifton, Marion P., 155, 168, 191, 193, 197, 203–4, 240, 249, 251, 253, 259
Clifton, Wallace, 243, 250
Coates Opera House, Kansas City, MO, 154, 235, 244, 261–62
Cogswell, W. J., 112, 153
Collier, James Walter, 10, 36, 41, 50, 52, 84, 87–88, 112, 117, 119–20, 122–26, 130–37, 139, 146n5, 151, 159, 174, 196, 201, 232, 275, 277
Columbus Theatre, Harlem, NY, 237
Continental Theater, Philadelphia, 79
Cooper, James Fenimore, 35
Coote, Charles, 267
The Count of Monte Cristo, 229, 261
Cowell, Anna, 115
Coyne, J. S., 21
Crabtree, Lotta, 3, 84, 116–17, 122, 125–26, 131–32, 135, 138, 151–52, 155, 157, 163, 169–70, 174, 180, 184, 186, 191–92, 210, 213, 221, 223, 231, 234, 242, 246, 259, 264, 268, 274, 279
Crane, William H., 192
Cricket Lodge, Long Branch, NJ, 153, 171, 224, 250, 258–59, 267, 278–79
The Cricket on the Hearth, 29, 61, 83
Crisp, William, 46–47, 51, 57n7
Crisp's Gaiety Theatre, Memphis, 46
Curley, H. C., 175
Curtis, Maurice Bertram, 191
Cushman, Charlotte, 53, 72, 102–3, 196
Custer, George, 120

Dale, Alan (Alfred J. Cohen), 226
Daly, Augustin, 120, 185, 221, 274
The Daughter of the Regiment, 19

Dauvray, Helen, 210
Davenport, A. H. ("Dolly"), 50, 84, 87
Davenport, Edward Loomis, 52
Davenport, Fanny (Mrs. E. L.), 119, 221
Davis, Jefferson, 70
Davis, L. Clarke, 86
Davis, Rebecca Harding, 274
Dawes, Gertrude, 12
Dazey, Charles Turner, 18, 211, 265, 268
Dean, Julia, 53, 64
DeBar, Benedict, 33, 35, 54, 56, 61–64, 68, 70, 72, 78–80, 82, 96, 106, 111, 115, 124, 141, 144, 155, 157–58, 161, 173, 178
DeBar, Blanche Booth, 82–83, 92n16
De Marguerities, Noemil, 116
Denin, Kate, 105
Denin, Susan, 36
De Vere, Nellie Mortimer (Mrs. George F.), 259
De Walden, Thomas, 35, 42n19
Deyo, George W., 251, 263–64, 267
Dickens, Charles, 29, 251
Don Cesar de Bazan, 13
Donizetti, Gaetano, 19, 98
Donnelly, Thomas L., 188, 198, 202
Doud, Fred, 233
Douglas, 13, 47, 71
Douglas, Stephan A., 22
Drew, Louisa Lane, 88, 195
Dudley Hall, Lynchburg, VA, 50
Duff, James, 99, 118, 139–40
Duffield, Benjamin J., 39, 114
Duncan, Charles C., 129
Durivage, Oliver E., 27

Eagle Theatre, Boston, 14
East Lynne, 122
Eberle, Eugene A., 175, 183
Eberle, Mary, 175, 225, 233
Eddy, Edwin, 11–12
Edwards, Welsh, 211, 213
Elliott, W. T., 191
Ellis, Sidney R., 221
Ellsler, Effie (Euphemia), 15, 160, 170

Ellsler, Effie (Euphemia)(daughter), 177, 184
Ellsler, John A., 15–16, 19, 40–41, 45, 50, 52, 101, 106, 157–58, 160–61, 170, 177, 202, 223, 275
Ellsler's Atheneum, Columbus, OH, 106
Ellsler's Opera House, Pittsburgh, 151, 157
Elmore, Marion, 210
Elsa, 211–13, 230
Emerson, Edwin A. (Ned), 112
Emerson, Ralph Waldo, 99
Enos, Albert G., 171, 189, 191, 193, 211, 216
Erckmann, Émile, 192
Estelle, Kate, 111
The Eton Boy, 17, 20, 28
Evans, Lizzie, 223
Eveleen Wilson, 14

Farren, Mary Ann Russell (Mrs. George P.), 112, 117–18, 120
Fay, 150–51
Field, Eugene, 226, 282
Fiends in Human Form, 12
Fisher, Amelia, 106, 109n31
Fisher, Clara. *See* Maeder, Clara Fisher
Fisher, Jennie, 168, 171
Fisk, J. R., 96
Fiske, Minnie Maddern. *See* Maddern, Minnie
Fleming, William, 22, 53
Florence, William J., 10, 17, 84
Flotsam and Jetsam, 190, 192
Floyd, W. R., 124
Forbes, William C., 29, 30, 35, 40
Ford, Annie, 121, 137, 145, 150, 171
Ford, Blanche Chapman, 1, 113, 171
Ford, Harry Clay, 1, 113, 171
Ford, John T., 1, 29 30, 32, 35, 39, 48–50, 52, 81–82, 88, 89–90, 97, 99, 101–2, 106, 112–13, 119, 122, 124, 131, 137, 145, 149–51, 161–62, 171, 184, 189, 191, 210, 275
Ford's Atheneum, Washington, DC, 88

Ford's Grand Opera House, Baltimore, 150, 158, 160, 170, 177, 184
Ford's Opera House, Washington, DC, 170
Ford's Theatre, Washington, DC, 1, 89–90, 102–3, 111–12, 115–16, 124
The Forest Rose, 13
Forrest, Edwin, 4, 84, 103, 112, 123, 155, 195, 234
Foster, Joseph C., 20, 31, 40–41
Four Sisters, 27–28, 34, 45–46, 48–50, 53, 83, 87, 89, 104
Fourteenth Street Theatre, New York, NY, 247, 252
Fox, George L., 131–32
Frémont, John C., 72
The French Spy, 28–29, 32–34, 36, 38, 45–47, 49, 52, 54–55, 63, 69, 78, 80, 84, 90, 111
Fuller, George F., 202, 205, 209–11
Fuller, Richard, 145

Gaiety Theatre, Bloomington, IL, 36
Gaiety Theatre, Memphis, 47
Gaiety Theatre, Nashville, 47
Galloway, Mr. and Mrs. James T., 211, 216, 225, 233, 240–41, 249
Garfield, James A., 138, 170, 172, 204, 209
Garrettson, M. Augusta, 51, 53
Gayler, Charles, 37, 42n26
Gebhardt, Freddy, 245
Die Geier Wally, 211, 213
Germon, Jane, 150
Gerth, Frank, 259–62
Getz, Charles, 102, 162
Gilliss Opera House, Kansas City, MO, 224, 235, 237n9
A Glance at New York, 14
Glenn, Samuel W., 11, 15, 36–41, 45–47, 49–50, 52, 81, 119, 159
Glessing, T. B., 159
Globe Theatre, Boston, 202
Goethe, Johann Wolfgang von, 175, 179
Golden, Bella, 131
Gomersal, Mr. and Mrs. William, 124

Goodall, William, 10, 12, 15–16, 20
Goode, Lizzie, 221, 225
Gordon, Archibald, 195
Gordon, M. E., 124
Gould, Howard, 263
Gourlay, Jeannie, 124
Graham, Benjamin R., 221–22, 225
Grand Opera House, Brooklyn, NY, 253
Grand Opera House, Cincinnati, 178, 189, 204
Grand Opera House, Columbus, OH, 193
Grand Opera House, Harlem, NY, 237
Grand Opera House, New York, NY, 188, 198, 202, 209, 217, 234, 256
Grand Opera House, Pittsburgh, 178
Grand Opera House, St. Louis, 154, 161, 223
Grand Opera House, St. Paul, MN, 226
Grand Opera House, Toronto, 264
Grand Opera House, Wilmington, DE, 160
Grant, Ulysses S., 104, 115, 138, 160, 167, 204
The Grasshopper, 184
Grattan, Mrs. H. P., 84, 140
Gray, Alice, 103, 155
Green Bushes, 37
Greenhalgh, Joseph Dodson, 130
Green Mount Cemetery, Baltimore, 1
Green-Wood Cemetery, Brooklyn, 237, 278
Griebel, George H., 251, 258
Griffiths, George H., 167–68
Grover, Leonard, 102, 119–20, 131
Guenn: A Wave on the Breton Coast, 227
Guiteau, Charles, 209

Haines, John Thomas, 28
Hale, Charles, 123–24
Halevey, Ludovic, 184
Hamblin, Thomas S., 5, 11–12, 15, 19, 24nn8–10, 50, 143, 209, 280
Hamlet, 16, 72, 265
Hammerstein, Oscar, 237, 251
Hanchett, David, 43n39

Harold, Maggie, 229
Harris, Augustus, 29, 39
Harris, Charles Mitchell, 277
Harris, William, 145, 155, 157, 160–61, 167–71, 174–78, 180, 183, 185–91, 193, 195, 197, 201–2, 277
Harris, William Averell, 277
Hart, Josh, 237
Harte, Bret, 199
Hartsell, Harold, 249
Hay, John, 89–91, 103
Hendershott, Robert Henry, 129, 146n1
Henderson, Ettie, 95
Henderson, William, 79–80, 95, 138, 184–85
Henley, Marie, 192, 195, 204
Herbert, Florence, 210
Hermance, the Child of Fortune, 96–98
Herne, James A., 101, 103, 274
Heron, Matilda, 83
Hewitt, John Hill, 82
The Hidden Hand, 52, 60, 63
Hight, Jennie, 116
Hind, Adeline Knight, 64, 68, 81, 84, 87, 123–24, 132, 135–36
Hind, Thomas James, 66, 84
Hinton, Lillie, 230
H.M.S Pinafore, 190–91, 199
Hoey, Josephine, 138
Holden, Luther, 12, 95, 254n33, 258
Holden, Mrs. Luther, 258
Holliday Street Theatre, Baltimore, 32, 35, 38–39, 41, 48, 50, 52, 81–82, 99, 103, 113, 119, 131, 144, 188–89, 195, 240
Hollingshead, John, 184
Home, John, 13
Hood, John Bell, 114
Hooley's Theatre, Chicago, 192, 202, 206, 270
Hough's Varieties, Lexington, KY, 35
Howard, Blanche Willis, 227
Howard Athenaeum, Boston, 52, 96, 98, 125
Hudson, Eliza S., 225, 227, 229, 233, 251

Hudson, Harry B., 150
Hudson, Mel, 235
Huguley, Harrison, 107, 109n31
A Husband at Sight, 17, 23, 28, 41, 50, 71, 106, 114

Ibsen, Henrik, 274
In-Go-Ma, 27
Ingomar the Barbarian, 27, 121, 169
Iolanthe, 190
Ion, 22, 83
Ireland as It Is, 31
Irving, Henry, 223–24, 232
Irving, J. Edward (Ted), 171
Ives, Cora Semmes, 73n7

Jack Sheppard, 13–14, 21, 53
Jackson, Daniel H., 279
Jackson, T. E., 168–69
James, Henry, 96
Jarrett, Henry C., 119, 121
Jefferson, Joseph, III, 4, 15, 31, 35, 142, 180, 185, 195, 229
Jessie Brown, 39
Johnson, Andrew, 133, 136
Jones, Joseph S., 11

Karfa, 12
Katty O'Sheal, 17, 30–31, 36–38, 45–46, 49–51, 55, 60, 63, 78, 82–83, 87, 101, 106, 111, 114, 139
Kean, Mr. and Mrs. Charles, 122
Keene, Laura, 20, 37, 77, 83, 86, 88, 96, 118–19, 131, 143–44, 167, 280
Keiller, David T., 261
Kelley, James, 60
Kellogg, Clara Louise, 185
Kennark, Jennie, 213, 223
Kimball, Moses, 73
Kingsbury, Alice, 105–6, 111, 131, 187, 262, 264
Kingsley, Sidney, 274
Krampa, Maria, 266
Kunkel, George, 45–46, 48, 50–52, 81–82

The Ladies' Stratagem, 22, 28, 45, 49
Lady Morgan (Sydney Owenson), 39
The Lady of Lyons, 12, 15–16, 27, 36, 121
The Lady of the Lions, 27–28, 36
Lady Tom, 264, 266–67
Lamb, Edward, 169
L'Ami Fritz, 192
Lander, Jean Davenport, 259
Lanergan, Mrs. J. W., 111
Langdon, Harry, 35
Langtry, Lillie, 245, 263
Lanning, John E., 251, 255
Laura Keene's Varieties Theatre, New York, NY, 77, 83
Leah the Forsaken, 120
Le Claire, Laura, 204, 206
Lee, Robert E., 88, 115
Leland Opera House, Albany, 175, 183
Leslie, Harry, 121–22
Lewis, Ida, 210
Lewis, James, 59
Library Hall, Pittsburgh, 184
Lincoln, Abraham, 1, 55, 71, 88–91, 93n40, 103, 115–16, 132
Lincoln, Mary Todd, 138
Lind, Jenny, 11, 18, 27
Linda di Chamounix, 98
Linen, James, 160
Lingham, Matt, 162
The Little Maverick, 265, 268
The Little Mother, 202–3
The Little Savage, 49, 205–11, 216, 218n9
The Little Sinner, 243–46
The Little Treasure, 29–30, 122, 124
The Loan of a Lover, 113
Locke, Annie, 222
Logan, Olive, 184, 192, 197
Lomax, John H. *See* Mitchell, John H. Lomax
Lomax, Joseph, 9, 23n1
Lomax, Joseph D. *See* Mitchell, Joseph D. Lomax
London Assurance, 28, 53
Long, John D., 103

Long Branch, NJ, 6, 138, 142, 146, 149, 153, 158, 164, 167, 171, 174, 181, 184, 186, 189, 193, 198, 201, 204, 208, 210, 217, 221, 224–30, 232–33, 237, 239, 242, 245, 250, 257, 258, 263–64, 267, 270, 273, 276–79
Longfellow, Henry Wadsworth, 196
Lorne, John Douglas Sutherland Campbell, Marquis of, 192
Lorton, John T., 54
Lothian, Charles, 211
Lothian, Napier, 140, 162, 167, 169, 180, 232
The Lottery Ticket, 14
Louise, Duchess of Argyll, Princess, 192
Louisville Theatre, Louisville, KY, 54, 96
The Love Chase, 16
The Love of a Prince, 37
Love's Telegraph, 54–55
Lowell, Benjamin Franklin, 134–42, 145–46, 151–54, 158
Lubin, Frederick, 116
Lykens, Will S., 240, 242, 244, 247, 250–51, 259–62, 264
Lyon, Nathaniel, 72

Macauley, Bernard, 134, 141
Macfarland's Metropolitan Theatre, Detroit, 20
Mackay, Frank F., 10
Mackay, Steele, 274
Maddern, Emma, 40, 111, 130, 136, 176
Maddern, Lizzie, 40
Maddern, Mary, 40, 64
Maddern, Minnie, 40, 210, 231, 240, 262, 264
Madison Square Theatre Company, 213
Maeder, Clara Fisher, 106, 281
Maeder, Fred, 133, 168
Maeder, Maria Farren, 120
Maggie Mitchell Dramatic Association, 209
Maggie the Midget, 227–33
Magoffin, Beriah, 71

The Marble Heart, 32, 34–35, 53, 60
Marchant, George F., 47
Marchant's Concert Hall, Augusta, GA, 47
Marchant's Thalian Hall, Wilmington, NC, 48
Marchant's Varieties, Savannah, GA, 48
Margot the Poultry Dealer, 35
Marlitt, Elsie (Eugenie John), 145, 150
Marlowe, Julia, 277
Married Life, 174
Marsh Troupe, 13, 48
Marshall, Perry, 34
Marshall, Wyzeman, 96, 98, 103–4, 106–7, 119
Marshall Theatre, Richmond, 30, 37, 45, 48
Mashey, Harry Paddock, 215, 276
Mashey, Mr. and Mrs. George N., 215
Masks and Faces, 29, 31, 47, 90
Mather, Margaret, 210
Mayhew, Katie, 160, 250
Mayo, Frank, 119, 121
Mazeppa, 24n24, 84
McAllister, Phosa, 168
McClannin, Robert F., 31, 46, 54, 56, 64, 188, 191, 193, 195–97, 203–4, 221–22, 225, 228, 233, 240, 244, 249, 251, 253, 264, 269, 275
McClellan, George B., 88
McCollom, J. C., 106
McConnell, H. S., 80–81, 92n10
McCormack, W. C., 130
McCullough, John, 152, 186, 234
McGill, Alexander T., 255, 258
McManus, Jennie Johnson, 64
McPherson, James B., 177
McVicker, James H., 33, 49, 96, 114, 138, 143, 149, 153–54, 157, 162–64, 174, 180, 244
McVicker's Theatre, Chicago, 54, 100, 105, 114, 117, 133, 140, 142–43, 154, 162, 168, 178
Meech, Henry, 21
Meilhac, Henri, 184

Melville, Emilie, 116, 120, 124, 130
Memphis Theatre, Memphis, 34, 38, 51, 53
Menken, Adah Isaacs, 84
Methua, J. G., 96
Metropolitan Hall, Indianapolis, 100
Metropolitan Theatre, Buffalo, 78
Metropolitan Theatre, Detroit, 20, 79
Metropolitan Theatre, Sacramento, 187
Metropolitan Theatre, San Francisco, 153
Metropolitan Theatre and Museum, New York, NY, 135
The Middy Ashore, 12, 18, 20, 28
Midland Theatre, Kansas City, MO, 261
A Midsummer Night's Dream, 132
The Mighty Dollar, 180
The Mikado, 190
Miles, Robert E. J., 162, 178, 205
Miller, Annie, 62
Milly, the Maid with the Milking Pail, 17–18, 21, 30, 39, 45, 47, 71, 78, 90
Miner, Henry, 246
Mischief Making, 33
Mitchell, Alfred, 24n10, 53, 113
Mitchell, Anna (Hannah) Dodson Lomax, 9–16, 18, 20–22, 23n1, 24, 27–28, 31, 33–34, 36, 45, 50–51, 53, 63–64, 69, 71, 77–78, 80–83, 87–90, 96–97, 99, 101, 106–7, 113, 118, 129–30, 137, 139, 146n5, 237
Mitchell, Charles S., 9, 23n1, 53, 101, 172, 223, 236–37
Mitchell, Charles S., Jr., 9, 18, 53, 74n14, 140, 188, 193, 198, 201, 207, 221, 226, 229, 236–37, 258, 277
Mitchell, Dodson Lomax, 188, 233, 277
Mitchell, Emily, 9
Mitchell, Emma, 9, 23, 32, 40, 50, 53, 59, 70–71, 81–84, 90, 139, 146, 172, 178, 188, 201, 277
Mitchell, John H. Lomax, 9, 52, 74n14, 172, 183, 188
Mitchell, Johnny H., 188

Mitchell, Joseph D. Lomax, 9, 53, 74n14, 136, 236, 277
Mitchell, Julian Bugher, 24n10, 131, 139, 172, 177, 184–85, 191, 193, 195, 197, 204–5, 207, 210, 233, 274–75, 277–78
Mitchell, Margaret (Maggie): and Abraham Lincoln, 1, 91, 103; attainment of stardom, 17–19; birth and childhood, 6, 9–13; charity, 2, 32, 41, 79, 107, 112, 121, 149, 163, 167, 171, 178, 180, 202, 217, 224, 232, 246, 258, 276; death, 278; debut of *Fanchon*, 64–69; debut of *Jane Eyre*, 143; debut of *Little Barefoot*, 99; debut of *The Little Savage*, 205–6; debut of *Lorle*, 132–33; debut of *Maggie the Midget*, 228; debut of *Mignon*, 175; debut of *The Pearl of Savoy*, 98–99; debut of *Ray*, 249–50; demeanor, 2–5, 34, 89; divorces, 89–90, 93n33, 93n35, 251, 255–58; illnesses and injuries, 2, 22, 35, 39, 96, 102, 130, 136–37, 151, 155, 162–63, 170, 174, 176, 178, 183–85, 196, 202, 207, 217, 223, 253, 262, 269, 278; and John Wilkes Booth, 1, 45–46, 48, 50–51, 73nn2–3, 80, 82–83, 92n14, 96, 98, 105, 107, 109n31, 113, 115–16, 137, 147n17, 155, 204–5; and Julian Mitchell, 24n10, 24n13, 131, 278; marriage to Charles Abbott, 258; marriage to Hank Paddock, 136; marriage to William Virgil Wallace, 89–90; physical characteristics, 2, 5, 13, 22, 29–30, 37, 49, 63, 130, 171, 260, 263; real estate investments, 101, 134, 138, 153, 167, 181, 186, 193, 198, 208, 221, 224, 247, 256, 259, 263, 276, 279; religion and morality, 5–6, 9, 34, 38, 87, 91, 145, 163, 188, 215, 225, 241; retirement from the stage, 250, 261, 270–76; secessionist sympathies, 1, 54, 61–63, 71–72, 73n7, 74n14, 79, 105, 114, 116, 118, 122; wealth, 41, 97, 101, 104, 107, 119, 125, 138–39, 153, 180–81, 192–93, 195, 198, 204, 207–8, 221, 224, 232, 242, 263, 268, 276
Mitchell, Mary Lomax (Collier Albaugh), 9, 13, 23, 35–36, 39–41, 50–52, 59–60, 70, 73, 77, 79, 81, 90, 105–6, 111–16, 122, 131, 138, 144, 170, 172, 277
Mitchell, Sarah Constance, 9, 139, 146, 153, 170, 172, 188, 277
Mitchell, Sophia Lomax, 9, 24n10, 53, 113, 172, 188, 277
Mitchell, Willie, 172, 183, 188
M'Liss, 199
Modjeska, Helena, 213
Montague, H. J., 186
Montez, Lola, 42n19, 152
Montgomery Theatre, Montgomery, AL, 59, 79
Moore, Andrew, 70
Moore, John, 10–14
Moore, Minnie E., 214, 224–25, 247, 251, 255–56
Moore, Ovanda E., 255–56
Moore, William A., 125
Morris, Clara, 45, 106, 160–61, 179, 202, 241, 258, 280
Morris, Thomas E., 117
Mortimer, Annie, 193, 204
Morton, Edward, 17
Morton, John Maddison, 28, 49
Mount Morris Theatre, Harlem, NY, 230
Moxley, Thomas, 45–48, 50–52
Mozart Hall, Louisville, 39
Murdoch, Harry S., 150, 178
Murdoch, James E., 10, 12, 72, 150
Muzzy, Helen, 49, 101, 103, 112, 136, 141

Myers, J.C., 97
My Son Diana, 39
The Mysterious Stranger. See Satan in Paris

Nagle, Joseph E., 114
Nan, the Good for Nothing, 14
National Theatre, Boston, 22, 45
National Theatre, Cincinnati, 122, 131
National Theatre, New York, NY, 23
National Theatre, Washington, DC, 30, 124, 131, 136, 141, 151, 160, 177, 184, 195, 240
Neilson, Adelaide, 164
Nelson, Virginia, 251, 259
New Bush Street Theatre, San Francisco, 262
New National Theatre, Pittsburgh, 40
New St. Charles Theatre, New York, NY, 13
New Theatre, Nashville, 104
Newton, Kate, 99
Newton, T. W., 41
Niblo's Garden, New York, NY, 50, 84, 111–13, 116–17, 119–20, 122, 159, 214
Nichols, E. T., 16
Nichols, H. P., 278
Niobe, 265–67
Noah, Mordecai, 40
North's National Theatre, Chicago, 37, 40
Novissimo, Arthur, 229

An Object of Interest, 17, 21
O'Brien, Frank, 73n7
Odell, George C. D., 4, 119
Oliver Twist, 12, 20
Olympic Theatre, New York, 131–32
Olympic Theatre, St. Louis, 136, 161, 189–91
O'Neill, Eugene, 274
O'Neill, James, 157, 162, 229, 261
Our American Cousin, 31
Our Maggie, 32, 34–35

Overall, John W., 56, 58n34, 63–64, 69–70, 75n47, 91n2
Over Yonder, 145
Owens, John E., 4, 15, 31, 62, 70–71, 107, 116, 119, 122, 124, 167, 192
Owens, Tom, 15

Paddock, Fanchon Marie, 138–39, 153, 164n1, 172, 188, 207, 221, 225, 242–43, 245, 250, 259, 264, 270, 273, 276–78
Paddock, Henry M. (Harry), 149, 153, 164, 167, 172, 188, 207, 221, 242–43, 250, 258–59, 264, 270, 276–78
Paddock, Henry T. (Hank), 19, 40, 89, 134–37, 142, 147n17, 161, 163–64, 168, 171–72, 175, 178, 181, 184–86, 190–93, 197–98, 201, 204, 207–8, 214, 222, 224–26, 229, 235, 239–40, 242–44, 247, 250–51, 255–58, 260, 277
Paddock, Mary Ann, 134
Paddock, Thomas, 134
Palmer, Minnie, 210, 223
Parkhurst, George, 225, 233, 244
Park Theatre, Boston, 214, 233
Park Theatre, Brooklyn, 130, 159, 169, 183, 194, 209, 222, 240, 275
Park Theatre, New York, NY, 10, 118, 211
Park Theater, Philadelphia, 260
Patience, 190
Patterson, Martha Johnson, 136
The People's Lawyer, 31
People's Theatre, Cincinnati, 30
People's Theatre, New York, NY, 246–47
People's Theatre, St. Louis, 22, 32
Perkins, Walter, 240, 243
Perry, Agnes Land, 79
La Petite Marie, 103
The Pet of the Petticoats, 20
Pfeiffer, Charlotte Birch, 64, 113, 133, 218n27

Phillips, Henry B., 184, 188
Phillips, Mrs. I. B., 48
Phoenix Hall, Petersburg, VA, 48, 50
Pickford, Mary, 3, 275
Pike's Opera House, Cincinnati, 105, 151, 162
Pilgrim, James, 13–14, 17, 22, 32, 37, 39, 42n26, 45, 49, 83
Pine Street Theatre, Providence, RI, 50
The Pirate of the Isles, 11
Pirates of Penzance, 190
Pixley, Annie, 199, 202, 210, 223, 259
Planché, J. R., 13, 51
Poland, Edward, 263–64
Poole, John F., 188, 202
Pope, Charles, 56, 64, 72, 134, 155
Postlewait, Thomas, 28
Prescott, Marie, 184, 186–87, 275
Price, Fannie B., 130
Prior, Louisa (Mrs. James J.), 211, 222
Provost, Mary, 10, 167
Purdy, A. H., 13
Putnam, Katie, 131, 157, 184, 264

Queen, Frank, 82
Queen, Fred, 227, 233, 240
The Queen of the Abruzzi, 21, 55
Quinlan, James, 16, 20–21

Rafaelle, the Reprobate, 60
Rand, Olivia, 189
Rankin, Kitty Blanchard, 84, 115–16
Rapley, William H., 131
Ravlin, N. F., 163, 167
Ray, 243, 249–53, 257–66
Raymond, John T., 101, 103, 112
Read, Alvin, 64
Reade, Charles, 29
Redding, J. H., 193, 204–5
Reeves, Marian Calhoun Legare, 173–74
Rehan, Ada, 175–77
The Rendezvous, 90
Rice, John B., 21, 34
Rice's Theatre, Chicago, 31, 33

Richard III, 10, 12, 60
Richings, Caroline, 62, 79, 84
Rip Van Winkle, 31, 229
Robertson, Agnes, 16, 19, 21, 23, 28, 30, 34, 39, 84, 86, 100
Robinson, James Hall, 13–14
Robinson's Opera House, Cincinnati, 161
Robson, Stuart, 35, 50, 79, 192
Romeo and Juliet, 13, 113
Rosewald, Jacob H., 133, 150
The Rough Diamond, 13
Rowe, Mrs. J. H. (Georgie Dickson), 191
Rowson, Susanna, 14
Runnion, James B., 175–79
Rush, Cecile, 105
Russell, Richard Fulton, 176–77, 201–4, 206, 210–13, 221
Russell, Tommy, 258

St. Charles Theatre, New Orleans, 33, 56, 62, 69, 144
St. Clair, Sallie, 20
Salt Lake Theatre, Salt Lake City, 262
Samuel, A. R., 159
Sand, George, 64, 74n22
Sands, Will A., 204–6
Sanford, Harry E., 221, 228, 236, 240, 242, 244, 247–48
Satan in Paris, 19, 21, 28, 33, 45, 47, 50–51, 80, 90, 111
Saville, John G., 160
Scallan, William, 99, 117–18
Schoeffel, John B., 178
Schratt, Katharina, 210
Scott, Rufus, 192–93, 204, 207
Seebach, Marie, 143
Selby, Charles, 19, 32, 34, 54
Semmes, Thomas Jenkins, 73n7
The Seven Sisters, 77, 83
Seward, William H., 132, 136
Shannon, Charles, 21
Shannon, Lavinia, 213, 216, 221
Shaw, George Bernard, 274
Shepherd, Alexander Robey ("Boss"), 160
Sheridan, W. E., 118, 159–60

Sherman, John, 193
Sherman, William T., 104, 114, 117, 129, 133, 177
Shewell, Linington R. ("Len"), 30, 150–58, 162, 167, 169, 180, 183, 190, 204–5, 207, 211, 275
Sickles, T. E., 152
Siddons, J. H., 17
Simmonds, Morris, 134–42, 145–46
Simon, William, 104
Sinn, William E., 121, 169, 183–84, 188, 190, 209, 222, 240, 275
Sixteen String Jack, 11
Skerrett, Emma (Mrs. George), 10, 22, 112, 117
Smith, Albert R., 27, 29
Smith, Charles T., 21–22
Smith, Harry A., 269
The Soldier's Daughter, 10
Sothern, Edward Askew, 31, 107, 185, 192
Southworth, Emma, 52
Spalding, W. E., 131
Spencer, Edward, 173
Standard Theatre, New York, NY, 184
Stanton, Edwin, 107
Stevens, John A., 154–55
Stirling, Earle, 244, 251
Stirling, Edward, 13, 17
Stoddard, Susan Flood, 171
Stoddart, Adele, 84
Stoddart, James H., 84
Stoddart, Matilda, 84, 116
Stone, Amy, 124
The Stranger, 13, 15
Strong, Almira, 244
Suck, George F., 103
Sullivan, John L., 270
Sutton, J. P., 139
Sylvester, Louise, 131

Tabor, Horace A. W., 228
Tabor's Opera House, Denver, 235, 244
Tabor's Opera House, Leadville, CO, 228, 244

Talfourd, Thomas, 22, 83
Tayleure, Clifton W., 122, 131, 143, 162, 173, 177
Taylor, Benjamin F., 282
Taylor, Howard P., 243
Taylor, James, 204
Taylor, Laurette, 278
Taylor, Nellie, 226, 239, 258
Taylor, Tom, 23, 29, 54, 133
Teal, Benjamin F., 249–50, 263, 265–68, 275
Temple, Shirley, 3
Terry, Ellen, 223–24, 232
Theatre Comique, Harlem, NY, 237, 240
Thérèse, 19
Thom, Reuben, 61
Thomas, Ambroise, 175
Thompson, Charlotte, 95, 106, 111, 119–20, 155–57, 170, 210
Thompson, William C., 51, 53
Thumb, Tom (Charles Sherwood Stratton), 56, 215
Tootle's Grand Opera House, St. Joseph, MO, 154
To Parents and Guardians, 23
Townsend, George Alfred, 38
Trix, 195, 214, 216
Tucker, Winfield, 276
Tupper, Sheridan, 251, 264
Twain, Mark (Samuel Clemens), 129
Tweed, William ("Boss"), 208, 255
Twelfth Night, 41

Ugolino, 13
Uncle Tom's Cabin, 16, 23, 52, 113, 122
The Unequal Match, 133
Union Square Theatre, New York, NY, 232

Van Deeren, Mrs. D. B., 204, 211, 216, 233
Vandenhoff, Charles, 131, 141
Vane, Alice, 131

Varieties Theatre, New Orleans, 62, 70, 124
Varrey, Edwin, 171
Venice Preserved, 29
Vernon, Ida, 111
Vider, Louis, 186
Vincent, Charles T., 264
The Vivandiere, 82, 90
Vogler, Otto, 225, 259
Von Hillern, Wilhelmine, 211, 218n27

Waldauer, August, 63–64, 68–69, 71, 80, 82, 87, 91n2, 92n16, 95, 99, 106, 161, 176, 184, 275
Wallace, William Virgil, 90, 93n34
Wallack, Ann Waring, 50
Wallack, Fanny, 12, 37
Wallack, James W., Jr., 50, 138
Wallack, Lester, 215, 245, 275
Wallack's Theatre, New York, NY, 84, 135
Waller, Emma, 53
Walnut Street Theatre, Philadelphia, 21, 51, 185, 202
The Wandering Boys, 40, 50, 53, 81, 83, 90, 106
Ward, William Melmoth, 150
Ware, J. F. W., 145
Warren, Effie, 150
Warren, Lavinia, 215
Washington Theatre, Washington, DC, 46, 52, 97
Wearithorne (Nannette o'), 173–74, 211
Webb, Ada, 111, 124
Webb, Emma, 124
Weiss, John, 107
Wells, Mary, 117–18, 135, 159
Wemyss, Kate, 143
The Wept of Wish-Ton-Wish, 35, 37, 45, 47, 49–50, 63, 69–70, 78–79, 81, 90
West End Theatre, Harlem, NY, 237, 251, 256, 258
Wheatley, William, 112, 117–18, 120
Wheelock, Joseph F., 152

Whiting, Nellie, 191
The Wild Irish Girl, 39, 55–56, 78, 90, 106
Wilhelm Meister, 175–76
Williams, Barney, 23n4, 125
Williams, Mollie, 111
Williams, Mr. and Mrs. Frederick, 150
William Tell, 12
The Willow Copse, 13
Wilson, Charles Henry, 22
Wilson, Garff, 280
Wilson, Robert, 89
Wilson, William, 259
Wilton, Emily, 140
Wilton, George, 140, 145
Winter, William, 102, 132
Wise, Henry Alexander, 30, 51
Wister, Annis Lee, 150
Withers, William, 52, 89, 102–3
The Wizard's Tempest, 84
Wood, Allen H. (Charles W. Hahr), 251, 258
Wood, George, 30, 32–33, 39, 46, 49, 81, 105, 114, 122, 135
Wood's Theatre, Cincinnati, 50, 79, 81, 96, 100, 105, 113, 144
Wood's Theatre, Louisville, KY, 112, 114
Wood's Theatre, St. Louis, 46
Woodworth, Samuel, 13
Wright, Stephen, 259
Wyatt, Carrie, 204–5, 211–13
Wyndham, Alice, 171

Yancey, William Lowndes, 56
Young, Brigham, 262
The Young Actress, 28, 30
The Young Scamp, 13, 28
Youth, 229
The Youthful Queen, 21
The Youth Who Never Saw a Woman, 13

Ziegfeld, Florenz, 274

www.ingramcontent.com/pod-product-compliance
Lightning Source LLC
Chambersburg PA
CBHW022010300426
44117CB00005B/108